TO THE Hartford Convention

TO THE
Hartford Convention:

The Federalists

and the

Origins of Party Politics

in Massachusetts,

1789-1815

James M. Banner, Jr.

New York: Alfred · A · Knopf

1 9 7 0

THIS IS A BORZOI BOOK
PUBLISHED BY ALFRED A. KNOPF, INC.

First Edition

Library of Congress Catalog Card Number: 75-88753

Manufactured in the United States of America

TO

L. W. B.

Preface

To our age of nation-building, ideological politics, and revolution, few moments in the national history are as compelling as the early years of the republic. Those years witnessed the consolidation and institutionalization of the first anti-colonial revolution in Western history. Americans then wrestled with the implications of a republican ideology altogether as momentous and pervasive as the French revolutionary ideology in its own time and the Marxist system of beliefs in ours. The nation then suffered the trials of most newborn states, including critical contests for legitimacy, repeated threats of nullification and secession, and the recurring danger of civil war. And it was during that age of revolution that Americans formulated the nation's three most enduring bequests to posterity: the first constitutions drafted in popularly elected conventions and ratified by popular referendums, an applied scheme of republican government, and the first modern political parties in the West. This book is an exploration into the history of one of these parties, the Federalist Party, by way of examining its most important constituent branch, the Federalist Party of Massachusetts.

The Federalist Party played a central yet ambiguous role in the history of the day. Celebrated for its aversion to "factions," it nevertheless became an organized political power. Acclaimed as the champion of strong national government, it fathered the first coherent regionalist movement in the nation's history. Vehicle of the grand visions of Washington, Hamilton, Marshall, and John Adams, it yielded to the insular secessionist schemes of Timothy Pickering and the sulphurous jottings of Fisher Ames. Enemy of doctrines, dogmas, and theories, it gave rise to a commanding political ideology.

It was in New England—and above all in Massachusetts—

that the Federalist Party became most deeply entrenched, enjoyed its greatest electoral triumphs, and played out its final battles. It was there that it took the form, espoused the policies, and gave voice to the particularistic aspirations which culminated in the Hartford Convention. It was there that Federalism revealed those patterns of party growth and that ambivalence between national and regional identification which bear such resemblance to political movements in other youthful nations. And it was in Massachusetts that the party and its ideology received their richest articulation.

I began this study with an interest in the Hartford Convention. Here was an event of dramatic appeal and recognized political significance whose basic history, though reasonably well known, had never been examined in detail. In the last days of 1814, twenty-six New England Federalists had gathered in Hartford, Connecticut, to protest against the inept Republican management of the war with Great Britain and the whole system of Republican administration since Jefferson's election. The war had gone badly, New England had been invaded in 1814, and the Republican-controlled federal government had failed to come to the defense of the Northeast. Unprotected, shocked by the course of the war, desperately in need of military aid, New England Federalists called the Hartford Convention to demand redress for their long-standing grievances and to force the federal government to provide defensive help. Conceived at a time of national crisis and held amidst rising clamors for nullification and outright secession, the meeting understandably aroused great alarm outside New England Federalist circles.

Yet the convention adjourned without action, and for all its high-toned style its report was conciliatory. While implying that, if reconvened, the convention would adopt some measure of interposition or secession, its report merely "recommended" amendments to the Constitution and changes in the system of military defense. While condemning Madison's direction of the war, convention members made known their wish to bargain with the administration and to avoid embarrassing it during the delicate peace negotiations then taking place at Ghent. Drama and politics there were. But why, one might reasonably ask, so much bluster and so little action? Why the impassioned rhetoric coupled with such cautious tactics? Why such moderation in the face of such violent public demands?

It was in a preliminary attempt to answer such questions that I came to a number of unforeseen conclusions. The first was that the Hartford Convention was a product neither of the war years nor of the politics of all New England. Rather, it was almost entirely a Massachusetts affair whose antecedents were to be found at least as far back as the decade before Jefferson's election. Moreover, I came to see that the convention represented the culmination of one stage in the state's political development. Neither the Hartford Convention nor early Massachusetts politics could be understood without the other. Thus what commenced as a study of a discrete event assumed broader dimensions from the start. It turned into an examination of the Massachusetts Federalist Party.

This party was many things: an expression of political and regional culture, an institution which evolved in response to specific legal, ideological, and social conditions, and a mechanism which existed—in the behaviorist sense—to get people elected. In order to understand how this party operated I was led to unravel and explore the genetics of its organization and some of its hidden dynamics. I was also brought to examine the sociological, religious, and legal setting of Massachusetts politics before 1815 and the contribution of a two-party system to the process of political democratization and representative government.

It also became clear to me that neither the Hartford Convention nor Federalist Party development could be understood apart from the context of the larger political community of Massachusetts. Like any political party, the Massachusetts Federalist Party could not remain isolated from the larger society of which it was a part. It was never able to immunize itself from its heterogeneous clientele—a group of adherents, spread across Massachusetts proper and the District of Maine and made up of a varied cross-section of the state's population, which was not of one mind regarding the party's course. Party leaders differed, sometimes bitterly, over the direction of party affairs. But the effect of these disagreements was minor, compared with the consequence of a wider division between two generations of practicing politicians on the one hand and powerful groups of Federalists outside the party organization on the other. Men whose interpretations of contemporary events were virtually indistinguishable could not manage to agree upon the means the party should adopt to save Federalism and with it, they hoped, the American republic. This conflict between active and would-be politicians after 1795 forms one of the major themes of Massachusetts political history.

Finally, in order to understand the history of the Hartford Convention, I have explored the ideology of Massachusetts Federalism. Massachusetts Federalist thought bears examining for its contribution to the American mind and for the light it throws upon the history of such conceptions as democracy, leadership, community, and the state. Many Federalist ideas are part of a long critical tradition in our history. But in investigating the Massachusetts Federalist mind, I have also tried to single out those additional attitudes and issues which were especially relevant to early American politics, and, in so doing, I have examined some areas of thought often neglected in characterizations of the American mind. I emphasize this to underline the fact that this is, in the first instance, an essay in causation. It has been my aim to take a single event—the Hartford Convention—and to suggest how this one episode, an act of political desperation, revived an older and once effective political style, articulated a whole tradition of regional thought, and reflected the enduring concerns of all Americans.

For, like so many events in the early history of the republic, the Hartford Convention was an incident in the larger eighteenth-century revolution of the Western world. Resounding with the echoes of distant warfare, it was deeply rooted in the half-century-long crisis in Western institutions. It signaled an important moment in the protracted struggle to define the meaning of the republican experiment and to defend it in a hostile and unstable world. And, above all else, it gained inspiration from the native revolution of 1776.

A study of politics in the early republic makes vividly clear the continuity of attitude and action within the entire half-century after 1765. What agitated most Americans in the 1770's continued to agitate them in 1810; what they fought for at Lexington they believed themselves to be fighting for at New Orleans. What is more, the tone and style of American politics altered little in fifty years. The frenzied political climate before 1776 recurred in the 1790's and continued unabated after 1800. Believing that these continuities reveal much about politics in the early nation, I have emphasized the historical kinship between the events which opened the early history of the republic and those, like the Hartford Convention, which helped close it out. In doing so I hope I have made evident that the Federalists of Massachusetts did not reject the American Revolution. They embraced it.

The political history of Massachusetts Federalism, as some will not fail to discern, bears many striking resemblances to the political history of recent times. After 1812, one party dedicated itself to ending a war initiated by the other. The war was dividing American society and re-ordering its politics. It was centralizing American life at the same time that it was shattering national unity. Against this war—against the suppression of civil liberties, against its divisive impact, against the wisdom of the entire military effort—Massachusetts Federalists protested in passionate tones.

Yet this study began before any such historical bonds between the two eras could be discerned. Affected by the ideological debates of the Progressive and New Deal periods and the enduring controversy surrounding the work of Charles A. Beard, I suspected that the first party schisms represented something other than the conflicts of aristocracy and yeoman democracy, of capital and labor, or of agrarian and mercantile wealth. I wished to learn more about the way democracy in America had developed and functioned and to re-examine the historic role of the voter, of public opinion, and of ideology in the political process. Rather than assuming, as have some historians, that partisan politics were extraneous to the way American life really functioned, I assumed that politics, in the broadest sense, lay at the center of our national experience. In this way, I hoped to reopen questions long left closed and to revise the older formulations of our political history. And yet it is not too much to say that what stands out in far sharper relief than anticipated are the similarities between some of the concerns of the early republic and those of our own age. In the end, this is just as well. For if Massachusetts Federalists deserve a hearing for other reasons, they surely demand attention for raising enduring questions—some of them for the first time—about the conduct of American government and the shape of the American polity, both in and out of war.

James M. Banner, Jr.

Princeton, New Jersey
May 15, 1969

Acknowledgments

Fᴏʀ their generous assistance and for permission to examine and use quotations from their collections, I am grateful to the staffs of the Beineke Library and the Historical Manuscripts Division, Sterling Library, Yale University; Houghton Library, Harvard University; Firestone Library, Princeton University; the Southern Historical Collection, University of North Carolina at Chapel Hill; the American Antiquarian Society; the New York Public Library; the New York Society Library; the Library of Congress; the Connecticut Historical Society; the Connecticut State Library; the Massachusetts State Library; the Boston Public Library; the Rhode Island Historical Society; the Pennsylvania Historical Society; the Library Company of Philadelphia; the Forbes Library, Northampton, Massachusetts; the Essex Institute, Salem, Massachusetts; the Dedham, Massachusetts, Historical Society; the Beverly, Massachusetts, Historical Society; and especially to Mr. Kenneth A. Lohf of the Special Collections Division, Butler Library, Columbia University; Miss Winifred Collins, Mrs. Gertrude A. Fisher, and Mr. Warren G. Wheeler of the Massachusetts Historical Society; Mr. James E. Belliveau of the Boston Athenaeum; Mr. Leo Flaherty of the Massachusetts State Archives; and Miss Shirley Beresford and Mr. Arthur J. Breton of the New York Historical Society. Richard B. Morris kindly permitted me to use materials from the John Jay Papers at Columbia University. Quotations from the Adams Papers are from the microfilm edition, by permission of the Massachusetts Historical Society.

A Research Training Fellowship from the Social Science Research Council enabled me to concentrate on the research for this manuscript, especially for Chapters VI and VII, at a crucial stage in its preparation. The support of the Department of History at Princeton University and of the Inter-University Consortium for Political Research also aided my researches at other times. Mrs. Susan O'H. Bordeaux provided essential aid in preparing the statistical material in Chapter VII on the composition of the Massachusetts General Court, and Mr. Michael D. Carrigan has been of great assistance in the final stages of my work. Mrs. Helen S. Wright and Mrs. Laura Bell gave generously of their time in typing drafts of the manuscript.

I am also grateful to James B. Bell, Wesley Frank Craven, Otis L. Graham, Jr., Ashbel Green, Linda K. Kerber, Robert A. Lively, Donald G. Mathews, John T. McAlister, Jr., Allan A. Silver, and Chilton Williamson, who read all or parts of the manuscript and whose counsels were in every case of great assistance.

I should especially like to acknowledge here my indebtedness to five others who, directly and indirectly, have contributed to this study. Winton U. Solberg first transmitted to me the excitement of American history, and Robert D. Cross, by unrelenting criticism and undeviating fairness, awakened me to the rigors of historical writing and analysis. Eric L. McKitrick's probing questions and unerring observations sustained my efforts and contributed in countless ways to my arguments and presentation. And by the example of his own unfailingly high accomplishments of style and interpretation, his many suggestions, his constant encouragement, and his respect for independent intellectual endeavor, Richard Hofstadter has deeply influenced my work throughout. My wife, Lois W. Banner, whose own researches into American religion after the Revolution I have drawn upon and acknowledged elsewhere in this work, has aided and counseled me at every stage of my research and writing. As a critic, she has few peers.

Contents

CHAPTER I • *page 3*
The Ideological Origins of Massachusetts Federalism

CHAPTER II • *page 53*
Massachusetts Federalism and the New Order

CHAPTER III • *page 84*
Massachusetts Federalists and the Union

CHAPTER IV • *page 122*
Federalist Leadership: Politicians
and the Federalist Clergy

CHAPTER V • *page 168*
The Social Sources of Massachusetts
Federalism

CHAPTER VI • *page 216*
The Genesis of Party Organization

CHAPTER VII • *page 268*
The Fruits of Organization: Democracy
and Republicanism

CHAPTER VIII • *page 294*
To the Hartford Convention

Appendices • *page 351*

A Note on Sources • *page 369*

Index • *follows page 378*

TO THE Hartford Convention

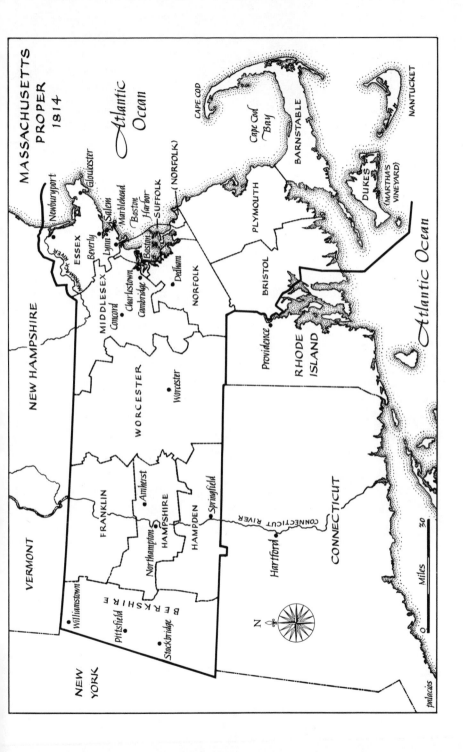

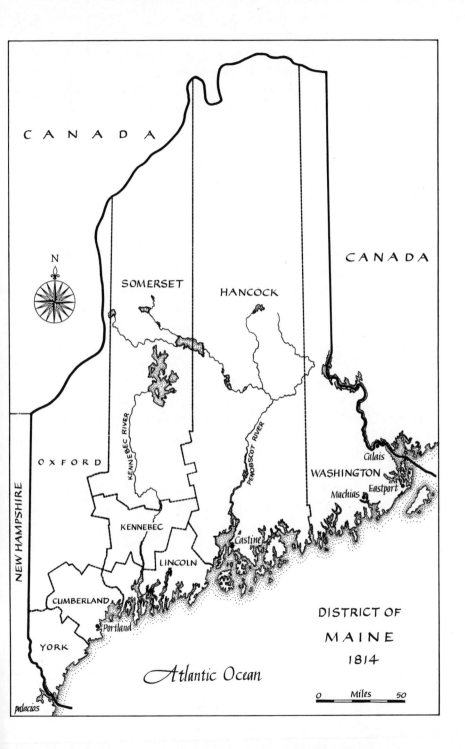

CANADA

N

CANADA

SOMERSET

HANCOCK

OXFORD

KENNEBEC RIVER

PENOBSCOT RIVER

Calais

WASHINGTON

NEW HAMPSHIRE

Machias   Eastport

KENNEBEC

Castine

LINCOLN

CUMBERLAND

Portland

YORK

DISTRICT OF

MAINE

1814

palacios

Atlantic Ocean

0   Miles   50

I

The Ideological Origins of Massachusetts Federalism

I

MASSACHUSETTS Federalism was a way of thought before it was a way of politics. From its origins in the early 1780's, it embraced a large cluster of beliefs, expectations, attitudes, and myths which, when transposed into the formulations of politics and injected with the Federalists' characteristic ardor, went to make up a full-fledged political ideology. As just one expression of American thought, this ideology was not without some kinship to Republican thinking nor to the general system of attitudes which went to make up the Massachusetts mind. In Massachusetts, Republicanism and Federalism shared a similar intellectual heritage and possessed many of the same traits. Yet by 1800 the two had become sharply discordant in their emphases and appeals. Passionately articulated, energetically disseminated, tenaciously believed, Massachusetts Federalism had become a coherent and comprehensive pattern of social and political thought.

To speak of a party ideology is not, however, to suggest a body of rigorously consistent ideas, confined, as so much of the historical literature would have us believe, to questions of constitutional construction, economic development, and international affairs. The component ideas of the Massachusetts Federalist ideology were shared by people of all ages, callings, and estates and spanned the broadest range of human concerns. Some Federalists, it is true, engaged in formal thinking. The trained and experienced intelligences among them were often given to long and deep reflection about the state of their society. And if Massachusetts Federalists produced no single

3

authoritative statement of principles and aims—where has there ever been an American version of Calvin's *Institutes* or of Marx's *Communist Manifesto?*—most Federalists gained inspiration from the substantial body of native republican thought developed since the 1750's, and some of them made noteworthy additions to American political writing.

Yet, for all this, few were original thinkers, and few could rival in keenness of intellect or breadth of vision such party figures as Hamilton and Marshall and the quasi-Federalist, independent-minded Adamses, father and son. None essayed a fully reasoned critique of American society. Most of what they wrote took the form of letters, fugitive lines for the partisan press, and electioneering puffs and handbills. Even the most talented tended to rehearse the ideas of the past. Indeed, most of the constituent elements of the Massachusetts Federalist ideology had become part of the common currency of thought long before 1790. Such themes as pride of race, distrust of money-getting men, fears of "leveling," and suspicion of aliens had been in evidence as early as the 1630's and were known to most Americans by 1776 as Massachusetts traits. But it was not until the first decade of the national government that these strands of belief gained what they had not earlier possessed: timeliness, unity of expression, and the coherence of a regional intellectual system.

Why this provincial political ideology arose in the 1790's and not at another time is a problem central to Federalist history. But to account for it, as others have done, by reference to the outbreak of partisan warfare is to invoke the very development which itself demands explanation. Party politics followed—they did not precede—the growth and definition of political ideology. The reasons for the emergence of a coherent body of Massachusetts Federalist thought lay not so much in the demands of partisanship as in the changing situation of Massachusetts in the union, the altered arrangements of social forces within the state, and the swiftly mounting clash between native and foreign world-views throughout the nation.

By almost any reckoning, Massachusetts occupied a front

4

and honored rank among the states in the 1790's. One in seven Americans—roughly 15 per cent of the nation's population—made his home in the Commonwealth, either in the downstate counties or in the vaster but more sparsely settled District of Maine. Virginia alone—and then only by counting her slaves—was more populous. And only Virginia, by virtue of the Constitution's three-fifths clause, which enabled the slaveholding states to count five slaves as three free men for apportioning representation in the lower house of Congress, held more seats in the first House of Representatives.

Massachusetts also ranked among the principal states in commerce and shipping. She led the nation in registered tonnage, was third in gross customs collections, and stood fourth in the value of her exports. Her tangible wealth proved no less substantial: the first direct tax levied under the Constitution found the Commonwealth second only to Virginia in total apportionment. And the allocation of power in the first administration reflected these relationships: John Adams of Massachusetts became vice-president to Virginia's George Washington.[1]

To such measurable determinants of influence, Massachusetts added a famed and worthy history. Second oldest of the principal mainland colonies, proclaimed as the "Cradle of Liberty" for her defiant posture during the heady days of Independence, recognized throughout the Western world for the first modern constitution to be drafted by a representative convention and ratified by the people, celebrated as the home of Joseph Warren, Sam Adams, John Hancock, and John Adams—for all these reasons the old Puritan Commonwealth held the respect of most Americans. Shays's Rebellion of 1786—the armed protest of interior county farmers against an insupportable burden of taxes—had briefly shattered the state's tranquillity and had come to symbolize for refined intelligences

---

[1] U.S. Bureau of the Census, *Historical Statistics of the United States, Colonial Times to 1957* (Washington, 1960), pp. 13, 693; and Timothy Pitkin, *A Statistical View of the Commerce of the United States* (Hartford, Conn., 1816), pp. 51, 323, 347, 391.

the perils of lawlessness, disorder, and mobs.[2] But in the flush of ratification and in the renewed prosperity of trade and agriculture which followed Washington's inauguration, no more than its recollection remained to trouble the people.

In the new nation, moreover, the new state promised to remain in good hands. To replace the aging talents of Hancock, James Bowdoin, and Sam Adams, new and younger leaders were coming forth. The elder among them—George Cabot, Elbridge Gerry, Theophilus Parsons, Timothy Pickering, Theodore Sedgwick, James Sullivan—had lived through the Revolution and were confident of their ability to define its meaning and govern in its moderate spirit. The younger—John Quincy Adams, Fisher Ames, Harrison Gray Otis, Josiah Quincy, Joseph Story—were hardly less experienced for their age and had before themselves equally brilliant futures in public life. The well-placed members of Massachusetts society never ceased to praise them: Edmund Burke, said one, was the "Fisher Ames of Europe."[3] Most were to become Federalists.

These men, older and younger, anticipated careers of national prominence and power. They were confident of their state's commanding stature and certain that they represented not one interest group, not one class, but the interests of all the people of the state. And their assumptions were more than wishful thinking. For at the time of ratification, the belief that Massachusetts possessed, for all its diversity, great social homogeneity—more than most of the other leading states—had considerable justification in fact.

More disproportionately than the citizens of New York, Pennsylvania, or Virginia, the people of Massachusetts in 1790 were almost uniformly of English descent. Unlike middle-state

---

[2]On Shays's Rebellion, see George R. Minot, *The History of the Insurrection in Massachusetts in the Year 1786* (Worcester, Mass., 1788); Richard B. Morris, "Insurrection in Massachusetts," in *America in Crisis: Fourteen Crucial Episodes in American History*, ed. Daniel Aaron (New York, 1952), pp. 21-49; and Robert J. Taylor, *Western Massachusetts in the Revolution* (Providence, R.I., 1954), pp. 128-67.

[3][Boston] *Columbian Centinel* (hereafter *Centinel*), July 23, 1814.

6

and Southern inhabitants, only a small number counted Ulster
County Scots among their ancestors, and fewer still traced
their lineage to Germany and France.[4] The overwhelming
proportion had families in England and envisaged their past
in English hues.

Homogeneity of religion mirrored that of ethnic origins.
Except for a scattering of Catholics in the coastal towns, all
Massachusetts residents claimed nominal adherence to some
form of Protestantism.[5] Few were communicants of the three
principal dissenting sects—Baptist, Methodist, and Quaker—
and few had religious ties with Presbyterianism. Most belonged
to societies of the established Congregational faith, and a large
proportion of these—from orthodox believers on the one hand
to Unitarians on the other—would not have believed the pre-
diction that within a quarter-century the unity of Massachusetts Protestantism would be shattered beyond repair.

Homogeneity of origin and religion was just one manifestation of the comparative unity of Massachusetts society.
The absence—whether from the perspective of wealth, class,
trade, or section—of any clearly defined and effective divisions
within the statewide community was another. For although
men, interest groups, and regions were constantly at odds, they
continually associated and re-associated in a kaleidoscopic pattern which prevented the formation of permanent divisions.

Take, for example, the mistrust between eastern and western Massachusetts. An indelible theme of Massachusetts history,
this regional tension remained a salient feature of the state's
religious, cultural, and political affairs after the Revolution.
Yet neither during the debates over the state and federal constitutions nor during Shays's Rebellion were the two sections

---

[4]Clarence L. Ver Steeg, *The Formative Years, 1607-1763* (New
York, 1964), pp. 167-68; John A. Krout and Dixon Ryan Fox, *The
Completion of Independence, 1780-1830* (New York, 1944), pp. 5, 8;
and Oscar Handlin, *Boston's Immigrants: A Study in Acculturation*
(rev. ed., Cambridge, 1959), pp. 25-26.

[5]I discuss the religious composition of Massachusetts more fully
in Chap. V, Sec. iv.

pitted consistently against each other. Over the votes on ratifications, east-west tensions were minor: within both the eastern and western counties the leading men were divided in their support of the constitutions. Yet over Shays's Rebellion these same men, in both the east and the west, were almost unanimously opposed.[6]

The Commonwealth's husbandmen were similarly at odds. Although the mass of the people made their living from the soil, the yeoman majority—divided by regional tradition, proximity to market, size of farm, and type of crop production—never acted together. Farmers in the interior were never able to unite against what they felt to be the disproportionate political influence of the maritime towns. They fell out even more when it came to supporting or rejecting the two constitutions and the Shaysites. And the same farmers who later joined the Federalists in protesting against the centralizing policies of Jefferson's Embargo and the War of 1812 supported the federal government's assumption of state debts in 1790 as a way of relieving them from property taxes—a policy which many others protested as too great a step toward national consolidation.

Moreover, the farmers never identified their interests with those of the artisans, mechanics, and laborers of the seaboard. The two groups fell out over matters relating to General Court representation, commodity prices, and taxation. The workers in the commercial towns for their part took offense at the overrepresentation of inland farming interests in the state legislature. They regularly identified their own interests with those

---

[6]Oscar and Mary F. Handlin, "Radicals and Conservatives in Massachusetts after Independence," *New England Quarterly*, XVII (Sept. 1944), 343-55; H. A. Cushing, *History of the Transition from Provincial to Commonwealth Government in Massachusetts* (New York, 1896); and Samuel Bannister Harding, *The Contest Over the Ratification of the Federal Constitution in the State of Massachusetts* (New York, 1896), esp. pp. 99-100. On the long history of east-west tensions within Massachusetts, see Taylor, *Western Massachusetts in the Revolution*, pp. 52-74 *passim;* and Lee N. Newcomer, *The Embattled Farmers: A Massachusetts Countryside in the American Revolution* (New York, 1953), *passim.*

of the merchants—most conspicuously during the ratification debates of 1788. And as for the business and professional men, creditors were frequently at odds over Hamilton's funding, assumption, and national bank plans, while the merchants continually squabbled over tonnage rates and discriminatory tariffs.[7]

Men's positions in the social hierarchy proved no more significant as permanent causes of division than the relationships of occupational and interest groups. In 1790, the fluidity of wealth and class which had resulted from the dislocations of Independence remained everywhere in evidence. Most of the Patriot families which had been eminent in the pre-Revolutionary years retained their social and governing positions into the early 1790's. But many people who had held substantial inherited wealth on the eve of the Revolution—like Tristram Dalton and the Jackson and Tracy families of Newburyport—had lost it by 1790. In place of the old wealth, new fortunes appeared and upon these fortunes new careers, until men of recent distinction came to fill most of the topmost echelons of government, business, and the professions.

Like Governor Hancock and ex-Governor James Bowdoin, many members of this *arriviste* elite benefited from the flight of Tories and British officials to gain the power and recognition which family, wealth, or personal ambition had led them to seek but which English rule had denied them. Like George Cabot, others of respectable but more modest origins seized the occasion of war and commercial disruption to reap vast profits in privateering, war contracts, and legitimate commerce and thus to establish themselves upon the peak of the state's financial and governing elite. Like William Bartlett, the humble cordwainer and candy vendor who rose to become Newburyport's richest townsman, still others found their fortunes in trade and currency dealings in the 1780's and rose

---

[7]Oscar and Mary F. Handlin, "Radicals and Conservatives in Mass."; and Paul Goodman, *The Democratic-Republicans of Massachusetts: Politics in a Young Republic* (Cambridge, 1964), Chaps. II & III *passim*.

swiftly to the summit of social and political power.[8] Such examples encouraged others to follow suit, and the early 1790's—especially after the outbreak of war in Europe had offered the unexampled opportunities of neutral trade—were filled with success stories of similar magnitude.

The considerable fluidity of social and economic relationships not only contributed to the maintenance of social tranquillity, but it also kept vigorously alive a faith in the solidary character of Massachusetts society—in the unity of ruler and ruled, of church and state, of east and west, of farmer and merchant. As long as one could rise from humble birth and obscure position to fortune and power, from the place of "inferior" to that of "better," who would not believe in a harmony of interests and the continuities between classes and interests? And why should not the well-endowed subscribe to a belief that the best men might be recruited "from the plough, from the mechanick's bench, from behind the counter"?[9] To have faith in the equal opportunity to gain learning, wealth, and respectability meant to have equal confidence that those who governed deserved the respect they received and that they indeed spoke for the whole community. The universal code of deference which helped cement Massachusetts society and which for so long helped moderate the relations between the classes owed as much to the genuine and visible promise of social mobility and betterment as it did to the "false consciousness" of the lower classes or to willful upper-class efforts to keep the lowly in line.

Such faith in the unitary character of Massachusetts society received striking emphasis in the consistent political apathy of the Massachusetts voter. How many adult males were qualified to vote in 1780 under the Massachusetts Constitution of 1780 is difficult to ascertain; yet in that year only

---

[8]Benjamin W. Labaree, *Patriots and Partisans: The Merchants of Newburyport, 1764-1815* (Cambridge, 1962), pp. 84-91, 94-97; and Oscar and Mary F. Handlin, "Radicals and Conservatives in Mass."
[9][Jonathan Jackson], *Thoughts Upon the Political Situation of the United States of America* . . . (Worcester, Mass., 1788), p. 70.

17 per cent of the adult white males in the state—probably somewhere in the vicinity of one third of the qualified voters—turned up at the gubernatorial polls, and most towns refused to meet the constitutional obligation to send representatives to the General Court. Given the chance to participate, few people seized it. Except when Shays's Rebellion briefly shattered the harmony of the state and an unusually high 28 per cent of the adult white males voted, most potential electors were satisfied enough with the status quo to defer to those who had traditionally governed in the name of the common good.[1]

Thus, from ratification on, all Massachusetts retained an abiding interest in preserving the substance and symbols of social solidarity. Nowhere was this concern more vividly manifested than in the realm of politics. Public figures at all levels of government joined in efforts to create a harmony which compensated in appearance for whatever it lacked in reality. The results were for a time impressive. To secure John Hancock's crucial support for the Constitution, for instance, his detractors not only pledged themselves to support a Bill of Rights but also agreed to offer him their political backing in the state, a bargain which kept Hancock in the governor's mansion until his death in 1793. In the same kind of effort—this time to conciliate the traditional mistrust of eastern and western Massachusetts—the General Court selected an inhabitant of the Connecticut River Valley, Caleb Strong, and a maritime figure, Tristram Dalton, to represent Massachusetts in the first United States Senate. Not even the debates over

---

[1]On the arguments, with which I disagree, for widespread "democracy" in Massachusetts at least until 1780, see Robert E. Brown, *Middle-Class Democracy and the Revolution in Massachusetts, 1691-1780* (Ithaca, N.Y., 1955); and, for a recent critique of this formulation, see Michael Zuckerman, "The Social Context of Democracy in Massachusetts," *William and Mary Quarterly* (hereafter *WMQ*), 3rd Ser., XXV (Oct. 1968), 523-44. For figures on electoral participation in Massachusetts after 1780, see J. R. Pole, "Suffrage and Representation in Massachusetts: A Statistical Note," *ibid.*, XIV (Oct. 1957), 560-92, as corrected in "Letters to the Editor," *ibid.*, XV (July 1958), 412-16.

commercial duties, funding, assumption, and a national bank could do more than briefly ruffle the harmony among men and interests. Well into the 1790's, no lasting divisions on matters of national or international significance were to be found.[2]

By no means did Massachusetts politics avoid all tension and animosity. The uproar over Shays's Rebellion and the deep suspicion of Hancock, as much for his grandiose style of life as for his politics, are sufficient evidence to the contrary. Yet what dissension there was arose chiefly from clashing personal ambitions and loyalties rather than from differences of principle. The unity of pro- and anti-Constitution camps, just like the unity of Patriot forces earlier, dissolved quickly after 1788 into complex factions of interchangeable parts. And after 1788, the basis of political differences remained, as it had been, factional division. Since the early 1780's, at least three different factions—loose and transitory coalitions of well-circumstanced men who lacked ideology, organization, and wide popular support—had vied for personal preferment. As the 1790's opened, the same three eastern-led "connexions"—John Hancock's statewide following, James Bowdoin's Essex County faction, and the urban-based coalition behind Sam Adams, Elbridge Gerry, and James Warren—continued to joust for patronage and office. Yet their contests, like all others throughout the state, remained localized; and the political groupings themselves remained fluid and unstable. Factional affiliations had little effect upon social relationships, and business and professional affairs proceeded without recognition of political difference. On the larger issues, Massachusetts presented a united front. Her national position and her leaders' places in the councils of government seemed secure.[3]

Yet within five years these promises of national leadership lay shattered. Massachusetts became powerless to affect the nation's course. Her interests stood imperiled, her leaders re-

---

[2]Goodman, *Democratic-Republicans of Mass.*, pp. 18-26, and Labaree, *Patriots and Partisans*, pp. 76-80, 98-99.
[3]Goodman, *Democratic-Republicans of Mass.*, pp. 25 ff., 31-46, 50-51.

buffed, her internal tranquillity all but forgotten. How this shift in the state's fortunes affected the thought and politics of the Commonwealth's majority and how it gave rise to a powerful regionalist movement is my central concern. But the combination of domestic and foreign events which occasioned the emergence of a distinctive party and ideology requires some elaboration first.

To begin with, the state's comparative leadership in population and wealth was declining. From the outset of the national government, the densely populated, relatively unarable Commonwealth, characteristically unreceptive to immigrants, was at a disadvantage to the other states. Faced with a rate of emigration which offset both births and immigration, Massachusetts was one of the slowest-growing states in the union. Internal migration from downstate towns to the Maine wilderness was considerable. But most opportunity-seekers, especially the young, left the state in increasing numbers for the open lands and less restrictive communities of the New York, Pennsylvania, and Ohio frontiers. Foreign immigrants, few as they were, circumvented the austere soils and atmosphere of New England for the more promising lands to the south and west. And men drawn off the farm into the cities directed their courses more to New York and Philadelphia than to Boston and Salem. Partly as a result, the value of the tangible resources of the state slipped from second to fourth place between 1790 and 1813. And by 1820, Massachusetts had also fallen from second to fifth place in population, ranking behind New York, Pennsylvania, Virginia, and youthful Ohio. Twice the number of Massachusetts' congressmen represented Pennsylvania in Washington, and more than twice as many sat for New York.[4] It is scarcely any wonder that by the early 1800's, three of the central demands of Massachusetts Federalism had become the control of immigration, repeal of the three-fifths clause, and a limit to territorial expansion.

---

[4]U.S. Bureau of the Census, *Historical Statistics of the United States*, pp. 13, 693, and Pitkin, *Statistical View*, p. 327.

The decline in the Commonwealth's comparative standing among the states swiftly reflected itself in the decline of her political power. Whereas she once offered her vice-president to Virginia's president and then witnessed his succession to the chief-magistracy, between 1800 and 1824 the state was unable to offer a serious candidate for the White House. No representative of the Commonwealth held a principal cabinet post until after the War of 1812; and save for John Quincy Adams toward the close of the war, none made a signal mark upon the national scene after 1800. Even more telling was the state's impotence to affect the course of national policies. First Jefferson's election in 1800, then his purchase of Louisiana in 1803, next his Embargo of 1807, and finally the Madison administration's declaration of war against Great Britain all vividly attested to the contempt with which dominant opinion in the nation had come to hold the commercial and regional interests of Massachusetts as her own Federalist majority defined them— a majority which, worst thing of all, was itself threatened.

Furthermore, at the very time that other states began to rival and surpass the old Bay Colony, her own internal homogeneity began to dissolve. Although the consistency of the state's ethnic composition was not to be disturbed until the commencement of Irish immigration in the 1820's, her religious uniformity—or at least the almost universal commitment to Congregationalism—fell under assault much sooner. First, the spread of deism and the defection of many from the orthodoxy of the Congregational establishment to a more liberal Calvinism, Unitarianism, or Universalism began seriously to undermine the prerogatives of the traditionalist Congregational clergy. In addition, the migration of people and the dogged perseverance of itinerant Baptist and Methodist preachers led to a burgeoning of dissent. Although the law burdened all dissenting religions with heavy liabilities, nothing could impede their increasingly rapid growth. They found such a mounting receptivity to their doctrines and styles within the borders of the state that they were able to expose the established church to increasingly effective moral, legal, and political challenge and thus to weaken its authority on all fronts.[5]

The rise of religious pluralism coincided with a rapid broadening of economic opportunities. First with the return of confidence in government, then with the outbreak of war in Europe in 1793 and the opening of neutral commerce, unforeseen opportunities in oceanic trade and in the associated activities of banking, insurance, shipbuilding, and merchandising lured new men, often of humble origins and little capital, into the coastal towns and into participation in their affairs.[6] If profits increased for everyone, so did competition and risk. The brittle arrangements of society suffered for the second time in twenty years the destabilizing effects of new fortunes. While assuaging the worries of some, prosperity also intensified the apprehensions of others. If new men might move upward, older wealth might once again slip down.

The return of good times had its effect everywhere. But whereas commercial prosperity dominated the concerns of maritime Massachusetts, in the interior and in Maine the land question became uppermost. By the mid-1790's, men had settled the remaining tracts in western Massachusetts and most of the arable areas everywhere in the downstate counties. Growing numbers of downstate families flocked to the Maine frontier of Massachusetts, to the Vermont and New Hampshire forests, or farther west beyond the Alleghenies into the Northwest. These demographic shifts, growing every year more significant, created all the potentialities for social disequilibrium and political tension usually associated with population movements and the settlement of virgin territories: new demands for services upon government, battles over land ownership, pressures upon traditional institutions and ideas transferred to a new environment, resentments caused by the failure to give leading men in the newly settled regions their recognition in

---

[5]See Chap. V, Sec. iv.
[6]See, e.g., Labaree, *Patriots and Partisans*, pp. 94-97.

the larger statewide community, resistance to the demands of the new frontier settlements by those left behind, and the resulting widening gap between the old society and the new. Long before the end of the century, rising demands were heard for the separation of Maine from downstate Massachusetts, or, barring that, for an increase in Maine's political power commensurate with her growth. Not only was Maine threatening to hold the balance of power between eastern and western Massachusetts, but her people were putting to a test the state's traditionally fragile regional cooperation.[7]

Such developments—the rise of religious pluralism, changes in the state's economy, and shifts of population—consolidated the state's impermanent political alliances and fluid social arrangements. More clearly defined and more comprehensive social and economic cliques—and, ultimately, political parties—were the result. Partly from the insecurities which afflict most *nouveaux arrivés*, partly from the ruling elite's attempt to preserve its competitive advantage, and partly because of the contemporaneous rise of partisan division, the demarcation between classes stiffened and the unity and trust within the community deteriorated. What once were commonplace maneuverings for profits and respectability hardened into contests for political mastery and social control with deep ideological overtones. Men had previously arranged business partnerships on the basis of capital need and with little relationship to social pedigree or factional allegiance. Now business groups closed out men of differing social rank or political identification, and separate Federalist and Republican banks, insurance companies, turnpike corporations, and the like came into existence. Charitable projects, historical societies, and dance assemblies initiated social, religious, and political tests. No groups escaped

[7]Goodman, *Democratic-Republicans of Mass.*, pp. 118-27; William Allen, "Bingham Land," *Collections of the Maine Historical Society*, VII (1876), 353-60; and *William Bingham's Maine Lands, 1790-1820*, ed. Frederick S. Allis, Jr., in *Publications of the Colonial Society of Massachusetts*, XXXVI & XXXVII (Boston, 1954).

the corrosive effect of class consciousness, and few avoided the tests of political purity.[8]

No doubt, the disruptive forces at work within Massachusetts society would sooner or later have led of themselves to the breakdown of factional coalitions and to the formation of genuine political parties and ideologies. But by giving new significance to all other events, the French Revolution measurably hastened the emergence of new politics and new persuasions. Nothing struck such a decisive blow to community harmony than the emotions loosed by the Revolution. Not again until the twentieth century did foreign events create such deep convulsions in American thought nor more sharply divide one American from another. And in no region were the political and intellectual consequences of the Revolution more severe than in New England and in no state more than in Massachusetts.

Yet the entire Commonwealth welcomed its early phases. Some deplored the outbreak of war in Europe in 1793 and regretted the beheading of Louis XVI, but most acclaimed the birth of a sister republic and exulted in the prospects of neutral trade. "Not withstanding the late excesses of the Republican party in France," a newspaper commentator wrote, "the cause of the French is still that of humanity—is still the cause of freedom."[9] Even the Congregational clerics, buoyed by what they judged to be its republicanism and anti-Catholicism, felt moved as late as 1795 to extol the Revolution in France as "a continuation of the late American war" and as one "among other causes, under heaven, of our present tranquillity."[1] Not even Citizen

---

[8]Labaree, *Patriots and Partisans*, pp. 136, 139 ff. On the breakdown of community harmony in one large town, see William T. Whitney, Jr., "The Crowninshields of Salem, 1800-1808: A Study in the Politics of Commercial Growth," *Essex Institute Historical Collections*, XCIV (Jan. 1958), 1-36; (April 1958), 79-118.

[9]*Centinel*, Oct. 10, 1792.

[1]Quoted in Gary B. Nash, "The American Clergy and the French Revolution," *WMQ*, 3rd Ser., XXII (July 1965), 396; and Anson E. Morse, *The Federalist Party in Massachusetts to the Year 1800* (Princeton, N.J., 1909), pp. 90-91. For the pre-1795 approbation

Genêt's brazen attempts to enlist American privateers in French service in contravention of Washington's neutrality policy injured the general enthusiasm. Although Genêt antagonized many informed men in 1793, the rising maritime depredations of Great Britain rapidly offset his actions in the public mind. Not surprisingly, some of the state's leading lay and clerical figures held suspect what they called "French principles" and the "Jacobin mode" from the earliest days of the Revolution and nourished a suspicion of anyone, especially James Madison, whom they thought evinced an "excessive partiality" for France.[2] Nevertheless, even the most violent phase of the Revolution in 1793, though condemned by many, failed to divide Massachusetts.

What finally brought home the full significance of the Revolution was the impact of a series of domestic events. First, the rapid growth of deistic religion directly implicated the Rev-

---

of the French Revolution in Massachusetts generally, see Nash, "American Clergy and the French Revolution," pp. 393-97; Morse, *Federalist Party in Mass.*, pp. 69-74; Harrison Gray Otis in *The Debates and Proceedings in the Congress of the United States* (Washington, 1834-56), usually cited as *Annals of Congress* (hereafter A/C), 5th Cong., House, 1st Sess., p. 105; Goodman, *Democratic-Republicans of Mass.*, pp. 55-56; and Labaree, *Patriots and Partisans*, pp. 106 ff.

[2]See, e.g., Cabot to Samuel Phillips, Mar. 8, 1794, in Henry Cabot Lodge, *Life and Letters of George Cabot* (Boston, 1878), pp. 77-78: French principles "are more to be dreaded, in a moral view, than a thousand yellow fevers in a physical." In fact, some of those who came to be Federalists by the mid-1790's mistrusted France even before the French Revolution. As early as 1787, for example, two years before the Tennis Court Oath, Stephen Higginson suspected France of trying to frustrate American independence and decried her "weighty influence" in national affairs. Moreover, the future Federalists were on guard against Madison right from the start of the federal government. In 1789, Ames considered him "very much Frenchified in his politics." See "Letters of Stephen Higginson, 1785-1804" (hereafter "Higginson Letters"), ed. J. Franklin Jameson, in *Annual Report of the American Historical Association for the Year 1896* (2 vols., Washington, 1897), I, 713-39 *passim*; and Ames to George R. Minot, May 3, 1789, in *Works of Fisher Ames*, ed. Seth Ames (2 vols., Boston, 1854), I, 35. See also Ames to John Lowell [Sr.], Dec. 6, 1792, Misc. MSS Colls., Library of Congress (hereafter LC); and Theodore Sedgwick to Henry Van Schaack, Feb. 13, 1790, Sedgwick MSS, Massachusetts Historical Society (hereafter MHS).

olution and revealed to Federalist minds its evil effects. Deistic notions had long circulated in the United States. But not until 1794, with the appearance of Tom Paine's *Age of Reason,* did the defenders of the old Calvinist faith recognize deism's full threat to the old faith. Drawing a connection between revealed religion on the one hand and corrupt and tyrannical government on the other, Paine denounced all conservative and established confessions. Inexpensively published and widely read, his book offered to the public an engaging defense of the French Revolution as an antireligious exercise. Not surprisingly, the vocal Congregational clergy leaped to the defense of their traditional prerogatives and, joined by others of like mind, condemned the French Revolution, the "detestable principles of an atheistical philosophy," and the "scene of horrid blasphemy and abominable wickedness, which stands unrivaled in the annals of history."[3] When justified as an act of republicanism, the Revolution could win their praise. But once it was portrayed as an antagonist of religion, the clergy's reaction was foregone. After 1794, no deeper foes of France, nor of the Revolution's American sympathizers, could be found.

The outspoken assault upon revealed religion coincided with an outbreak of domestic turmoil and debate more severe than any other experienced since the American Revolution. The "Whisky Rebellion" of 1794—the protest of Pennsylvania farmers against the national excise tax—not only recalled Shays's Rebellion but in conservative opinion posed an even graver threat to the national well-being. Moreover, the establishment of Democratic Clubs in Boston and elsewhere in 1793 conjured up the most lurid visions of "Jacobin" anarchy.

---

[3]Nash, "American Clergy and the French Revolution," p. 398; and Morse, *Federalist Party in Mass.,* p. 81. I have been greatly benefited in my own thinking by Nash's examination of the effects of the French Revolution, deism, and Tom Paine's writings upon the Congregational clergy in Massachusetts. See also Charles Downer Hazen, *The French Revolution as Seen by Americans of the Eighteenth Century* (Baltimore, Md., 1897); G. Adolph Koch, *Republican Religion: The American Revolution and the Cult of Reason* (New York, 1933); and Herbert M. Morais, *Deism in Eighteenth Century America* (New York, 1960).

But the domestic event which most directly catalyzed sentiment against the French Revolution and most deeply affected the history of the early Massachusetts parties was the debate over Jay's Treaty with Great Britain. When the unfavorable terms of this agreement became known early in 1795, Massachusetts men condemned them as prejudicial to the national interest, and the Boston town meeting went on record in the summer of 1795 against its provisions. Among other things, the treaty failed to open trade with the West Indies except under the most humiliating terms, and it prohibited direct trade in American vessels to Europe. It failed to satisfy American desires for a narrow definition of contraband cargo, and it recognized the British right to seize contraband goods from neutral ships. Yet, despite the treaty's objectionable provisions, Massachusetts opinion veered sharply in favor of its ratification by the end of the summer of 1795.[4]

Why it did so has never been precisely clear. No major events, no local political developments, intervened. Second thoughts convinced many influential merchants that in a time of exciting commercial prospects an imperfect treaty served their interests better than no treaty at all. Many more were thrown back to a defense of the treaty by the verbal attacks upon commerce and shipping launched by the agrarian South. Moreover, the Senate debates over ratification and the struggle in the House over treaty appropriations threw into sharp relief the long-brewing antagonism between New England and the plantation owners. But above all, the question of the treaty raised more vividly than at any other moment since the Peace of 1783 the matter of America's own republican future in a hostile and warring world. Those who identified themselves with Federalism became convinced that trade and friendship with England, under whatever conditions, was the only path

---

[4]On the effects of the Jay Treaty upon opinion, see Joseph Charles, *The Origins of the American Party System* (Williamsburg, Va., 1956), Chap. III; Goodman, *Democratic-Republicans of Mass.*, pp. 57-59; and Labaree, *Patriots and Partisans*, pp. 111-12. On the Democratic Clubs, see Eugene P. Link, *Democratic-Republican Societies, 1790-1800* (New York, 1942).

to the preservation of the national autonomy and, equally important for the fate of mankind, of the only remaining republic in the world.

To contemporaries, this consideration transcended all others. Matters of religion, trade, expansion, mobility, voting, and immigration all became infused with theoretical and practical questions of republicanism. Could a republican society whose very basis was virtue and religion tolerate the distribution of antireligious tracts? Could a nation dependent upon trade for its well-being risk its delicate commercial relationships, even in the name of republican principle? Could America fly in the face of experience by extending republican government halfway across the continent and inviting foreigners to participate in its affairs? Was the only genuine republic in the world well served by free criticism of its public officials? Such questions and others like them had been raised before but never so universally and never to the minds of contemporaries with such momentous implications for the national future.

The Massachusetts Federalists' negative response to all these questions was inspired not simply by the crabbed self-interest for which historical tradition too easily indicts them, but also by a generous vision of the national destiny. Their difficulty was that this vision was now contested: the commitment to republicanism which had united men in 1776 now divided them. And it was this renewal of intense ideological debate over the meaning of republicanism that generated the outlines of a two-party system.

In the mid-1790's, the political system remained inchoate and undifferentiated. But as a result of the sudden intrusion upon the Massachusetts consciousness of the unsettling events in France, the erosion of the delicate bonds of social unity, and the beginning of a decline in the Commonwealth's relative weight in the union, Federalism swiftly gained dominion over the state. The party was not the agent but the beneficiary of change.

Of the two political alternatives which emerged by the end of the century, Federalism came to dominate Massachusetts because it offered reassurance to a people abruptly cast loose from the securities of the past. As an alternative to Jeffersonianism, with its emphasis on mobility, opportunity, and self-reliance, Federalism offered a social ideal which emphasized stability, tradition, dependence, and the common good. It fed upon provincial illusions and fears and expressed a powerful regional culture. To a people resentful of their state's loss of influence and of their own loss of standing within society, frightened by the specter of an unparalleled revolution abroad, provoked by the domestic hostility of religious dissenters, factional adversaries, and men on the make, frustrated by the failure of their own revolution to bear out its promise, and simply unable to understand change—to these people the Federalist Party gave a powerful voice and held a great appeal.

The party won the adherence of all sorts of men: the high and low, western farmer and eastern merchant, Boston deist and Connecticut Valley Calvinist, the learned and the ignorant. And more effectively and more passionately than its Republican opposite, it identified itself with New England's worthy past. By the 1790's, a half-century before the movement for Southern independence, a strong traditionalist and regionalist movement had taken root in Massachusetts. From its beginnings in the 1790's, when factionalism was on the rise and the French Revolution had laid bare the crisis of Western institutions, this movement sought definition, expression, and political form. And before 1800 and the abrupt and irreversible destruction of Federalist political power at the national level, it found all three in the Federalist Party.

II

IT IS DIFFICULT to recapture the intensity of feeling which quickly accumulated behind the Federalist Party in Massachusetts after 1795 and the excessive manner in which it was expressed. Yet few features of that formative era of American politics are so striking as the impassioned and envenomed quality of its political rhetoric. Soon after the measured debates on the Constitution, political discourse took on a rancor and coarseness of tone rarely equaled in our national history. Mutual trust gave way to bitter recrimination, hope yielded to anxiety, and violence of deed came to match violence of word. Rare was the issue of the public press which did not record instances of personal abuse, politically motivated duels, threats of nullification, armed rebellions among the populace, and brawls on the floor of Congress. Few contemporaries escaped the bitter spirit.[5]

The Federalists absorbed this extremist political style more fully than did their Republican adversaries. They were far more abusive in their partisan assaults. Their rhetorical violence spanned a longer period. And they delivered their crisis prophecies with a force of invective unmatched at the time and seldom since surpassed. But why they did so—indeed, why there occurred such a rapid deterioration of civic morale and tranquillity and why long-standing differences of social and political philosophy, of personal ambitions, and of sectional and economic rivalries provoked greater political heat in the 1790's than before—remains to be accounted for.

To cite in explanation for the Federalists' political rancor the novelty of partisan conflict, the destruction of community harmony, or the extraordinary impact of the French Revolution is to give an elliptical answer. One wishes to know why, at that moment and not another, parties themselves became subject to fierce condemnation, why men began to voice such bitter lamentations over the evaporation of mutual trust, why quondam friends—former comrades-in-arms, old associates in Independence and constitution-making, "Founding Fathers"—

---

[5]For a general review of the violence of politics in the 1790's, see the three articles by Marshall Smelser: "The Jacobin Phrenzy: Federalism and the Menace of Liberty, Equality, and Fraternity," *Review of Politics*, XIII (Oct. 1951), 457-82; "The Jacobin Phrenzy: The Menace of Monarchy, Plutocracy, and Anglophilia, 1789-1798," *ibid.*, XXI (Jan. 1959), 239-58; and "The Federalist Period as an Age of Passion," *American Quarterly* (hereafter *AQ*), X (Winter 1958), 391-419.

suddenly assailed each other as dishonest traitors, why the French Revolution assumed such outlandish proportions in the debates of the day. Likewise, to suggest that the Federalists drew more alarmist meaning from events because of their limited receptivity to change or their economic and social position is to provide only a partial explanation of their supercharged style. One needs to make sense not only of the quality and content of their violent rhetoric but also of its structure and imagery.

Any explanation of Federalist political rhetoric begins in paradox: the passions generated by political division originated in ideological consensus. Massachusetts Federalists shared a commitment to republican ideology altogether as deep and encompassing as their Republican opponents. No matter their age or circumstance, they were steeped in the lore of the republican way, having imbibed its assumptions from family tradition, through formal schooling, and most directly through the momentous flux of public affairs. After more than a half-century of development, the republican ideology had by the 1790's become a secular faith for all Americans, commanding all the psychic investment of loyalty and belief required of all such systems of political ideas. Federalists and Republicans embraced its tenets with equal fervor, and each outdid the other in professions of their faith. Yet their testimonials, rather than conveying a sense of assurance, possessed unmistakable strains of anxiety and fear. For if in the end these political antagonists could agree upon nothing else, they could agree upon one fact: the republic was in peril.[6]

---

[6]The ideological basis of the day's politics is emphasized in John R. Howe's brief but valuable "Republican Thought and the Political Violence of the 1790's," *AQ,* XIX (Summer 1967), 147-65. As will be apparent throughout, I have been greatly stimulated by this and the following studies: Bernard Bailyn, *The Ideological Origins of the American Revolution* (Cambridge, 1967), *The Origins of American Politics* (New York, 1968), and "Political Experience and Enlightenment Ideas in Eighteenth-Century America," *American Historical Review,* LXVII (Jan. 1962), 339-51; Gordon S. Wood, *The Creation of the American Republic, 1776-1787* (Chapel Hill, N.C., 1969), and "Rhetoric and Reality in the American Revolution,"

I: *Origins of Massachusetts Federalism*

The times contained enough foreign danger and domestic confusion amply to justify such a concern. But the fears of Massachusetts Federalists stemmed not only from the events of the moment but also from the long tradition of republican philosophy. Their political and social thought, like that of classical republican theorists, originated in a sobering premise: although exalted in conception and unique in promise, republics were unsurpassed in fragility, vulnerability, and impermanence. "It is the lot of free republican government," noted Federalist Samuel Taggart, "to be but of short duration." "A republic," ventured Fisher Ames, "wears out its morals almost as soon as the sap of a white birch rots the wood." And the survival of only a few small republican states in Europe recalled the vain hopes of earlier republican philosophers and statesmen.[7] How could the United States—though isolated by oceans and sustained by a unique constitution—expect to escape the fate which beset all states of its kind: internal division, moral corruption, political tyranny, and external assault?

WMQ, 3rd Ser., XXIII (Jan. 1966), 3-32; and Cecelia M. Kenyon, "Republicanism and Radicalism in the American Revolution: An Old-Fashioned Interpretation," *ibid.*, XIX (Apr. 1962), 153-82.

I challenge, however, the implications of Howe, Smelser, and others that the problem of political violence ended with the 1790's. The violence continued after 1800 and, though often altered in style and content, has become a recurrent element of American politics since then. Moreover, like the violence itself, the ideological strains of American politics were continuous from the pre-Revolutionary years at least until 1815. Contrary to Bailyn's argument (*Ideological Origins*, pp. 20-21) to the effect that the three principal creative periods of the Revolutionary era ended with the formation of the national government, the attempts of Jefferson, Hamilton, Washington, Adams, and others to define the republican experiment in a revolutionary context after 1790 represent equally creative moments of an Age of Revolution which extended at least until 1815. The Virginia and Kentucky Resolutions, the Louisiana Purchase, the Embargo, the War of 1812, and the Hartford Convention, each in their way, were efforts to work out the implications, many of them not manifest earlier, of the American revolutionary ideology.

[7]Samuel Taggart, *An Oration Delivered at Conway, July 4, 1804* . . . (Northampton, Mass., 1804), p. 5; Ames to Pickering, Jan. 12, 1807, *Works*, I, 386; and Caleb Strong, *Patriotism and Piety, The Speeches of his Excellency Caleb Strong, Esq.* . . . *from 1800 to 1807* (Newburyport, Mass., 1808), p. 115.

The ambitiousness of America's republican designs only increased the dangers. This was to be a confederated republic, lacking both a strong central authority and a standing military arm. It was to be a large republic, dependent for its cohesion more upon men's loyalties than upon force and legal restraint. It was to be an open republic where ideas would circulate freely and the most humble would have the opportunity to gain standing and wealth. Could such a society prevail?

According to the republican canon and the Massachusetts Federalist ideology, four conditions were essential for the survival of the republican state. The first was public and private virtue. "It has ever been an acknowledged maxim in the science of politics," declared an anonymous Federalist writer, "that virtue is the only permanent basis of a republic." The Reverend David Tappan, a stout defender of the Federalist faith, reminded his congregation "that the most celebrated states and kingdoms of the earth have arisen by virtue and fallen by vice." "It will be difficult to find an instance," Governor Caleb Strong agreed, "where a free and civilized people have been conquered who had not degenerated from that virtue, by which their liberty was established." Permit the slightest intrusion of dishonesty or corruption, and a republic was doomed.[8]

In the thinking of Massachusetts Federalists, virtue flourished when men sacrificed personal advantage for the general welfare and displayed a disinterested concern for the good of all. "True republican rulers," noted the Reverend John Thornton Kirkland, "are bound to act, not simply as those who appoint them *would*, but as they *ought*." But virtue, above all, implied dedication to religion. "Religion makes men republi-

---

[8][Boston] *New England Palladium* (hereafter *Palladium*), Apr. 1, 1806; David Tappan, *A Discourse . . . on April 5, 1798* (Boston, 1798), quoted in J. Earl Thompson, Jr., "A Perilous Experiment: New England Clergymen and American Destiny, 1796-1826" (unpub. Ph.D. dissertation, Princeton Univ., 1966), p. 269; and Strong, *Patriotism and Piety*, p. 113. See also *ibid.*, pp. 15, 120; *Palladium*, Mar. 31, 1807; and Abraham Haskell, *Oration, Pronounced at Fitchburg . . . July 4, A.D. 1814* (Worcester, Mass., 1814), pp. 21-22, 30-33.

cans," declared Nathaniel Emmons, an outspoken clerical adherent of Federalism. Piety and good morals, wrote Tappan, "invariably lead to national honor and prosperity, and in the ordinary course of things will ultimately secure them." But "every species of irreligion and vice contributes, either directly or remotely, to disgrace, enfeeble, and destroy a community."[9]

Beyond virtue, the republican commonwealth rested upon internal unity, a balance of social forces, equilibrium among the branches of government, and a harmony between classes and sections. To the Massachusetts Federalist way of thinking, the qualities of unity and balance were essential republican traits. They had equally to do with the national compromise of regional and economic interests and the local "harmony of good neighborhood." They depended upon the very conditions which Massachusetts was believed recently to have displayed and the Constitution to have preserved: homogeneity of race and religion, continuity up and down the social scale, and a spirit of mutual concession and commitment to the general good. "The strength of a republick," Governor Strong reminded the General Court, "consists in the mutual dependence and agreement of its several parts." The Constitution, Timothy Pickering noted, reflected just such qualities: it was "the result of compromise—of mutual sacrifices, of State interests, of local wishes, and attachments, to the common good."[1]

From such considerations it followed that republics required compactness, political unity, and ethnic purity. "A republican government, the nature of which being mild,"

---

[9]John Thornton Kirkland, "Memoir of Fisher Ames," in Ames, *Works*, I, 21; *The Works of Nathaniel Emmons, D. D.*, ed. Jacob Ide (2 vols., Boston, 1842), II, 246-47; and Thompson, "Perilous Experiment," p. 267. See also Samuel Kendall, *Religion the Only Sure Basis of Free Governments* . . . (Boston, 1804); and Timothy Pickering's toast, "Religion and Morality, essential supports [of] a free government," [Boston] *Repertory*, Mar. 9, 1804.

[1]Strong, *Patriotism and Piety*, p. 156; *The Patriotick Proceedings of the Legislature of Massachusetts, During their Session from Jan. 26, to March 4, 1809* (Boston, 1809), p. 62; and Pickering in *A/C*, 8th Cong., Senate, 1st Sess., pp. 195-98. On the republican notion of balance, see Bailyn, *Ideological Origins*, pp. 73 ff.

wrote the party's chief publicist and pamphleteer, John Lowell, Jr., "is much less calculated for a very extensive country, than any other." Territorial expansion scattered the population, augmented sectional tensions, and attenuated the already weak authority of government over the people. Large republics, Federalists believed after Montesquieu, tended to disintegrate, and if they managed to retain their cohesion they did so only under the corrective force of military despotism. "All history," Federalists agreed, "showed that great empires, whether monarchies or republics, had ultimately broken to pieces by their magnitude." Before 1815, no Massachusetts Federalist was known to accept Madison's bold thesis, best expressed in the *Tenth Federalist*, that large territorial boundaries might be the very guarantor of republican government.[2]

Nor did the Massachusetts Federalists accept the Madisonian notion of an inevitable, if manageable, struggle between the elements of a pluralistic society. They denied the existence of a natural contest between the upper and lower orders of society, between the productive classes, or among sections, religions, and different types of property. "Our interests when candidly considered are one," Theophilus Parsons declared. The inhabitants of remote agricultural towns often complained that disregard for commerce and shipping brought ruin to the whole republic. Northampton memorialists who petitioned Congress against the declaration of war in 1812 pointed out that "residing in the interior of the country" they had no direct interest in opposing the government's trade restrictions. "But the interests of the merchant are so closely blended with those of the mechanic and husbandman, that any measures, hostile to the rights and happiness of either, maintain the same character in relation to all."[3]

---

[2][John Lowell, Jr.], *Thoughts in a Series of Letters in Answer to a Question Respecting the Division of the States, by a Massachusetts Farmer* (n.p., 1813), p. 8; and Samuel Thatcher in *A/C*, 8th Cong., House, 1st Sess., p. 456.

[3][Theophilus Parsons], *Result of the Convention of Delegates Holden at Ipswich in the County of Essex . . .* (hereafter *Essex Result*), (Newburyport, Mass., 1778), pp. 11-12; and *Proceedings of*

I: *Origins of Massachusetts Federalism*

The immigration of foreigners also found a place in the Federalist catalogue of anti-republican evils. For as men "who have little interest in, and less attachment to the country," aliens threatened the cohesiveness and solidarity of republican society. Likewise, political parties were destructive of republican unity. By disrupting mutual harmony and consolidating the divisions within the community, the growth of faction— "an adherence," according to the Federalist definition, "to interests foreign to the interests of the State"—weakened a republican nation and exposed it to domestic and foreign intrigues.[4]

If moral rectitude and social equilibrium sustained a republic, then power imperiled it. Nothing in the whole system of republican thought was more axiomatic than the belief that republican prospects hung upon men's success in checking power's compulsive advance. Carefully allocated, wisely used, and jealously checked, nothing better enhanced man's estate or contributed to the general welfare. But, far from inert, power was, in the words of Caleb Strong, "of an encroaching nature," naturally aggrandizing and heedless of its legal bounds.[5]

Even more important, men naturally sought power. "The love of power," Federalists believed, "is congenial to mankind; this desire seems to be interwoven with human nature." Moreover, the designing and ambitious sought it only for their own advantage at the expense of the commonweal. Given their

---

the *Town of Northampton*, dtd. July 1, 1812, Misc. Broadside (hereafter "Bdse.") Coll., Forbes Library, Northampton, Mass. See also Strong, *Patriotism and Piety*, pp. 72, 74; Pickering, "Memorandum," dtd. *ca.* 1812, Pickering MSS, MHS; *Centinel*, May 1, 1811; *Palladium*, Feb. 26, March 26, 1811; *Patriotick Proceedings*, pp. 101, 128; Benjamin Pickman in *A/C*, 11th Cong., House, 1st Sess., p. 186; and the Memorial of Gorham, Maine, Aug. 29, 1808, in Hugh D. McLellan, *History of Gorham, Me.* (Portland, Me., 1903), pp. 153-54.

[4]Ames, *Works*, II, 118.

[5]Strong to Pickering, Feb. 7, 1815, Pickering MSS, MHS. The continuities of ideology are revealed vividly in the notion of power's "encroaching nature." The same phrase was used by Americans before 1776 (Bailyn, *Ideological Origins*, p. 56) and by James Madison in the *47th Federalist*. On the place of "power" in the republican ideology generally, see Bailyn, *Ideological Origins*, pp. 55 ff., and Wood, *Creation of the American Republic*, pp. 18-23, 36-43.

ambitions, wrote Theodore Lyman, "men are seldom content to stop at any stage of power." Once having enjoyed a taste of dominion over others, they sought more and more power until, from the contest of their ambitions, despotism emerged and the fragile structure of republicanism disintegrated.[6]

Yet the ambitious designs of men from within America offered no greater a threat to the republican state than did foreign attacks. For by disrupting the normal course of society, the wars which followed external assaults gave rise to immorality, destroyed social intercourse, and weakened religion. By calling for unaccustomed concentrations of civil and military authority, wars loosened the delicate fetters upon power. War would "shake down the feeble and then unbraced structure of our government." But this was just the dilemma: while by their very fragility republics invited attack from without, for their very survival these attacks had to be forestalled by the use of power. Although no republic could afford to antagonize another nation, much less to seize the initiative and make war, neither could a republic remain defenseless. Passivity encouraged peace, but military impotence invited war.[7]

Such, then, were held to be the principal qualities of a republican society: virtue, harmony, carefully limited power, and an avoidance of foreign wars and entanglements. Between Independence and the Constitution, this general system of republican beliefs became the unofficial civic creed of all Americans, rigidly adhered to and fiercely defended.[8] Yet for all its appeal, the republican ideology, like the republic which it helped undergird, was brittle and provocative. Because it contained only the barest guidelines to the implementation of the republican scheme, it invited conflicting interpretations as to its implications at every point. It suggested what an ideal re-

---

[6]Samuel Taggart in *A/C*, 8th Cong., House, 1st Sess., p. 732; Ames, *Works*, II, 418; and Theodore Lyman to Pickering, Feb. 29, 1804, Pickering MSS, MHS.

[7]Ames in *A/C*, 4th Cong., House, 1st Sess., p. 1262.

[8]The speed and tenacity of Americans' commitment to republicanism are emphasized by Kenyon, "Republicanism and Radicalism in the American Revolution," pp. 165-67.

public might be, but not how to achieve it. Given the tenacity of men's republican faith, how could a sincerely motivated difference over its meaning be kept from appearing a departure from its principles or a perversion of its goals? Given the general terms in which its central premises were couched, who was reliably to say what constituted a wise use of authority and what a dangerous extension of power, what a useful foreign involvement and what an invitation to war, what virtue and what vice? Like all ideologies, this one inspired more debate than consensus.

If the nature of republican ideology placed a heavy burden upon national harmony, the universally held belief in the unique role of America's republican effort made this burden insupportable. In the tumultuous days of Danton and Robespierre, Austerlitz and Trafalgar, it was easy to assume that with the fate of the United States rode the fate of republicanism everywhere. America in American eyes became the final barrier to English monarchical power and French revolutionary despotism. America, contemporaries believed, was "the world's last hope of a republick." Massachusetts Federalists concurred. The nation, warned a typical Federalist commentator, had only two options: it must either erect the noblest edifice of man's history or "blast . . . the fairest hopes of creation." "Should this last hope of freedom fail, this only republican government on the face of the earth be subverted," echoed the Massachusetts General Court, "there is little probability that the experiment would ever be repeated."[9]

Here lay the crux of the matter for thoughtful contemporaries: the American republic was, in their oft-repeated word, an "experiment"—untried, unprecedented, unpredictable.[1] Given the attacks of a hostile world, there was no telling that this far-flung confederated empire would survive. It was

---

[9]*An Address to the Citizens of the County of Plymouth* (n.p., 1812), p. 3; Thomas Danforth, *An Oration, Pronounced July 4, 1804* . . . (Boston, 1804), pp. 9-10; and Strong, *Patriotism and Piety*, p. 121.

[1]William Cunningham, Jr., *An Oration, Pronounced at Fitchburg, July 4, 1803* . . . (Leominster, Mass., 1803), p. 12; and Ames, *Works*, II, 129.

certain only that its failure would end the hopes and aspirations of all peoples for all time. Bearing such a commission for posterity, men understandably differed as to what constituted virtue, equilibrium, power, and the rest. In turn, because they believed that with each small act rode man's fate, they not surprisingly showed an unusual inclination toward mistrusting each other's motives and intentions and toward an excessive defensiveness and assertiveness—toward all the attributes of what has been called the paranoid style.[2]

Yet as much as Federalist paranoia grew out of the republican faith, it was also related to other—and more venerable—modes of thought. In the special imagery of Federalist rhetoric and in the distinctive Federalist interpretations of events are to be found the unmistakable influence of the Puritan jeremiad and of American revolutionary thought.

The Puritan jeremiad had not died with Independence. During the era of the French Revolution, the New England countryside rang with dark prophecies of heaven-sent punishment against erring men. "We are a people," it was repeatedly lamented, "in an uncommon degree laden with iniquity." For their transgressions against the Holy Spirit, neither citizen nor nation was to be spared Almighty judgment. Thundering from the Congregational pulpits of New England, the jeremiad evoked for thousands of parishioners the spirit of their forefathers and helped them reaffirm their solidarity with the hoariest traditions of the Puritan state. As delivered by the Congregational clergy, the jeremiad above all expressed men's fears for the republic and their condemnation of the course of national events since the mid-1790's, "all those atrocious enormities," in the words of the Reverend David Osgood, which "are still crying to Heaven for vengeance."[3]

---

[2]In borrowing the useful notion of a "paranoid style" from Richard Hofstadter, *The Paranoid Style in American Politics and Other Essays* (New York, 1965), I mean to suggest a quality of thought which revealed the very structure of ideology.

[3]Samuel Austin, *A Sermon, Preached in Worcester, Massachusetts . . . July 23d, 1812* (Worcester, Mass., 1812), p. 9; David Osgood, *A Discourse Delivered at Cambridge . . . April 8, 1810* (Cambridge,

I: *Origins of Massachusetts Federalism*

The jeremiad was so effective in arousing men from the 1790's on because its themes of corruption and potential destruction exactly coincided with major themes of the republican ideology which the clerics and the general public had so thoroughly assimilated. In particular, the jeremiad possessed a close affinity with the cyclical theory of history deeply imbedded within republican thought. The jeremiad assumed a process of decline, a falling-off of virtue from some higher state of rectitude and religiosity. The cyclical theory assumed a similar process of decline: nations successively rose and fell, first to dominate over others, then to fall subject to them. This ebb and flow was intimately related to the virtue and prosperity of the people. Though powerless to initiate the growth or to prevent the decay of their society, a people might, through vigilance and moral uprightness, prolong a nation's days of full development or, through corruption and impiety, hasten its fall.[4]

The Federalists of Massachusetts had never seen any reason to doubt these truths. They fully expected the inexorable cycle of history eventually to work its way. Writing as early as 1778, young Theophilus Parsons of Newburyport, a rising legal talent and soon-to-be Federalist, explained that "the most

---

1810), p. 17; William Bentley, *The Diary of William Bentley, D.D.* (4 vols., Salem, Mass., 1905-14), II, 423; and *Autobiography of Amos Kendall*, ed. William Stickney (New York, 1949), pp. 72-73.

Perry Miller, "From the Covenant to the Revival," in *The Shaping of American Religion*, eds. James Ward Smith and A. Leland Jamison (4 vols., Princeton, N.J., 1961), I, 322-68, has examined the jeremiad in the Revolutionary and post-Revolutionary years and has shown the part played by the clergy in accommodating the secular revolutionary ideology within the religious context. On the earlier history of the jeremiad, see Miller, *The New England Mind: From Colony to Province* (Cambridge, 1953), Chap. II and *passim*. Bailyn, *Ideological Origins*, has also demonstrated the intimate link between religious convictions and political ideology before 1776. For considerable evidence of the healthy state of the jeremiad until at least 1815, see Thompson, "Perilous Experiment"; Morse, *Federalist Party in Mass.*; and Vernon Stauffer, *New England and the Bavarian Illuminati* (New York, 1918), *passim*.

[4]Stow Persons, "The Cyclical Theory of History in Eighteenth-Century America," *AQ*, VI (Summer 1954), 147-63.

virtuous states have become vicious. The morals of all people, in all ages, have been shockingly corrupted." Was America to differ? "Shall we long boast an exemption from the general fate of mankind? Are our private and political virtues to be transmitted untainted from generation to generation, through a course of ages? Have we not already degenerated from the pure morals and disinterested patriotism of our ancestors?" Thirty years later, Federalist convictions had not changed. "The history of the world is a history of revolution," Abijah Bigelow noted in 1808. "Nations, like individuals, have their rise and fall." Prosperity and wealth, the Reverend David Tappan reasoned, were high and estimable ends; but they invariably defeated themselves by corrupting men's morals and drawing them towards "pride and avarice, luxury and dissipation, idleness and sensuality, and too often into practical or scornful impiety. These, with other kindred vices, hasten their downfall and ruin." The cycle of history had then been completed.[5]

Yet, if most men agreed on the cause and inevitability of decline, they differed over the agency which brought it about. Where the secular spokesmen of the republican faith tended to ascribe the deterioration of national dignity and prosperity to the workings of the natural law, the spiritual leaders of the established Congregational church saw a divine hand at work. To them, corruption and immorality called down upon themselves the unappeasable force of divine anger. "The voice of God to us . . . is emphatically this," they declared in 1799. "Come out of the infidel, antichristian world, my people; that ye be not partakers of her sins, and that ye receive not her plagues."[6]

When pressed to indicate the signs of heavenly retribution, the clerics found them at every hand. Take, for example, they said, Thomas Jefferson, whom they likened to Jereboam,

---

[5][Parsons], *Essex Result*, p. 32; Abijah Bigelow, *An Oration, Delivered at Bolton, July 4, 1808* (Leominster, Mass., 1808), p. 3; and David Tappan, *A Discourse, Delivered . . . on April 5, 1798* (Boston, 1798), pp. 18-19.

[6]Quoted in Stauffer, *Bavarian Illuminati*, p. 101.

Absalom, and Beelzebub the Anti-Christ: "If a whole nation prefer a wicked man, it demonstrates the wickedness of the nation. . . . God does not send a wicked ruler to a good people; he never did. A good people will not endure a wicked ruler; they never did." Or the existing national government: it revealed "falsehood, fraud, and treachery," induced "oppression and barbarity," aimed at "discord, slavery, and ruin among the nations. . . . Thus we harmonize with spiritual Babylon. . . . The same moral putrefaction covers the land with the damps of death." Or the War of 1812: God permits nations to go to war "to act out the perverseness of their nature" and "to punish them for their sins."[7]

By the time the jeremiad had come back into its own around 1800, it was difficult to distinguish the clerical arraignments of a corrupt people from the invective of the secular politician. Few party orators could equal the bitter spirit of the clerics who called the Republicans "men of hardened hearts, seared consciences, reprobate minds, and desperate in wickedness," or who likened the presidency to a "vast, noxious lake, bursting its barriers, overflowing all the springs and rivers of the country, communicating its own malignity wherever it extends." For their part, lay Federalists in the Commonwealth began to see in the nation's difficulties what Fisher Ames, not the most ardent of believers, called "God's displeasure." And a newspaper writer urged his readers in 1801 to the same view: "If we are doomed to be bestrode for a time by the mortifier Jacobinism, let us confess that it is but a just punishment for neglecting our God and our country." Two violent and impassioned styles had assimilated each other.[8]

Although these lay and clerical diatribes were inspired in the first instance by the rhetoric of the earlier Puritan divines, a more encompassing and more recent tradition lay

---

[7]Thompson, "Perilous Experiment," pp. 109, 148, 164.

[8]David Osgood, *A Solemn Protest Against the Late Declaration of War* . . . (Cambridge, 1812), pp. 14-15; Thompson, "Perilous Experiment," p. 109; Ames, *Works*, II, 133; and "Latitudinarian" in *Centinel*, Jan. 10, 1801.

behind them. They carried with their condemnation of corruption not only the emphases of Puritan theology but the clear overtones of American revolutionary thought. To read the products of the Massachusetts Federalist mind after 1795 is often to believe oneself transported to the Boston of the Tea Party and the Port Bill. Old images, old symbols, old charges abound, appropriately refurbished to fit a new setting, but otherwise calling to mind, as they called to the minds of contemporaries, the same fears of tyranny, the same visions of depravity, the same threats of conspiracy, and many of the same canons of the political science of that former day.

Like the revolutionary generation, the Federalists of Massachusetts looked back to an Augustan age of virtue and achievement. Especially after 1800, when the presidency and the Congress had been swept from their control, they came to idealize the unembellished Constitution of 1787 and the era of the first two presidents, just as the Whig opposition in England and the American colonists had often sanctified the ancient English constitution and ancient English liberties. "The period of the two former administrations," it was commonly believed, "was the golden age of America." From impotence, depression, and disunity, the nation had risen to a state of power and wealth without precedent in the annals of the past. "No parallel can be found in history, of a transition so rapid as that of the United States from the lowest depression to the highest felicity—from the condition of a weak and disjointed republic, to that of a great, united, and prosperous nation." Under Federalist auspices, "our national association was a compact of virtue." Government was benign, liberty secure, and justice universal. "Beyond the example of any former period . . . the people enjoyed every thing they wished, the nation every thing it required."[9]

---

[9]*Patriotick Proceedings,* p. 116; *Proceedings of a Convention of Delegates . . . convened at Hartford, in the State of Connecticut, December 15th, 1814* (Hartford, 1815) (hereafter *Hartford Convention Report*), p. 4; Sedgwick in *A/C,* 4th Cong., House, 1st Sess., p. 530; and *Address to the Friends of Independence, Peace, and Union*

I: *Origins of Massachusetts Federalism*

Then, after 1800, occurred what the cyclical theory predicted. The nation started on what George Cabot called its "natural downward course" toward impiety and vice. It was now America's turn to re-enact the history of other free states: "In the fate of the European Republicks," warned Harrison Gray Otis, "we might read our own." This, then, was the meaning for Federalists of what they called the "revolution of 1800": it signaled not merely the triumph of a new political ideal but the termination, as they had experienced it, of the republican experiment. The specter of corruption, tyranny, and warfare as destructive to American republican liberties as the Jacobin Terror had been to the republican glories of the early French Revolution opened before them. Jefferson's election appeared to them no mere change of administration, no modest introduction of new policies, "no little cabinet scene, where one minister comes into power and another goes out," in the words of Fisher Ames, "but a great moral revolution proceeding from the vices and passions of men, shifting officers today, that measures, and principles, and systems, may be shifted to-morrow."[1]

The corruption behind the nation's decline had many sources. Some believed it to have originated in French "Jacobinism," an ill-defined system of politics and morals "coeval with man's first transgression." Others attributed it to the deliberate

---

in the County of Middlesex (n.p., 1812), p. 1. On the contemporary belief in the Federalist era as an Augustan age, see Linda K. Kerber, *Federalists in Dissent: Imagery and Ideology in Jeffersonian America* (Ithaca, N.Y., forthcoming), Chap. I, which the author was kind enough to allow me to read in manuscript. For interminable substantiation of the following pages, also see Morse, *Federalist Party in Mass.*, and Stauffer, *Bavarian Illuminati, passim.*

[1]Cabot to Pickering, Apr. 9, 1808, Lodge, *Cabot*, 391-92; Otis in *A/C*, 5th Cong., House, 2d Sess., p. 1962; and Ames, *Works*, II, 129. See also Cotton Tufts, Jr., *Oration, Pronounced Before the Federal Republicans of Charlestown, Massachusetts, July 4, 1814* (Charlestown, Mass., 1814). For the Federalist notion of a revolution of 1800, see, e.g., *Centinel*, June 15, 1811, and Ames, *Works*, II, 129. The same sense before 1776 of a sharp decline in the quality of life and politics after a period of splendor and accomplishment is discussed in Bailyn, *Ideological Origins*, pp. 130-43.

efforts of wicked and infidel men, among whom the foremost was an irreligious president. "Corruption," wrote Timothy Pickering in echo of the revolutionary generation, "is the object and instrument of the Chief, and the tendency of his administration; for the purpose of maintaining himself in power, and for the accomplishment of his infidel and visionary schemes. The corrupt portion of the people are the agents of his misrule. . . . Virtue and worth are his enemies—and therefore he would overwhelm them." Many found the origins of corruption in democracy. Popular rule, wrote Ames, was no less tyrannical than military despotism: "The tyranny of what is called the people, and that by the sword, both operate alike to debase and corrupt, till there are neither men left with the spirit to desire liberty, nor morals with the power to sustain justice."[2]

Parties, too, shared the blame. Their leaders "cry 'liberty,' but mean, as all party leaders do, 'power.' " Party collisions had "cast a shade over our national character, wasted our strength, endangered our union, assaulted the basis of our constitution, and placed in jeopardy our existence as a nation." Partisan divisions had contributed to the atomization of society. They had disrupted harmonious social arrangements "and all the endearing charities of life between ancient friends and neighbors." Formerly, stated the members of a Federalist caucus, "individuals drawn together by many and serious concerns in life, and there possessing accurate knowledge of the talents and virtues of their fellow-citizens" had been able to choose their own companions and associates. But now men separated and joined together in strange combinations. They had become "strangers to each other, and . . . have nothing in common." The social fabric had deteriorated under the corrupting influence of party development.[3]

---

[2]Cunningham, *Oration at Fitchburg, July 4, 1803*, p. 12; Pickering to Rufus King, Mar. 4, 1804, Pickering MSS, MHS; and Ames, *Works*, II, 382.

[3]Ames to George R. Minot, May 3, 1792, *Works*, I, 118; *The Panoplist*, II (May 1807), 570; Speech of Governor Christopher Gore,

Few policies in any way associated with the opposition escaped the Federalist indictment. "The pursuit of wealth and pleasure," the destruction of what Theodore Sedgwick called "the aristocracy of virtue," the open door to immigrants, the president's patronage policies, the expansion of the national territory—all were at once causes and consequences of moral decay. And all marked the doom of the republic: "All history lies open for our warning," Ames cried out in anguish, "—open like a churchyard, all whose lessons are solemn, and chiselled for eternity in the hard stone,—lessons that whisper, O! that they could thunder to republics, 'Your passions and vices forbid you to be free.' "[4]

What from Ames's perspective could have devolved into an enervating political fatalism turned instead into an enveloping moral crusade.. The republic might be in dire circumstances, but this was all the more reason to embark upon a campaign of redemption. Indeed, the more the Federalists of Massachusetts became convinced that "the Degradation of our Nation and the corruption of the public mind & of the Morals of Individuals are constantly increasing," the harder they joined battle against these forces of evil. For as they saw it, they were engaged not in a limited struggle of party or policy but in "a contest of Vice against Virtue." "Good is set against evil," they reminded each other, "and none but the illnatured and unthankful can refuse to acknowledge it." And if the struggle was awesome, there was nevertheless something comforting and exhilarating in the Manichean thought that they were doing battle for the side of Right and Justice, that "the struggle with our Jacobins is like the good Christian's with the evil

---

June 7, 1809, *Resolves of the General Court of Massachusetts*, 1809, p. 305; *Patriotick Proceedings*, p. 99; and *Protest in the House of Representatives of the Commonwealth of Massachusetts*, dtd. Feb. 20, 1812. For an analysis of attitudes toward parties in the early republic, see Richard Hofstadter, *The Idea of a Party System: The Rise of Legitimate Opposition in the United States, 1780-1840* (Berkeley, Calif., 1969).

[4]Ames, *Works*, II, 352; and Sedgwick to Rufus King, Dec. 14, 1801, King MSS, New York Historical Society (hereafter NYHS).

one." Whatever successes the Federalist Party gained within Massachusetts owed not a little to this apocalyptic mentality.[5]

When they turned from the fact of moral corruption to explain its effect upon the nation, Federalists also drew upon the ideological inheritance of the revolutionary years. The decline of virtue which had begun in the 1790's and gained momentum after 1800 signaled the onset of a domestic political tyranny altogether as fearful as the worst of foreign despotisms. Given the Republican Party's known links to France, given the recent example of Napoleonic tyranny, was anyone now to doubt that with Jefferson's election another dark stage in the American experience had been reached? Could one fail to see in the Republicans' single-minded campaign for the executive chair, their attacks upon the federal judiciary, their appointment policies, their purchase of the trans-Mississippi West, and, worst of all, their embargoes and the war all the classic signs of despotism: tradition ignored, laws flouted, power consolidated, and, finally, freedom destroyed? By 1804, the issue was already closed: "Liberty is no longer the question," explained Ames in words reminiscent of 1776; "to mitigate the rigors of despotism is all that is left to us."[6]

Such a charge may no longer seem worthy of serious attention, yet Massachusetts Federalists considered it indisputable. The question of an American despotism seemed no less relevant to their own concerns than the issue of monarchy had seemed thirty years before. From their special perspective, Massachusetts Federalists viewed their declining influence in the nation as evidence not of their own impotence but of some malevolent political force. "Instead of free republicks united by solemn compact, under a federal government with limited powers," they agreed, "we have become a consolidated empire

---

[5]Christopher Gore to Rufus King, Nov. 11, 1810, King MSS, NYHS; "Electioneering Minutes, April 1810," Misc. MSS, Beverly, Mass., Historical Society; Higginson to Pickering, Nov. 22, 1803, Pickering MSS, MHS; and Ames to Gore, Dec. 18, 1798, Ames, *Works*, I, 245.

[6]Ames to ?, Feb. 6, 1804, Ames MSS, Dedham, Mass., Historical Society.

under the absolute controul of a few men—we have sunk into the deep abyss of a frightful despotism." The contest they waged was a struggle *"of the oppressed against the oppressor, of virtuous opposition against systematic tyranny."*

This tyranny, they said, in words which recalled the 1770's, was like that of the Star Chamber, disturbing the delicate balance between Congress, the president, and the courts and threatening to render Americans *"slaves,* and to no very desirable masters." The Embargo, "more unfeeling and odious than the Boston Port Bill," was "the utmost streak of despotism." The Constitution had turned into "a formidable engine of tyranny, adopted to carry into effect the cruel system of the French ruler." Because the government had fallen into the hands of a faction—a portion of the people which "conspires against the rights of the citizens, or the honor and independence of the nation"—it deserved another name: "In the uncourtly dialect of '75, we should call it *tyranny."*[7] In the final analysis, the whole effort of the Virginia presidents—"the people's present *royal* family," in Ames's words—was to reconstitute a central power no less concentrated or highhanded than the worst of legitimate monarchies. "This is the point," thundered Josiah Quincy in speaking of Madison and Monroe in 1813, "on which the projects of the Cabinet for the three years past have been brought to bear,—that James the First should be made to continue four years longer. And this is the point on

---

[7]*Patriotick Proceedings,* p. 90; *The Ordeal: A Critical Journal of Politicks and Literature,* ed. Joseph T. Buckingham (Boston, 1809), Apr. 1, 1809; *Boston Town Records, 1796-1813* (Boston, 1905), pp. 240-45; Edmund Quincy, *Life of Josiah Quincy* (Boston, 1868), p. 212; MSS Report on Memorials from Deerfield, etc. . . . Feb. 18-20, 1814, and MSS Memorial from Deer Isle, Jan. 31, 1814, Senate Docs. 4820/1 and 4820/16, Mass. Archives, Mass. State House; *An Address to the People of the County of Hampshire* (Northampton, Mass., 1809); and Tufts, *Oration . . . July 4, 1814.* See also Ames to Oliver Wolcott, Jr., Dec. 2, 1803, Wolcott MSS, Connecticut Historical Society (hereafter CHS): "The alternative is republicanism or military despotism"; and *Patriotick Proceedings,* p. 130. On the meaning of the oft-used notion of "slavery" before 1776, see Bailyn, *Ideological Origins,* pp. 232 ff., and on the concept of a balance of governmental and social forces, *ibid.,* pp. 272 ff.

which the projects of the Cabinet will be brought to bear for the three years to come,—that James the Second shall be made to succeed, according to the fundamental prescripts of the Montecellian dynasty."[8]

Behind this tyranny, in Federalist minds, lay the invidious thrust of democracy. By what they called "uncontroulled democracy" or "excessive democracy" they had in mind many things: unlimited suffrage and all the manifestations of electioneering; contempt for the learning, taste, and experience of the better sort; general degradation and disorder. Nothing could be more fearful than when "the passions of the multitude form the source of power, when democracy, under the mask of liberty, stalks among mankind, dealing out license to her infuriated progeny, to gorge in human misery their mad desires."[9] But in the revolutionary context of their thought, nothing about democracy was more fearful than its inevitable degeneration into absolute rule: "In all times there is in all popular governments, a natural tendency, to a state of things, which constitutes tyranny." "Between uncontroulled democracy and uncontroulled despotism in any other shape," warned Samuel Taggart, "there is but a very narrow dividing line." This darkest hobgoblin of the Federalist mind thus gained its sinister aspect because it was anti-republican: democracy, said one Federalist, had made the government "a despotism beyond rule, not a republic confined to rule." Where for the most

---

[8]Ames to Henry [?] Van Schaack, Mar. 7, 1801, Misc. MSS Colls., LC; and Edmund Quincy, *Josiah Quincy*, p. 294.

[9]Samuel Taggart to Rev. John Taylor, Jan. 20, 1805, in "Letters of Samuel Taggart, Representative in Congress, 1803-1814" (hereafter "Taggart Letters"), ed. George Henry Haynes, *American Antiquarian Society Proceedings*, XXXIII (Apr. 1923), 148; Cabot to Gore, Oct. 11, 1800, Lodge, *Cabot*, p. 292; and Danforth, *Oration, Pronounced July 4, 1804*, p. 9. For brief reviews of the variant uses and connotations of the word "democracy" in both Europe and America in the 1790's, see Robert R. Palmer, *The Age of the Democratic Revolution*, Vol. I: *The Challenge* (Princeton, N.J., 1959), pp. 13-20; by the same author, "Notes on the Use of the Word 'Democracy,' 1789-1799," *Political Science Quarterly*, LXVIII (June 1953), 203-26; and Roy N. Lokken, "The Concept of Democracy in Colonial Political Thought," *WMQ*, 3rd Ser., XVI (Oct. 1959), 568-80.

ardent Republicans the growth of social and political democracy had become the symbol of a revolution achieved, for the Federalists of Massachusetts it stood as the hallmark of a revolution corrupted—and, for some of them, an encouragement to a new revolution.[1]

Yet when it comes to the continuities between the Federalist and revolutionary ideologies, nothing more vividly exposes the pre-1776 origins of post-1790 rhetorical violence than the Massachusetts Federalists' recourse, when seeking to make sense of the day's events, to conspiratorial explanations. Just as the conspiracy theory became a staple ingredient of thought for the colonists before the Revolution, so it became a central explanatory principle for people trying to understand the disturbing turn in national affairs after 1795. By then, Americans of all political stripes had comfortably slipped into the practice of ascribing the day's tumultuous and perplexing affairs to the workings of designing men and clandestine conclaves. Not that the nation lacked for real plots: Aaron Burr's stillborn effort to separate the trans-Appalachian West from the maritime states and Timothy Pickering's periodic schemes for New England secession all smacked of the secret and cabalistic. By charging the Federalists with attacks against popular liberties, the Republicans themselves helped to nourish the conspiracy theory. Moreover, for men of both parties, the theory was lent greater weight by their inability to recognize the legitimacy of the opposition.

But because of their ultimate failure to stay the triumph of the opposition party and because of their relative loss of national influence, Massachusetts Federalists were more susceptible to seeing plots and secret plans in the most innocent acts. From the farcical Bavarian Illuminati scare of the late 1790's—when select Massachusetts Federalists unearthed a plot among Bavarian-based Masons to subvert the liberties and religions of the Western world—to the more widely experienced fears

---

[1]*Centinel,* Jan. 23, 1813; Ames, *Works,* II, 347; John Thornton Kirkland, "Memoir of Fisher Ames," *ibid.,* I, 21-22; and Taggart to Rev. John Taylor, Jan. 20, 1805, "Taggart Letters," p. 148.

that Republican administrations were in league with France, party members spotted "secret and systematic means," an "intrigue," a "fixed determination," a "settled purpose," a "deep and well-digested design," and an "unseen hand behind the curtain" in event after appalling event.[2]

These purported conspiracies had no fixed origin and no single aim. Plots were laid within the cabinet, in midnight caucuses of "Jacobin" malcontents, in Napoleon's carriage somewhere in Europe. There were conspiracies of "internal foes" and of "external enemies." There were small conspiracies to seize elections and larger "secret and systematic" foreign intrigues "by wicked and artful men, in foreign countries" to "undermine the foundations of [Christian] Religion, and to overthrow its Altars." But to anxious Federalists, the conspiracy which best accounted for the tumults of the age was the "understanding" between the governments of America and France. "I have no doubt," declared Harrison Gray Otis during the quasi-war with France in 1798, "that regular information and instruction are conveyed from this country to influence the measures of the Directory and impede our attempts to negotiate with success." As in other republics, it appeared in ours "that secret corruption and foreign influence had completed their work." Timothy Pickering, not inexperienced in such affairs himself, uncovered "a secret stipulation" between Jefferson and Napoleon to maintain the Embargo of 1807. And the Newburyport town meeting expressed its apprehensions

---

[2]Jedidiah Morse, *A Sermon, Preached at Charlestown, November 28, 1788* (Boston, 1788), pp. 20-22; [John Lowell, Jr.], *Perpetual War, the Policy of Mr. Madison . . . by a New-England Farmer* (Boston, 1812), p. 107; *Hartford Convention Report,* p. 17; [Samuel Dexter and John Lowell, Jr.], *Mr. Dexter's Address to the Electors of Massachusetts. To Which is Added a Temperate Examination of Said Address by a Citizen of Massachusetts* (Boston, 1814), p. 16; Cabot to Pickering, Nov. 7, 1798, Lodge, *Cabot,* p. 181; and *Palladium,* Apr. 1, 1808. On the Illuminati frenzy, see Stauffer, *Bavarian Illuminati,* and on the long history of conspiracy theories in England and America, see Bailyn, *Ideological Origins,* pp. 94-159, *Origins of American Politics, passim,* and Wood, "Rhetoric and Reality in the American Revolution," *WMQ,* 3rd Ser., XXIII (Jan. 1966), 3-32.

about the administration's "intention . . . to league itself with
the French Nation in a war with Great Britain." When that
war finally came in 1812, its most ardent opponents were quick
to discern "a secret arrangement with the French cabinet."
And by those whose credulity rebelled at mere bi-partite plots,
the war was explained as "a license given by a Virginia vassal
of the French Emperor to the English authorizing them in
legal form to destroy the prosperity of New-England."[3]

To dismiss these impassioned charges of corruption, despotism, and conspiracy as so much partisan hyperbole would
be seriously to misinterpret the central thrust of the Massachusetts Federalist ideology. For if Jeffersonian policy was neither
tyrannical nor cabalistic, neither was it in the best interests of
New England as the Federalists of Massachusetts—farmers,
merchants, lawyers, clerics, and artisans—defined them. That
Jefferson was known to be deeply hostile to the Congregational
clergy and the long-rooted religious sensibilities of the majority
of New England's inhabitants was bad enough. That he scorned
the wisdom of republican theorists by open resort to party
management, empire-building, and risky foreign ventures was
worse. That he consorted with the corrupt, stirred up the
vicious, and applauded the levelers was equally unforgivable.
But what was intolerable was that, on top of all this, he seemed

---

[3]Ames to Pickering, July 10, 1798, Ames, *Works*, I, 233; Morse,
A Sermon, Preached at Charlestown, November 29, 1798, pp. 21-22;
Samuel Eliot Morison, *The Life and Letters of Harrison Gray Otis,
Federalist, 1765-1848* (2 vols., Boston, 1913), I, 70; Pickering to Rufus
King, Feb. 3, 1809, King MSS, NYHS; *Newburyport Resolutions*
(n.p., 1809), p. 4; *Proceedings of a Convention of Delegates from
Forty One Towns in the County of Worcester* (n.p., 1812), p. 11;
and Elijah Parish, *A Protest Against the War. A Discourse Delivered
at Byfield, Fast Day, July 23, 1812* (Newburyport, Mass., 1812), p. 23.
It was Parish who likened the Republicans to Anti-Christ in *ibid.*,
p. 11. See also *A Review of the Rise, Progress and Tendency of the
Present System of National Policy . . .* (Boston, 1808); MSS Report
on Memorials from Deerfield, etc. . . . Mass. Archives; and Pickering
to Gore, Jan. 8, 1809, Pickering MSS, MHS. Morison has recently
revised his earlier work on Otis—without significant additions regarding Federalist politics—as *Harrison Gray Otis, 1765-1848: The
Urbane Federalist* (Boston, 1969). I have used the original edition
throughout.

bent upon diminishing the influence of Massachusetts in the nation. Thus the violent nature of the Federalists' assault upon Democratic-Republican policy grew out of the convergence of two equally powerful strains of thought: a pattern of provincial beliefs and the permeating current of republican and revolutionary ideology.

Yet, to forge the disparate strands of particularistic and republican thought into the potent political ideology of Massachusetts Federalism required a central unifying belief. And this was provided by the conviction, universal in Massachusetts Federalist circles shortly after 1800, that the federal government, in estranging itself from New England, had become an alien force.

The Commonwealth's experience with British government in the 1770's had made the people of Massachusetts continually sensitive to the distance and unresponsiveness of their rulers. During the 1780's and early 1790's, the fear that the national government might not answer to the Northeast had emerged as a distinct concern of most of the state's leading men. Yet during those years, the administrations of Washington and Adams had appeared aware of the needs of New England. Hamilton's financial policies had buttressed the activities of a trading commonwealth. And the Jay Treaty, no matter how corrosive of national harmony, had preserved the state's essential commercial links with Great Britain.

Moreover, as the Massachusetts figures on the national scene were keenly aware, the government had resided in a city, like Boston and Salem, of merchants and lawyers. The tone of Philadelphia was that of trade and affairs. Government sat within sight of the wharves. Commerce intruded upon administration, and agriculture appeared only an adjunct of trade. Furthermore, the government was heavily dependent upon the capital's commercial and financial elite. It was to them that merchants and ship captains transmitted information from Europe and elsewhere; it was they who released this information to the public. And with these men such Massachusetts Federalists as Otis and George Cabot, Stephen Higginson and

46

Theodore Sedgwick, were on intimate terms. This was a city in which no Massachusetts man need feel out of place.

Yet even under such circumstances, few Federalists enjoyed life in the capital city. Few escaped deep and nagging doubts about the effectiveness of the new government. Experience had demonstrated the need for a bond between government and citizen, but was not this government too distant? A government must hold the confidence of the people, but were New Englanders to respect a government with which they had only minimal contact and which was exposed to influence from the South and West? Such questions, joined with fears for the stability of the republic, gave rise as early as Washington's first term to a concern that no government situated outside New England could retain the region's loyalty and esteem. By 1792, Fisher Ames had concluded that "the government is too far off to gain the affections of the people."[4]

More than republican theory, however, led men to feel estranged from the government, to escape quickly from Philadelphia at the close of congressional business, to leave their families at home, and to complain constantly about society on the banks of the Delaware. The life of the government official at Philadelphia remained unsatisfying because it seemed strange and foreign to the New Englander. Despite a constant round of official fetes and dinners, Massachusetts congressmen repeatedly bewailed the quality of life in the Pennsylvania city. Despite their local friendships they felt cut-off and homesick. Despite their stature at home they felt frustrated in attempts to gain entrée to the city's prestigious circles. Perhaps nothing better illustrates the feelings of boredom and alienation felt by the New Englanders than Otis's mounting complaints to his family and friends about the burdens of public life and his detestation of life away from Boston amidst the Quakers and Philadelphia cosmopolitans.[5] If this urbane gentleman, so

---

[4]Ames to George R. Minot, Feb. 16, 1792, Ames, *Works*, I, 113.
[5]For Otis's complaints and his reports of Sedgwick's wretchedness in Philadelphia, see Otis to Sally Foster Otis, Dec. 10, 1797, to Elizabeth Gray Otis, Feb. 11, 1798, Otis MSS, MHS. Other evidence

accomplished in any society, came so deeply to dislike his situation, could anyone take satisfaction from public service with the national government? Add to such feelings the bitterness which accompanied the breakdown of social intercourse with the rise of parties, the insecurity of tenure now that partisan challenges awaited most congressmen at the polls, and the constant attacks upon men's character in the public press, and most of the makings of a full-fledged anti-government impulse already existed. Long before the transfer to Washington, the leading figures of Massachusetts found service in the government a "splendid torment."

When the capital moved to the Potomac wilderness in 1800, these sentiments rapidly intensified. Government not only shifted farther away from the people, but it moved into the South, away from the salutary influence of commerce, and to a spot devoid of comfort and society. The new federal city was the mere skeleton of a community, isolated from the citizenry, removed from the established channels of communication and information, and thrown in upon itself at a time of extreme and bitter partisan division.[6] Moreover, the government which inhabited the new town had fallen into the hands of infidel, anti-commercial, anti-New England Southerners. It seemed now a government not merely isolated from the people

---

of the breakdown of society in Philadelphia is the remark of Mrs. George Logan that Philadelphia was in "a state of society destructive of the ties which in ordinary times bind one class of citizens to another," quoted in Alexander DeConde, *The Quasi-War: The Politics and Diplomacy of the Undeclared War with France, 1797-1801* (New York, 1966), p. 82. See also Thomas Jefferson's comment from Philadelphia in 1797: "Men who have been intimate all their lives cross the streets to avoid meeting, and turn their heads another way, lest they should be obliged to touch their hats." Jefferson to Edward Rutledge, June 24, 1797, *The Writings of Thomas Jefferson*, ed. Paul Leicester Ford (10 vols., New York, 1896), VII, 155.

[6]Edmund Quincy, *Josiah Quincy*, pp. 131-32, 186-88. For a stimulating analysis of the effect of the isolation of government from citizen upon the government, see James Sterling Young, *The Washington Community, 1800-1828* (New York, 1966), which has greatly aided my understanding of the reactions of the Massachusetts Federalists to the events of the time. My interest, however, has focused upon the effect of this separation upon the citizen.

but, like that of the British king and ministry in 1774, actively hostile to Federalist Massachusetts.

That fewer Massachusetts Federalists sat in Congress or occupied executive posts after 1800 only hardened the conviction that the government had withdrawn its concern and protection from the Northeast. Many former congressmen and a number of new aspirants to congressional seats suddenly found their careers altered and limited to the orbit of state affairs after 1800. Some, like Otis, had already felt the deterioration of life at the capital and had willingly retired from Congress at the time of Jefferson's election. Others, like House Speaker Theodore Sedgwick, had given up their seats in the erroneous expectation of being succeeded by members of their own party. Still others, like the young Josiah Quincy just starting out on an illustrious career, had lost out to Republicans in their bids for Congress. For different reasons then, some of the most talented and ambitious men of the age—frustrated by defeat, chastened by their experience in government, and convinced that the nation had fallen into evil hands—found themselves collected in Massachusetts after 1800, cut off from the federal government and separated from the broadening environment of its affairs. From Boston, Worcester, and Northampton, they watched over the national scene and grew increasingly convinced that it was their task to redeem the republic.

For it soon seemed to Massachusetts Federalists that the Republican administrations, especially in their contempt for commerce, had clearly lost touch with the people and had turned their backs upon the wisdom of republican experience. As much from a concern for republicanism as from a fear for their personal interests, rural Federalists like Sedgwick and Strong joined maritime leaders like Otis and Cabot in protesting that shipping and trade were the bulwarks of the fragile union. Commerce, they argued, reached beyond the confines of any single interest group or section to lend its enlarging and vitalizing force to all enterprises and all regions. A healthy commercial sector insured the order and prosperity of the entire nation. As trade and shipping prospered, every member of

49

society benefited. The farmer found a market for his goods, and the workman found an outlet for his skills.[7]

By ignoring the interests of the commercial Northeast, the Jeffersonians revealed how faulty was their understanding of the nation's economy, how little they knew of what was needed to sustain the American commonwealth. They claimed to protect trade by retaliating against the British Orders in Council, yet had they consulted the people most concerned? Had they considered how, by altering the existing patterns of trade with discriminatory tariffs and embargoes, they might injure the trade-dependent South? Had they measured the danger to republicanism everywhere of offending the world's mightiest maritime power and the nation's leading trading partner? Clearly they had not. "To make our trade more free," Ames pointed out, "it is to be embarrassed and violently shifted from one country to another, not according to the interest of the merchants, but the visionary theories and capricious rashness of the legislators." While "Great Britain is fighting our battles and the battles of mankind, and France is combating for the power to enslave and plunder us and all the world," the Republicans were attacking England and rewarding France. Was this not precisely the way to invite economic ruin and open warfare from one quarter, despotism and corrupton from the other? No republic could withstand the onslaught of so many evils at once.[8]

---

[7]For the Federalist views, see, e.g., *Patriotick Proceedings, passim*, and Samuel Taggart in *A/C*, 10th Cong., House, 2d Sess., p. 871. The recent work of Douglass C. North lends substantial credence to the Federalists' economic arguments and to their emphasis upon trade and commerce as the foundation for growth in income and prosperity: "Early National Income Estimates of the U.S.," *Economic Development and Cultural Change*, IX (Apr. 1961), 387-96; *The Economic Growth of the United States, 1790-1860* (Englewood Cliffs, N.J., 1961), esp. Chaps. II-VI; and *Growth and Welfare in the American Past: A New Economic History* (Englewood Cliffs, N.J., 1966), esp. Chaps. II-V.

[8]Ames in *A/C*, 3d Cong., House, 1st Sess., p. 338, and Ames to Thomas Dwight, Oct. 31, 1803, Ames, *Works*, I, 330. See also Higginson to John Adams, July 1786, "Higginson Letters," p. 733, and Jabez Upham in *A/C*, 11th Cong., House, 2d Sess., p. 1036. For the general

Yet what did the Republican administrations do? In a manner strikingly reminiscent of British policy before 1776, they closed the ports in 1807, enforced the Embargo with Draconian intent, and scoffed at New England's claims of injury and ruin.[9] In vain the Massachusetts Federalists protested against such actions; in vain they pointed to their own economic stagnation and to the harm done the staple-crop, export-dependent South. By the time the Madison administration declared war on England in 1812, they had reached the end of their patience. It was not simply that the interests of New England had been ignored, but that within the constituted channels of government their efforts to protect these interests had been unavailing. Government was no longer responsive to the citizens. No matter how loudly they protested, no matter how forcefully they brought to bear upon the administration the mobilized force of public opinion in Massachusetts, nothing moved it from its determined course. By 1814, Massachusetts Federalists had come to view the government in Washington much as the colonists had earlier come to envisage the ministry at Whitehall: distant, alien, determined upon obedience, and heedless of the public will.

That the United States might somehow escape the burdens which had afflicted other nations—that republican laws and a republican constitution might somehow prevent the alienation of government and citizen—had been the chief hope of the Massachusetts Federalists since the Revolution. But now, these hopes dashed, they began to seek recourse through their own government in Boston. The violence of their political rhetoric and the mounting threats of nullification and secession toward the close of the war should thus be seen as more than symptoms of frustration. In large part, they were efforts to

---

conviction that England alone could preserve the republic, see also Ames to George R. Minot, July 2, 1789, Ames, *Works*, I, 57-60; Ames to Wolcott, Mar. 26 and June 9, 1798, Wolcott MSS, CHS; and Ames to Quincy, Feb. 12, 1806, Nov. 11, 1807, Quincy MSS, LC.

[9]On the harsh enforcement of the Embargo Acts, see Leonard W. Levy, *Jefferson and Civil Liberties: The Darker Side* (Cambridge, 1963), Chaps. V and VI.

awaken the administration in Washington for the last time to the danger of further ignoring the political majority of Massachusetts and to signal the Federalists' readiness to replace the authority of an isolated government with a government more responsive and closer to home.

In the end, however, the violence of Massachusetts Federalism by the last months of 1814 revealed more than the frustrations of a regional majority lacking influence on the national scene. It exposed as well the intellectual foundations of Federalist politics in the dominant republican ideology of the age. If the Hartford Convention accomplished little else, it revealed some of the otherwise hidden potentialities of American revolutionary thought. It was not that the Massachusetts Federalists absorbed the ideological legacy of the Revolution more fully than the Republicans but rather that, because of their historical and provincial situation, their thought remained more rigidly confined to the original categories of revolutionary thought. In protest against their plight, they were working out some of the darker and more violent implications of that revolutionary ideology. From this perspective, the Hartford Convention of 1814 stands out as one of the culminating episodes in the American phase of the age of the democratic revolution.

II

Massachusetts Federalism and the New Order

I

HARMONY, unity, order, solidarity: these were the basic motifs of Massachusetts Federalist thought. Finding distant inspiration in Harrington and Newton, Massachusetts Federalists saw society both as a structure of harmonious and mutually interdependent interests and as a collectivity in which individuals, by occupying fixed places and performing specified tasks, contributed to the health and prosperity of the whole community. "The social body," explained one cleric, "is composed of various members, mutually connected and dependent. Though some be deemed less honourable, they may not be less necessary than others. As the eye, the ear, the hand, the foot of the human body, cannot say one to the other, I have no need of you, but all in their respective places have indispensable uses; so in the Commonwealth, each citizen has some gift or function, by which he may become a contributor to the support and pleasure of the whole body."[1]

Yet as this clerical pronouncement makes so clear, the

---

[1] John Allyn, *A Sermon, Preached in the Audience of His Excellency Caleb Strong, Esq. Governor . . . May 29, 1805* (Boston, 1805), p. 13; and Caleb Strong, *Patriotism and Piety, The Speeches of his Excellency Caleb Strong, Esq. . . . from 1800 to 1807* (Newburyport, Mass., 1808), p. 156. See also *ibid.*, pp. 98, 115; [Jonathan Jackson], *Thoughts Upon the Political Situation of the United States of America . . .* (Worcester, Mass., 1788), p. 131; and the Preamble and Article VII of the Bill of Rights of the Massachusetts Constitution of 1780, a text of which will be found in Francis Newton Thorpe, *The Federal and State Constitutions . . .* (7 vols., Washington, 1909), III, 1888-1923.

theme of organic balance went beyond mere republican concerns to reveal an older and more conservative preoccupation with the maintenance of fixed relationships among men. When Federalists envisaged a general equilibrium, they had in mind inequality as well as interdependence, deference and denial as well as agreement and compromise. "In all societies," said a newspaper writer parroting the words of Edmund Burke, "some must be uppermost. The levellers only change and pervert the natural order of things." To Massachusetts Federalists, raised on the Aristotelian notion of superior and inferior roles and functions, the social harmony presupposed natural distinctions among men and, what is more, unprotesting submission to one's place in the social hierarchy—"each one learning his proper place," in Jonathan Jackson's words, "and keeping in it."[2]

The trouble was, however, that what Jackson called the "habits of subordination" were not inheritable.[3] They had to be learned anew by each generation and taught afresh to every man. Such, moreover, was human nature that an education in self-denial and subordination could not begin too early nor be repeated too often. The best place, thought Federalists, to initiate this training in deference was in the tightly regulated and patriarchal family circle, where age differences assumed the same significance as distinctions between social classes in the general society. Children must be taught to honor and obey their elders, control their whims, and restrain their youthful energies in the general interest of the whole household. It was within the home that the growing child must first be exposed to the necessary distinctions among men and taught that only a few possess the privilege to rule.

This kind of education was expected of all classes. Instruction in the niceties of generational and social station was

---

[2][Boston] *Columbian Centinel* (hereafter *Centinel*), Oct. 21, 1801; [Jackson], *Thoughts*, p. 49; and *Works of Fisher Ames*, ed. Seth Ames (2 vols., Boston, 1854), II, 210. Burke is quoted in almost the same words in Allen Guttmann, *The Conservative Tradition in America* (New York, 1967), p. 8.

[3]The phrase is from [Jackson], *Thoughts*, p. 131.

not to be restricted to the homes of the less fortunate. How could the well-placed learn to exercise authority without first having experienced the discipline of obedience and submission themselves? Children must be taught "proper subordination," declared Jonathan Jackson, "for they, who were never learned to obey, must govern very badly." In many families of the Federalist elite, children bowed before their parents and called them by a deferential "Honored Papa" and "Honored Mamma."[4]

What family training initiated, formal schooling was to reinforce. And where the lessons of the home emphasized deference to age and parental authority, the schools were meant to broaden the objects of respect to include the rulers of the state and the leaders of society. "The people," said Stephen Higginson, "must be *taught* to confide in and reverence their rulers." "It is not enough," reasoned Caleb Strong, "to teach children to read and write, and understand the first rules of arithmetic; it is also of importance to habituate them to restraint." The whole purpose of education, intoned one Federalist minister, is "to inculcate on their expanding minds the necessity of sub-ordination and obedience to their superiors."[5] Schools were not meant to enlighten and liberate the mind but to discipline the spirit and train the will.

Where the family and schools happened to fail, the militia, the press, the party, and the pulpit were heavy weapons in reserve. Federalists looked upon militia service as an indispensable guarantor of public order, inasmuch as it not only protected the community from enemies without but also provided a school of discipline for the disorderly within. Frequent military training, annual musters, ceremonial parades enforced

---

[4]*Ibid.*, p. 27; and Josiah P. Quincy, "Social Life in Boston," *The Memorial History of Boston*, ed. Justin Winsor (4 vols., Boston, 1883), IV, 1-24. On the intractability of adults, see Allyn, *Sermon . . . May 29, 1805*, pp. 17-18.

[5]Higginson to Pickering, May 27, 1797, Pickering MSS, Massachusetts Historical Society (hereafter MHS); Strong, *Patriotism and Piety*, pp. 40, 42, 45, 117; and Alden Bradford, *An Oration, Pronounced at Wiscasset, on the Fourth of July 1804* (Wiscasset, Me., 1804), pp. 13-14.

"that most important thing . . . *that discipline of the mind—subordination.*"[6] Through the use of rank and uniform, the militia organization made clearly visible the distinctions of station and power within the state. The citizens' guard was a training ground for natural commanders and an arena in which the common militiaman learned order and submission.

Similarly, the clergy were expected—and expected themselves—to help maintain the spirit of deference and submission. "The business of religious teachers perfectly coincides with the business of civil rulers," declared Nathaniel Emmons. "It is the ultimate design of civil magistrates to restrain the external actions of men; and so far as religious teachers restrain their internal corruption, just so far they aid the civil powers, and contribute all their influence to promote the good of civil society." What better forum existed for instilling the values of order and acquiescence than the pulpit? Ministers, declared the Federalist state senate with this in mind, are "eminently useful in preserving the blessings of good government, and upholding the order of society."[7]

For their part, the Congregational clerics were not loath to indulge the invitation to support the state which gave them special privileges. They zealously pressed religion into service as the guarantor of stability. Indeed, no one articulated the elitist definition of social harmony better than the ministers of the established church. We benefit our community, noted the cleric John Allyn, "by only pursuing with zeal and fidelity the business of our respective vocations. . . . Every one, in all times, by well discharging the duties of his sphere and station, may build up the interests and increase the happiness of his country. . . . Keeping in the line, that nature and providence have marked out for us, we may effect a multitude of purposes." Allyn thought his lessons no less just for being harsh. "The rich would be less happy without the poor to administer to their leisure and ease; and the poor in turn are profited by the

---

[6][Jackson], *Thoughts*, p. 158.

[7]*The Works of Nathaniel Emmons*, ed. Jacob Ide (2 vols., Boston, 1842), II, 239; and Strong, *Patriotism and Piety*, pp. 117-18.

stewardship of the rich, whose enterprize, providence, and economy enable them to reward their labour, and relieve that indigence, which springs from indolence, wastefulness, and vice, or from sickness and misfortune."[8]

Allyn's was no isolated clerical construction of the harmonic ideal. Jedidiah Morse unhesitatingly lectured a congregation of Boston Negroes on the natural hierarchy among men. "Distinctions of rank and condition in life," he declared, "are requisite to the perfection of the social state. There must be rulers and subjects, masters and servants, rich and poor. The human body is not perfect without all its members, some of which are more honourable than others; so it is with the body politic." John Sylvester John Gardiner, Boston's outspoken Episcopal pastor who out-Federalized even the Congregational clergy, repeatedly cautioned his worshipers against vain strivings for distinction outside one's appointed station. It had pleased God, he said, "to place mankind in different stations, and to distinguish them from each other by a diversity of rank, power, and talent." The ardent Elijah Parish admonished his Byfield parishioners to remember that "order is the glory of the universe. The excellence of creation results from the subordination of the parts to the whole. Revolving worlds move in obedience to fixed laws. In civil government, the people obey, the magistrates rule, and order and security follows."[9]

It was government, however, which most Federalists agreed must in the final analysis be the mainstay of order. Without the exertions of the civil magistracy, families broke apart, schooling was ignored, and religion was disdained too

---

[8] Allyn, *Sermon . . . May 29, 1805*, pp. 13, 14. See also Thomas Barnes *v.* Inhabitants of the First Parish of Falmouth, *Reports of the Supreme Judicial Court of Massachusetts* (hereafter *Mass. Reports*), VI (May 1810), 409.

[9] Jedidiah Morse, *A Discourse, Delivered at the African Meeting House, in Boston, July 14, 1808* . . . (Boston, 1808), p. 6; John S. J. Gardiner, *Address, Delivered Before the Members of the Massachusetts Charitable Fire Society . . . May 28, 1803* (Boston, 1803), p. 4; and Elijah Parish, *A Sermon, Preached at Boston . . . Upon the Annual Election, May 30, 1810* (Boston, 1810), p. 3. See also Emmons, *Works*, II, 253.

often to insure that liberty could be maintained. Some institution had to possess ultimate responsibility for restraining the
turbulent, denying the ambitious, and exacting obedience from
all. Some men had to have the authority to see that "every
citizen shall sustain his just part, and keep his proper place."
Government must take over where other expedients fail. It
must establish the perfect tranquillity "in which no one un-
punished can step out of his place to the annoyance of another." It must impose, if it cannot teach, "the habits of just
subordination." It must guarantee liberty, which consists "not
so much in removing all restraint from the orderly, as in imposing it on the violent."[1]

The ultimate test of good government, according to the
Massachusetts Federalist ideology, was its ability to preserve
the rights of property. "The essence, and almost the quintes-
sence, of a good government," wrote Ames, "is to protect
property and its rights." Jonathan Jackson concurred: "The
right of property is a sacred right," he wrote, and because in
the United States "the acquisition and secure holding of property is one of the first and most darling objects of pursuit,"
and because "property is the object of the great mass of any
faction," one of the primary ends of government must be to
insure property against violation and destruction.[2] Most
Massachusetts Federalists, like articulate Americans of all persuasions, considered these propositions, combining the authority
of political theory, the wisdom of empirical science, the whis-
pering of divine sanction, and the heady optimism of the
American experience, to be beyond dispute.

Where the Massachusetts Federalists divided with their
Republican opponents, however, was not over the matter of
official protection of property but over the role government
was to assume in encouraging and ensuring its distribution.
Commonwealth Republicans, the victims of political discrimi-

[1][Jackson], *Thoughts*, pp. 6, 172; Ames, *Works*, II, 221.
[2]*Ibid.*, II, 166, 368; and [Jackson], *Thoughts*, pp. 35, 133. See
also Seth Spring *v.* Sylvanus Lowell, *Mass. Reports*, I (May 1805),
430.

nation when it came to obtaining bank charters, land patents, corporate franchises, and the like, called for a positive use of official authority. They agitated for a government which would preserve free access to all property and take positive steps to equalize opportunities for its acquisition and use.

Federalists, on the contrary, had become the champions of negative government. They believed positive official action ill-conceived, not merely because it was unnatural, but because it was unnecessary. According to the Federalists' proto-Spencerian calculus, government intervention in the affairs of property might affect its use, but government could not reverse the inexorable decree of nature that property always be unequally distributed. Except for preventing the flagrant abuse of property, the magistracy must encourage nature's ways by obligingly standing aside. "The inequality of property," Caleb Strong reminded the General Court, "arises from the nature of things, and not from any defect in the form or administration of government. All that the best government can do, is to prevent that inequality which fraud, oppression, or violence would produce; to encourage frugality, and as far as justice and the constitution will permit, to restrain luxury and profusion; and to protect the lawful possession of every man, so that each may enjoy the fruits of his labour in perfect security."[3]

Bleaker and more rigid standards of negative government are scarcely conceivable, and they illustrate the distance that had come to separate Massachusetts Federalism early in the nineteenth century from the Hamiltonian tradition of positive government. Yet what made Strong's defense of government inaction so irresistibly compelling to Massachusetts Federalists, and what blinded such men to Republican charges of favoritism toward privilege, was that they assumed society and the state to be indivisible and coextensive. The state did not serve the privileged. It was at once the mirror and the highest manifestation of the social order.

---

[3]Strong, *Patriotism and Piety*, p. 99.

To men who controlled so much landed and commercial property, these assumptions seemed reasonable enough. There was no disjunction between their interests and the government they managed, and it was difficult to understand that there ever could be. Under their enlightened guidance, government's sole responsibility toward property would be to perform none but the most limited custodial functions in line with the general welfare, to prevent the unlimited and speculative acquisition of property, and to guard against the indiscriminate and injurious use of real and chattel possessions. Laissez-faire propositions had been invoked, not to preserve the equality of opportunity, but to prevent it.

II

WHETHER FOR THE PROTECTION OF PROPERTY, the maintenance of the natural hierarchical order among men, or the preservation of some real but intangible harmony of interests, the Massachusetts Federalist ideology presupposed the need on the part of all citizens for some act of sacrifice. Reasoning that social harmony could not be assured nor the common good encouraged without a widespread willingness to relinquish immediate and remote satisfactions, Federalists spiritedly rejected the argument that the general welfare of a republican society was enhanced by uninhibited competition and the pursuit of self-interest. The ideal of a prosperous, enlightened, and beneficent commonwealth was not, they believed, forwarded by discord and competition but by a disavowal of gain, abstention from the contest for preferment and distinction, and a renunciation of ambition. "The path to every great public good," Fisher Ames declared in 1795, "is obstructed with great obstacles and to surmount them requires some vigor of exertion, some firmness of self-denial."[4]

---

[4] Ames in *The Debates and Proceedings in the Congress of the United States* (Washington, 1834-56), usually cited as *Annals of Congress*, 3rd Cong., House, 2d Sess., p. 1104.

It seems hardly necessary to dwell upon the elitist implications of the Federalists' call for sacrifice. As hostile contemporaries saw, as historians have emphasized, and as anyone familiar with the literature of Federalism must concede, it had all the earmarks of a defense of privilege by men whose station made a donation of time, effort, and fortune relatively easy. Federalist interest in convincing people to renounce ambition and abandon the search for personal advantage was motivated as much by a desire to buttress what they conceived to be their high place in the social order as by a wish to promote the general harmony. Sacrifice meant good-natured subordination to the natural aristocracy; it meant deferring to the larger interests of the common good, defined and enunciated by a privileged elite. Rather than trying to better his condition, a man was to keep his place; rather than striving to transcend his station, he was to transfer to his betters the authority to decide at what moment he was to be permitted to rise. He could best serve his own and the common interest by realizing that equality of station and possession was an idle dream.

It is not my purpose to deny that the Federalist emphasis upon sacrifice was part of the strategy of rationalizing upper-class rule. But we seriously misrepresent the Federalist ideology if we insist on believing that it was no more than this. An inspiring secular and religious tradition called upon all men of good will to give up something to the commonweal. The postponement of personal advantage was meant to apply with equal force to rich and poor, well born and humble. And because of their more refined talents and their greater experience with human affairs, men of education and high station were expected to fulfill their duties with greater responsibility and, if need be, with greater sacrifice to their own interest. The injunction to abjure ambition and to serve the greater good was thus meant as a reminder to the wealthy and well placed that, more than most, they had large obligations to country and commonwealth. Gentlemen of the best sort were expected to come to the defense of principle regardless of the cost, to "suffer much for [their] country, and permit no one to do anything against it," and "to sacrifice, when necessary, their health, their property, and even their lives, in defence of its rights and liberties."[5]

Among the most important obligations to society which wealth and position incurred, according to Massachusetts Federalist thought, were charity and a responsible use of private property. Custom and moral duty obliged the rich and leisured to supplement what society already provided in the way of support for paupers, the sick, and the disaster-ridden. Federalists found few things more contemptible than the misuse of wealth for luxury or ostentation. One's fortune must be productively and charitably used. Since vice often accompanied excessive fortune, an important way to preserve social virtue was to donate individual wealth to charity. Being "a peculiar token of [God's] favor to his peculiar friends," said more than one cleric, wealth must be spent "to the glory of God, and to the good of mankind."[6]

Federalists were not unaware that charitable giving accomplished more than simply relieving the plight of the unfortunate. It disclosed the virtue of the natural aristocracy, demonstrated that the well-endowed served the interests of the people, and thus gained the affection of the common man. Benevolence protected the well-stationed against their enemies and religion against the unbelievers. "If those who profess to be better than others would do more than others in acts of kindness and charity," declared one minister, "they would exhibit that evidence of the reality, the beauty, and the importance of the Christian religion, which none of the ungodly world can gainsay or resist."[7]

---

[5]Ames, *Works*, II, 376; and Abijah Bigelow, *The Voters' Guide* . . . (Leominster, Mass., 1807), pp. 113-14. See also Emmons, *Works*, II, 252, in which Emmons defines a man of disinterested benevolence as one "willing to give up his private right, or his personal interest, whenever the public good requires such an act of self-denial."

[6]Nathaniel Emmons, *The Giver More Blessed Than the Receiver* . . . (Boston, 1809), pp. 11-12.

[7]*Ibid.*, p. 15.

Charitable good works were by their nature voluntary and, because of inequalities of wealth, not expected in the same measure of all citizens. But Massachusetts Federalists took a different view toward the duties of property. In contrast to private giving, the obligation to employ personal property in a fashion useful to society and not injurious to its interests was, according to Federalist thinking, more universally incurred and, because less easily defined, clearly within the orbit of official scrutiny. The same men who pronounced the right of property to be a sacred right and advocated the principles of negative government nevertheless maintained that the public good always took precedence over the private interest of the property owner. Theophilus Parsons, who spent most of his life trying to institutionalize and protect what he called the "sacred" rights of property, denied that they were inalienable. By his membership in society, a man surrendered the "sovereign" right of controlling his person, his land, and his chattels. With the exception of the right to conscience, Parsons argued, these other rights, while "natural," were also "alienable," subject to majority control exercised through the legislature. However, they were alienable only "when the good of the whole demanded it."[8] The Massachusetts Bill of Rights, among other basic documents of the state, gave official sanction to these views.

The reports of the Massachusetts Supreme Judicial Court, of which Parsons was the chief justice after 1806, bear testimony to the Federalists' convictions on this point. Speaking for the Court in 1805, Theodore Sedgwick noted that while the sacred rights of private property "are not usually to be violated," they are subject to invasion "for obvious and important purposes of public utility." In an 1810 decision, the Court offered as succinct a statement of the Federalist attitude toward the relationship between private and public interest

---

[8][Theophilus Parsons], *Result of the Convention of Delegates Holden at Ipswich in the County of Essex* . . . (Newburyport, Mass., 1778), pp. 14, 21.

as can be found: "As every citizen derives the security of his property, and the fruits of his industry, from the power of the state, so, as the price of this protection, he is bound to contribute, in common with his fellow-citizens, for the public use so much of his property, and for such public uses, as the state shall direct."[9]

As spelled out by the courts and the legislature, these principles meant in practice that the state widely construed its power of eminent domain, especially in the construction of roads and canals; it meant also that the General Court could set up codes of uniform standards to prevent frauds and adulterations, develop inspection procedures to protect the quality of finished goods, prohibit the sale of many products deemed injurious to health, and regulate toll schedules for ferries and turnpikes. The General Court always claimed the right to grant privileges for competing enterprises—basing its arguments on the need not only to end monopoly but to serve the general public. And, until the traditional concept of the corporate rights of society received a heavy blow in the 1819 Dartmouth College case, the government possessed the power not only to grant charters but to terminate them.[1] The acquisition of private property might be a "sacred" right with which the government could not interfere, but the use of property always remained open to government investigation and intervention.

---

[9]Seth Spring *v.* Sylvanus Lowell, *Mass. Reports*, I (May 1805), 430; and Thomas Barnes *v.* Inhabitants of the First Parish of Falmouth, *ibid.*, VI (May 1810), 408-09.

[1]Oscar and Mary F. Handlin, *Commonwealth: A Study of the Role of Government in the American Economy, Massachusetts, 1774-1861* (New York, 1947), *passim*, esp. pp. 67 ff., 116, 119, 162-63. See also Micah Hamilton *v.* Josiah Borden, Jr., *Mass. Reports*, I (Sept. 1804), 50-53; Benjamin Landon Hood *v.* Proprietors of Dighton Bridge, *ibid.*, III (Oct. 1807), 263-68; Isaac Riddle *v.* Proprietors of the Locks and Canals on the Merrimack River, *ibid.*, VII (Oct. 1810), 169-88; Maine Bank *v.* Samuel Butts, *ibid.*, IX (May 1812), 49-55; Inhabitants of Arundel *v.* Hugh M'Culloch, *ibid.*, X (May 1813), 70-72; and Nickerson *v.* Brackett, *ibid.*, X (June 1813), 212-17.

II: *Massachusetts Federalism and the New Order*

My purpose in dwelling on the way Federalists defined their sentiments toward charity and property responsibilities is only in part to suggest the range of their notions of obligation and sacrifice. My principal concern is with the Federalists' attitude toward the larger issue of public service, beneath which they arranged the somewhat narrower questions of property use and benevolence. For while they insisted that charitable giving was an important contributor to the common good and that society was the better for restraints placed upon the use of property, on the whole these were secondary themes in the Federalists' definition of social responsibility. By the time of Jefferson's presidency, the Federalists of Massachusetts were far more concerned about the obligation of the individual's public service. Disturbed by what they thought to be a general flight from civic responsibility and aroused by the declining quality of public officials, they were particularly dismayed that the falling-off reached into the Federalist camp. According to the Federalist ideology, the common good required that men of learning and experience assume the burdens of leadership. The Commonwealth's well-being was directly proportionate to the participation of the better sort in public affairs. An active concern for matters of politics and government did not guarantee the community's health, but without it no republic could prosper.

That the Federalists equated dedication to the common good with service to the party and dereliction in the party's cause as a disservice to the entire community should occasion no surprise. By the late 1790's, the party had become for them the mainstay of public order and the guarantor of social harmony. To serve the party was to serve the Commonwealth. As thoughtful Federalists saw it by 1800, however, the trouble was that men of good will were not turning out for the party. They refused to run for public office, turned down posts in the party organization, failed to turn up at the polls. John Quincy Adams spoke for concerned Federalists throughout Massachusetts when he charged that "many of them are too much devoted to personal and selfish views to make any sacrifice to party purposes."[2]

Party purposes! Here was the new guide to action, the new criterion of judgment. The call to sacrifice had been transmitted into the call of party. Where before to acknowledge partisan sentiments smacked of indiscretion, now to do so was invested with honor and high purpose. Consecration to the party's goals had become among men's chief responsibilities, devotion to partisan affairs a surrogate for service in the general interest of society.

Massachusetts Federalists had always thought of themselves as heirs and spokesmen of a worthy tradition of public service. Upper-class custom decreed that the best men devote their time and fortune to the rule of mankind. Civic affairs were the province of the better sort, government the responsibility of the rich, well born, and able. "In this wicked world," wrote Pickering, "it is the duty of every good man, though he cannot restore it to *innocence*, to strive to prevent its growing worse." Impelled by such convictions, men like Cabot, Gore, and Ames reluctantly but repeatedly emerged from retirement to serve the Commonwealth and the party.[3]

The 1780's and 1790's appeared to be a time when men's dedication to service approximated the Federalists' high ideals. But after Jefferson's election the natural aristocracy seemed

---

[2]John Quincy Adams to Josiah Quincy, Dec. 4, 1804, Edmund Quincy, *Life of Josiah Quincy* (Boston, 1868), pp. 63-65. See also Adams to William Branch Giles, Dec. 26, 1808, reel 135, Adams Family Papers microfilm (hereafter Adams microfilm).

[3]Pickering to Lowell, Nov. 7, 1814, Henry Cabot Lodge, *Life and Letters of George Cabot* (Boston, 1878), p. 542. Although both Cabot and Gore fled from continued public service, especially under highly charged partisan conditions, they could not in the end resist the stirrings of conscience and ancient ideals. Cabot's reluctance to serve in any capacity is well known, but what is significant is that in the end he served. See, e.g., Ames to Pickering, Dec. 2, 1805, Ames, *Works*, I, 342, and Gore's explanation for his return to public service in a letter to Rufus King, Apr. 15, 1806, King MSS, New York Historical Society (hereafter NYHS), where he says that "Men of Consideration should not resign the Government into the Hands of a different Class" nor desert friends and nation in parlous times "when our Advice & Experience may be of use to them & ourselves."

suddenly to default on its obligations to lead. Thoughtful Federalists became deeply troubled by what they imagined to be a headlong retreat from public service and an alarming rise of indifference to the public interest. They bemoaned the apathy of the well placed in both generations and saw in it nothing but fearful portents for the future. The best men had become "moonstricken." "Lounging cavillers," Otis called them. "It is impossible," wrote Higginson, "to alarm, much less to convince, a large portion of the Federal Party here of their danger." To Josiah Quincy, the worthy were paralyzed: "Men who hesitate at everything contend at unequal odds with men who stick at nothing." Cabot noted that "men of consideration" had "lost more of their vivacity than of their numbers." Ames, notable for his energy, was scoffed at by his friends, "a terrible proof, how low is our degradation and how terrible and hopeless is our fall." "I am alone and unaided," he complained, ". . . and not a soul will help me. They sometimes yield to, but oftener stare at, my zeal, and oftener still, laugh at my means."[4]

What Federalists took to be a plummeting of public spiritedness among the better sort originated, they almost universally agreed, in one source: the search for gain. Drawing upon a Puritan ethic suspicious of the monied and commercial trades, they charged that money-getting deflected attention from the momentous issues of national survival and political morality. What Sedgwick called the "spirit of avarice" they thought atrophied the spirit of selfless dedication to the common good.[5] It explained Federalism's impotence in the face of

---

[4][Jackson], *Thoughts*, p. 24; Thomas Dwight to Sedgwick, Jan. 19, 1801, Joseph Lyman to Sedgwick, Dec. 25, 1800, Sedgwick MSS, MHS; Otis to Quincy, Feb. 24, 1812, Edmund Quincy, *Josiah Quincy*, p. 249; Higginson to Pickering, Mar. 17, 1804, Cabot to Rufus King, Mar. 17, 1804, Lodge, *Cabot*, pp. 453, 345; Quincy to John Quincy Adams, Nov. 23, 1804, reel 403, Adams microfilm; Gore to Rufus King, Apr. 15, 1806, King MSS, NYHS; Ames to Wolcott, Mar. 9 & Apr. 4, 1804, Wolcott MSS, Connecticut Historical Society; and Ames to Gore, Dec. 14, 1802, Ames, *Works*, I, 312.

[5]Sedgwick to Rufus King, Dec. 14, 1801, King MSS, NYHS. See also Strong, *Patriotism and Piety*, pp. 48-49, 94.

Jacobinism and infidelity, the growing defections to Republican ranks of the men of good principle, and the general deterioration of public and private virtue. Indeed, it explained almost all the party's troubles and in the process foretold the doom of the republican experiment itself.

In the minds of concerned Federalists, the indictment of avariciousness and self-interest fell most heavily upon the men of business, the merchants and bankers. Young William Smith Shaw, John Adams's nephew and secretary of the early state party organization, observed how the most alarming events could no longer arouse public concern. "As for the merchants, public affairs and the national interests were always subjects of too insignificant consideration to engross much of their attention." Cleric Jedidiah Morse concluded after a review of the political situation that hope for Federalism was slim. "It is no easy matter to rouse men who are devoted to the acquisition or the enjoyment of wealth, to act vigorously in any cause. Such is the case with too many of our patriots." "Patriotick motives," wrote the young publicist John Lowell, Jr., "are cold and inoperative against the seducing and tyrannical influence of a love of increase and gain."[6]

Fisher Ames, the exemplary republican among Federal-

---

[6]William Smith Shaw to John Quincy Adams, Feb. 25, 1804, reel 403, Adams microfilm; Morse to Joseph Lyman, Dec. 27, 1804, Morse MSS, Yale; and [John Lowell, Jr.], *Perpetual War, the Policy of Mr. Madison . . . by a New-England Farmer* (Boston, 1812), p. 116. Cf. Theodore Lyman to Cabot, Feb. 29, 1804, Lodge, *Cabot,* p. 447, deploring "a large class of valuable men, whose business takes up the principal part of their attention, and who scarcely ever cast their eye toward the political horizon of their country." Otis to Robert Goodloe Harper, Apr. 19, 1807, Samuel Eliot Morison, *The Life and Letters of Harrison Gray Otis, Federalist, 1765-1848* (2 vols., Boston, 1913), I, 282-83: "It is the principal misfortune of our country that all avenues to great and liberal and patriotic objects are shut against the noble and high-minded; and that the ardour and genius which were naturally to sway the affairs of state, are forced into competition with mercantile and landjobbing projectors. Hence money is the object here with all ranks and degrees." Ames to Gore, Nov. 16, 1803, Ames, *Works,* I, 332: "Our people are not for [public business]. To get money is our business; the measures of government and political events, are only our amusements."

ists, expressed most vividly this point of view. Part of the trouble, he reasoned, was that the United States was in the midst of unexampled prosperity. "In prosperous times," he wrote, "when men feel the greatest ardor in their pursuits of gain, they manifest the most callous apathy to politics. Those who possess nothing, and have nothing to do but to manage the intrigues of elections, will prevail against five times their number of men of business." This was before Jefferson's inauguration. Two years later, after numerous attempts to arouse a Federalist following behind a program of action, Ames was nearing the end of his patience. "The fact is," he wrote, "our folks are ten times more weary of their politics, than anxious about their results. Touch our pockets directly, or our pleasures ever so indirectly, then see our spirit." Shortly before his premature death in 1808, Ames delivered himself of a final bitter condemnation of the public mood. "Glory was the object of the Roman republic," he wrote in an essay entitled "Lessons from History," "and gain is of ours. A Roman felt as if the leprosy had broken out in his cheek when his country was dishonored; and *we charge it to our ledger.* To Rome it cost blood; to us, ink or tribute."[7]

---

[7]*Ibid.*, II, 137, 333; and Ames to Thomas Dwight, Nov. 29, 1803, *ibid.*, I, 333-34. How great were the tensions between the attractions of private gain and party persuasion is best seen in the flounderings of many Federalists when it came to deciding whether to invest in war loans after 1812 or to scorn personal advantage for party principles. Some invested, others did not. See Robert A. East's illuminating "Economic Development and New England Federalism, 1803-1814," *New England Quarterly*, X (1937), 430-46; Paul Goodman, "Ethics and Enterprise: The Values of a Boston Elite, 1800-1860," *American Quarterly*, XVIII (Fall 1966), 437-51, for a review of the continuing tensions between old-style values and the demands of money-making in a new economic era; and also Eliza S. M. Quincy to Josiah Quincy, Feb. 3, 1813, in Eliza S. M. Quincy, *Memoir of the Life of Eliza S. M. Quincy* (Boston, 1861), p. 169; Israel Thorndike to Otis, Apr. 23, 1814, Otis MSS, MHS; and J. D. Forbes, *Israel Thorndike, Federalist Financier* (New York, 1953). The sensitivity of Federalists to the charge of profiteering is vividly revealed in Lewis Tappan's strained defense of his wartime gains as "accidentally experienced." Lewis to Benjamin Tappan, Dec. 27, 1813, Tappan MSS, Library of Congress (hereafter LC).

Degeneration among the Jacobins and democrats was bad enough. But how frightening to discover it among men of good principles to whom it was given to rule! Was there no future for moral integrity, no hope for honorable conduct? Was Massachusetts herself, the citadel of good principles, to fall before the all-consuming search for the main chance? Was there to be no refuge from the scourge of ambition, no defense of old values, no shelter for the wise and good?

What is striking is the unanimity and universality of these fears among thoughtful and articulate members of the Massachusetts elite. The leading sign of the advancing moral revolution was not so much that people were seeking to gratify their ambition, but that while indulging their self-interest they altogether neglected the over-arching claims of public good. Here was a new spirit, they repeatedly complained, heedless of community welfare and concerned only with self-advantage. It was indifferent to the ancient and epochal struggle between vice and virtue. It ignored the obligation to use property wisely and, what was worse, it was disdainful of party regularity when it stood athwart the way to profit. Its guide was not moral principle but commercial value.

That the Massachusetts Federalists were sincere in their concern for the state of society, that they were able accurately to identify a marked and accelerating change in the attitudes of men, no one is likely to deny. Yet it is not being unduly critical of their powers of discernment to interpret what they construed as a seismic moral crisis as in reality something quite different: as the beginnings of what would soon become the full-blown, nineteenth-century entrepreneurial spirit. Seen in this light, Massachusetts Federalism was not only a reaction against the reallocation of power and preferment in society, but a protest against the gathering forces of unfettered middle-class capitalism.

In this, as in so many other matters, the Federalists' Utopia was not before them but in the past. Much as they idealized the 1780's, Federalists looked back to a half-real, half-imaginary time when enterprise was governed by moral precept and consecrated to community well-being. Trade and commerce, agriculture and the artisans' crafts, as the Federalist recollection had it, then prospered all ranks and filled the legitimate needs of society for goods and services. The business calling, if not the most worthy, was nevertheless respectable. To Cabot, Higginson, the Jacksons, and the Lees it ranked among the other high professions; the merchant, like the lawyer, teacher, and cleric, was a member of the natural aristocracy, a man of proven integrity and talents. Men of business—modest, charitable, responsible—stood out as exemplars of the prudential virtues. Ideally, enterprise was subservient to upper-class values and subject to the oversight, at once encouraging and restraining, of government. Moreover, because business was the purview of the few, competition was kept to a minimum and the elevated guidance of the wise and good was preserved.

The acquisitive spirit was a denial of all this, a disavowal of the corporate nature of society. It pitted man against community and man against man. The money-getting impulse was essentially anarchic and, as such, not amenable to the usual cautionary restraints of moral preachment and civil law. It gave rise to contempt for the natural order of social rankings and made men victims of the pernicious notion that fortune is a sign of worth.

Indeed, Federalists were not unaware of the link between democracy and economic individualism. They recognized in the democratic and egalitarian ethic the signal of the beginning of a competition for power and esteem based on success in the accumulation of wealth. They perceived that economic equality was to be the demand of those so long denied the advantage of rank, family, and office. Not only would unrestrained competition undermine the harmonious republican structure of the Commonwealth, but the contest for gain, once under way, and once coupled with the subversive notion that wealth should fall within the reach of all men, would respect no boundaries of status, party, or class.

Confronting this onrushing shift in values, Massachusetts

Federalists transformed the notion of sacrifice from an ideal befitting a stable, deferential society in which there existed a general consensus as to each man's role into an ideal which was supposed to be a corrective to the enterprising spirit of the new age. The Federalist ideology in Massachusetts became more than a New England complement to the yeoman democracy and agrarian capitalism rising out of the South and West. It became a remonstrance against the unrestrained liberal capitalism of the middle class.

Rather than the political counterpart of commercial capitalism, rather than an elaborate apologetic of those who somehow succeeded in enforcing their pattern of thought upon a society as differentiated as Massachusetts, the Massachusetts Federalist ideology was in fact a criticism of the entrepreneurial impulse. Moreover, it gained in appeal precisely in those areas where the commercial life appeared to pose the greatest dangers to traditional values and associations. The broad appeal of the ideology lay in expressing for the commercial East its keen resentment of Jeffersonian trade policies and also in enunciating for men of an agrarian bias who harbored a deep suspicion of the capitalist values their not unjustified fear of losing out to the forces of unrestrained petty capitalism. In these two manifestations of Federalism—one opposing Republican pretensions to share the fruits of prosperity and opportunity, the other arrayed against the entire competitive spirit of the new age, Republican and Federalist alike—are to be found the wide range of the early republic's conservative mood.

III

ONE WAY TO UNDERSTAND what the Federalists were protesting against is to compare their self-characterization with their description of the Republicans. The true Federalist was an elevated spirit, an "enlightened and virtuous" character, a man of "sobriety, frugality, and regard to the publick welfare," one who knew his place and stuck to it, "unambitious, disinterested, religious." He possessed an abiding respect for the past, honored his forebears, drank deeply of tradition, resisted change, fought against "the insidious encroachments of *innovation*," and adhered "to the good old *school*" of his fathers. Much as David Riesman has described the inner-directed man, the Massachusetts Federalist believed himself guided by internal norms, a set of values implanted in youth, nurtured in maturity, and serving as a standard against which all actions and motives could be judged. He was a man willing to "preserve unimpaired the institutions which have been transmitted to us by the wisdom of our ancestors, and retain their purity of manners, and the lessons which they inculcated."[8]

The Federalist, by definition, spurned self-interest. Independent, self-reliant, and scornful of popular esteem, he stood above ambition. He was a man of erect and independent mind, "too proud to flatter the people, and too honest to deceive them." Time and time again, Federalists testified to their ability to withstand the seductions of gain and popularity and restated their firm adherence to principle. They prided themselves on having bested the diabolical impulse to conform their actions to the voguish fashions of public opinion. "Fortified by a sense of duty to myself and my country," reported one Federalist, "I had no hesitation to take the course of *true* courage." "I should always wish," remarked another, "to have my political conduct be such as to meet the approbation of my constituents, but this wish should never induce me to act contrary to the dictates of my conscience." A Federalist could pay no higher compliment to another man than to say, as Samuel Taggart did of one of his House colleagues, "Party or no party, he will act his own opinion."[9]

---

[8]Bradford, *Oration . . . at Wiscasset*, p. 12; Strong, *Patriotism and Piety*, pp. 96, 112; *Centinel*, Jan. 7, 1801, Aug. 14, 1802; William Baylies, *An Oration, Pronounced at Middleborough . . . July 4, 1808* (Middleborough, Mass., 1808), p. 23; and Jedidiah Morse, *A Sermon . . . in Boston, June 6, 1803* (Charlestown, Mass., 1803), p. 27.

[9]Baylies, *Oration . . . at Middleborough*, p. 23; Josiah Quincy to Eliza Susan Quincy, Jan. 20, 1809, Edmund Quincy, *Josiah Quincy*, p. 178; Abijah Bigelow to Hannah Bigelow, July 4, 1813, "Letters

At greater length than most and with utmost fidelity to the Federalist self-image, Josiah Quincy was frequently given to reflecting on what guided his public actions. A government career had never appealed to him, he said retrospectively. "I had no desire to make my course upward in political life." He conceived his public station "only as a means and opportunity of serving my country, with no wish or intention of continuing in it one moment longer than it was the unsolicited wish of my fellow-citizens." Once in the public eye, it was difficult, he lamented, to keep aloof from speculators, stockjobbers, lobbyists, and the rest. One was pulled this way and that by blandishments and petitions, by the subtle corruptions of constituent pressures. Fortunately, however, in the end "the temperament of my mind did not permit me to submit." Holding fast to the time-tested ways of New England's great figures, Quincy was repelled by influence-peddlers, popularity-seekers, and vain theorists—the sort of men one encountered in Washington. "With men of such states of mind and temperament, men educated in the strictness and under the laws which regulate New England debates could have little pleasure in intercourse, less in controversy, and of course no sympathy."

Quincy continued, however, to do his duty, reassured by the inner voice and reinforced by a sense of personal worth. With somewhat greater consistency and independence than most, he deeply admired John Quincy Adams's own independent spirit, stood by him after he left the party, and tried for a while to pattern his life after the party's most famous apostate. "I mean to identify myself with no set of men," he reflected in 1808. "I shall do my duty openly, virtuously, and as intelligently as Heaven permits me. I shall not seek to please by any sacrifice of my real opinion. I shall not fear to offend any, if a just view of my country's interest obliges me to declare truths

---

of Abijah Bigelow, Member of Congress, to his Wife, 1810-1815," *American Antiquarian Society Proceedings,* IV (Oct. 1930), 366-67; and Taggart to Rev. John Taylor, Jan. 13, 1804, "Letters of Samuel Taggart, Representative in Congress, 1803-1814," ed. George Henry Haynes, *ibid.,* XXXIII (Apr. 1923), 123. See also Sedgwick to Rutledge, June 27, 1801, Rutledge MSS, Univ. of North Carolina.

which will have that effect. This course of conduct may not secure me place, of which I am less than ever solicitous, but it will secure me that sense of a right to personal honor of which I am daily more and more solicitous."[1]

As to popularity, Quincy agreed fully with his friend Adams. "It is indeed very apparent," the younger Adams wrote to his father, "that popularity bears a very strong resemblance to the itch, by its contagion." But Quincy, disdaining what he interpreted as the arrant and misguided pride of those who judged their successes and failures by the ephemeral tides of popular opinion, thought the matter more than a bawdy joke. "The course of my education," he explained, "has inculcated other sentiments and instilled different feelings. I have been taught that the just pride of life is only attained by acquiring real honor among honorable men; and that this can only be affected by an undeviating course of public and private conduct, directed by sound principle, and terminating in a fulfillment of duty. . . . I shall not, in order to gain the temporary applause of men whom I cannot respect, forfeit the esteem of those whose good opinion is my most precious reward in this life."[2]

Set against this austere and self-esteeming characterization, others understandably failed to measure up, and none, of course, more so than the followers of Jefferson. In looking for the Federalist portrait of a Republican, it is useful to go back to the period in which the image was set; and a good starting point is Stephen Higginson's 1789 series of letters signed "Laco," a none-too-subtle attack upon the character of John Hancock.[3] In Higginson's mind, here was the antithesis of the wise and good man. The popular governor had gotten a bad start by inheriting a large estate from his uncle, "without any labour or exertions of his own." This accounted for his

[1]Edmund Quincy, *Josiah Quincy*, pp. 88, 124, 186-88.
[2]John Quincy Adams to John Adams (Nov. ? 1804), reel 403, Adams microfilm; and Edmund Quincy, *Josiah Quincy*, p. 180.
[3][Stephen Higginson], *The Writings of Laco* (New York, 1789), *passim*.

Southern manners and courtly living, especially when contrasted with "the manly simplicity and firmness" of the best New Englanders. Perhaps Hancock's fortunate origins helped explain his lack of courage and resolve in directing the affairs of men. Called upon "to plan the MAN," he regularly failed. Here Higginson contrasted the masculine and prudential virtues of the true leader with Hancock's feminine traits, his popularity "in polite circles," his desire to be "flattered and pampered" by dependents. These were "some of the exterior graces necessary to form a popular character," but hardly the attributes befitting the governor of men.

Indeed, what troubled Higginson more than anything was Hancock's obvious search for popular esteem. Rather than devoting "his time, his health, and his estate to the publick service," he courted "popular applause" and made it the sole object of his pursuit. The general good of mankind had no influence upon his political conduct. Fired, like all popularity seekers, with ambition, Hancock could not afford to rely upon his own judgment nor, for that matter, tolerate self-reliance in others. "He cannot brook anything like independence . . . and always frowns on that man that has any opinion or will of his own." The governor had evidently never learned that, of all the tides in the affairs of men, "there is none so irregular and uncertain in its motions as that of popular applause and affection." "Popular demagogues" are borne upon this tide. "Men of character" resist it. Higginson was willing to admit that to win the respect and attention of "eminent and worthy characters" is a fitting and useful goal. But, as in Hancock's case, this could easily turn into a "too great reliance on exterior appearances and too implicit a conformity to popular opinion." What was needed was the steady and independent man who could teach "by precept and example, to practice those virtues proper to their situation, and necessary to their safety and happiness— such as temperance, frugality, prudence, and a love of their country."

Much of what Higginson found in Hancock before the rise of parties Massachusetts Federalists soon discovered in all their political enemies. Republicans to a man were "destitute of private virtue and of public spirit," "inveterate anti-federalists and men desperate in their circumstances." Their self-seeking masqueraded as service in the general interest. They were flatterers whose title to place arose not "from a consideration of services rendered to the Publick," but from successful promotion of their private interest. They were "creatures who, under pretence of serving the people, are in fact serving themselves." While Federalists acted to preserve principle, Republicans strove "to obtain office, and change the customs and habits of the country." "Our combination," said an early Federalist campaign circular, "is to preserve principle, theirs to obtain office." Republicans were "the enemies of order who are seeking their own emolument in the confusion of innovation & misrule," the "modern Reformers" who were "shaking old Massachusetts to the base . . . disturbing the institutions of your ancestors, and . . . engrossing all power in their hands."[4]

Moreover, Republicans sought the ephemeral plaudits of popular favor rather than the abiding satisfactions of self-esteem. Nothing set them apart in the Federalist view more than their eagerness for public approval. With no values of their own, they guided themselves by the opinions of others. Disregarding the lessons of their youth and deaf to the voices of the past, they went about conforming their lives to momentary fashion in a vain search for advancement and recognition.

Or was it vain? It was—if one adhered to the old criteria which rewarded true worth and gave preferment to men who bore their lot until bidden to move ahead by others. But this is exactly what so disturbed the Federalists: these criteria them-

---

[4]Ames, *Works*, II, 127; Higginson to Hamilton, Aug. 24, 1793, Hamilton MSS, LC; *Bristol County Resolutions*, dtd. Mar. 12, 1812, Misc. Broadside (hereafter "Bdse.") Coll., Rhode Island Historical Society (hereafter RIHS); Edmund Quincy, *Josiah Quincy*, pp. 220-22; Joseph Lyman *et al.* to ?, Mar. 1805, in *Centinel*, Mar. 30, 1805; "Federalist Caucus Resolutions," dtd. Feb. 1806, in William Smith Shaw MSS, Boston Athenaeum; and *Address to the Free and Independent People of Massachusetts*, dtd. Feb. 12, 1812.

selves seemed to be going out of fashion. People were now advancing by other routes. They were marching to the commands of the people rather than to the wisdom of the polite and high born. Nothing is more dangerous, exclaimed one Federalist, than "the novel doctrine of new-fashioned republicans, that the hasty opinions of the populace are infallible" nor the opinion *"that characters should be tried at the bar of public opinion.* What senseless jargon! The decision would frequently be against the truly meritorious, and in favor of the most worthless."[5]

If Federalists displayed little respect for the man who seemed naturally attracted to the party of Jefferson, they reserved their most bitter contempt for the apostate from Federalism. The naturally turbulent and seditious spirit could be expected to join the ranks of the opposition. But how explain the defection of one who had exhibited all the attributes of probity and virtue and then gone over suddenly to the other side, the old party stalwart who joined up with the Jacobin crowd? Apostasy made staunch Federalists nearly apoplectic with anger and resentment. That they recognized in it a visible sign of their deteriorating power and appeal, a rebuke to their principles, a sign of the advance of democratic and leveling principles, a traitorous act, the enemy's capture of a hostage— all these constructions go far to explain the intensity of their reaction to it. But no Federalist could bring himself to believe that an act of apostasy was a manifestation of the tensions between regional and national identification or was motivated by anything but the basest principles.

Federalists spiritedly protested that by an apostate they did not mean someone who had chosen to leave the party after a fair and honest examination of political principles. Yet they were never known to find anyone who fit this description. To their minds, the typical apostate was one who had quit the

---

[5]Bradford, *Oration . . . at Wiscasset*, pp. 9, 12. Cf. Isaac C. Bates, *An Oration, Pronounced at Northampton, July 4, 1805* (Northampton, Mass., 1805), p. 9: *Vox populi vox Dei* is "an apothegm that has gone hand in hand with destruction."

party in order to gain "political and pecuniary distinction and reward." Moreover, his apostasy was total, "not to federalism merely, but to virtue, and to religion, and to good government." About the characters of democrats, according to Pickering, there was never any question. But "if they were once federalists, & have apostatised in order to acquire popularity, influence, power & office—all such men are clearly dishonest; and entitled to no credit, whatever may be their professions. They are *bribed*—no matter whether by gold, or an office which produces *gold;* or by *power* which is the bribe to their ambition."[6]

To admit that apostasy might be reasoned and honest was to acknowledge both the legitimacy of the opposition and the validity of its principles. Since such an acknowledgment was inconceivable, defection could only be the result of caprice or depravity. Of John Quincy Adams, for example, it was continually repeated that he had renounced the Federalist position on the Embargo in order to gain high rank in Republican circles and enhance a darkening political future.

> *Unhappy he, by glare of office lur'd,*
> *Renounced the truth, and federal faith abjur'd!*

Long after Adams had left the party, bitter Federalists continued to say that his defection had "gained him the high object of his selfish ambition, the presidency of the United States."[7]

It could easily enough be said of Adams that, like his independent and unpredictable father, he was "a kite without

---

[6]*Centinel,* Feb. 1, 1812; Pickering to Cabot, Jan. 29, 1804, Pickering MSS, MHS; Pickering to Samuel W. Dana, Feb. 17, 1812, Gratz Coll., Pennsylvania Historical Society.

[7]William Cullen Bryant, *The Embargo* (2nd ed. corrected and enlarged, Boston, 1809), p. 17; Pickering to Thorndike, Sept. 19, 1827, to Francis Baylies, Feb. 23, 1828, Pickering MSS, MHS; and Josiah Quincy, *Memoir of the Life of John Quincy Adams* (Boston, 1858), pp. 42-43. See also [Boston] *New England Palladium,* Apr. 20 & May 10, 1808; [John Lowell, Jr.], *Remarks on the Hon. John Q. Adams's Review of Mr. Ames's Works* (Boston, 1809), pp. 36-37; and, by the same author, *An Appeal to the People, on the Causes and Consequences of a War with Great Britain* (Boston, 1811), p. 35n.

a tail.'"[8] But in the demonology of recreants from Federalism, Salem's William Gray was a figure whose apostasy was inexplicable unless motivated by self-interest. Reputed to be the wealthiest merchant in America, Gray, said all warm Federalists, had attached himself to Jefferson's minions in order to spare his property in the coming Jacobin holocaust. It was bad enough that he had enhanced his fortune by selling a large inventory of Russian and Indian goods as prices shot up during the Embargo. But what Federalists found beneath contempt was, first, his desertion to Republicanism and, then, his exertions to maintain the Embargo. He had left the party, they were convinced, to build a fortune upon the people's sufferings. "To lend himself to a party & *such a party*! against whom he has opposed himself for 20 years," thundered a Maine Federalist, "to become a flaming Democrat, & to sacrifice everything on the Altar of his Ambition & Avarice display such a profligacy of character & such a contempt of all decency as is perfectly astonishing."[9] Just as Boston greeted the turn-coat Adams in silence, Salem Federalists refused to speak to Gray, harassed him with libel suits, and threatened never to hire employees who had worked for him. Respectable Massachusetts meant to quarantine this traitor to his kind.

There was always hope of preventing apostasy, but there was no escaping the Republican. And the Republican was so fearsome because he was more than a mere party adherent: Massachusetts Federalists saw him as a different human being, a separate character type. Republicans were "another class," "quite a distinct order of men." They were the antithesis of everything the Federalists thought themselves to be. They guided themselves by the external world and repudiated the values instilled by their fathers. They were unaffected by conscience, unapproachable through reason, unamenable to educa-

---

[8] Higginson to Pickering, Feb. 15, 1804, Pickering MSS, MHS.
[9] Samuel Sumner Wilde to David Cobb, Apr. 26, 1810, Cobb MSS, MHS. See also *An Address to the Electors of the County of Plymouth* (n.p., 1811), p. 9; and [John Lowell, Jr.], *Gov. Strong's Calumniator Reproved* . . . (Boston, 1814), p. 5.

tion, contemptuous of restraint, devoid of moral sense, heedless of the common good, mesmerized by the glitter of popular esteem, devoted to their own self-advantage. "Naturally," wrote one Federalist, "there can be but two parties in a Country; the friends of order and its foes. Under the banners of the first are ranged all men of property, all quiet, honest, peaceable, orderly, unambitious citizens. In the ranks of the last are enlisted all desperate, embarrassed, unprincipled, disorderly, ambitious, disaffected, morose men." These traits were not minor deficiencies but defects of character, rooted in the very nature of man. Irredeemably lost and permanently unregenerate, the Republicans could "never be reformed by good example or good company. Their quarrel is with nature and is eternal."[1]

Some Federalists went even further and, much as Tocqueville and other visitors were later to do, depicted Republicans not simply as an inferior order of men but as altogether "new men" who meant to found a "new order of things."[2] A large concentration of men of the Jacobin stamp, who clamored for popularity, danced attendance on the mob, and lusted after material gain, had been unknown in early America. The people's genteel poverty, the guiding hand of the well endowed, and a homogeneity of manners and circumstances had preserved a deep-rooted community harmony and encouraged among all men similar notions of the good and fruitful life. But under the corrupting stimuli of the French Revolution and unprecedented domestic prosperity, old standards had deteriorated and new ones had taken their place. Now all men—and, what was worse, all kinds of men—believed riches and privileges within their reach. Men satisfied previously with humble

---

[1]*Centinel,* Mar. 28, 1812; *Bristol County Resolutions,* dtd. Mar. 12, 1812, Misc. Bdse. Coll., RIHS. See also Baylies, *Oration . . . at Middleborough,* pp. 12-13.

[2]The first official circular of the Federalist Party leaders warned party workers against the assaults of "new men." Unsigned printed circular letter (Sept. 1804), Misc. Bdse. Coll., American Antiquarian Society. See also *Public Documents of the Legislature of Massachusetts* (Boston, 1813), p. 26.

station and simple means had suddenly become infected with an avaricious spirit and the expectation of great gain. Men who had quietly sought the private respect of their fellow citizens now courted the mob. Not only had there occurred a transformation of character on a grand scale, but the novel types had united to form a discrete party whose aims encompassed nothing less than the revolution of all society and the recruitment under its standard of all men. The new party had taken upon itself to make the new man.

Implicit in these ideas was both a theory of party development and a theory of character change. On the one hand, in saying that the Democratic-Republican Party was the repository of the morally diseased, Federalists were describing what they thought to be a causal relationship between character type and party affiliation. In this view, men were Republican because they were morally corrupt. Republicanism was the political expression of defective character. A political opposition had emerged, Federalists thought, in the train of a vast dislocation of standards and values. The Republican Party did not offer responsible means to achieve justifiable ends. It bore no relation to the greater needs of the whole republican society. Neither history nor experience nor necessity could legitimize it. It was simply the manifestation of the growing strength of a new breed of men, avid to destroy all vestiges of the old order.

While suggesting, moreover, that politics was the testing ground for moral systems and an expression of character, Federalists were also saying that the new politics had bred a new character type. Rather than seeking direction from internalized standards, the Republican took his cue from the majority upon whom he then became dependent. Unsure of his values, he derived them from what would gain him personal advantage and then came to believe that what worked was of the highest value. Unable to win the respect of the high born, he sought recognition through a party and then assumed himself to be the equal of his neighbors. This, to the Federalist mind, was the Republican, and it was the party which best accounted for him and which he best accounted for. By putting a premium on popularity-seeking, rewarding the gregarious, recruiting the disdainer of traditional authority, instilling a hope of social and economic advance, and holding out the prospect of equality, the Republican Party had both created the very man to whom it appealed and become the vehicle by which he emerged.

We may dismiss the Federalists' own evaluation of their society. Yet we cannot dismiss their assumptions about the relationship between institutions and character type, between status and life style. Nor can we ignore the possibility that, by creating a new kind of politics and new institutions, by nourishing different expectations, by rewarding men of different station, professional attainment, and religion, and by variously emphasizing the values of stability and change, harmony and conflict, deference and equality, the parties differentially created and recruited men of different character. Might it be that in the dynamics of the early party system is to be found the outline of the American, this new man?

III

Massachusetts Federalists and the Union

I

IN THE minds of Massachusetts Federalists, few beliefs were more compelling or pervasive than what I have chosen to call the myth of New England exclusiveness.[1] The myth was a kind of mental shorthand for a constellation of attitudes and ideals at whose core was the conviction that the people of New England, and none more so than those of Massachusetts, were somehow set apart from the rest of the nation. From the earliest days of the Bay Colony, members of the Puritan community had found reassurance in the thought of the surpassing quality of New England life. By 1790, few doubted that they were morally superior, ethnically more distinctive, socially more integrated, and economically and politically more advanced than the inhabitants of any other part of the union. An anonymous commentator summoned the myth when he wrote, "The God of nature, in his infinite goodness, has made the people of New England to excel every other people that ever existed in the world."[2]

The myth came to Massachusetts Federalists out of their

---

[1] In using the term myth, I mean to cast no reflection on the validity of the beliefs incorporated by it. In the era of Jefferson, the myth of New England exclusiveness, to the degree that it dealt with race and class distinctions, bore a reasonable correspondence with reality, and as long as Federalists directed the state, it tended to be self-fulfilling. But what is important is that, true or false, the myth vividly reflected the spirit of Massachusetts Federalism. Through it Federalists perceived their world, and its effects upon their behavior were abundant.

[2] "Warren," in [Boston] *Columbian Centinel* (hereafter *Centinel*), Feb. 2, 1814.

intellectual heritage, and they accepted its truth as readily as they accepted the truths of Christianity. In a world of turmoil, it was easy to believe, as their ancestors had long done, that Massachusetts was a favored land, a perfect society in which "the principle of equality among the citizens is recognized and established by the constitution," where there existed a perfect "equality of rights" which guaranteed to everyone equality before the law, and where "the way to honour and preferment is open to every one; and the pretensions of no citizen are limited, except by the distinction of merit and capacity."[3]

As the myth had it, the Commonwealth's distinctive civilization had been inaugurated by a special breed of founders who had selected New England as the site of a unique social and religious experiment. Pious men of vision and integrity, they were "of a totally different character from many adventurers both in ancient and modern days, who have been so polluted with crime, they were compelled to flee their native country, and seek a residence in distant and foreign lands." The fathers of Massachusetts succeeded in establishing a culture distinctive by its "homogeneity of habits, manners, language, government and religion." Over a long period of time, the province had become the special home of liberty, which, said one commentator, seemed "always to have flourished best in the North. The enervating heats of the South appear unfriendly to her constitution." In contrast to slave society, she had nurtured the masculine virtues among a people who prospered "*with the labor of their own hands,—with the sweat of their own brows.* . . . And by this their habitual mode of hardy industry, they acquire a vigor of nerve, a strength of muscle, & a spirit & intelligence somewhat characteristic." Indeed, Massachusetts had taken on the qualities of a nation: "New England now contains a million and a half of inhabitants," wrote Fisher Ames, "of all colonies that ever were founded, the largest, the

---

[3]Caleb Strong, *Patriotism and Piety, The Speeches of his Excellency Caleb Strong, Esq. . . . from 1800 to 1807* (Newburyport, Mass., 1808), pp. 98-99. See also the House's answer to Strong's 1803 address in *ibid.*, p. 83.

most assimilated, and to use the modern jargon, nationalized, the most respectable and prosperous, the most truly interesting to America and to humanity, more unlike and more superior to other people, (the English excepted,) than the old Roman race to their neighbors and competitors."[4]

The exclusivist theme became prominent at the very time that nationalism took on a Republican and Southern hue. As long as their weight seemed to preponderate in the councils of government, Massachusetts Federalists eagerly supported nationalizing endeavors. But once their influence, reckoned in personal as well as political terms, began to decline and a new breed threatened to replace them, they had new and deep misgivings about the role of their section in the larger union. By the early part of the nineteenth century, Massachusetts Federalists had become convinced that the triumph of Republicanism signaled an irrevocable eclipse of New England's moral and political ascendancy and a permanent lapse in the Commonwealth's fortunes. "We are parties in name to a confederacy," testified an anonymous pamphleteer, "over which we have no influence, nor control, nor effective voice in the national councils, and the wishes and the policy of New England are only known as they furnish themes for the invective and irony of those who rule the nation."[5]

---

[4]Alden Bradford, *A Sermon Delivered at Plymouth, December 21st, 1804* (Boston, 1805), p. 7; William B. Sprague, *The Life of Jedidiah Morse, D.D.* (New York, 1874), pp. 137-39; Timothy Bigelow, *An Address, Delivered on the Third Anniversary of the Washington Benevolent Society, April 30, 1814* (Boston, 1814), p. 12; Edmund Quincy, *Life of Josiah Quincy* (Boston, 1868), p. 158; *Works of Fisher Ames*, ed. Seth Ames (2 vols., Boston, 1854), II, 134; and John S. J. Gardiner, *An Address, Delivered Before the Members of the Massachusetts Charitable Fire Society . . . May 29, 1803* (Boston, 1803), p. 9.

[5]*A Defence of the Legislature of Massachusetts, or the Rights of Newengland Vindicated* (Boston, 1804), p. 4. Senator James Lloyd was of the opinion that "it is written in the volume of fate, that a President is never again to come from New England." Lloyd to Otis, Dec. 27, 1810, Otis MSS, Massachusetts Historical Society (hereafter MHS).

III: *Massachusetts Federalists and the Union*

Nothing in the Federalist experience prepared them to account for such a reverse, and the myth, refurbished to fit contemporary canons, became the inspirational theme for people no longer confident of the national experiment nor of their places in a changing world. Its appeal was in part rhetorical; it was an element of expression, the custom of an occasion, one of the modes of Federalist style. Just as tradition required some verbal genuflection toward the fathers of the Commonwealth, so tradition called for an allusion to New England's distinctiveness in every election sermon, Thanksgiving discourse, and Fourth of July oration. But even more, the myth was a badge of party identity. One demonstrated his Federalism and signified membership in a select circle by referring to the superior virtues of the people of Massachusetts. For partisan purposes, there was no underestimating the value of the myth in identifying the party with the oldest interests and transcendent character of Massachusetts civilization.

Because of its orientation toward the past, the myth exerted a powerful restraint against accommodation with the rest of the nation and with the advancing forces of democracy and enterprise. But it also evoked visions of an ideal society which somehow had to be regained. To reassert the strength of New England, to cleanse it of alien and modern influence, to save the nation from its errors were obligations which in the minds of Massachusetts Federalists remained compelling. Rather than inclining them to resignation and fatalism, the myth was a powerful stimulus to unremitting efforts to restore New England to her rightful place in the national firmament as the paladin of Christian and republican institutions.

It was in making a last stand against all anti-republican perils that Massachusetts Federalists believed they could vindicate the party's way to man. Like the revolutionaries before them, they sought to regenerate a whole people. By defending the American mission, Massachusetts could man the barricades for all mankind. "Rule, New England! New England rules and saves," was the refrain of a popular contemporary ode recited proudly at party gatherings. All Federalists concurred. "It depends more upon Massachusetts than any state in the Union," wrote Manasseh Cutler, "to save us from civil war, and, in the event, a despotic government."[6] It was only a short distance from this conviction to the belief that the Federalist Party, as special guardian of New England's interests and highest exemplar of her exclusive claims to leadership, was the last bulwark against national disaster. "If the Federal party can save itself it will save the country," was Ames's conviction. "It lies with the [Hartford] Convention," Joseph Lyman wrote in 1814, "as God's Instrument to save our country in this hour of her greatest distress and peril."[7]

Faced with the twin problem of justifying their own political activities and of providing for a community deeply suspicious of politics and power an appropriate rationale for going to the polls, active and articulate Federalists sought to make voters understand that a ballot cast for a Federalist was not a mark of confidence in the candidate nor a choice of one

---

[6]Cutler to Ephraim Cutler, Mar. 14, 1802, in William Parker Cutler and Julia Perkins Cutler, *Life, Journals and Correspondence of Rev. Manasseh Cutler, LL.D.* (2 vols., Cincinnati, Ohio, 1888), II, 98. See also Otis *et al.* to John Holmes, Mar. 8, 1809, John Holmes Papers, New York Public Library (hereafter NYPL); Otis *et al.* to Timothy Bigelow, Feb. 9, 1810, Misc. MSS Colls., MHS; Joseph Hale to Rufus King, Apr. 13, 1802, King MSS, New York Historical Society (hereafter NYHS); Ames, *Works*, II, 131; *Centinel*, Mar. 2, 1805; and *The Patriotick Proceedings of the Legislature of Massachusetts, During their Session from Jan. 26, to Mar. 4, 1809* (Boston, 1809), p. 99.

[7]Ames to Wolcott, Dec. 2, 1802, Wolcott MSS, Connecticut Historical Society (hereafter CHS); and Joseph Lyman to John Treadwell, Dec. 14, 1814, Samuel Eliot Morison, *The Life and Letters of Harrison Gray Otis, Federalist, 1765-1848* (2 vols., Boston, 1913), II, 187. Compare the statement of a Federalist writer in 1809: "The legislature is destined, we believe, to rescue our country from destruction; at least, if the nation is to be saved, we think this great result can only be produced by the operation of all the talents, all the resources, all the energy, and all the virtues of Massachusetts." The General Court, it is hardly necessary to note, was in Federalist hands. *The Ordeal: A Critical Journal of Politicks and Literature*, ed. Joseph T. Buckingham (Boston, 1809), Feb. 18, 1809.

party over another but a vote for New England civilization itself. "The preservation of the sacred fire of liberty, and the destiny of the republican model of government are deeply, and perhaps *finally* staked, on the question now to be decided by the Electors of Massachusetts," read a party circular of 1812.[8] Conceived in the provincial terminology of New England Federalism, the party's role was to be the Redeemer of the American Dream.

II

In conformity to the exclusivist myth, the Federalists of Massachusetts placed great emphasis on the ethnic and cultural homogeneity of New England, an emphasis most vividly expressed in the nativist thrust of the Federalist ideology. Historians have by and large ignored the anti-foreign sentiment which flourished among New England Federalists in the years following the Alien and Sedition Acts and have suggested, by resuming the chronicle of nativism with the emergence of primarily anti-Catholic attitudes in the 1820's, that dislike and fear of the alien had vanished in the intervening decades.[9] Yet

---

[8]Nicholas Tillinghast *et al.* to Oliver Harvey, Nov. 7, 1812, Broadside Coll., Library of Congress (hereafter LC). "It is impossible not to see that the salvation of our Country, *may* depend on our success," stated a more cautious production of the party leadership, "while its misery and ruin may be the consequence of our defeat." Otis *et al.* to John Holmes, Mar. 8, 1809, Holmes MSS, NYPL.

[9]On the history of American nativism, see John C. Miller, *Crisis in Freedom: The Alien and Sedition Acts* (Boston, 1951); James Morton Smith, *Freedom's Fetters: The Alien and Sedition Laws and American Civil Liberties* (Ithaca, N.Y., 1956); Ray Allen Billington, *The Protestant Crusade* (New York, 1938); and John Higham, *Strangers in the Land: Patterns of American Nativism, 1860-1925* (New Brunswick, N.J., 1955). For examples of nativistic rhetoric among Massachusetts Federalists before 1800, see Anson E. Morse, *The Federalist Party in Massachusetts to the Year 1800* (Princeton, N.J., 1909), Chap. VII *passim*.

Federalist nativism did not die with the Adams administration, and its endurance well into the nineteenth century provides a revealing insight into the way the notion of exclusiveness and a belief in Massachusetts' redemptive capacities permeated Federalist thought.

Nativism was nowhere more tenacious after 1800 than among the Federalists of Massachusetts. Beset by frustration on every hand, they fell back upon the reassuring exclusivist belief that New Englanders were choice offspring of the choicest people, unpolluted by foreign blood. Disenchanted with the national purpose and estranged from the nation at large, they succumbed easily to the notion that their ills were occasioned by the foreigners within, by their corrupting revolutionary doctrines, their conspiracies with foreign potentates, their attempts to democratize native citizens, and their unaccustomed manners and ways. Federalists came to subscribe almost unanimously to the view that "the grand cause of all our present difficulties may be traced . . . to so many *hordes of Foreigners* immigrating to America."[1] Their party became the first in the nation's history to base its popular appeals upon an exclusionary and nativist motif.

Among Massachusetts Federalists, nativist ideas were universally shared. When Jedidiah Morse informed the readers of his *Compendius History of New England* that New Englanders, unlike the inhabitants of other sections, were "almost universally of English descent," he was enunciating a creed as well as a fact. So too was Jonathan Mason, exulting that "we have good habits, good industry, few or no great families & no foreigners." Young Federalist William Cunningham spoke for all his fellow partisans in reminding a patriotic gathering that "our progenitors were choice scions from the best English stock. They were not plucked up and thrown upon these wilds to live or die, as the convicts at Botany-Bay and other parts of New Holland. Nor did their natural wants force them here

---

[1]William Smith Shaw to Abigail Adams, May 20, 1798, quoted in Smith, *Freedom's Fetters*, p. 24.

for subsistence, like the wild *Irish* and sour *Germans* in *Pennsylvania*."[2]

Accuracy was never at issue here. In the matter of the racial composition of the New England population, reality and creed coincided: all but a minute fraction of New Englanders traced their lineage to the British Isles. Neither was pride in the bonds of ancestry new to Massachusetts thinking. From the earliest days of the Bay Colony, her inhabitants had taken satisfaction in their English genealogy, falling back in times of trouble and bewilderment upon the conventional attitudes of distinctiveness so neatly expressed in William Stoughton's celebrated remark: "God sifted a whole Nation that he might send choice Grain over into this wilderness."[3] What is significant is that exclusivist and nativist beliefs blended easily into a pride in racial homogeneity.

It was a nativism which, however, in comparison with the strident and paranoic racism of a later and less genteel age, was noteworthy for its restraint. What saved Massachusetts Federalists from indulging in the kind of virulent and far-reaching xenophobia of post-Civil War generations was their lack of even the most rudimentary theory of race and the absence of a sizable foreign-born group among them. Instead of being able to point to any inherent racial defects in the small immigrant population, Federalists could only summon the superior virtues of English civilization, with which they identified their own society, and compare them with the deficient cultural belongings of the non-English stock. From the superior spiritual and institutional heritage of Britain, they argued, "we derive all that is valuable in religion and morals, the common

---

[2]Jedidiah Morse and Elijah Parish, *A Compendius History of New England* (2nd ed. rev., Newburyport, Mass., 1809), p. 329; Jonathan Mason to Gouverneur Morris, June 2, 1803, Gouverneur Morris Coll., Columbia; and William Cunningham, Jr., *An Oration, Pronounced at Fitchburg, July 4, 1803* . . . (Leominster, Mass., 1803), p. 5.

[3]William Stoughton, *New-England's True Interest* (Cambridge, 1670), quoted in Perry Miller, *The New England Mind: From Colony to Province* (Cambridge, 1962), p. 135.

law, the habeas corpus, the trial by jury, and that spirit and those principles of freedom, which led to the establishment of our independence. Had we been the sons of Frenchmen, we could have inherited none of these blessings."[4] Aliens were to be feared, not because they polluted the blood of Americans, but because they carried with them ideas and institutions foreign to the predominant English culture of New England.

If we add to such aroused pride of culture the Massachusetts Federalists' declining faith, once out of power, in the national experiment, it is not difficult to understand why nativist thinking, like the more comprehensive myth of exclusiveness, was confined to the Federalist ideology. As the foremost student of nativist patterns in the United States has observed, hatred and distrust of minority groups on account of their foreign associations has gone hand in hand with difficulties in defining the meaning and character of the nation.[5] To those with an optimistic vision of the republican future, nativism has had little appeal. Jefferson's party, buoyed by political victories, had a robust confidence in the republican experiment, accepted the pluralism of American society as its

---

[4]John S. J. Gardiner, *A Discourse Delivered at Trinity Church, Boston, April 9, 1812* . . . (Boston, 1812), pp. 12-13, and *A Sermon Preached at Boston, December 1, 1808* . . . (Boston, 1808), pp. 15, 21. The Federalist ideology, which betrayed only an inchoate and polite feeling of national origins superiority, was soon enough outdistanced by the xenophobic hysteria which mouthed the vocabulary of racism. Yet the more sophisticated forms of the post-Civil War nativist impulse surely owed something to the ideas expressed decorously by Gardiner, Pickering, and others. It was not altogether accidental, for example, that Henry Cabot Lodge, the descendant and filiopietistic biographer of George Cabot, himself a nativist in the genteel manner, should write in 1878, "We of the English race . . . can best appreciate the task with which our ancestors grappled. . . . With no undue national pride, we can justly say that the adoption and support of the Constitution offer an example of the political genius of the Anglo-Saxon race to which history cannot furnish a parallel." Henry Cabot Lodge, *Life and Letters of George Cabot* (Boston, 1878), pp. 270-71, 414-15.

[5]Higham, *Strangers in the Land*, pp. 4-5. See also Marcus Lee Hansen, *The Atlantic Migration, 1607-1860* (Cambridge, 1940), pp. 67-70.

greatest strength, and perceived no conflict, real or potential, between sectional, national, and political loyalties.

In contrast, Massachusetts Federalists had by 1800 become a conscious minority, disassociated from their nationalist past and determined to preserve what remained to them of their waning powers and privileges. Internal alien influence appeared to them a cause of their plight. They were certain that New England was being overwhelmed by the South and West and that "foreign fugitives" in those sections were largely responsible for the declining Northern weight in government. "The influences of emigrants prevail over those of the ancient natives," declared Josiah Quincy. Federalists' fears and confusions led them to believe that "the voices of our Representatives will be drowned amid the discordant jargon of French, Spanish, German and Irish delegates, chosen by slave owners, in a disproportionate ratio." The Louisiana Purchase confirmed their worst anxieties. It intensified their sense of isolation from the sources of national power, deepened their conviction that the balance of sectional power had tipped permanently away from New England, and seemed to substantiate their charge that Republicans were heedless of the national harmony of interests. The Purchase seemed also to cap years of Republican efforts to provide a sanctuary for the worst elements of European society, "the *Gallo-Hispano-Indian omnium gatherum* of savages and adventurers, whose pure morals are expected to sustain and glorify our republic."[6]

Those who had recently come to the New World, they had little doubt, had imported with them the baggage of European revolution. Federalists constantly echoed the alarm sounded in 1797 by the then freshman-Congressman Harrison Gray Otis in support of a proposed tax on naturalization cer-

---

[6]*Defence of the Legislature of Mass.*, p. 8; Ames to Thomas Dwight, Oct. 31, 1803, Ames, *Works*, I, 329; and Edmund Quincy, *Josiah Quincy*, p. 313. The Federalists were fully alive to the fact that immigrants were not only circumventing New England but that the foreign-born vote was going to the Republicans. See, e.g., [Boston] *New England Palladium* (hereafter *Palladium*), Aug. 13, 1805; *Centinel*, July 1, 1801, Jan. 16, 1802.

tificates: the measure, he said, would "tend to foreclose the mass of vicious and disorganizing characters who can not live peaceably at home, and who, after unfurling the standard of rebellion in their own countries, come hither to revolutionize ours. I feel every disposition to respect those honest and industrious people . . . who have become citizens . . . but I do not wish to invite hordes of wild Irishmen, nor the turbulent and disorderly of all parts of the world, to come here with a view to disturb our tranquillity after having succeeded in the overthrow of their own governments."[7] Furthermore, immigrants were dangerous democrats as well as revolutionaries. The welfare of the republic, warned Fisher Ames, "plainly requires the power of expelling or refusing admission to aliens, and the rebel Irish," whose principal belief, he wrote, was that "a mob should govern us."[8]

The Federalists of Massachusetts, whose own allegiance to the union was not without qualification, were nevertheless quick to call into question the foreign-born's fidelity to the national purpose. They poured contempt upon Albert Gallatin, the "Frenchified Genevan" who "keeps de veels of government going."[9] The Louisiana Purchase "introduced a population alien to [the Constitution] in every element of character, previous education, & political tendency" and obligated the nation

---

[7]Morison, *Otis*, I, 108. As Howard Mumford Jones has pointed out, Englishmen had feared the savage, uncivilized "wild Irish" since the bloody wars of the sixteenth century, when the term used here by Otis and echoed by countless other Federalists first came into use. Once the Federalists had taken the part of England in her war with France, the perennial struggle to subdue Ireland, now enlisted on the French side, crossed the ocean and entered a new phase. Jones, *O Strange New World* (New York, 1964), pp. 167 ff.

[8]Ames to Gore, Dec. 18, 1798, Ames, *Works*, I, 247-48, II, 212. At times, rather than playing upon anxieties of revolution and democracy, Federalists sought to arouse the old fears of monarchy and aristocracy. See, e.g., the electioneering pamphlet which berated Jefferson for admitting "this mass of unsound and aristocratic material" and "the debauched and leprous outcasts of the royal potentates of Europe" who import "the monarchical habits and institutions" of the Continent. *A Political Sermon Addressed to the Electors of Middlesex* (n.p., 1808), p. 29.

[9]*Palladium*, Feb. 24, 1809; *Centinel*, Aug. 19, 1809.

to assimilate "a number of French and Spanish subjects, whose habits, manners, and ideas of civil government, are wholly foreign to republican institutions." The Hartford Convention pressed the administration to explain its inattention to the immigrant problem: "Why admit to a participation in the government," asked the convention report, "aliens who were not parties to the compact—who are ignorant of the nature of our institutions, and have no stake in the welfare of the country but what is recent and transitory?"[1]

To the argument about foreigners' disloyalty, Massachusetts Federalists added other staple nativist complaints. Immigrants would deny the native-born his landed inheritance, "the soil, which will soon be wanted by posterity." Moreover, as Otis had reminded the nation at an early date, only the dirty and turbulent quit their homelands; the best sort remained behind. "The mass of foreigners, who have sought asylum in the United States, have been compelled to that measure by their poverty or their crimes."[2] These peevish utterances all added up to a rapidly diminishing faith in the ideal of an American sanctuary. "Our extended empire," wrote the young Peter Oxenbridge Thatcher, "ought not to hold out to every profligate, discontented citizen of the old world, the language of inspiration: 'Come unto me all ye that labour, and I will give you rest.'" "Let us no longer pray," warned William Smith Shaw, "that America may become an asylum to all nations."[3]

---

[1] Edmund Quincy, *Josiah Quincy*, pp. 89-91; and *Political Sermon Addressed to the Electors of Middlesex*, p. 29. See also Ames, *Works*, II, 377-78; Abijah Bigelow, *An Oration Delivered at Boston, July 4, 1808* (Leominster, Mass., 1808), pp. 12-13; and [John Lowell, Jr.], *Peace Without Dishonour—War Without Hope . . .* (Boston, 1807), p. 30.

[2] *The Monthly Anthology and Boston Review* (hereafter *Monthly Anthology*), I (July 1804), 415. See also *Political Sermon Addressed to the Electors of Middlesex*, pp. 27-28; Ames, *Works*, II, 255; and Thomas Danforth, *An Oration Pronounced July 4, 1804* (Boston, 1804), p. 15.

[3] *Monthly Anthology*, I (July 1804), 415; and William Smith Shaw to Abigail Adams, May 20, 1798, quoted in Smith, *Freedom's Fetters*, p. 24.

A little-publicized treatise on political economy written in 1809 by Federalist Loammi Baldwin, then twenty-nine and soon to be a famed civil engineer, reveals the depths of Federalist disillusionment. To all outward appearances, his *Thoughts on the Study of Political Economy* was a dispassionate evaluation of the relationship between government and the production and distribution of resources and wealth.[4] Not only did Baldwin disdain an interest in partisan debate, but unlike most Massachusetts Federalists he welcomed the Louisiana Purchase. He saw in the expansion of the country a source of future wealth and power, and, in contrast to those Federalists who still trembled at the thought of territorial expansion and population growth, he confidently predicted that the nation could support an immensely expanded land and people. In the spirit of the political economist, he linked the growth of population with the growth of national wealth. "Considering the extent and physical aspect of North America, and the numerous channels of industry, which the soil and productions of the United States afford," wrote Baldwin, "there is certainly very little to fear from a want of comfortable support for even a vastly extended population."

Beyond this, however, Baldwin's trust in the nation's absorptive capacities stopped. Population growth must above all be orderly, he insisted, and by this he meant that immigration must be strictly limited and population expansion grounded solely upon the natural increase of the native inhabitants. "The union of the sexes is the most important, and, in a political view, the only desirable source of population to a state," he declared soberly, "for though immigration will afford a temporary accession of physical, it is by no means a certain source of political power." Like other Federalists, who identified the foreign-born with social and political instability and the disruption of orderly government, Baldwin also questioned the new inhabitants' loyalty to their adopted land. "Foreigners

---

[4]*Thoughts on the Study of Political Economy, as Connected with the Population, Industry, and Paper Currency of the United States* (Cambridge, 1809).

who leave their native land, generally do it in order to seek a more flattering field for the exercise of their ingenuity and industry, without relinquishing their early associations, and seldom become wholly domiciliated in the one they adopt. As members of the national family they cannot possess the interest and attachment to the prosperity of their new country." In sober professional tones, Baldwin cautioned his countrymen to beware the alien in their midst.

As the Federalist politicians who, like Baldwin, had once accepted a responsibility to socialize the immigrant grew cold to his presence, they began to seek to close off the flow of immigrants, or, barring that, to keep them powerless once they had settled permanently in the country. Some, like Harrison Gray Otis, dallied with denying the vote to the foreign-born. "If some means are not adopted to prevent the indiscriminate admission of wild Irishmen & others to the right of suffrage," wrote Otis at the height of the Hibernian frenzy in the 1790's, "there will soon be an end to liberty and property."[5] But most were satisfied with proposals to keep the foreign-born from holding public office. As early as 1797, they sought by constitutional amendment to make ineligible for the presidency, the Senate, and the House all foreigners naturalized since the Declaration of Independence; later they softened their plan to embrace only those naturalized citizens who had not been in the country for fourteen years. Their briefly successful at-

---

[5]Morison, *Otis*, I, 107; and "A New-England Man," *Palladium*, Mar. 2 and 12, 1802. The Federalist interest in excluding the immigrant and denying him the vote was a product only of the late 1790's. In the earlier part of that decade, before the implications of the French Revolution and the Jeffersonian challenge had fully struck home, many Federalists went so far as to encourage foreign immigration. In 1793, Jedidiah Morse and others founded the Massachusetts Society for the Information and Advice of Immigrants whose prospectus, while recognizing the value of a homogeneous population, argued that humanity and self-interest together required a change of policy on the part of the Commonwealth. By the late 1790's, however, as most immigrants turned south, the Society was moribund and Morse himself, like his son Samuel F. B. Morse later on, became a nativist. William B. Sprague, *The Life of Jedidiah Morse, D.D.* (New York, 1874), pp. 137-39.

tempts at the same time to increase the period of naturalization have been amply documented.[6]

Although the election of 1800 dashed their hopes of constitutional and statutory revision, they perisisted throughout the Jeffersonian era in their plans. The Hartford Convention culminated their efforts to gain a hearing for an amendment to prohibit naturalized citizens from holding "any civil office" under national authority. In the convention report which it is generally agreed he wrote, Otis, the undisputed champion of American nativists, attacked "the easy admission of naturalized foreigners, to places of trust, honour or profit, operating as an inducement to the malcontent subjects of the old world to come to these States, in quest of executive patronage, and to repay it by an abject devotion to executive measures."[7]

In Massachusetts, the political contest imposed no restraints upon nativist appeals. Where so few aliens troubled the domestic scene or threatened retaliation at the ballot-box, Federalist leaders had an unlimited opportunity to play freely

---

[6]Smith, *Freedom's Fetters*, pp. 27-29; Robert Treat Paine, Sr., to Samuel Sewall, Aug. 7, 1810, Paine MSS, MHS; Benjamin Pickman, Jr., to Nathan Read, Dec. 28, 1800, Read MSS, Essex Institute; Miller, *Crisis in Freedom*, pp. 47-49; Herman V. Ames, *The Proposed Amendments to the Constitution of the United States During the First Century of its History* (Washington, 1897), pp. 30, 74; *Resolves of the General Court of Massachusetts*, June 20, 1804; Theophilus Parsons, [Jr.], *Memoir of Theophilus Parsons* (Boston, 1859), pp. 126-28; and Morison, *Otis*, I, 107-09.

[7]*Proceedings of a Convention of Delegates . . . Convened at Hartford, in the State of Connecticut, December 15th, 1814* (Hartford, 1815), pp. 18-19. In Massachusetts itself, Federalists in control of the state government were able to enforce their system of exclusiveness. Under an act of 1794 immigrants could be deported from the Commonwealth upon complaint of the overseer of the poor; the aim of the law was to relieve the burden of poor relief, but the effect was to provide a pretext and mechanism for excluding the foreigner. The Boston Town Meeting, not content with the workability of the law, tried in 1802 to obtain an amendment to the poor laws "to prevent Foreigners of idle immoral and dissolute character from being brought to the Town from other countries." *Commonwealth History of Massachusetts*, ed. Albert Bushnell Hart (3 vols., New York, 1927-30), III, 509; and *Boston Town Records, 1796-1813* (Boston, 1905), pp. 115-16.

upon the anxieties of the potentially dispossessed.[8] Much of their political appeal within the state and most of their partisan oratory moved to a nativist cadence. Party leaders carefully exploited the theme that the Republican Party "gives foreigners our loaves and fishes" to the neglect of the native-born, and they organized election campaigns against the "too indiscriminate naturalization of *foreigners* in the Southern states."[9]

Such was the temptation to make the foreigner a surrogate target of animosities built up against native-born political opponents, that Massachusetts Federalism often had all the aspects of a full-blown anti-foreign crusade. In the process of investing the alien with incredible power and accusing the Republican Party of a subversive solicitude for the foreign-born, Massachusetts Federalists went far toward establishing a nativist tradition in American politics. And in doing so, they paid a high price. Having once identified themselves with a nativist program, they forfeited all claims to the allegiance of the immigrant. The erosion of their position among the foreign-born before 1815 made impossible, when the immigrant tide swelled rapidly after 1820, the re-creation of the party's national base.

III

THE NATIVIST TIDE which Federalists imagined to be sweeping the nation seemed all the more threatening when viewed as an element in a larger Southern plan to destroy the sovereignty and independence of the Northeastern states and to subjugate New Englanders to the "Virginia interest." A

[8]John A. Krout and Dixon Ryan Fox, *The Completion of Independence, 1780-1830* (New York, 1944), pp. 5, 8; Miller, *Crisis in Freedom*, p. 43; and Oscar Handlin, *Boston's Immigrants: A Study in Acculturation* (rev. ed., Cambridge, 1959), pp. 25-26.

[9]Otis *et al.* to Thomas W. Ward, Feb. 26, 1813, Misc. Bdse. Coll., AAS. See also William Ladd, *An Oration, Pronounced at Minot, Maine, on the Fourth of July, 1814* (Portland, Me., 1814), p. 13.

Southern conspiracy, Federalists felt sure, had long been afoot to penalize them, as it were, for their superiority. "The Virginia faction have certainly formed a deliberate plan to govern & depress New England," declared Stephen Higginson. The Old Dominion was still smarting from a "mortifying and alarming truth" learned in the Revolution: that in the Northern states lay the union's strength, that New England possessed the greatest militia and maritime power, the largest fortunes, and the best talents. Therefore, "From the peace to this time, it has been [Virginia's] main object, to depress the northern States, to secure the influence & safety of the south."[1]

Belief in a Southern conspiracy to humble the North came easily to men who confused sectional with party interests. The Massachusetts Federalists' inability to distinguish between what was Southern and what Republican in the political forces arrayed against them repeatedly dogged their efforts to come to terms with the national experiment and, as much as the passions and prejudices aroused by the Virginia and Kentucky Resolutions, seriously compromised the union's integrity. For in fact, measured by congressional strength rather than executive control, Southern influence in the national government had already begun to slip. With the rapid growth after 1788 of New York and Pennsylvania, the South never possessed a majority in the national House of Representatives and, except in 1800, the three-fifths clause did not play a major role in electing a Virginian to the presidency. The proportion of Southerners in the House actually declined after 1800; while Massachusetts' representation increased, Virginia's remained steady.[2]

---

[1]Higginson to Pickering, Nov. 22, 1803, Pickering MSS, MHS. Those who tried to discover alternative explanations most commonly pointed to the debilitating effects of partisan conflicts within New England and to the slow pace of population growth in the state. "A.B.," *Centinel*, Dec. 15, 1813; John Quincy Adams to William Plumer, Aug. 16, 1809, reel 135, Adams Family Papers microfilm; and Rodolphus Dickinson, *A Geographical and Statistical View of Massachusetts Proper* (Greenfield, Mass., 1813), p. 38.

[2]Albert F. Simpson, "The Political Significance of Slave Representation, 1787-1821," *Journal of Southern History*, VII (Aug. 1941),

III: *Massachusetts Federalists and the Union*

Following Jefferson's election, the population of the North and Northwest above the Mason-Dixon Line began rapidly to outpace the Southern population. Furthermore, New England was amply, if not abundantly, represented in the high councils of Congress and the executive branch.[3] The "Southern" policy which Massachusetts Federalists decried was a Republican policy enacted with the enthusiastic support of much of Northern Republicanism. But in this mental world of intrigue and conspiracy, beliefs took on their own life. Massachusetts Federalism helped habituate three generations of New Englanders to view every misunderstanding between the two major parties as the trumpet of a conflict pitching one section against the other, a conflict which would force one section—New England—to withdraw from the union.

As the Massachusetts Federalists saw it, the only way to forestall the coming clash between North and South was to remove what they judged to be the source of Southern domination over the rest of the nation: the three-fifths clause. Like all Americans, they had an affecting faith in the Constitution

---

315-42. Figures are derived from U.S. Bureau of the Census, *Historical Statistics of the United States, Colonial Times to 1957* (Washington, 1960), p. 693; in the South, Delaware and Kentucky are excluded and Maryland included. See also Staughton Lynd, "The Abolitionist Critique of the United States Constitution," in *The Anti-Slavery Vanguard: New Essays on the Abolitionists*, ed. Martin Duberman (Princeton, N.J., 1965), pp. 209-39.

[3] Three New Englanders (Postmaster Gideon Granger of Connecticut, Attorney General Levi Lincoln of Massachusetts, and Secretary of War Henry Dearborn of Maine) sat in Jefferson's cabinet; two others (John Langdon of New Hampshire and Jacob Crowninshield of Massachusetts, both slated for Navy Secretary) declined to serve when asked. The Commonwealth was represented in Madison's administration by two men (Secretary of War William Eustis and Secretary of the Navy Benjamin W. Crowninshield), and Madison's second vice-president was Massachusetts elder statesman Elbridge Gerry. In the House, Berkshire's Barnabas Bidwell and Salem's Jacob Crowninshield served briefly as Republican floor leaders after being specifically sought out by Jefferson, and Joseph B. Varnum was president pro-tem of the Senate after serving as House Speaker in the Tenth and Eleventh Congresses. Noble E. Cunningham, Jr., *The Jeffersonian Republicans in Power: Party Operations, 1801-1809* (Chapel Hill, N.C., 1963), pp. 88-91.

and in the ability of constitutional amendment to remedy their distress. And by 1804, it was their fixed belief that defects in the fundamental document accounted for the fruition of the South's nefarious plans.

Pointing to what they conceived to be their predominant role in securing ratification in 1788, they argued that the privilege of counting five slaves as three white for the purposes of representation had been exacted from the North by Southern members of the Constitutional Convention. Northern indulgence had given the South an advantage which it had not deserved in the first place; now, the privilege abused, Massachusetts Federalists wanted it back. Josiah Quincy's assertion that "the slave representation is the cause of all the difficulties we labor under" went undisputed. "By means of the representation of slaves," declared the Northampton meeting which helped set in motion the convention movement of 1814, "the southern states have an influence in our national councils, altogether disproportionate to their wealth, strength, and resources; and we presume it to be a fact capable of demonstration, that for about twenty years past, the United States have been governed by a representation of about two-fifths of the actual property of the country."[4] The constitutional compromise had betrayed New England's interests. It was time to reopen the question of its utility.

As early as 1802, Federalists thought of proposing a repeal of the offending three-fifths clause; by 1804, they began actively and concertedly to seek it. On all occasions, an obdurate opposition rebuffed them. The General Court in June, 1804, passed a resolution calling for the apportionment of representation and direct taxes on the basis of the free population of all the states, but the United States Senate abruptly

---

[4]*Synopsis of Debates, in the Massachusetts Legislature* (Boston? 1814), p. 20; and Noah Webster, *A Collection of Papers on Political, Literary and Moral Subjects* (New York, 1843), pp. 312-13. See also *Public Documents of the Legislature of Massachusetts* (Boston, 1813), pp. 81-82.

tabled it, and all states save Federalist Connecticut and Delaware summarily rejected it. Again, during moments of national crisis in 1809 and 1812, they listed the amendment as the nation's most pressing need; the Hartford Convention Report named it first among seven proposed constitutional changes.[5] It was, of course, just as well that the amendment was rejected, for the Northeast was gradually falling into the hands of the Democratic-Republicans. The enhancement of New England's influence would have meant a sharp rise in Republican fortunes.

Yet baneful though the three-fifths clause was, the ruling-class gentlemen of Massachusetts knew that it was, at bottom, the manifestation of a deeper evil. Slavery, not the Constitution, was to blame for Northern impotence. Contemporaries of both sections did not forget that the Philadelphia Convention had been threatened with paralysis until the issue of the slave representation was resolved. Since that time, there had been no contesting the proposition that slavery was the basis of sectional tensions and disagreements. In the continuing debates over the slave trade in the decades after 1787, neither North nor South was permitted to forget the price each had paid to the peculiar institution. Northerners of whatever political and moral disposition could hardly look with kindness upon that system which had forced the North to surrender a significant

---

[5]Among those who took the lead, as early as 1804, in trying to secure an amendment were John Quincy Adams, Pickering, and Quincy, men of dissimilar careers and attitudes. Simpson, "Political Significance of Slave Representation"; *Centinel*, May 26, 1802; Morison, *Otis*, I, 260-64, II, 193-95; Ames, *Proposed Amendments*, pp. 45-46, 326; John Quincy Adams, "Publius Valerius" (Oct. 1804) and Draft of a Speech on the "Ely Amendment" (Dec.? 1804), reel 403, Adams microfilm; *Defence of the Legislature of Mass., passim; Patriotick Proceedings*, pp. 52-53, 126; Massachusetts (pseud.), *The New States* (Boston, 1813); Ephraim Lock to Cyrus King, Oct. 18, 1814, Cyrus King MSS, Columbia; *Proceedings of a Convention of Delegates . . . convened at Hartford, in the State of Connecticut, December 15th, 1814* (Hartford, 1815), pp. 19-20; Pickering to Lowell, Nov. 28, 1814, Lodge, *Cabot*, p. 543; and Samuel Taggart, *An Oration Delivered at Conway, July 4, 1804 . . .* (Northampton, Mass., 1804), pp. 15-18.

proportion of its political power to the South. The Union existed by virtue of a concession to slavery, and now the North was mortgaged to the masters of the blacks.[6]

The three-fifths compromise was no less galling for being morally repellant. Early in the nation's life, spurred on by revolutionary idealism, men who were to become prominent in both parties made repeated attempts to ease the effects of slavery and the slave trade and to abolish both practices altogether. By the 1790's, such leading Massachusetts Federalists of the older generation as Jedidiah Morse, Nathan Dane, Samuel Dexter, Theodore Sedgwick, and George Thacher could look back upon more than a decade of public effort to secure these ends.[7] Some Republicans, such as Barnabas Bidwell and Joseph B. Varnum, were also in the forefront of this early antislavery campaign; but by and large, embarrassed by their partisan connection with Southern slaveholders, they were in a poorer position than Federalists to exploit Northern hostility to slavery. What remained of the antislavery cause in the North therefore passed into the Federalist Party.

One might have supposed that Massachusetts Federalists would turn the Republican predicament to good account by launching a full-scale moral assault against slavery to discredit their opponents, awaken New England's well-developed sense of moral rectitude, and enhance the stature of Federalism. They might also have attempted to capitalize on Northern distaste for slavery in order to split Northern from Southern Republicans. But as it happened, by 1815 the antislavery cause in Massachusetts was dead, a victim of political needs and moral indifference.

---

[6]For a review of these attitudes in the post-Revolutionary decades, see Lynd's suggestive essay, "Abolitionist Critique of the United States Constitution."

[7]Mary Stoughton Locke, *Anti-Slavery in America from the Introduction of African Slaves to the Prohibition of the Slave Trade (1619-1808)* (Boston, 1901); H. D. Sedgwick, "The Sedgwicks of Berkshire," *Collections of the Berkshire Historical and Scientific Society*, III (1900), 91-106; Sprague, *Morse*, pp. 141-48; and Ames, *Proposed Amendments*, pp. 326-27.

III: *Massachusetts Federalists and the Union*

Even before 1800, the antislavery streak in Massachusetts Federalism had been cautious and restrained. After Jefferson's election, it became so muted as to raise serious questions about the commitment of Federalism and the entire North to the antislavery cause in the whole half-century after Independence. Save for a few isolated leaders, no one spoke out vigorously and continuously in defense of manumission, nor did the successful campaign against the slave trade engage the public interest or enter to any substantial degree into partisan debate.[8]

Even younger Federalists failed to become concerned about the Negro. Though they detested slavery, they said little about it in public and left the burden of the dying cause upon the older Federalists tired of the battle. Once abolition was accomplished in Massachusetts during the 1780's, the state's small and unimportant abolition society no longer sent delegates to the annual abolition convention in Philadelphia. And it was during the years of Federalist ascendancy in Massachusetts that communities tightened their poor laws, warned more Negroes from their boundaries, and established segregated schools and churches.[9]

---

[8]Locke, *Anti-Slavery in America.*

[9]*Ibid.*, pp. 99, 109, 115-16; *Minutes of the Proceedings of a Convention of Delegates from the Abolition Societies Established in Different Parts of the United States, Assembled at Philadelphia, 1794-* (Philadelphia, 1794-   ); Josiah Quincy, *A Municipal History of the Town and City of Boston* . . . (Boston, 1852), p. 21; Jedidiah Morse, *A Discourse, Delivered at the African Meeting House, in Boston, July 14, 1808* (Boston, 1808), *passim;* George H. Moore, *Notes on the History of Slavery in Massachusetts* (New York, 1866), pp. 229-37; and *Centinel,* Mar. 24, 1802, Oct. 4, 1809. For the most recent reviews of discriminatory attitudes and actions toward Negroes in the early nation—discrimination which in Massachusetts was shared by members of both parties but by all indications before 1820 was most frequently expressed, actively fostered, and in the end codified into law and municipal regulation by Federalists—see Winthrop D. Jordon, *White Over Black: American Attitudes Towards the Negro, 1550-1812* (Chapel Hill, N.C., 1968), esp. Parts IV and V; Arthur Zilversmit, *The First Emancipation: The Abolition of Slavery in the North* (Chicago, 1967); and Leon Litwack, *North of Slavery: The Negro in the Free States, 1790-1860* (Chicago, 1961), pp. 16-17, 33-34, 104 ff., 114, 121, 136-37, 169-70. Although, as Litwack argues, Massa-

One key to Federalists' indifference toward the black population was their recoil from all people who had the misfortune to lack an English ancestry. Another was their attitude toward equality. Despite their detestation of slavery, they could not fail to note the parallel between their contest with social and political upstarts and the Southern gentleman's anxieties about the pretensions of the freed slave. Furthermore, Massachusetts Federalists had learned with keen chagrin that liberty was all too frequently equated with equality. Might not the Negroes of Massachusetts, now given their freedom, demand an equal station not only with the whites but with those whites who were distinctly their social betters? Some feared as much. Cleric Jedidiah Morse, for example, in a discourse before the Negro congregation of Boston's African Meeting House, admonished his hearers to "be ambitious to make the best use of your liberty and privilege. Make them not a cloak for licentiousness. Shew to those around you, that you are worthy to be free. Be contented in the humble station in which Providence has placed you. By your decent, respectful, regular, industrious, quiet behavior, authorize your friends still to shew themselves friendly. . . . Be sober, be temperate, be pious."[1] At the heart of the Federalist persuasion, where the battle between a moral abhorrence of slavery and an aversion to equality raged, the defense of inequality gained the upper hand.

Political apprehensions further dampened the Federalists' interest in the antislavery cause. After 1800, the Southern wing of the party had weakened almost to the point of extinction, and a public demonstration of abolitionist sentiment in the North would only have added to the infirmities of Southern Federalism. If the Federalist Party was to be reconstructed on the national level, the abolitionist cause would have to be sac-

chusetts Negroes "advanced more rapidly toward equal rights than in any other state" by 1860, progress was in no case rapid and most of what advances in civil rights there were occurred after 1820. *Ibid.*, pp. 94, 104, 110, 143. See also the well-meaning but discriminatory provisions of *Acts and Laws Passed by the General Court of Massachusetts*, 1787, Chaps. 48 and 54; and *Centinel*, Oct. 9, 1802.

[1]Morse, *Discourse . . . July 14, 1808*, p. 18.

rificed. Furthermore, as the century progressed, Massachusetts Federalism came to owe much of its appeal to the creation of a case against any external interference, French or Southern, in the political and economic affairs of New England. To have claimed that they had the right to meddle with the property of slaveholders, no matter how indefensible the ethics of slave ownership, Federalists would have risked an inconsistency injurious to their own interests.[2]

Finally, Massachusetts Federalists could not have failed to see that manumission would be followed by an immediate surge of Southern congressional representation and a relative diminution in New England's influence. Freed, it appeared, the Negro was more of a political threat than enslaved. What the Federalists wanted, and what their assaults upon the three-fifths clause were designed to gain, was not the abolition of slavery but the abolition of Negro representation.

By this, one should not infer that Massachusetts Federalists had become altogether callous toward the tragedy of slavery nor that after the 1790's they never publicly assailed the Southern masters, but only that antislavery sentiments had come to occupy a marginal position in the Federalist ideology and that, when attacking slavery, Federalists attacked it obliquely. After all, even if the antislavery impulse was politically vulnerable, it remained of considerable utility in reminding those accustomed to their own superiority of the moral shortcomings of others: "The planters are generally extremely ignorant, excessively idle, and addicted to all the low vices of drinking, gambling, etc. . . . Supported entirely by the labour of his slaves, under the direction of an overseer, the planter reclines at his ease and can live in luxury without any personal exertion."[3] Reassured of his own probity, the typical Federalist was likely to forget the slave.

---

[2]Morison, *Otis*, II, 220-21, 263. Otis was the staunchest defender of the South's property rights over the rights of slaves.

[3][Newburyport] *Herald*, Mar. 13, 1798, quoted in Benjamin W. Labaree, *Patriots and Partisans: The Merchants of Newburyport, 1764-1815* (Cambridge, 1962), p. 127.

It was not for some time that a general concern for the Negro bond servant reawakened in Massachusetts. And when it did, abolitionism took on much of the character of a crusade to impose the prudential Yankee virtues of industry, thrift, and renunciation upon a resistant South. In the age of Jefferson, the surviving thread of abolitionist sentiment already had the recognizable tone of cultural *amour-propre*. Federalist anti-slavery arguments, few as they were, served much more to reinforce the myth of New England exclusiveness than to bring about a change of Southern heart or the manumission of the slaves.

The passing of early Massachusetts abolitionism also meant that many New Englanders who came to maturity after 1790 were taught to look upon the slave question in a largely political light and were raised upon antislavery thinking which was principally exclusivist and opportunistic. They did not at first know how to react to the new abolitionists in the 1830's. Many, like Harrison Gray Otis, for whom antislavery remained linked to the specter of Southern Negro votes, scorned as they had three decades earlier the idea of freeing the slaves.[4] Yet, in fortifying the anti-Southern bias of the North, the larger Federalist ideology which encompassed such sentiments taught a third generation of political leaders to understand that slavery lay at the root of New England's powerlessness.

That so many sons of Federalist fathers assumed leading roles in the abolitionist crusade after 1815 was certainly not coincidental.[5] When they entered battle with the slave masters,

---

[4]Morison, *Otis*, II, 219-31, 263-74.

[5]Among the more renowned were William Cullen Bryant, William Pitt Fessenden, Hannibal Hamlin, James Russell Lowell, Wendell Phillips, Edmund Quincy, Robert Rantoul, Theodore Sedgwick, Jr., and Lewis Tappan. The long-lived Josiah Quincy himself became a member of Lincoln's Republican Party and an anti-slavery-ite. William Lloyd Garrison, whose father disappeared early in the youth's life, received his first employment at an early age as apprentice at the Newburyport *Herald*, where he imbibed the principles of Timothy Pickering and reverenced with youthful ardor the image of Harrison Gray Otis. Later, he advocated Northern secession from the South. John L. Thomas, *The Liberator: William Lloyd*

they rehearsed once again the principles of their fathers' politics and fought as much against the South and for New England as against slavery and for the slave. Indeed, the abolitionist historians of the 1830's looked upon the events of the century's early years from a vantage unmistakably reminiscent of Federalist thought. They claimed that the three-fifths clause had made possible Jefferson's election and looked upon the Hartford Convention's proposal to amend it as a high point in a continuous campaign against Negro bondage. They argued that the election of 1800 betokened a triumph for slavery and that the Louisiana Purchase was a victory not of American imperial aspirations and national security but of forces scheming to extend slave territory and Southern power.[6] It was not only genuine abolitionism, then, which challenged the South in the 1830's, but New England sectionalism and the Massachusetts Federalist ideology come back to life.

IV

As THE YEARS of Republican ascendancy lengthened and as New England's relegation to permanent impotence seemed clear, Massachusetts Federalists began to reopen the entire question of the national union. But what eventuated in a searching re-examination of their allegiance to the union stemmed from more than a simple concern for their own place in it. It arose as well from a concern for the state of the union itself, for its moral character, the quality of its leadership, the effect

---

Garrison, A Biography (Boston, 1963), Chap. II. Opponents of abolition later tried to discredit the reform cause by linking it to Federalism. See, e.g., [Charles Gordon Greene], *The Identity of the Old Hartford Convention Federalists with the Modern Whig, Harrison Party* (Boston, 1840), p. 9, charging that the convention call for repeal of the three-fifths clause "proves that old Tory Federalism was the father of *Abolitionism.*"

    [6]Lynd, "Abolitionist Critique." On efforts in 1819 and 1820 to link the opponents of Missouri statehood with the Hartford Convention, see Glover Moore, *The Missouri Controversy, 1819-1821* (Lexington, Ky., 1953), *passim.*

of its politics, and the extent of its foreign entanglements. Federalists wondered if a nation so morally diseased and so poorly governed could survive. They grew convinced that the country would split apart and, what is more, that it would have to split apart for its own survival. Disunion, they came to believe, would preserve not only New England but the entire republican experiment. What historians have customarily overlooked, however, is that, when speaking of disunion, Federalists were not only thinking about New England separation. They were thinking of the West as well. From an early date, Federalist thought was caught up in the ebb and flow of the expansionist mood.

Unlike the Jeffersonians, who boldly contemplated the future of an extended agrarian empire stretching into the western interior and who dedicated their party to the proposition that republicanism and democracy could survive and flourish side by side in a continental nation, Massachusetts Federalists envisaged a republic bound to the ocean. They had little sympathy for the agrarian ethos of the South and West. They disdained the settlers of the frontier and resisted the beckonings of the western land mass. This is not to say that Federalism had no appeal among the farmers of the Massachusetts hinterlands; for, on the contrary, much of the party's strength was to be found among the people of the farming interior. But Federalism's attraction lay among a special sort of farmer: resistant to change, unventuresome, satisfied with a static life, unmoved by the spirit of agrarian enterprise, fearful of competition, and not yet taken by land speculation. If this farmer's vision extended beyond the confines of the town, it turned to the seafaring communities, where confidence in national survival was based upon faith in ocean power and where men's thoughts turned away from the land. To the majority of Federalists, whether merchants or farmers, the sea and commercial society set the terms of life, provided markets and resources, offered jobs and opportunity. When after 1815 the spirit of Federalism eventually went west, it went not to subdue the new land but to reform the lives of those who had turned their backs upon the Atlantic.

Federalists' antipathy to the West and their attacks upon the Louisiana Purchase, the Republican Florida policies, and the War of 1812 rehearsed the traditional apprehensions of republican theorists. Samuel Taggart cautioned an audience to fear the addition of the trans-Mississippi West, for "in a territory so extensive as the United States, comprising within its limits, perhaps, nearly all the varieties of the human species, to be found in the civilized world, peoples whose sentiments, habits, manners, and prejudices, are very different, and whose local interests and attachments are various, it is not strange that the seed of division should exist."[7] Others assailed the admission of Louisiana to statehood, charging that it violated the principle that unanimity among member states was required to enlarge the Union. Josiah Quincy questioned the loyalties of the "wild men on the Missouri" and the "Anglo-Hispano-Gallo-Americans who bask in the sands in the mouth of the Mississippi." The addition of new lands, others argued, placed an unendurable strain upon the fabric of union by reducing the power and privileges of its original components. New lands to the west depopulated New England, threatened to reduce her proportional weight in Congress, forced land prices down along the New England frontier. The growing West had become the symbol of New England's impotence, and it did not escape the attention of Federalists that the society of the West was appreciably more democratic—and Republican—than that of Massachusetts.[8]

Federalist hostility toward the West and the Federalist belief in a fundamental antagonism of interests and cultures on

---

[7]Taggart, *Oration . . . at Conway*, pp. 7-8.

[8]Pickering to Winthrop Sargent, Jan. 6, 1804, Pickering MSS, MHS; Quincy to Wolcott, Sept. 5, 1803, Wolcott MSS, CHS; *Speeches Delivered in the Congress of the United States: by Josiah Quincy . . . 1805-1813*, ed. Edmund Quincy (Boston, 1874), p. 216; *Defence of the Legislature of Massachusetts*, p. 13; and *Political Sermon Addressed to the Electors of Middlesex*, pp. 27-28.

both sides of the mountains finally gave rise to the conviction that the nation would—and should—divide at the Appalachians. Caleb Strong spoke the mind of most Federalists in declaring that "the territory of the U.S. is so extensive as to forbid us to indulge the expectation that we shall remain many years united."[9] Strong, like most Massachusetts Federalists, differed from other Americans not in fearing disunion but only in anticipating it. For him the central question was never so much whether the Union could be held together but when, given its constant expansion, it would split apart. Disunion, Federalists liked to point out, had often been contemplated and already attempted—and not by New Englanders. The Western territories had threatened secession in the 1780's, Virginia and Kentucky had scarcely veiled their disunionist sentiment in 1799, and Burr's plot had more recently implicated the Western settlers. Could one reasonably expect that the West would continue bound to the East?

Federalist hopes that the West would secede presupposed a basic mutuality of interests between North and South. As their fears of the West mounted, Massachusetts Federalists made concerted efforts to define a case for North-South harmony and to convince the South that her best interests lay with the North. "The great and essential interests of the people," wrote Otis in the Hartford Convention Report, "are common to the south and to the east." The threat to them both arises from beyond the mountains, and nothing could be more foolish than for the South to unite with the West to govern the East: "The western states, multiplied in number, and augmented in population, will control the interests of the whole."[1]

---

[9]Strong to Pickering, Feb. 7, 1815, Pickering MSS, MHS. From the moment Jefferson was elected, Federalists thought a division of the union was imminent. See, e.g., Thomas Dwight to Jedidiah Morse, Dec. 19, 1800, Norcross Papers, MHS.

[1] See also *Patriotick Proceedings*, p. 128; [John Lowell, Jr.], *Thoughts in a Series of Letters in Answer to a Question Respecting the Division of the States* ... (n.p., 1813), pp. 18, 34; [Samuel Dexter], *Mr. Dexter's Address to the Electors of Massachusetts* (Boston, 1814), p. 7; Timothy Bigelow, *Address* ... *April 30, 1814*, p. 14; and Gore to Rufus King, Nov. 1, 1803, King MSS, NYHS.

The fullest presentation of this argument was made by the young Federalist pamphleteer, John Lowell, Jr. Condemning the thought of a division of the original states, Lowell urged that positive consideration be given to a division at the Alleghenies. The original states, he argued, were large enough—indeed, almost too large—for a successful republican government. The Louisiana Purchase not only violated the compact between the states and endangered the republican experiment, but it denied God's design in erecting the mountain barrier to separate the people on either side and to protect the Eastern republic. A despotic government, "where the remote parts are governed by viceroys or satraps," is better suited to a territory as vast as the enlarged United States. But in a republic "where general opinion governs, it is necessary that the people should be less extended, and more enlightened, and that there should be some similarity in their manners, habits, and pursuits."

The Westerners, the writer went on to argue, would wish to move the capital away from the coast, place heavy taxes on the East, and ignore the interests of the original states. Moreover, wondered Lowell, why worry about the West? Because the Westerners' economy was principally agricultural, they had nothing that the East required. Besides, they were jealous of the commercial prosperity of the original coastal states. Both sections would benefit by a separation, he concluded. And, in order to hasten the day, the South should throw in its lot with the North, in return for which New England would be willing to retain the three-fifths clause for some time longer.[2]

Lowell was not alone in sharing an aggressive attitude toward the West and combining it with pleas for a North-South *rapprochement*. Thomas Dawes foresaw the day when the original states would sicken of expansion and "tell the

---

[2][Lowell], *Thoughts in a Series of Letters, passim*. See also Taggart, *Oration . . . at Conway*, p. 26; Pickering to Edward Pennington, July 12, 1812, Pickering MSS, MHS; and *Report of the Committee* [of the General Court] *Appointed to Consider . . . An Expansion of Territorial Limits*, dtd. June 4, 1813.

Western folk as Abraham told Lot." Some urged that the states which had been represented at Philadelphia simply draft a new government—on the New England plan, most hastily added, with "no Negro voters, nor naturalized voters, nor alterations without the consent of all the States"—and restrict membership to the old thirteen states. Then, "in less than 12 months we should see the whole Atlantic States again united happy & prosperous." What was behind such thinking was bluntly revealed by one proponent of the scheme: "The Northern sections w'd soon have the ascendancy and control over the others, and thus govern, instead of being governed by a people half-civilized."[3]

Even Timothy Pickering, whose vain plottings traditionally have been dismissed as unrepresentative of Federalism or, obversely, as typical of party sentiments, was affected enough by fear of the West to foresee a North-South reunion. From the time of the ratification of the Louisiana Purchase to the beginnings of Madison's presidency, Pickering was hard at work to bring about a separation of New England from what he called "*the aristocratic democrats* of the South. . . . The white and black population will mark the boundary." But around 1810, like other Federalists, Pickering grew alarmed at Western growth. The admission of Louisiana to statehood in 1812 satisfied him that the West intended to gain equality with the original states, to ally itself with the South in order to annihilate New England's remaining power, and then, itself grown dominant, to cast off the Southern alliance and tyrannize the entire East. If the West failed in its designs, it would simply withdraw from the union, leaving the East to defend itself alone and pay its own debts.

Under the circumstances, Pickering hoped the South would discern the danger and re-cement itself to the North,

---

[3]Thomas Dawes to Noah Webster, Feb. 17, 1814, Webster MSS, NYPL; Ephraim Lock to Cyrus King, Oct. 18, 1814, Cyrus King MSS, Columbia; and Kenneth Wiggins Porter, *The Jacksons and the Lees: Two Generations of Massachusetts Merchants, 1765-1844* (2 vols., Cambridge, 1937), I, 114.

not only to protect the entire East but to convince the West to secede. If the South and North, he reasoned, were to lay an equitable burden of taxes and duties upon the Western states, the new territories would leave the union. "Entertaining this opinion, I cannot think of course, that a separation at this time would be an evil; on the contrary, I believe an immediate separation would be a real blessing to the 'good old thirteen states,' as John Randolph once called them."[4] It is in the light of this concern to mend fences with the South that we must understand the Federalists' frequent protestations that they meant no harm to union—that is, the union of the original thirteen states.

Federalists' opposition to expansion and their fears of Western hegemony left a powerful legacy of suspicion and hostility which was resurrected in varying guises in New England until the Civil War and later found its way into the Whig persuasion. Yet, in the end, the Federalists' anti-Southern bias emerged triumphant. Despite the Federalists' repeated avowals of a concern to preserve the union of the original states and to see the West take itself out of the republic, they were increasingly taken with the necessity of separating themselves from the remainder of the nation.

From at least 1786, the Commonwealth had been the special spawning ground of disunionist schemes.[5] The most

---

[4]On Pickering's early disunionist phase, see, e.g., Pickering to Richard Peters, Dec. 24, 1803. But even at that time, Pickering entertained deep suspicions of Western motives. See Pickering to Cabot, Jan. 29, 1804, to King, Mar. 4, 1804. For an early statement of his conviction that the West would secede, see Pickering to Strong, Nov. 22, 1803. And for his later sentiments, see Pickering to Edward Pennington, July 12, 1812, to George Logan, July 4, 1813, and to Lowell, Nov. 28, 1814, and Jan. 23, 1815. These letters are in the Pickering MSS, MHS. See also Pickering to Strong, Jan. 9 and 10, 1815, in Lodge, *Cabot*, pp. 557-59.
[5]On the early interest in a separate New England confederacy, see, e.g., Robert A. East, "The Massachusetts Conservatives in the Critical Period," in *Era of the American Revolution*, ed. Richard B. Morris (New York, 1939), pp. 372-75; Morison, *Otis*, I, 69, 267n; Labaree, *Patriots and Partisans*, p. 70; and Sedgwick to Strong, Aug. 6, 1786, "Letters to Caleb Strong, 1786, 1800," *American Historical Review*, IV (Jan. 1899), 328.

serious separation plans, those under Pickering's inspiration, were, however, launched after the turn of the century.[6] The first, a secret and misguided effort in 1804 restricted to a small circle of ineffective and marginal political figures such as Jedidiah Morse and Manasseh Cutler, never got far and remained unknown to all but a few men for many years.[7] The second in 1808, because it exploited the widespread misery of the Embargo crisis, was a more serious affair; yet it, too, failed for lack of sufficient popular support after the Embargo's repeal early in 1809.

Even at the height of Pickering's machinations, most Massachusetts Federalists professed an attachment to the union —"the Anchor," said the Massachusetts House, "of our present hope, and the ARK of our ultimate security, as a nation." Most Federalists throughout the Commonwealth condemned "impetuous and irregular efforts to which despondency and despair might impel." The townspeople of Beverly, for instance, declared that they saw "with anxiety and concern the Union of these States, dissolving as fast as under the old confederation— a Union so infinitely essential to their best interests and to their high rank among the nations."[8] These were not the sentiments of secessionists.

Yet few would have been able to agree with old patriot John Adams when he said that "I have been so long accus-

---

[6]On these abortive plots, see David Hackett Fischer, *The Revolution of American Conservatism: The Federalist Party in the Era of Jeffersonian Democracy* (New York, 1965), pp. 175-77; Morison, *Otis*, I, 264-68; *Documents Relating to New England Federalism, 1800-1815,* ed. Henry Adams (Boston, 1905), *passim;* Henry Adams, *History of the United States of America During the Administrations of Jefferson and Madison* (9 vols., New York, 1889-98), II, 160-69; Herbert L. Fader, "Design for Disunion: The Abortive Federalist Intrigue of 1804" (unpub. M.A. essay, Southern Illinois Univ., 1958); and Lynn W. Turner, *William Plumer of New Hampshire, 1759-1850* (Chapel Hill, N.C., 1962), Chap. VIII.

[7]See Morse to William Plumer, Nov. 16, 1803, Plumer MSS, New Hampshire State Library; and Morse to Plumer, Feb. 3, 1804, Plumer MSS, LC.

[8]Strong, *Patriotism and Piety*, pp. 4, 119; and *Centinel*, Mar. 2, 1814.

tomed to consider the American Confederation as one . . . that the habit is become a Second Nature." For the great majority of Massachusetts Federalists, theirs was a conditional unionism, avowed in prosperity, questioned in adversity, and always at odds with an abiding affection for the state. In any conflict between the two loyalties, wrote John Lowell, Jr., "it is our duty, our most solemn duty, to vindicate the rights, and support the interests of the state we represent." Pickering bluntly put it another way: his affections, he wrote, still flowed "in what you will deem their natural order—toward Salem, Massachusetts, New England, the Union at large."[9]

Yet men who retreated from change and revolution did not tranquilly contemplate rebellion against the Constitution. "It is an event we do not desire," wrote the editors of the Federalist *Centinel* in 1812, "not because we have derived advantages from the compact, but because we cannot foresee or limit the dangers or effects of revolution." When, however, they finally came to confront the possibility of disunion, they considered it an ultimate step, compelled only by republican self-preservation. "We have always been led to believe that a separation of the States would be a great evil," wrote a Newburyport editor in 1813. "We still think it an evil. But rather than prosecute the present war, which will eventuate in the ruin of the Northern and Eastern States . . . we think it by far the least of the two evils."[1] These were the sentiments of reluctant disunionists.

---

[9]John Adams to Seth Sprague, Oct. 26, 1812, reel 414, Adams microfilm; [John Lowell, Jr.], *Remarks on the Hon. John Q. Adams's Review of Mr. Ames's Works* (Boston, 1809), p. 39; and Henry Cabot Lodge, "Timothy Pickering," in *Studies in History* (New York, 1884), p. 220. See also Pickering to Edward Pennington, July 12, 1812, Pickering MSS, MHS, and the revealing verse quoted by Samuel Eliot Morison in the *Maritime History of Massachusetts, 1783-1860* (Cambridge, 1921), p. 212:

> Amy Kittredge is my name
> Salem is my dwelling place
> New England is my nashun
> And Christ is my salvation.

[1]*Centinel*, Jan. 13, 1813; and Labaree, *Patriots and Partisans*, pp. 184-85.

While frowning upon the extreme of secession, however, the majority of Massachusetts Federalists did not give up the search for a defense of their minority interests. This they found in the more moderate course of state interposition. The Federalist theory of interposition, so widely held after 1808, was rooted in the premise that the nation was a collection of "several independent confederated republics," a "league" of equal and sovereign states which had surrendered only a portion of their authority to the central government under the Constitution. In constitutional arguments sharply reminiscent of the Virginia and Kentucky Resolutions which they had only a few years earlier rejected, Federalists declared that the Constitution was variously a "treaty," "contract," or "association." Each state was a free republic "united by a solemn compact under a federal government of limited powers." These sovereign republics, and not the people, had been represented at Philadelphia, and the nation's sovereignty derived directly from the sovereignty of the states.

Federalists concluded from these propositions that since the states had negotiated the Constitution, the states alone could determine when a national law violated the compact, when its obligations under the Constitution ceased, and when to denounce it. From this it irresistibly followed that if a state nullified a law, interposed its authority between the people and the national administration, or in the extremity seceded, it would not commit treason. The state would merely assume to itself its full sovereign powers as a republic, a remedy "prescribed by the law of nations."[2]

[2]Frank Maloy Anderson, "A Forgotten Phase of New England's Opposition to the War of 1812," *Mississippi Valley Historical Society Proceedings*, VI (1912-13), 176-88; Edward St. Loe Livermore, *Mr. Livermore's Speech, in the House of Representatives . . . On the Bill from the Senate, Making Further Provisions for Enforcing the Embargo Law* (n.p., 1809), p. 4; [Josiah Quincy], *An Address of Members of the House of Representatives of the Congress of the United States, to their Constituents, on the Subject of the War with Great Britain* (Boston, 1812), p. 5; *Patriotick Proceedings*, pp.

III: *Massachusetts Federalists and the Union*

Many Federalists were convinced that the theory of a confederated republic justified secession, yet it is a measure of their caution that they showed a distinct preference for the alternative of interposition. Here was a moderate approach to the assertion of state interests, more effective than mere petitioning, yet less drastic than outright secession. It was also a constitutional posture which could be adopted selectively in order to protect specific interests. Disunion risked annulling all laws, even beneficial ones, and it raised the threat of civil war. Interposition, on the other hand, merely placed the state's sovereign authority between the national government and the people. Rarely defined with precision, it variously meant the negative expedient of refusing to recognize the validity of national tax laws within state borders or the positive act of legislating for commercial regulation and external affairs without regard to Congress and the President.

Whatever its specific implications, the majority of Federalists who considered interposition as a practicable alternative to acquiescence in repugnant measures did so because it was of a lesser order of radicalism than secession. While declaring, for example, that the people plan to "seek redress in every legal and constitutional method" and that they looked to the General Court "as our last resort," the Federalist Newburyport town meeting pledged itself no less determinedly "to abstain from every form of violent opposition." It was interposition and nothing more which a Newburyport writer had in mind when he warned that in addition to remonstrating, "we can submit, if it be not strictly constitutional, to do something more."[3] The very imprecision of the doctrine was its strength; it was a threat rather than a plan. It signaled at once New England's sense of outraged exclusiveness and her hope for reconciliation.

23, 30-31, 90; Massachusetts (pseud.), *New States*, p. 31; [Lowell], *Remarks on Adams's Review*, p. 38; and [Newburyport] *Herald*, Feb. 3 & 24, 1809, quoted in Labaree, *Patriots and Partisans*, p. 168.

[3]Labaree, *Patriots and Partisans*, pp. 159, 163, 165-66; *Patriotick Proceedings*, p. 52; *Newburyport Resolutions*, dtd. Jan. 12, 1809.

Amidst the clamorous politics of the new century, one group above all—the leaders of the party organization—steadfastly resisted the mounting call for separate state action and remained resolutely opposed to disunion. Until 1814, they answered secessionist and interposition plans with almost universal disapprobation. They placed Pickering under the severest pressures in 1804 and 1808 to renounce his disunionist schemes, reminded him of the weakness of Federalism in the Jeffersonian South, and made known their belief that his conduct was both irregular and deeply embarrassing to the party. "It will be well," Cabot heatedly wrote him in Congress in 1808, "to pass some very decided resolution on the importance of maintaining the Union inviolate under every trial." Ames, no less disturbed, was described as urging from his deathbed that every effort be bent to avoid separation. "Rather than that the Union should be endangered, every sacrifice . . . should be made—every evil submitted to. *For his part . . . he would stand by the ship to the last—he would pump so long as a single plank could be kept above water.*"[4]

It is indicative of the organization leaders' known opposition that Pickering's plannings never provided for their participation. In fact, Pickering's actions were directed toward wresting the control of New England Federalist policy from the political moderates who controlled it—cautious men who maintained a studied silence in the face of the rising furor. It was not until the movement for a New England convention was well under way in 1814 that the leading politicians began to support even interposition plans and then, as I shall have

---

[4]Cabot to Pickering, Oct. 5, 1808, Lodge, *Cabot*, p. 398; and Winfred E. A. Bernhard, *Fisher Ames: Federalist and Statesman, 1758-1808* (Chapel Hill, N.C., 1965), p. 342. For Cabot's, Ames's, and others' ultimately successful efforts to rein in Pickering, see also Lodge, *Cabot*, p. 394, and Adams, *New England Federalism*, pp. 353, 365, 380-81. In the South, the Federalists managed to hold roughly one third of the vote in North Carolina until after 1815, possessed considerable support only around Charleston in South Carolina, and had some strength in the Tidewater and, especially, the Shenandoah Valley of Virginia. Elsewhere, Southern Federalism scarcely existed.

occasion to suggest, primarily in their own defense, not New England's.[5]

By their failure actively to encourage and join the public call for open state action against federal encroachments— whether, as in most cases, it was a demand for state interposition, or, as it sometimes became, a cry for secession—the captains of the party organization evinced more than a reluctance to give official or party sanction to seditious and extralegal acts. They demonstrated their estrangement from those Federalists who, spurred on by editors, publicists, local conventions, and the increasingly clamorous clergy, had begun solidly to embrace the prospect of interposition and, by 1814, were threatening to go beyond.

Driven by the war to take a stand in defense of New England's exclusive interests which they neither welcomed nor were prepared for, the likes of Cabot and Otis had to adopt a strategy they feared. They had to accommodate public opinion and act the part which party leadership conferred upon them— or relinquish control of the party to less moderate figures. The bonds which had strengthened the Federalist community in time of peace were, during the emergency of 1814, put to the test. And while Federalists with one voice deplored the straitened condition of New England, their disagreements over strategy stood exposed. At issue, as the Hartford Convention members seemed to understand, was the control and direction of New England Federalism.

---

[5] See, e.g., Otis to Rutledge, July 31, 1812, Rutledge MSS, University of North Carolina.

IV

Federalist Leadership: Politicians and the Federalist Clergy

I

FROM the beginning of its history, the Massachusetts Federalist Party spoke with many voices, not one. It was a coalition of men, interest groups, religious persuasions, and regional blocs which attracted a heterogeneous following, pitched its message to a wide assortment of people in all quarters of the state, and moved to the commands of a variety of men. Because we have grown accustomed to confining our vision to the limited context of party activity and because we have for so long ignored the remarkable growth in voting participation after 1800, it has been easy to believe that Massachusetts Federalism was under the lone direction of experienced politicians somehow isolated from the society about them. But party leaders never alone controlled the party's fate, and none were immune from popular sentiment. Beyond the orbit of the party organization were many well-placed and would-be statesmen, only remotely experienced in partisan politics, who aspired to direct the temporal affairs of men. Important differences existed between those on the one hand whose distinguishing and shared trait was seasoning in the political arts, and those on the other who had little knowledge of secular politics and less sympathy for its concerns. These differences arose less from age and ideology than from calling and station in the larger community. And in the dissimilarity of the politicians' and would-be politicians' roles lay one of the principal features of the history of Massachusetts Federalism.

IV: Federalist Leadership

For a quarter-century after Independence, the dominant figures of Massachusetts Federalism were the original members of the original party. Known in their own day as "gentlemen of the old school," they were the party's elders, esteemed for talent and integrity and set apart in men's minds by the eminence which accrues to a life of accomplishment and service.[1] With age, they had developed a distinctive manner of expression and a characteristic bent of mind which set the party's tone and deeply affected the thought and action of a younger generation of leaders. To the nation at large, they were the party's most representative and prestigious type.

Yet style and state of mind were not the chief sources of their commanding position. What gave them a superior claim upon the loyalty of other Federalists, and what explains the unique station they occupied, was that they had been "young men of the Revolution," the makers of rebellion and the architects of independence.[2] Their good fortune to have just entered upon their mature careers when war broke out and when the demand for capable and industrious leadership was so acute says much about their rapid rise to prominence and their influence in party affairs long after they had retired.

Born before 1760, the old-school gentlemen had come of age by the time of Yorktown and had taken part in the heady events of the Revolutionary cause. Capable and worthy of preferment in their own right, benefited by family, genteel comfort, and education, they had been in an unparalleled position as young men to exploit the opportunities of rapid change and to assume leadership in the young nation. By any measure they were cautious rebels who from the beginning frowned on the excesses of revolution and lent their efforts to the mainte-

---

[1] For the Federalists' own use of the designation "old school," see David Hackett Fischer, *The Revolution of American Conservatism: The Federalist Party in the Era of Jeffersonian Democracy* (New York, 1965), p. 1*n*.

[2] I borrow the term "young men of the Revolution" from Stanley Elkins and Eric L. McKitrick, "The Founding Fathers: Young Men of the Revolution," *Political Science Quarterly*, LXXVI (June 1961), 181-216.

nance of domestic stability and tranquillity. From an early age they were drawn to order and repelled by variety and change.

In any other revolutionary setting their moderation would have impeded their advance, but in the American Revolution it only helped their rise to positions of power and strategic advantage. Indeed, such was their prudence that their Revolutionary record comes as a disappointment. A few of the future old-school gentry, like Henry Knox, Benjamin Lincoln, and Timothy Pickering, assumed military command and hazarded their lives for the republic. But for the most part, the party's future captains preferred, like Francis Dana, Nathan Dane, John Lowell, Theophilus Parsons, and Caleb Strong, to remain conveniently close to the centers of power and preferment, or they tried, like George Cabot, Benjamin Goodhue, Stephen Higginson, and the Derbys of Salem, to do well while doing good.[3] When peace came, these someday Federalists were better stationed than they had been before the war. They had advanced further than most contemporaries, and they confidently expected to rule the new nation. They had become early manifestations of a recurrent breed of American: upward-moving beneficiaries of change and new opportunity, eloquent in justification of the new order and jealous of their new-found place.

Not only did the Federalists-to-be possess that hypersensitivity toward change and that pervasive fear of competition characteristic of the *arriviste*, but they had a pride of unique station. Because of their intimate association with the events of the Revolution, these old-school figures enjoyed an advantage which comes to few men. They possessed a clearly defined and exclusive status. It could not be shared, nor passed on, nor reproduced. Successors might invoke the Revolution, but they, after all, had made it. And they believed it their right to define what it meant. "The American Revolution was in

---

[3]Fischer, *Revolution of American Conservatism*, Appendix II *passim.*

fact, after 1776," wrote Fisher Ames, "a resistance to foreign government." Its purpose was not to reshape society but to preserve it. Moreover, the claim of what Timothy Pickering called the "antifederalist-republican-democrats" to the succession of the Founding Fathers was illegitimate. "Who adopted the National Constitution?" inquired a Federalist legislator. "Federalists. Who opposed it? Democrats."[4]

In addition to trying to monopolize the definition of the national purpose, the old-school gentry believed that their very membership in the circle of men who had helped establish the institutions of the new nation gave them a transcendent claim upon public office. In the new governments they came to occupy official posts almost by prescriptive right. Unlike their successors, they did not have to "run" for office; they "stood" for it, certain of long tenure and contemptuous of those who questioned their qualifications. Because they staffed the governments they had constructed, they also refused to acknowledge a distinction between the government and its personnel. Assaults upon their administration of affairs appeared to them as attacks upon the framework of government. Republican opposition to their policies and against their repeated candidacies seemed more than a slur upon their class. It was an affront to the whole Revolution.

Yet the same experiences that made the old-school gentlemen resistant to change also made them sensitive and responsive to it. As trustees of the new government, their job was not only to preserve it but to make it work. In this endeavor, the setting and direction of their lives predisposed them to pragmatism and flexibility. Before the emergence of parties, these old-school patriots had become public figures, accustomed to

---

[4][Boston] *New England Palladium* (hereafter *Palladium*), June 7, 1808; Ames, "Political Thoughts," *Monthly Anthology and Boston Review* (hereafter *Monthly Anthology*), II (Nov. 1805), 566; and Pickering to Samuel Williams, Jan. 9, 1810, Pickering MSS, Massachusetts Historical Society (hereafter MHS). For the latter-day statement of the Federalist argument, see Charles A. Beard, *Economic Origins of Jeffersonian Democracy* (New York, 1915).

the arena of state and national affairs. First as merchants and lawyers, then as political leaders, they had developed friendships and connections in distant towns and cities and had begun to move, if they did not already do so, in national and cosmopolitan circles. Their practice at the bar, their commercial transactions, their investments, and their travels were to an ever-mounting degree premised on the existence of a national community, national laws, and national institutions, which gave them a perspective on public affairs which transcended the parochial boundaries of village and town.

The men of maritime Massachusetts, born and raised in the varied and informed world of the coast, adapted perhaps most easily to the enlarged perspective of affairs. But others did so no less completely. The greatest change of view took place among the leading men of the interior, whose provincial beliefs were sharply challenged in the orbit of state and national politics. After a few years of life in the large commercial towns where governments convened and people from all over the world congregated, men like Caleb Strong and Theodore Sedgwick found their views altered and their affinity for local politics considerably diminished. They had become members of a national political elite, responsible to larger constituencies and charged with governing the new national order.

Whatever the varied forces which elevated these Revolutionary figures to positions of responsibility, the fact is that their rise was capped by the achievement of great authority. And the possession of such power at the meridian of their careers could scarcely fail to have an effect upon their attitudes toward government and leadership. Most political figures of the early republic may have deeply mistrusted the uses of power; yet as men practiced in the business of public affairs, the old-school Federalists, like many good Jeffersonians, never showed quite the same fear of it when they held it as when they did not. When Caleb Strong wrote that power was "of an encroaching nature," he added, as much in the spirit of confession as rebuke, that "we think there is no danger from it while it is exercised by us, or by those in whom we have great confidence, and are apt to forget it may soon pass to others with whom we should be unwilling to trust it."[5]

Thus, as much as they decried the abuse of power, by the 1780's they had become experienced in its application and confident of their ability to use it wisely. As framers of the new order, they were unable in good conscience to escape involvement in its government. Indeed, their belief that the wise and good alone must direct the affairs of men was accompanied by a compulsion to govern, a habit rooted in the long tradition of stewardship upon which they had been raised. Old-school gentlemen may have recoiled from the idea of politics in a partisan sense, but they were never known to disdain the idea of politics conceived as impartial statesmanship. And much as they assailed the costs and burdens of public service, it never crossed their minds that it was a defective calling, unworthy of their participation.

The old-school politicians were deeply committed to the notion that effective government was the essential guarantor of public order and happiness. Though they called for education and moral discipline and worried that a society so deeply shot through with moral transgression could not survive, they doubted that regeneration of the spirit could rescue the nation unless its government were first reformed and "an aristocracy of experience" placed in charge. There are many ways to read the Federalist proposition that men capable of governing the state are to be found only among the "natural aristocracy," "those, and those only, who by nature, education, and good disposition, are qualified for government."[6] But if by this they meant to offer a justification for upper-class rule, they also had in mind the virtues of government by students of political science and men of practical experience. What we can expect from the natural aristocracy, Theophilus Parsons wrote, is "a thorough knowledge of the interests of their country, when

---

[5]Strong to Pickering, Feb. 7, 1815, Pickering MSS, MHS.
[6]The phrases are Jonathan Jackson's in [Jackson], *Thoughts Upon the Political Situation of the United States of America . . .* (Worcester, Mass., 1788), pp. 55, 57.

considered abstractly, when compared with the neighboring States, and when with those more remote, and an acquaintance with its produce and manufacture, or its exports and imports. All these are necessary to be known, in order to determine what is the true interest of any state; and without that interest is ascertained, impossible will it be to discover, whether a variety of certain laws may be beneficial or hurtful." In much the same vein, Parsons counseled young aspirants to public office to avoid an education in theoretical and useless subjects. "Look after the politics of the country," he admonished them, "as you look after your ships, your banks, your mills, your business." To parents, he gave the same utilitarian advice. "Educate your children in practical subjects," he told them, "and teach all those things . . . before Latin and Greek; or the calculus."[7]

This may sound like strange advice from one of the most learned men of Massachusetts, a master of ancient languages, astronomy, and mathematics. But Parsons' attitude was typical of most Federalists, and by 1800 one of the dominant motifs of the Federalist ideology was an attack upon politicians' visionary schemes. By then, the old-school gentry were convinced that the nation had fallen into the hands of impractical theoreticians who would toss away the experience of the ages to engage in the folly of social experimentation. Governing a republic called for caution and a regard for the accumulated knowledge of man's past, not for some utopian vision beyond the capacities of fractious, imperfect men. "One fact," said Ames, "is better than two systems." The Republican advocacy of popular rule of the state was the hallmark of "modern

---

[7][Theophilus Parsons], *Result of the Convention of Delegates Holden at Ipswich in the County of Essex* (Newburyport, Mass., 1778), pp. 18-20; and Theophilus Parsons [Jr.], *Memoir of Theophilus Parsons* (Boston, 1859), pp. 120-21. This point is made in a different context by Norman Jacobson, "Class and Ideology in the American Revolution," in *Class, Status, and Power: A Reader in Social Stratification,* eds. Reinhard Bendix and Seymour Martin Lipset (Glencoe, Ill., 1953), pp. 550-51, and Linda K. Kerber, *The Federalists in Dissent in Jeffersonian America* (Ithaca, N.Y., forthcoming), Chap. IV.

philosophism," and it caused old-school Federalists to assail the rationalist spirit and on their own behalf offer a defense of men who would "prefer the wisdom of *experience* to the illusions of *theory*."[8]

Jefferson gave them their chief target. They had many things in mind when they attacked him, but among their chief concerns was his supposed disregard for practical realities, well-tried procedures, and institutional forms. Jefferson seemed to them to ignore the restraints of law, to tamper lightly with the basic structures of government and society, to dabble in the curious and useless—all out of devotion to some philosophical vision. "Those are not the wisest of men who undertake to act always by rule," Fisher Ames reasoned with Jefferson in mind. "In political affairs there are no more self-conceited blunderers than the statesmen who affect to proceed, in all cases, without regard to circumstances, but solely according to speculative principles."[9] So well did they know Jefferson: inventor, architect, city planner, drafter of the decimal coinage system, and master politician!

If the old-school Federalists of Massachusetts assailed Jefferson's "philosophism" as the wellspring of his misguided attitudes toward executive leadership, they held it even more responsible for his supposed attachment to "levelling prin-

---

[8] [Boston] *Columbian Centinel* (hereafter *Centinel*), Aug. 14, 1802; and Ames in *The Debates and Proceedings in the Congress of the United States* (Washington, 1834-56), usually cited as *Annals of Congress*, 3rd Cong., House, 1st Sess., 330. See also the Federalist toast in *Centinel*, June 3, 1801: "May *experience exemplify* what *precept* has *promised*."

[9] *Works of Fisher Ames*, ed. Seth Ames (2 vols., Boston, 1854), II, 334. For Ames's comments in a similar vein on Madison, the "book politician," see *ibid*., I, 35-50 *passim*. And for a more extended analysis of the Federalist view of science and theoretical thought, see Kerber, *Federalists in Dissent*, Chap. III. See also Sedgwick to Harmanus Bleeker, Jan. 23, 1812, Sedgwick MSS, MHS: The Jeffersonian era shows "the dominion of philosophy in opposition to common sense, and of theory against experience." Cabot to Pickering, Feb. 17, 1806, Henry Cabot Lodge, *Life and Letters of George Cabot* (Boston, 1878), pp. 352-53: "Great philosophers and men of distinguished talents will be often found the most zealous defenders of the most monstrous follies,—a good lesson for human pride."

ciples." And of all the threats to republicanism in their thinking, popular government was among the most dangerous. Cabot spoke the mind of all Federalists in holding "democracy in its natural operation to be the *government of the worst.*" And Ames repeatedly warned that the nation would "sacrifice the essence of liberty to the spirit of democracy." Conceived in this way as an attitude of spirit rather than one of the institutional arrangements of society, democracy repelled every good Federalist of the state.[1]

Yet, when defined more strictly as limited participation in the electoral process, democracy was something which old-school Federalists endorsed. After all, government was built upon consent, and consent meant the approval of the citizenry. In this spirit, George Cabot admitted that "the people must have a share in every good government. . . . No government can be relied on that has not a material portion of the democratic mixture in its composition." But what Cabot had in mind as the "people" was not the whole body of adult males, nor did he mean by a "share" in government what we would call the opportunity to govern. Instead, he meant the concurrence of a limited portion of the adult male population in the selection of government officials. While on the one hand "I deprecate every system which should exclude the people from a share," he wrote, "I am satisfied that no system can stand where they preponderate," adding, "There is no security for a good government without some popular mixture in it; but there will be neither justice nor stability in any system, if some material parts of it are not independent of popular control."[2]

According to these standards, elections should, on the one hand, be referendums in which sober and responsible citizens signified their approval of the government's past actions and,

[1]Cabot to Wolcott, Aug. 3, 1801, to Pickering, Feb. 14, 1804, Lodge, *Cabot,* pp. 322, 341; and Ames to Thomas Dwight, Jan. 25, 1804, Ames, *Works,* I, 338; II. 228.

[2]Cabot to Pickering, Feb. 14, 1804, to King, Mar. 17, 1804, to Gore, Apr. 10, 1801, Lodge, *Cabot,* pp. 342, 345, 318; and Cabot to King, Nov. 6, 1801, King MSS, New York Historical Society (hereafter NYHS).

on the other, commissions to the wise and good to rule according to their own judgment. Democracy, thus conceived, was a legitimizing process. It was a procedure and not, as the Republicans emphasized, an end of government. To the old-school Federalist mind, democracy was little more than the appurtenance of the most rigid and elitist republicanism.

Old-school Federalists were satisfied that if democracy could be confined to its legitimate but narrow orbit, the threat of excessive leveling could be countered. Yet, in the light of what eventually occurred, their optimism was misplaced and their conception of democracy fatally flawed. In the first place, their definition of democracy as minimal participation did not resolve the troublesome question of how to make people accept their limited role. Elitists assumed without much question that a well-informed public, instructed in the dismal logic of the natural inequalities among men, would defer to their betters. Their political opponents, however, were quick to exploit the pluralization of Massachusetts society to demonstrate their error.

In the second place, by construing democracy principally as a measure of participation, Federalists became accustomed to encouraging greater voting participation. By defining elections as referendums, Federalists invited attempts to solicit votes in order to win them. Only Ames, with characteristic insight, saw—and despaired—that "the body of the Federalists were always, and yet are, essentially democratic in their political notions"; but, like the rest, even he surrendered to the temptation to act the democrat in political methods.[3] After 1800, most old-school gentlemen worked hard to get out the vote and demonstrate the people's consent to Federalist rule. As they would have occasion to ponder by 1814, the price of seeking consent at the polls was nothing less than excessive democracy, Federalist style.

Try as they might, the old-school gentry knew that theirs was a losing struggle. By the time of Jefferson's election, they

---

[3]Ames, *Works*, II, 348.

had few illusions about the irresistible advance of uncontrolled democracy. "We are sliding down into the mire of a democracy," groaned Ames, "which pollutes the morals of the citizens before it swallows up their liberties." Cabot agreed: "The spirit of our country," he wrote, "is doubtless more democratic than our principles; and those principles of necessity place power in the worst hands."[4]

Yet, pessimistic and bitter as they were, the party's elder statesmen never lapsed into hopelessness and apathy. If anything, the inroads of democracy only determined them all the more to impede its further advance. Here, two alternatives seemed to present themselves. The party could either try to modify the effects of democracy, a course which had by 1804 proven ineffective, or it could seek to capture democracy for elitist ends.[5] Of the practiced old-school statesmen, a few were of a mind to take the first course. Cabot, for example, flirted with the idea of placing tighter restrictions upon the suffrage. In addition, the old-school gentry who controlled the party caucus well past 1800 carefully, if misguidedly, preserved for themselves the right to select presidential electors in the General Court.[6]

Most old-school Federalists, however, and eventually even Cabot himself, recognized that these expedients, however desirable, could only offend the average voter and further sow the democratic germ. The problem, they were coming to see, was not to reduce the vote but to control it, not to prohibit the people's participation but to mobilize it. Whatever these practical statesmen might say about "our supreme Lord, the rabble," the people could vote; and the potentialities of the

---

[4]Ames, "Political Thoughts," in *Monthly Anthology*, II (Nov. 1805), 556; and Cabot to King, July 30, 1801, King MSS, NYHS.

[5]Their assumption was, of course, that the party was worth saving. We must, said Ames, "preserve our being as a party." Ames to Wolcott, Mar. 18, 1801, Ames MSS, Dedham, Mass., Historical Society. The party, he repeated on another occasion, is "our only resource." The question was how to activate it. Ames to Wolcott, Dec. 2, 1802, Wolcott MSS, Connecticut Historical Society (hereafter CHS).

[6]Cabot to Pickering, Feb. 14, 1804, Lodge, *Cabot*, p. 344.

suffrage had begun to impress all but the most rigid of the older men. So too the need for organization, used with such effectiveness in 1776 and 1788, which once again recommended itself as a means of putting down a threat. At the same time that Cabot was contemplating counting the people out, he was deeply involved in preparations for the election of 1800, co-ordinating efforts among Federalists in many states, trying in the face of party disintegration to develop some sort of national plan, and groping, perhaps not fully consciously, toward a realization of the need for further organizational innovations.[7]

Cabot was not alone. Theodore Sedgwick, among the most conservative of the old-school sort, spoke for many of his kind in writing that he "would treat the people as if they were wise and virtuous." He would propagandize them and seize the initiative from the Republicans. ". . . The federalists are not only torpid & indifferent but their principles of defense are of a nature to be eternally attended with disgrace and defeat. It is a mere system of defence against the attacks of their adversaries." Appeals to reason will be unavailing, for "the people have neither a heart to fail nor a head to understand." Revealing vividly how the impulse to action and organization might arise from the deepest antagonism to democracy, Sedgwick concluded that "the party which hopes for victory or even safety must apply to fears & jealousies; it must raise passion & direct it." Ames was of the same mind. "The agents that move politics," he wrote, "are the popular passions." "Truth ought to be made popular, if possible." The Federalists, he was convinced, had for too long concerned themselves with what had to be hindered, not what must be done. "We must

---

[7]See, e.g., Cabot to Rutledge, Oct. 22, 1800, Rutledge MSS, University of North Carolina (hereafter UNC). My argument in this chapter and elsewhere is at variance with that expressed by Max Weber that, especially in England and America, the members of the high social and political elite in the older static and deferential society (whom Weber called the "notables") were incapable of becoming "professional" politicians in an organization *outside* the legislature. See Weber, "Politics as a Vocation," in *From Max Weber: Essays in Sociology,* eds. H. H. Gerth and C. Wright Mills (New York, 1958), esp. pp. 102-03.

court popular favor, we must study public opinion, and accommodate measures to what it is and still more to what it ought to be."[8]

To Ames, it was also a question of action and organization. What was needed was something less than full-scale political mobilization but something considerably more than the mere elucidation of principle. "A party inactive," he declared, "is a party half-conquered." "Is it not, therefore, proper, and indispensably necessary," he asked, "to be active, in order to prevent the destruction of the feeble ties by which the federal party is held together?" The keys were energy and innovation; the public must be aroused; political resources must be organized; men must, above all, act. "We must animate the federalists. We must try to raise their zeal high."[9]

As early as 1798, Ames organized party festivities, wined and dined the community, entertained Dedhamites with toasts and speeches, and loftily announced, "The progress of Federalism seems to have begun." And it was Ames who, with Cabot's encouragement, took the lead in revitalizing a moribund Massachusetts newspaper and transforming it for a time, as the *New England Palladium,* into a vehicle for old-school politics. Party elders contributed discreet essays to its columns and underwrote efforts to give it the widest possible circulation throughout New England. Ames, a student of Jeffersonian practices, patterned his project after the Republican press, which he believed instrumental in securing the Presidency. He fully understood the role of popular attitudes. "Public opinion governs our country, the newspapers govern *it,* and it is very possible to govern the newspapers." He conceived of his newspaper

---

[8] Sedgwick to Rutledge, June 27, 1801, Rutledge MSS, UNC; and to Theodore Sedgwick, Jr., May 17, 1804, to Harmanus Bleeker, Jan. 23, 1812, Sedgwick MSS, MHS. On Sedgwick's highly practiced talent for politicking and manipulation, see Joseph Charles, *The Origins of the American Party System* (Williamsburg, Va., 1956), p. 114.

[9] Ames to Gore, Dec. 13, 1802, to Theodore Dwight, Mar. 19, 1801, Ames, *Works,* I, 309-11, 292; and to Thomas Dwight, Feb. 19, 1804, Ames MSS, Dedham.

as a defense against the party's "entire dissolution." It would be a first step in marshaling the "compactness, energy, and intelligence of the party."[1]

Although his project ultimately failed and Ames wearied of his participation in it, the effort was not in vain. In their desire to activate an apathetic following, to arouse popular understanding of the party position, and to coordinate party actions, Ames and other old-school figures revealed to their party the potentialities of the press as an instrument of political control. That their newspaper turned out to be a weak weapon in the party arsenal is not half so significant as the impulse behind it. By emphasizing action and seeking an appropriate response to the democratic spirit, the old-school gentlemen were laying the foundation of a new party-wide effort to update Federalist operations and discover a modus vivendi with democracy.

In this search, a partisan press was not their only contribution to Federalist politics. Another was the party's legislative caucus, which the old-schoolmen adopted initially in order to resolve a deep leadership crisis around 1800. Soon outgrowing its original function, the caucus wielded sovereign power over the Massachusetts party for roughly twenty-five years, and it called into being and ultimately controlled a broad committee hierarchy which had day to day administrative responsibility for Federalist affairs.

In other words, Massachusetts Federalism would not have lasted out Jefferson's administration without the constant en-

---

[1]Ames to Wolcott, July 6, 1798, George Gibbs, *Memoirs of the Administrations of Washington and John Adams* (2 vols., New York, 1846), II, 69; Ames to Wolcott, Mar. 18, 1801, Ames MSS, Dedham; to Wolcott, Dec. 2, 1802, Wolcott MSS, CHS; and Cabot to Gore, to Alexander Hamilton, Oct. 11, 1800, to Wolcott, Oct. 5, 1800, Lodge, *Cabot*, pp. 292, 294, 295. Early Massachusetts backers and contributors to the *Palladium* included elder Federalists Jedidiah Morse, Cabot, John Lowell, John Thornton Kirkland, Eliphalet Pearson, and David Tappan. Robert Edson Lee, "Timothy Dwight and the Boston *Palladium*," *New England Quarterly* (hereafter *NEQ*), XXIV (June 1962), 229-39.

couragement of the old-school gentry and without their willingness to assume places in the new committee system. Christopher Gore, one of the stiffest of the breed, became a member of the original state Central Committee, and Israel Thorndike, a realist of the old school, joined the Committee later on. Other party elders staffed the system's lower echelons. Fisher Ames was first chairman of the Norfolk County Committee, Stephen Codman became first head of the Suffolk Committee, and such others as old-school congressmen Dwight Foster and Elijah Brigham served regularly on county and town committees. For every old-school gentleman who refused to take part in new-style Federalism, there was one who joined and helped set the tone of organization politics.[2]

Most of those who failed to play a continuous and active role in the type of politics whose foundation they had helped lay withdrew from public life out of no quarrel with the new politics. Their disengagement was motivated as often as not by age, illness, or a desire to realize other ambitions. Cabot, for example, never known to enjoy public service, resigned his Senate seat in 1796 and retreated gloomy but rich to his Brookline estate at the age of forty-five. Many of his associates curtailed their activities for reasons of health and family. Cabot's Senate successor, Benjamin Goodhue, retired in 1800 after two decades of public responsibilities, ill and probably alcoholic at fifty-two. Nathan Dane, co-author of the Northwest Ordinance, member of the Continental Congress and the General Court, withdrew in 1797, afflicted with deafness at the early age of forty-five. Ames gave up his House seat in 1796, the victim at thirty-eight of chronic illness and depression. Some, of course, withdrew simply out of a refusal to suffer the trials and indignities of party strife. But most waited until worthy and willing younger men came along to take their places, and only then, like Parsons, Sedgwick, John Lowell, Samuel Sewall, Nathan Read, and George Thacher,

---

[2]I examine their participation in new-style politics in greater detail in Chap. VI.

exchanged the life of partisan politics for other promising and public careers.[3]

Because this was a time of shifting perspectives and new careers for all Americans, what is more noteworthy is the number of old-school gentlemen who did not withdraw from politics but remained active long after 1800. In addition to those who helped organize and administer the committee system, others served energetically for another two decades. Caleb Strong, governor for eleven years between 1800 and 1815, was succeeded by John Brooks, who served until 1823. Pickering was active in the federal House and Senate until 1817, and Samuel Taggart sat in the House for the same years. Many of those who intended to retire found, like Cabot, that they could not remain permanently inactive. They continued to exert considerable influence within party councils and maintained a link with affairs through correspondence, newspaper pieces, and occasional forays into the public forum.[4]

---

[3]Many of those who claimed to have retired for reasons related to the rise of democracy more probably did so for a complex set of reasons, many of them unstated. Sedgwick, for instance, declared in 1802 that he would not have abandoned his political post had he not been convinced that the people wished to experiment with democracy and that his comfort would have to be sacrificed. But a closer look at Sedgwick's actions suggests that he would not have given up his place in the House had he not been satisfied at having found a worthy successor to his Berkshire seat. Only when his Federalist successor failed to be elected did Sedgwick pour out his bitterness. Significantly, he could not himself resist public life and soon accepted an appointment to the Massachusetts Supreme Judicial Court. Sedgwick to Rufus King, Mar. 24, 1801, June 15, Aug. 24, 1802, King MSS, NYHS.

[4]In 1801, Cabot wrote that he had little contact with the world except, as he put it, through "*our own sect* exclusively." Cabot to Wolcott, Aug. 3, 1801, Lodge, *Cabot,* pp. 320-22. Yet Cabot's "sect" was a wide one, embracing the leading political figures of both generations. See Cabot to Wolcott, Mar. 26, 1798, Gibbs, *Memoirs,* II, 42-43, in which Cabot writes that despite his reclusiveness he retains a keen interest in public affairs, writes for newspapers, and speaks frequently to others. And for similar evidence, see also Lodge, *Cabot,* pp. 588-89, and Ames to Pickering, Mar. 24, 1806, Ames, *Works,* I, 378. Gore listed the most pragmatic reasons for his return to public life and office holding. Gore to Rufus King, Apr. 15, 1806, King MSS, NYHS.

None of them refrained from assailing the new politics and the slim rewards of public service, but we should not assume that by scoring democratic politics they meant to impugn the actions of their successors. What they lamented was the necessity for organized politics, not the fact that Federalist politicians engaged in it. There is every reason to believe that had a systematic party organization recommended itself at an earlier date, most of the old-school gentry would have become its officers. That they did not act to create a formal party system in the 1790's was not so much out of resistance to the idea of organized politics but because circumstances did not earlier force such a departure upon them.

Ultimately, old-school politics served as a bridge between the decorous deference politics of colonial America and the more modern and aggressive politics of the new generation. The old-school gentlemen trained their successors in the ethos of public service and gave them an example of pragmatic leadership. They suggested that action and style were two necessary ingredients of any politics, and they laid the groundwork for the organization which would emerge after 1800. They could take satisfaction in having created the practical and intellectual underpinnings for their successors' actions. Though they bemoaned popular government and regretted any flirtation with its ways, they nevertheless encouraged efforts to discover political weapons to combat the democratic disease. Resisting the twin snares of apathy and amateurism, they set the stage for Federalist ventures in organized popular politics.

II

As the party elders gradually vacated their places in public life, they were succeeded by younger men whose thinking bore the unmistakable stamp of the old school. The new party leaders identified themselves with the Revolutionary generation, spoke of themselves as members of a natural aristocracy, and deplored the pretensions of "the most profligate and contemptible portion of society." They assumed the justice of monopoly government by the wise and good and assailed "government by acclamation." Like the first Federalists, they claimed the Constitution for their own; it was, said young Josiah Quincy, "almost wholly the work of men called Federalists, and was also opposed, almost to a man, by those, who now a days call themselves Republicans." With an asperity equal to their fathers', they scored the muddle-headed theorizing of modern political scientists and called for a regeneration of practical statesmanship. The Hartford Convention Report, which Harrison Gray Otis reputedly wrote, reviewed "the state of this nation under the advantages of a wise administration, contrasted with the miserable abyss into which it is plunged by the profligacy and folly of political theorists" and called on the people to "discard the influence of visionary theorists, and recognize the benefits of a practical policy."

How stiff a draught of anti-rationalism young Federalists took in from their fathers is perhaps nowhere better exhibited than in the perverse and uninhibited verse of fifteen-year-old William Cullen Bryant. "Go, Wretch, resign the presidential chair," he admonished Jefferson in 1809:

> *Disclose thy secret measures, foul or fair.*
> *Go, search with curious eye, for horned frogs,*
> *Mid the wild wastes of Louisianan bogs;*
> *Or, where Ohio rolls his turbid stream,*
> *Dig for huge bones, thy glory and thy theme.*
> *Go, scan, Philosophist, thy [Sally's] charms,*
> *And sink supinely in her sable arms;*
> *But quit to abler hands the helm of state,*
> *Nor image ruin on thy country's fate!*

As Republicanism entrenched itself, contempt turned into deep pessimism. Between the resignation of old-schoolman Cabot and young Federalist Otis there was little difference. "The precipitate course of the dreadful torrent will finally overwhelm and perhaps destroy us," wrote Otis of the democratic advance. "You know I am a fatalist upon this subject. My fears are indeed great & my convictions strong: The struggle between a populace and the *natural aristocracy* of a country is a fearful clash, and where the latter is unsupported by a firm executive, it must fall."[5]

Yet if the young Federalists placed a rhetorical emphasis upon the coming national apocalypse, they were as cautious in action as their elders. Taking their cue from the old-school politicians, they conceived their stewardship of the common good in the most instrumental terms and devoted a major portion of their energies to the struggle for electoral success. And because they had come to political maturity within the party system and had adopted the norms of two-party politics from the earliest date, they readily appreciated the advantages of organized political activity and were little disposed to risk them for the alluring but vain prospects of nullification or disunion.

It is useful to compare these practical statesmen with those who might be called the true Federalist radicals, men who, like Pickering in Massachusetts and Roger Griswold in Connecticut, not only foresaw an apocalypse but did their best to provoke one. In almost all cases, the extremists who encouraged secessionist sentiment and countenanced plans for dis-

---

[5]Otis to Rutledge, Oct. 18, 1801, Dec. 2, 1804, Rutledge MSS, UNC; [Josiah Quincy], *An Answer to the Questions: Why Are You a Federalist? and Why Shall You Vote for Gov. Strong* (n.p., 1805), pp. 3, 5-6; and William Cullen Bryant, *The Embargo* (2nd ed. corrected and enlarged, Boston, 1809), pp. 12-13. Another of the poem's passages suggests the kind of sentiments toward democracy which Bryant imbibed from his father, a Federalist officeholder from the arch-Federalist town of Cummington in Berkshire County:

> Enter, and view the thronging concourse there.
> Intent, with gaping mouth, and stupid stare;
> While in their midst their supple leader stands,
> Harangues aloud, and flourishes his hands;
> To adulation tunes his servile throat,
> And sues successful for each blockhead's vote.

In later years, Bryant was embarrassed enough by the poem—on political grounds as well—to exclude it from his collected works; but he never explicitly repudiated it.

union were recruited from outside the ranks of the politically experienced young Federalists. Either, like Timothy Pickering, they had come of age well before the emergence of a party system and, differing from the likes of Cabot and Gore, had never succeeded in getting right with it, or, like amateur politicians, they had never been a part of the political system and had never known the restraints and sanctions of organized partisan activity.

In contrast, the young Federalists, as charter members of the party organization, quickly discerned its possibilities and understood its limits. Though they struck out at the misuse of power and scored the excesses of party, they perceived that, no matter its shortcomings, the party was one means to control and apply power efficiently and responsibly. They did not believe, as they suspected so many amateurs did, that power was an end in itself. To them, power and politics were instruments in the service of larger goals. Wise enough to fear the perversion of authority, they nevertheless believed that, on balance, they were its best custodians: well prepared, high stationed, skilled, and endowed for stewardship.

The young and old politicians' common attitudes toward government, democracy, and politics were reinforced by a sense of status solidarity. Young Federalists were as well circumstanced as their elders and were drawn from the same circles. Cabot and Otis in eastern Massachusetts, Sedgwick and Henry Van Schaack in the western towns frequented the same parlors, directed the same banks, placed their monies in the same lands and cargoes, and worshipped the same distant God. In the maritime communities and their hinterlands, the legal profession and mercantile trades provided the majority of the party's cadre, young as well as old, and in the interior the farming gentry joined the men of bench and bar to staff the party posts.

To the bonds of status and calling were added those of blood and family. Young and old party captains were bound together in a vast cousinage which reached across the Commonwealth and oiled the machinery of government and society. Within the party, fathers and sons, uncles and nephews, and cousins and brothers exchanged the same posts and enforced the same ethic. The party, as Republicans liked to point out, had many aspects of a fiefdom, and its roster was the state's social and professional register.[6]

That young and old-school Federalists shared so many of the same circumstances and attitudes is not to say, however, that they were indistinguishable. But it is to suggest that what marked them off from each other was a difference of degree rather than of kind, a difference not in their ideas about democracy but in their notions of what to do about it. More than anything, this was a distinction grounded in the peculiar circumstances of each generation's political baptism, revolving around tactics, not goals; means, not ends.

When the old-school gentlemen had received their initiation into public affairs, they had bent every effort to prevent the rise of parties and counted among the triumphs of the Constitution a division of powers so clear that national parties were unthinkable. It was not until the late 1790's, when their careers were already on the wane, that they began to perceive that in order to coordinate the separate branches of government and make the presidential system work, parties were not only inevitable under the Constitution but indispensable. This realization marked a signal change in their attitude toward party, but it came too late in their political lives for them to act. Before they retired they could make only tentative beginnings toward organizing the party system.

In contrast, the second-generation Federalists opened their careers confronted by organized opposition to the wise and good and the stark alternative of surrender to the adversary or combat on his novel terms. By the accident of birth, most second-generation Federalists were just entering politics for the first time around 1800.[7] Few were past their thirties.

[6]For further evidence, see Chap. V, Secs. ii and iii.
[7]For brief sketches of some of the state's leading young Federalists, see Fischer, *Revolution of American Conservatism*, Appendix II, pp. 262-77. I have benefited greatly from Fischer's suggestive and

IV: *Federalist Leadership*

Most had been born after 1760, had reached maturity only shortly before the Treaty of Paris and, even if they could recall the Revolution, had not taken part in it. Rather than making revolution, theirs was the different task of preserving and consolidating it.

Young Federalists justified their fitness to rule in the same elitist terms as their elders, but their availability was grounded in conditions altogether different from those of the old-school figures. Rather than getting in on the formation of a party and claiming their right to place and prominence, they had first to join the party and then prove their fitness to direct it. Rather than having created the government, they could only try to demonstrate superior talents in administering it. Instead of membership in the Patriot cause, they could only show membership in the Federalist Party. While their elders' careers depended on the success of the Revolution, their own rode with the success of a party. Under these conditions, they took their cue from their elders, moved beyond the old politics, and struck a bargain with the democratic way not because they wished to but because they had to.

Unwilling to preside over the liquidation of their party and desirous of protecting their own public careers, the young party captains had to give a new meaning to political action.

---

ambitious work. Yet as provocative as is his thesis of a marked division between the older and younger Federalist generations and as refreshing as is his rediscovery of Federalist Party politics, he seriously overstates the disjunction between political generations and fails to do justice to the dynamics and sociology of Federalism. There is little doubt, as Fischer argues and as I shall also have occasion to show in detail in Chapter VII, that an active two-party system was crucial to the process of political democratization and, even more, to the creation of truly representative government. Yet what is most arresting about the early politics of Massachusetts is the continuity between the political generations. Without the support of the old-school gentlemen, as much the seasoned practitioners of politics as any young contemporary, the efforts of their successors would have come to nothing. Rather than hobbling the organizational efforts of the young party captains, the old-school figures provided the intellectual foundations and the personal incentives for their successors' political departures and then joined them in fashioning a new-style politics for a new political age.

Such were the altered political circumstances of the new century that, in comparison with their elders' public careers, the young Federalists' commitment to politics had to be far more continuous, dedicated, and expert—in short, far more professional. It could be said of all, as Otis said of Josiah Quincy, that they "intended ab initio to pursue politics as a profession."[8] To a much greater extent than the old-school captains, they devoted most of their lives to politics. Like most other professionals, they were spurred on by an ideal of public service, considered their labors to be impartial, and came to believe that their calling demanded definable professional qualifications. Except for the remunerative occupations needed to support their families, politics was their chief activity and interest. For the energetic young politician, life was a ceaseless round of travels and meetings, planning and fund raising, correspondence and speechmaking. Most young Federalists not only served in elective or appointive office at one time or another but concurrently managed parts of the party organization.

Because they were convinced that the fate of the republic and of an entire class of men was at stake, they did not conceive of their political activities as a sacrifice. Nor was it necessary to do so, because political service was coming to have widespread advantages to young men on the make. A highly articulated organization brought them into frequent contact with men of similar economic interests in all parts of the Commonwealth. Politics gave them increased exposure in the centers of wealth and preferment and added new avenues of advance. The old restraints against political organization which had inhibited the old-school figures had diminished appreciably by 1800 and, given the Republican challenge, there were more compelling reasons than ever to go forward with party-building programs.

Thus the young Federalists gave a broader interpretation to action and propaganda than Ames and Sedgwick had done.

---

[8] Otis to John Phillips, 1818, Edmund Quincy, *Life of Josiah Quincy* (Boston, 1868), p. 376.

Considering the party caucus as only a first step toward a party system, they conceived the full panoply of organized politics: its pyramidal structure of committees, its calculated fund raising, its central direction. It did not concern them that organization and demagogy smacked of the very system they sought to destroy. After all, had not Federalism always taught that the people were docile and easily led? What better way to save Federalism than to embrace democracy?

Not surprisingly, some members of the two political generations distrusted each other. But we seriously misconstrue the history of Massachusetts Federalism to see a sharp disassociation between them. Many of the misunderstandings that existed can be credited to the natural differences between generations. Many others were limited to the strategic but relatively small circle of maritime Federalism. More important, most of the friction was personal, and rarely did it affect party operations.

The principal targets of old-school suspicions were Otis and Quincy, both eloquent and powerful representatives of the younger breed and both always suspected of opportunism. From the very beginning of his political career, well before the rise of the party apparatus which he came to direct, Otis— charming, polished, witty, urbane—was charged with uncommon ambition and aggressiveness. First the old-school gentry accused him of seeking Pickering's spot in the State Department. When that office went to John Marshall, it was rumored that Otis planned to resign from Congress to accept appointment under the Convention with France of 1800. He also lost favor for endorsing Adams's peace mission to France in 1799 and for standing by Adams during the bitter election of 1800. Stephen Higginson dourly warned his friends that Otis would betray any trust for preferment. "For the sake of an additional vote, or the rise of one grade in the scale of promotion, [he] would sell any and all parties or persons in succession till he reached the top. Whoever trusts him will be betrayed." Even Ames, who had better reasons to appreciate Otis's talents, thought him "ardent and ambitious," and "eager in the chase of fame and wealth. . . . He sighs for political office—he knows not what, and he will file off the moment opportunity offers."[9] Christopher Gore singled out Otis and Quincy for his scorn. He scoffed at their "anxiety for office, distinction, & popularity," assailed them for believing that by "courting the prejudices of the mob, they should enter the seats of office & direct the whirlwind & the storm," and accused them of trying to preempt party offices and keep them from their party rivals.[1]

In moments of pique, the young objects of old-school suspicion reciprocated these feelings. Otis had little sympathy for the silly casuistry of men who "would sacrifice their party to save their theory," and he once condemned them for lacking the politician's touch. But his condemnations were directed more against the extremist Pickering than against the moderate Ames and Gore, and he was quick to grant that the elder statesmen were men "of probity, of talent, of influence" indispensable to the party.[2] All things considered, there was relatively little friction between old-school and young Federalists when it came to initiating the new-style politics after 1800.

Moreover, the older men never challenged the younger men's leadership. And, for their part, the younger men sedulously cultivated the favor of their elders, encouraged their continued participation in party affairs, and left aside strategic

---

[9] Wolcott to Ames, Dec. 29, 1799, Gibbs, *Memoirs*, II, 315; Higginson to Pickering, Jan. 12 & Apr. 16, 1800, Pickering MSS, MHS; and Ames to Gore, Oct. 5, 1796, Ames, *Works*, I, 202. See also Samuel Eliot Morison, *The Life and Letters of Harrison Gray Otis, Federalist, 1765-1848* (2 vols., Boston, 1913), I, 166-67, 237-38. Higginson had a special dislike for Otis. See also Higginson to Pickering, May 11, 1797, Nov. 24, 1798, Pickering MSS, MHS.

[1] Gore to ?, May 7, 1822 (photostat), Misc. MSS Colls., New York Public Library; Gore to Rufus King, Oct. 5, 1812, King MSS, NYHS. How risky it is to hypothesize a clear split among generations is made apparent by examining the movement to line up Federalist support behind New York Republican DeWitt Clinton in 1812. George Cabot encouraged Otis's, Quincy's, and other young Federalists' participation in a Clinton convention, while Gore steadfastly refused to have anything to do with a scheme linking him with Otis. In Gore's case, like Higginson's, his distrust of the younger men was more personal than political. See Chap. VIII.

[2] Otis to Sedgwick, Apr. 13, 1800, Sedgwick MSS, MHS; and Otis to Quincy, [1811?], Edmund Quincy, *Josiah Quincy*, p. 242.

places for them in the party's highest councils. Quincy, for his part, stayed on close terms with Cabot, Ames, Parsons, and Higginson, and Otis remained an intimate of Cabot.[3] In return, as I have tried to indicate, the elder statesmen made important contributions to the new-style politics and, like Cabot, tried to dampen any signs of radicalism and extremism outside the party hierarchy. The older men continued well into the new century to serve throughout the committee system with the younger men and remained at their posts about as long as their younger colleagues. The schism within Massachusetts Federalism existed elsewhere.

III

BECAUSE THEY HAD LEARNED their politics from the old-school gentry, the young Federalist politicians administered the party in line with assumptions which had long animated the Massachusetts governing elite. Whatever their disdain for "politics," the typical party figures of both generations were politicians. They were versed in conciliation and compromise, practiced in the give-and-take of the party forum and the legislative chamber, and concerned as much to preserve the party as to further a set of principles. Though they believed government to be a moral trust, they also thought it a secular concern. They judged a life devoted to political statecraft worthy of the highest esteem, argued that party and government office was the preserve of professional students of government, and assumed the function of the ruler to be both lawmaker and moral preceptor to mankind.

These attitudes were not, however, everywhere shared. Partisan politics, a new educative force in America, still surrendered precedence to the authority of religion, the law, and

---

[3]See, e.g., Ames to Quincy, Jan. 20, 1806, Ames, *Works*, I, 349-50; and Edmund Quincy, *Josiah Quincy*, p. 42. For the close rapport between Ames and Quincy, see their correspondence during 1807-1808 in Quincy MSS, Library of Congress.

the schoolroom. The circle of practiced politicians was not yet large, and, in a pluralistic society just beginning to accustom itself to partisan strife, the political figure was not the public's sole source of signals for action and cues to the interpretation of events. Outside the party camp was a large group of energetic and well-meaning men who had always been arbiters of attitudes and who claimed with the approval of their communities the right to direct public affairs. Among them were to be found all sorts of people: men of letters, teachers in schools and colleges, retired leaders of the business and commercial trades, gentlemen farmers, and members of the clergy.

Typically, these men were occasional politicians who entered and withdrew from the public arena as the intensity of public affairs waxed and waned. Around 1800 and again in 1808 and 1814, they raised their voices, aroused their followings, and called for radical political action to alleviate New England's plight. At other times, they tended their private concerns. Moreover, they never accepted a formal role in party matters. In fact, they had no sympathy for organized political action. They devoted much of their endeavors to questioning all political pursuits and disparaging the work of the professional politician. Their spasmodic participation in public affairs, coupled with their coolness toward politics, earned them the mistrust of the party captains. What is more, their high-toned and unqualified responses to critical issues eventually precipitated a sharp clash between their own and the politicians' interests.

Take, for example, the Commonwealth's men of letters, a small group of men centered roughly around Harvard College, the Anthology Society of Boston, and the *Monthly Anthology and Boston Review*, the house organ during its eight-year life of the Federalist literary community.[4] Neither so

---

[4]The history of the Anthology Society and the *Monthly Anthology* may be followed in the *Monthly Anthology and Boston Review; Journal of . . . the Monthly Anthology & Boston Review*, ed. Mark A. deW. Howe (Boston, 1910); and the following works of Lewis P. Simpson: "The Era of Joseph Stevens Buckminster: Life and Letters in the Boston-Cambridge Community" (unpub. Ph.D.

numerous nor influential as the lawyers and ministers, the Anthologists were nevertheless amateur political observers who were almost without exception Federalists. A majority of them were in their twenties, few beyond their thirties. Most of them took no part in political affairs, and almost none were engaged in business or commerce. Many, like the youthful James Savage and William Tudor, Jr., were historians, legal writers, travelers, patrons of the arts and letters, and men of leisure. Others, like the young Joseph Stevens Buckminster, John Thornton Kirkland, and Samuel Cooper Thacher, were liberal clergymen of the Boston school who warmly supported Henry Ware's election to the Hollis Professorship at Harvard in 1805 and, like most Anthologists, were sympathetic to the growth of Unitarianism.[5] Despite their drift away from religious conservatism, however, their literary and political orthodoxy was unqualified, their social ideas almost reactionary. According to one, "It becomes the duty of every one to exert his talents for the preservation of what exists, and the renewal of what is past," an obligation which was clearly meant to extend beyond the precincts of literature.[6]

---

dissertation, Univ. of Texas, 1948); "A Literary Adventure of the Early Republic: The Anthology Society and the Monthly Anthology," *NEQ*, XXVII (June 1954), 168-90; "Federalism and the Crisis of Literary Order," *American Literature*, XXXII (Nov. 1960), 253-66; and *The Federalist Literary Mind: Selections from the Monthly Anthology and Boston Review, 1803-1811* (Baton Rouge, La., 1962).

[5]Simpson, "Literary Adventure," pp. 170-71.

[6]Arthur Maynard Walter in *Monthly Anthology*, II (Apr. 1805), 200. In Noah Webster, the Anthologists saw the archenemy of good literary principles. They were scandalized when he questioned the authority of Samuel Johnson's *Dictionary*, scorned his attempts to understand an American idiom which "sprang from the mouths of the illiterate" rather than from the pages of the English greats, and attacked his efforts to improve the American language as smacking of speculative reasoning and revolutionary innovations. There was much in this of *lèse majesté*: Webster was a mere Connecticut Yankee and refused to pay homage at the Boston court of literary orthodoxy. See *Monthly Anthology*, V (May 1808), 277, VII (1809) *passim*, and VIII (Feb. 1810), 80-89; "Restorator" [Warren Dutton], *Palladium*, Oct. 2 & Nov. 6, 1801; Harry R. Warfel, *Noah Webster, Schoolmaster to America* (New York, 1936), pp. 293-94, 315-23; and *Centinel*, Sept. 13, 1806.

Yet, the society of letters was their principal concern. In an unusually barren literary era in Massachusetts, the Anthologists conceived their calling to be the preservation in the young republic of the literary canons of Augustan England. They thought of themselves as the defenders of an aristocratic literary tradition imperiled by vulgar tastes and undermined by partisan conflict. As the historian of this early school of American criticism has pointed out, what the literati feared most was the debasing of humane letters by the intrusion of popular attitudes. "Through the innovating spirit of the times," declared a young contributor to the *Anthology*, "the *republick* of letters may have its dignity and prosperity endangered by sliding inadvertently into a *democracy*."[7] To these young men of letters, as to many with only a fugitive interest in political affairs, democracy and politics were synonymous; and because American politics were inherently democratic, one accomplished nothing by fighting the democratic spirit through political action. In order to eradicate democracy, one had to put an end to politics itself.

When the Anthologists lashed out at politics, they were acting on the premise that partisanship inevitably polluted this polite and aristocratic world of letters. As if this were not intolerable enough, they saw factional warfare luring writers and scholars away from literature and toward the day's mundane debates. They subscribed wholeheartedly to John Quincy Adams's belief "that literature was, and in its nature must always be, aristocratic; that democracy of numbers and literature were self-contradictory."[8] Significantly, however, Adams himself did not retain their favor. When he returned from Prussia

---

[7]Simpson, "Federalism and the Crisis of Literary Order"; and Theodore Dehon, "A Discourse Upon the Importance of Literature to Our Country," *Monthly Anthology*, IV (Sept. 1807), 472.

[8]John Quincy Adams, *Memoirs*, ed. Charles Francis Adams (12 vols., Philadelphia, 1874-77), IX (Oct. 21, 1837), 416. See also Simpson, "Era of Buckminster," pp. 378-93. The Anthologists' admiration for Adams's literary abilities was shaken by his political apostasy in 1807, and after that they had much difficulty in evaluating dispassionately his literary and scholarly productions.

and accepted election to the United States Senate in 1803, they lamented his disregard of the literary life, and later, when he left the party, they were horrified at what they took to be his warmth toward democracy.

The Anthologists also had trouble coming to terms with Fisher Ames. It was Ames who wrote that "in democracies writers will be more afraid *of* the people, than afraid *for* them. . . . It is the very spirit of a democracy, as in France, to proscribe the aristocracy of talents." Coming from a Federalist, such thinking was unimpeachable, but when Ames began to indulge his talents in political essays, the literati lost confidence in him. William Tudor, Jr., deplored the conditions which drew men like Ames into petty public affairs and diluted their talents. For Tudor, the lesson was clear: "At a period like the present, when all the Charities of Social Life are violated by the relentless Rage of Politicks, a private Station is the Post of Honour for every Man who considers Independence as the first & best of Heaven's Blessings.—And he who doesn't think so, is a Slave & deserves nothing." Ames the activist disdained such thinking as the naiveté of "literary fops."[9]

This is not to suggest that the literati condemned all organization. The Anthologists may have been opposed to politics, but they did not object to mobilizing men's energies for a specific task. Indeed, the impulse behind the founding of the Anthology Society in 1803 was similar to that which underlay the formation a few months later of the Federalist Party system, namely, a desire to band together in order to confront and

---

[9]Ames, *Works*, II, 439-41; William Tudor to John Adams, Feb. 13, 1801, reel 400, Adams Family Papers microfilm (hereafter Adams microfilm); and Ames to Quincy, Jan. 20, 1806, Ames, *Works*, I, 349-50. See also William Tudor, "A Discourse . . . ," *Monthly Anthology*, IX (Sept. 1810), 158. The Anthologists printed a few characteristically mordant pieces from Ames's pen during his lifetime, but toward its close they became disenchanted with him. In one instance, they almost refused to print what they considered a poor effort but went ahead because of Ames's standing and because they had solicited the piece in the first place. Winfred E. A. Bernhard, *Fisher Ames: Federalist and Statesman, 1758-1808* (Chapel Hill, N.C., 1965), p. 337 *n*.

turn back the tide of democracy. But in contrast to the politicians of their generation, who organized to fight democracy with democratic techniques, the Anthologists organized for refuge from politics itself. By cleansing the literary republic of extra-literary influence, they hoped to escape the corruptions of the world. They would energize men of letters, revitalize criticism, and, armed with words and definitions, preserve undefiled the aristocratic republic of letters. Little did they realize that, in a nation which had begun to politicize every circumstance, literature had come to serve political ends.

However revealing the political posture of the Federalist literati, in the full context of Massachusetts Federalism it is, of course, only a footnote to the larger chronicle. There were other far more strategically located groups which also failed to be fully integrated into the state's politics. Of these, the most representative, influential, and outspoken were the marginal politicians whom I have chosen to call the Federalist clergy.[1] By this term I do not wish to suggest any organized bloc of ministers. Although clerics who warmly supported the Federalist cause were in almost all instances Congregationalists, and virtually all Congregational ministers were Federalists, the label "Congregational" by 1800 covered a multitude of creeds, some of them mutually hostile.[2] Moreover, while the Federalist

---

[1] In the section which follows, I have benefited immensely from the detailed knowledge of religious belief and organization of Lois W. Banner. Much of my understanding of the relationship between religion and politics in Massachusetts stems from her researches into the rhetoric and operations of American religion after the Revolution.

[2] I examine the political affiliation of the denominations at length in Chap. V, Sec. iv. Remarking on the political allegiance of Congregational ministers, Paul Goodman has correctly argued that "there were influential and articulate Jeffersonian Calvinists in the Bay State." But in point of fact there were only a few of them. To Goodman's own list of six Republican Congregational clerics, I have been able to add only two more: Ebenezer Bradford of Rowley and John Giles of Newburyport. Paul Goodman, *The Democratic-Republicans of Massachusetts: Politics in a Young Republic* (Cambridge, 1964), pp. 90, 227 *n.*

clergy's center of power was outside the greater Boston and Essex County maritime community and concentrated instead in the Connecticut River Valley, some powerful examples of the type lived within a few miles of the capital, and others were scattered everywhere across the state. What is important is that no matter who they were or where they were located, they found most of the politician's experience and many of his attitudes foreign to their own. Why this was so, and how a large group of Congregational ministers came to compose an informally organized power bloc within the Federalist camp, forms one of the most significant yet unexplored chapters of Massachusetts Federalist history.

Many things linked the minister of the standing church to the statesman of the ruling party. Both traditionally occupied a high station in the social order. Both held to the republican ideology. They had a common interest in suppressing democracy and common fears of French-born revolution and atheism. Social change and religious ferment raised for each the specter of displacement, and the strong links between Jeffersonianism and religious dissent in New England intensified their rapport. They shared, moreover, a long tradition of mutual support. Long after political rights had ceased to derive from church membership, the state had continued to protect the privileges of Congregationalism, and the church in return had bestowed its spiritual blessings upon the secular rulers. While the officers of government had directed the state, the clergy had articulated the predominant values of the Commonwealth.

It was the Revolution which abruptly altered the position of the established church in Massachusetts and disturbed its relationship with the ruling elite. The war disrupted religious practices, shattered congregations, and left many ministers without their pulpits. Church membership and churchgoing declined. When, in the 1780's, Congregationalism seemed in a fair way to regain its station, the Baptist and Methodist confessions began to win adherents and to rival the established creed in many sections of the state. Within the Congregational fold itself, schism was gathering force. Edwardeans clashed with conservatives, and both had to face the growing challenge of liberal and Unitarian heresies.

It was some time after the Revolution before Congregationalism regained its balance and even longer before it tried to reassert its commanding station in the state. So intently did the established clergy seek to stand up for the cause of revolution and republican government that, like most New Englanders, at least until 1794, they welcomed the cause of France as the cause of mankind and, despite its obvious hostility to religion, interpreted the course of the Revolution as another triumph of republicanism. Then, like others, they began rapidly to turn against it.

Why they did so, after the most virulent anticlerical and antireligious phases of the Revolution had already passed, is to be explained largely by the same domestic conditions which unnerved other Americans. This was the time of Tom Paine's *Age of Reason*, of the Whisky Rebellion, and of debates over the Jay Treaty. Looking about at home, the clergy saw nothing but the burgeoning of deism, the progress of religious dissent, signs of outright irreligion, the emergence of threatening political forces, and social strife and disharmony. As soon as they recognized the implications of these developments for revealed religion and the stratified society in which they still claimed a privileged position, they marshaled their forces for a counterattack.

After five years of acclaiming the events in Europe, they began to pillory the French Revolution and its American defenders, assail its "levelling tendencies," and prophesy the doom of republican institutions should infidelity go unchecked. Because their attacks upon equality and democracy coincided with the political needs of Federalist Party leaders, their standing in Federalist circles quickly rose. They found themselves courted by party notables; their sermons were widely printed and distributed. It seemed as if two decades of uncertainty had come to an end: the established ministry had rediscovered its role and re-cemented its alliance with the rulers of the state.[3]

Yet, a genuine marriage of interest and purpose never really took place. For two or three years, the secular and religious leaders made common cause against the Jacobin menace. But, as early as 1798, what opportunity there had been for the clergy to reassert its authority and lead a combined host against the fountainheads of religious and political infidelity had already begun to evaporate. By 1800 it had disappeared.

In their effort to take command of the American counter-revolution, and in the belief, as the Reverend Jedidiah Morse put it, that their outspoken efforts did "a vast deal of good in a *political view*," the Federalist clergy made two grave errors.[4] First, they raised their anti-revolutionary attacks to such a pitch that the political leaders' control of the people appeared threatened—something which old-school and young Federalists alike could not tolerate. Second, and most important, they involved themselves in the hysterical and diversionary fight against the Bavarian Illuminati.[5] Not only did combat against this almost mythic conspiratorial foe ring false in a nation concerned with the more tangible problems of war and politics; not only was a strident campaign against the purported European-based cabal a less effective instrument for suppressing the opposition than the ill-conceived but genuinely menacing Alien and Sedition Acts; but the anti-Illuminati effort also implicated the Masonic Order, of which many of the state's and nation's leading Federalists were members.[6] And, as if subverting their

---

[3]These observations are based upon Gary B. Nash, "The American Clergy and the French Revolution," *William and Mary Quarterly* (hereafter *WMQ*), 3rd Ser., XXII (July 1965), although my inferences are substantially different from his.

[4]William DeLoss Love, Jr., *The Fast and Thanksgiving Days of New England* (Boston, 1895), pp. 371-72 quoted in Nash, "American Clergy and the French Revolution," p. 411.

[5]The standard account of the Federalist and clerical reaction to the Illuminati is Vernon Stauffer, *New England and the Bavarian Illuminati* (New York, 1918).

[6]Jedidiah Morse, reigning American expert on the Illuminati peril, indulged in lengthy disclaimers of his intention to impugn

standing among the well placed was not enough, the clerics undermined their influence among the general population. By transforming the sermon into an occasion for partisan attack, they cut themselves off from Federalist coreligionists who feared the pollution of religion by politics as well as from Congregationalists who happened to be Republicans.

Thus, on the eve of the new political order, the Congregational minister found himself resented more than ever before—by Republicans, for meddling in politics and on the wrong side; by Federalist politicians, for complicating the problem of political control; and by dissenters of all sects, for adopting the protective mantle of the state's reigning political persuasion for the apparent advantage of his own religion. It is scarcely any wonder that the Reverend John Eliot concluded about this time that "as an order of men the ministers are not respected in this country as they once were."[7]

The clergy's comparative loss of esteem was also due to the ascendancy of a set of values appropriate to an enterprising society and inconsonant with the ideals of the church. What particularly goaded the minister was that he no longer seemed to count outside the confines of organized religion. The community applauded the man who steered a banking bill through the General Court, resolved a dispute over land patents, estab-

---

American Masonry, at the head of which was none other than George Washington. *Ibid.*, pp. 229 ff. The *Centinel*, forced to choose between loyalties to religious orthodoxy and Masonry, chose the latter. Its editor, Benjamin Russell, was a Mason. So was the young party leader William Sullivan and the influential Tracys of Newburyport. *Ibid.*, p. 277n; John Quincy Adams to Louisa Adams, Sept. 23, 1804, reel 403, Adams microfilm; and Kenneth Wiggins Porter, *The Jacksons and the Lees: Two Generations of Massachusetts Merchants, 1765-1844* (2 vols., Cambridge, 1937), I, 119.

[7]Benjamin W. Labaree, *Patriots and Partisans: The Merchants of Newburyport, 1764-1815* (Cambridge, 1962), p. 145; and John Eliot, *A Sermon, Preached . . . at the Ordination of the Rev. Mr. Joseph M'Kean* (Boston, 1797), p. 33, quoted in Conrad Wright, *The Beginnings of Unitarianism* (Boston, 1955), p. 249. For many such comments, see Anson E. Morse, *The Federalist Party in Massachusetts to the Year 1800* (Princeton, N.J., 1909), and Stauffer, *Bavarian Illuminati, passim.*

lished a source of credit in London, created new channels of trade. These were the concerns of men on the make, of a society prospering on the profits of neutral trade and engaged in the search for the main chance. Except when prosperity waned and war came, religion often seemed irrelevant.[8]

The Federalist clergy acutely felt their estrangement from the state's center of power and, while holding the Republicans in large part responsible, blamed the Federalist Party captains too. They resented the politicians' arrogation of authority over the Commonwealth and what they saw to be the disassociation of the concerns of leadership from the moral concerns of society as a whole. And, in this, their attitudes paralleled those of thousands of ordinary Massachusetts citizens who faced with deep apprehension the growth of alien religions, the loss of relative influence in community affairs, and the progress of new ways in the mercantile centers of eastern Massachusetts. Jeremy Belknap spoke for the entire standing church when he struck out against "a monopolizing spirit in some politicians, which would exclude clergymen from all attention to matters of state and government; and which would prohibit us from bringing political subjects into the pulpit, and even threaten us with the loss of our livings if we move at all in the political Sphere. . . . I consider politics as intimately connected with morality, and both with religion."[9] "Though

---

[8]A distinction can be drawn here between the attitudes of the orthodox and Unitarians toward the ascendant ethos of an enterprising society. Where the Federalist clerics mistrusted utilitarian values and decried abundant wealth and luxury, the Unitarians, from the 1790's on, increasingly stressed pragmatic values, extolled worldly success, and moved rapidly away from the customary emphasis upon social hierarchy and harmony. This is not of course to say that the Unitarians encouraged luxury and display, which they did not. See Jane Maloney Johnson's suggestive study, "Through Change and Through Storm: A Study of Federalist-Unitarian Thought, 1800-1860" (unpub. Ph.D. dissertation, Radcliffe College, 1958). I disagree sharply with the author's belief that most Federalists were Unitarians. *Ibid.,* p. 7.

[9]Jeremy Belknap, *A Sermon, Delivered . . . in Boston, May 26, 1796* (Boston, 1796), pp. 15 ff., quoted in Stauffer, *Bavarian Illuminati,* pp. 94-95. See also *The Ordeal: A Critical Journal of Politicks*

politicians and moralists may read fine lectures upon the public
and private virtues," declared Nathaniel Emmons, "yet their
best speculations upon these subjects are totally destitute of
the force and obligations of religious discourses. . . . The more
learned any are in law, or in history, and yet deny the utility
of religious teachers; the more they discover a natural or
moral incapacity to draw just conclusions from the plainest
premises."[1]

After all, religion and elitism were mutually supporting.
Religion not only spoke for the timeless verities of social justice, but it was the last bulwark protecting the ordained stratifications of society. "Whenever religion spreads an universal
influence through society," wrote one Federalist cleric, "there
is nothing out of place; there is no crowding for the highest
seats. It teaches one to think others better than himself, and to
wait unambitious, till he is bidden to go up higher."[2] The problem, then, as the Federalist clergy saw it, was not only to regain
influence but to reestablish the unity of politics and morality
and then to reassert the primacy of religion over both. Ministers have a "right" to govern, declared one writer, because
"they have better information and greater advantage to know
the truth." The clergy agreed: "The duty and obligation of
all the ministers of the gospel [is] to exert all the power and
influence which their sacred office gives them, to prevent the

and Literature, ed. Joseph T. Buckingham (Boston, 1809), Jan. 7,
1809; Samuel Austin, *The Apology of Patriots . . . A Sermon . . .
August 10, 1812* (Worcester, Mass., 1812); and Abiel Holmes, *An
Address, Delivered Before the Washington Benevolent Society at
Cambridge, July 5, 1813* (Cambridge, 1813).

[1]Nathaniel Emmons, "Religious Instructors Useful to Civil Society" (1803), *The Works of Nathaniel Emmons, D.D.,* ed. Jacob Ide
(2 vols., Boston, 1842), II, 237, 240-41. See also Belknap, *A Sermon,
Preached at the Installation of the Rev. Jedidiah Morse* (Boston,
1789), p. 8, quoted in Wright, *Beginnings of Unitarianism,* p. 249;
and David Osgood, *A Discourse, Delivered at Cambridge . . . April
8, 1810* (Cambridge, 1810), pp. 8-9.

[2]Abiel Abbot, *A Discourse, Delivered at North-Coventry, July
4th, 1799* (Hartford, Conn., 1799), p. 8, quoted in Wright, *Beginnings
of Unitarianism,* p. 250.

ruin of the nation." Simply stated, the ministers' job, in the words of one, was to "cry aloud and no [one] spare."[3]

Yet, in spite of the relative lessening of their authority, the Federalist clerics retained a good deal of influence over men and affairs. No greater testimony to the continuing sway of the ministers need be mentioned than the Republicans' protracted campaign to destroy their privileged position. If the clergyman's stature in the community had declined appreciably since the Revolution, his persuasive influence in individual towns had in many cases grown. Especially where there happened to be few dissenters, his influence was unqualified. Politicians ran the party, but they did not alone arouse the people. In many cases, secular and religious leaders shared control of the individual town. And, in some instances, the ministers called the tune. Henry Adams saw strong vestiges of the old autocracy of the Congregational clergy outside maritime Massachusetts well into the nineteenth century. "Did an individual defy their authority, the minister put his three-cornered hat on his head, took his silver-topped cane in his hand, and walked down the village street, knocking at one door and another of his best parishioners, to warn them that a spirit of license and of French infidelity was abroad, which could be repressed only by a strenuous and combined effort."[4] For the average man, the clergy-

---

[3] *Centinel,* Feb. 10, 1802; Emmons, *Works,* II, 246; and Osgood, *Discourse . . . April 8, 1810,* p. 10. See also Jedidiah Morse and Elijah Parish, *A Compendius History of New England* (2nd ed. rev., Newburyport, Mass., 1809), p. 330.

[4] Henry Adams, *History of the United States of America During the Administrations of Jefferson and Madison* (9 vols., New York, 1889-98), I, 79. See also Morse, *Federalist Party in Massachusetts,* pp. 181 ff., and Stephan Thernstrom, *Poverty and Progress: Social Mobility in a Nineteenth Century City* (Cambridge, 1964), pp. 38-39. Cf. Eliza Buckminster Lee, *Memoirs of Rev. Joseph Buckminster, D.D., and of his Son, Rev. Joseph Stevens Buckminster* (Boston, 1851), p. 13, writing of the early years of the century: "It was then deemed proper, even indispensable, that ministers should preach upon all subjects of public and political interest, expressing their individual opinions with moderation, but with decision and independence; and it sometimes happened that they did not confine themselves to the bounds of moderation. There were at this time very few newspapers,—

man was still a powerful and sometimes threatening figure. Party handbills and party rallies may have provided political excitement and political cues, but the rewards and sanctions of political allegiance continued to be spelled out from the pulpit.

The assertion of clerical influence also took more genuinely religious forms than the personal suasion and pulpit harangues to which the Federalist clergy were given. Much of the clergy's hold over the popular mind arose from the series of religious revivals which periodically swept parts of the interior of Massachusetts from the 1790's on. This "Second Great Awakening" represented the beginnings of a reorganization of American Protestantism, out of which eventually emerged an array of new religious bodies and a new religious temper. Ministers found themselves at the head of revitalized congregations, men of restored authority in community life. Coinciding with the impulse to political organization, their revivals helped to reconstitute the whole of post-Revolutionary American society. But, by the same token, the revivals exposed the divergent perspectives of the political captains and the clerical arbiters of New England civilization.

Because they remained bystanders to the organized business of politics, the Federalist ministers looked upon the political style as alien and hostile. Isolated from the institutional climate of partisan conflict, they were unpracticed in the exchanges of secular politics and unexposed to the demands of popular election. Because of the nature of their calling and because they found themselves banished from the partisan political arena, they came to view politics not, as the party captains

---

no reading-rooms; the public press was just beginning to be the important instrument of good and of evil which it has since become, and the preaching of ministers, at least in country places, was one of the great means of instructing and informing the people in political affairs, as well as religious duties." One student of community sociology has called the towns in which ministers could hold such sway "a dense collective experience." Conrad M. Arensberg, "American Communities," *American Anthropologist*, LVII (Dec. 1955), 1143-62.

would have it, as an exercise in accommodation but as a moral crusade to redeem man from delusion and the republic from its foes. Good and evil were not by their lights subject to negotiation and compromise.

In addition, the Federalist cleric was immune in a special way from public sentiment. Even though the laws of religious establishment dictated that the minister be responsible to the entire community of Congregationalists and dissenters, the law also permitted dissenters to form their own religious societies. Thus, in his own ministerial work, the Congregational cleric had to make no concessions to the sectarians—that is, to the many new elements of the increasingly pluralistic society around him.[5] Though accountable to the dominant moods of his own congregation, the minister was in a position to create these moods himself, and he easily assumed that they represented the sentiments of the community at large. Speaking only for Congregationalists and only to Congregationalists, he could little understand the attitudes of the politician who represented varied interests and whose position depended more directly upon the vagaries of public opinion.

Moreover, Massachusetts Congregationalism had always been, and remained after 1800, a collection of autonomous churches. The Federalist cleric had limited opportunity to gain experience in the workings of larger associations of men, of delegate assemblies and hierarchical bodies. Viewing himself as leader of an independent congregation, the Massachusetts Congregational minister had successfully resisted the appeal of presbyterian church association. All attempts at forming a statewide general association of clerics on the Connecticut model were unavailing before 1815. The best that could be achieved were regional ministerial associations, consultative meetings with little or no binding power over their members.[6]

---

[5]Jacob C. Meyer, *Church and State in Massachusetts, from 1740 to 1833* (Cleveland, Ohio, 1930), pp. 134, 143. See also William G. McLoughlin, "The Balkcom Case (1782) and the Pietistic Theory of Church and State," *WMQ*, 3rd Ser., XXIV (Apr. 1967), 267-83.

[6]William B. Sprague, *The Life of Jedidiah Morse, D.D.* (New York, 1874), pp. 72-91.

Contrasted to this religious structure, the Federalist party system took the form of a highly coordinated statewide organization. Party loyalty replaced membership tests, sanctions for nonparticipation were minimal, dues were voluntary. The party was shaped along presbyterian lines: directed from the center, hierarchical in form, and, to a significant degree, representative. The party cadreman was the presbyterian of the secular order, recruited from a local constituency, yet answerable to higher authority. The party committees were the party synods, aggregates of interests not directly responsible to individual communities and immunized in part from pressure below.

Indeed, the political parties were harbingers of a national system of voluntary societies in the secular and spiritual domain. Local and provincial politics remained important; but, increasingly, a national order of politics, to be followed by national missionary and reform movements, was superimposing itself upon local and regional factionalism. As it did so, power gravitated inexorably away from the local source and toward the national center. Public attention could still be drawn to parish affairs, the town meeting, local elections. But more and more it was diverted in the direction of national issues such as debates over a national commercial policy, international relations, and the presidential contest—issues which it was in the nature of parties to exploit, to magnify, and even to create.

In many realms, the party was becoming the principal rival of the church. It enunciated the dominant values of the day, dramatized conflicting interests, and recruited the best talents.[7] Its rallies took the place of religious services, its picnics

---

[7]Edmund S. Morgan has noted the change after the Revolution from clerical to political leadership and from religion to politics in American life. "The American Revolution Considered as an Intellectual Movement," in *Paths of American Thought,* eds. Arthur M. Schlesinger, Jr., and Morton White (Boston, 1963), pp. 11-33. What is more, the Calvinist clerics had taught men so well to think in the categories of depravity, redemption, and the like, that when leadership passed into the hands of politicians, the political leaders took over the entire intellectual heritage of Calvinist religion and appro-

became counterparts of church outings, its workers were like ministers out on call. The politician played the role of secular preacher of the early republic. He was the "insider," every town's principal link with the greater life of the Commonwealth. He dealt with the state's leading figures and was the news bearer from the outside world. It is not without significance that one of the earliest actions of the Massachusetts Federalist Party organization was to furnish local ministers with free subscriptions to party newspapers.[8] From an early time, the minister was made dependent upon the meager and highly partisan provincial press and, almost without knowing it, was made an adjunct of the party's general staff.

On still other counts, the loyal Federalist cleric was bound to feel some mistrust of the Federalist politician. While the churchman offered the hope of eternal but distant salvation, the politician, in his search for votes, claimed to be able to deliver a more immediate benefit to this enterprising society in the form of favorable legislation, corporate charters, appointive posts, and the like. In addition, while Congregationalists quarreled over doctrinal points, the party captains ignored ideological refinements in their search for ballots. And not only were the politicians liberal in their attitudes toward political dissent, but they were also liberal in their religious sentiments. Most of the party leaders had drifted away from Calvinist orthodoxy. Some of them, like Harrison Gray Otis, not without an eye to political advantage, had befriended dissenters and even encouraged their religion.[9]

Indeed, it was just this kind of latitudinarianism on the

---

priated it to secular, profane, and partisan purposes. And of course by the 1790's the Federalist clerics had come to understand the irony of their position: the very Revolution which they had earlier supported had let loose the politics they now so much deplored.

[8]See, e.g., Ames to Wolcott, Mar. 18, 1801, Ames MSS, Dedham, in which Ames indicates that his projected newspaper is to be spread "especially among the clergy."

[9]Otis to Rev. Joseph Clay, Jan. 13, 1807, Otis MSS, MHS. See also William Ellery Channing to Otis, Jan. 23, 1803, Otis MSS, MHS.

part of the party figures which drove a wedge between them and the Federalist clergy. The easterners who managed the party apparatus were almost without exception infected with the Unitarian spirit.[1] Not surprisingly, the Congregational clergy were alarmed by this. Federalist cleric Jedidiah Morse summed up their feelings in equating religious liberalism with the leveling spirit. "I consider Unitarianism," he wrote, "as the *democracy* of Christianity."[2] If the Charlestown cleric felt this way, the Congregationalists of the interior did so even more. Their hostility to eastern liberalism paralleled the traditional suspicion of western Massachusetts for the refined pleasures, the theater, the anti-Sabbatarianism, the displays of luxury and dress of the eastern towns.

All of this is not to say that the Federalist clergy were totally unaffected by the example of politics, nor that their suspicion of the politician prevented them entirely from borrowing some of his methods. But only a small group of ministers fully appreciated the implications of political organization. Some were conservative advocates of Congregational association, who, like Jedidiah Morse, saw in closer formal unity the

---

[1] Pickering, e.g., defended Unitarianism against Trinitarianism throughout his life, believed that the Protestant churches taught "absurdities," and refused to teach notions of the Trinity and Divine Revelation to his children. Pickering detailed some of his attitudes, if one dare believe it, to Jefferson himself in a letter of Feb. 12, 1821, Pickering MSS, MHS. See also a memorandum dated Dec. 23, 1821 in Pickering's hand, *ibid.*; Herbert M. Morais, *Deism in Eighteenth-Century America* (New York, 1960), pp. 140-42; and Ames, *Works*, I, 25. Cf. also the following comment from *The Panoplist*, the journal of orthodox Congregationalism, Vol. III (May 1808), 555: "A preacher pays a visit to a wealthy, fashionable family. . . . If he should introduce a discourse upon the important subject of salvation, what would probably be the effect? The company would be struck dumb with astonishment at his rudeness."

[2] Jedidiah Morse to Joseph Lyman, June 15, 1805, Morse MSS, Yale. See also Higginson to Rufus King, Feb. 10, 1805, King MSS, NYHS; Alden Bradford, *A Sermon Delivered at Plymouth, December 21st, 1804* (Boston, 1805), pp. 9-10; and Morse to Lyman, Feb. 9, 1805, Morse MSS, Yale, in which Morse comments: "It is unfortunate that a number of the ablest federalists are engaged (with truly Jacobinic arts) in revolutionizing [Harvard] college, in which I am bound to oppose them."

only defense against the inroads of infidelity and dissenting creeds. It was these men, stung into action by their loss of the Harvard presidency and despairing over the failure of their plans for a statewide ministerial association, who led the movement to found the Andover Theological Seminary in 1808, to transform an old religious journal into the mouthpiece of conservative theology, *The Panoplist*, and to launch a large-scale missionary movement.[3]

As the reform and missionary impulse within the Congregational fold swelled after 1810, other religious figures took up where Morse's circle left off. These men—for example, Jeremiah Evarts and Samuel Worcester, the able secretaries of the American Board of Commissioners for Foreign Missions in its early years—drew upon the experiences of the political parties as they constructed an effective missionary movement to transform American religion and redefine its social purpose.[4] The problems they faced were not far different from those confronted by the young party chieftains after 1800. Despite revivals, religious apathy often prevailed. Individual clerical efforts were often insufficient. Except for the partially successful Massachusetts Missionary Society, no state or national organization existed to provide a cadre of missionaries, to raise funds, to distribute literature, and to coordinate policies for a far-flung movement. Much as the parties had to organize in order to arouse their apathetic followings, the churches even-

---

[3]Sprague, *Morse*, pp. 65-115. Morse quite clearly conceived of his plans for a journal of conservative religion, a theological seminary, and a general religious association as organizational means to develop a coalition and enforce a unity of purpose within the whole right wing of Massachusetts Congregationalism.

[4]See, e.g., Jeremiah Evarts to Rev. Samuel Worcester, Mar. 31, 1815: "We must exhibit some of that enterprise which is observable in the conduct of worldly men." Evarts to Worcester, June 1816: "It is a notorious truth, and one which we may speak to each other, that there is not in Massachusetts a single man capable of leading the moral exertions of the friends of religion and morality. I mean there is not a man in civil life, and known to the public, who can lead these efforts with a tenth part of the ability that Mr. Otis or Mr. Gore could display on political subjects." E. C. Tracy, *Memoir of the Life of Jeremiah Evarts, Esq.* (Boston, 1845), pp. 107, 109.

tually had to organize more fully to induce their members to participate in the religious enterprise.

This convergence of the practical interests of some Federalist clerics with those of the party captains helped postpone into the nineteenth century a serious clash between the religious and secular political styles. So, too, did the early Federalist triumphs at the polls. But as soon as the Federalist Party could no longer claim the allegiance of a majority of the inhabitants of Massachusetts and the nation, and as soon as the country drifted first into Embargo and then war, the clerics—indeed anyone—could well inquire whether the party captains could not have prevented the crises. As the Commonwealth's position in the nation appeared to deteriorate, as the docks stood silent and the administration made war upon the world's last bulwark of liberty and religion, were political considerations to be permitted to intrude into a matter of right and wrong? Was this not the moment to reassert the transcendent claims of conscience and justice in defense of the Founding Fathers' principles and to ignore the constraints of union and the niceties of constitutional prescription? As the most zealous defenders of the Federalist-Congregational way, the clerics had few doubts.

Nor did they hesitate to try to reimpose the stamp of orthodoxy upon a party whose leadership treaded perilously close to deism and Unitarianism. The schism within Massachusetts Congregationalism, muted before 1805, manifest after, lent a particular note of urgency to the high-toned appeals of conservative clerics. The distant rumble of political extremism rising up from interior Massachusetts contained more than a little hope that liberal Boston might be forced to yield the direction of state affairs to religious orthodoxy.

By trying, in the name of high principle, to reclaim their former weight in public affairs and by challenging the strategy and dominance of the pragmatic politicians, the Federalist clergy twice brought the party to the brink of ruin. During the Embargo crisis and the War of 1812, such was the clamor for drastic measures from constituencies under clerical sway

that the men who administered the party found to their morti-
fication that they did not control it. Little troubled by institutional checks upon their actions, freely counseling extreme
opposition to the administration and, it cannot be forgotten,
commanding congregations which still remained the most well-
disciplined organizations in Massachusetts, the clergy aroused
the population to fever pitch and drove the vulnerable politicians to take steps which, even if they did no immediate harm
to Federalist strength in Massachusetts, ultimately destroyed the
chance of a national Federalist renaissance.

It reached the point in 1809 and 1814 that, unless they
wished to lose control of the party, the politicians were forced
to follow excited popular sentiment. A few insightful Federalists had foreseen this danger. Early in the century, Cabot had
observed that "you see good men in high offices here, but these
men hold their powers upon the sole condition that they will
not use them, and the moment they shall dare to exercise them
with vigor, they cease to be popular, and of course cease to fill
the high offices they now hold."[5] What was true in a time of
relative tranquillity was even more true in a time of turmoil.

Without access to the party institutions, the clergy had
to raise their voices in order to be heard. Only by exploiting
to the utmost their own persuasive authority in the community
could they hope to regain leverage over public affairs. The
periodic crises which beset the party after 1800 arose from the
clash between two groups of determined men with conflicting
claims and expectations: the politicians, still trying to legitimate
their claims to leadership and obtain mastery over public opinion, and the Federalist clergy, who still commanded a wide
hearing from the pulpit and who sought to reinvigorate their
role in the larger society. Along with the force of republican
ideology and the growth of a party machine, the conflict between them turned out to be the principal dynamic of the
party's history after 1800.

---

[5]Cabot to Rufus King, Mar. 17, 1804, Lodge, *Cabot*, p. 345.

V

The Social Sources of
Massachusetts Federalism

I

MASSACHUSETTS Federalism had the adherence of a
large and heterogeneous following. Gentlemen
of standing and education may have shaped and articulated the
Federalist ideology, but they spoke for and depended upon
thousands of obscure and average men who considered themselves Federalists and who apprehended their world through
the attitudes, symbols, and style of that ideology.

The "typical" Federalist of Massachusetts was an elusive
figure who stood somewhere below Harrison Gray Otis and
George Cabot in the scale of men but not necessarily far above
the lower ranks of society. Occasionally, he was a local lumi-
nary—a selectman, a justice of the peace, an attorney-at-law—
who had a wider impact than most of his countrymen on the
day's events. But the party's ordinary adherent exercised no
authority, commanded no deference, and had no entrée to the
parlors of the polite and prosperous. On most occasions he was
excluded from actual participation in the affairs of the ruling
Federalist elite and, like the man who took his cue from the
Federalist clergy, was frequently at cross-purposes with it. He
was rarely a "party man," could not be trusted to turn up at
the polls, and was often loath, in an age that anathematized factions, to make known his political loyalties.

What drew such a man to Federalism was a mental association with established authority and an affinity for the fixed
and traditional. More than self-interest propelled him into the

party's ranks. Whether out of dependence upon the powerful or a conscious identity of interest, the typical Federalist was an "insider" who enjoyed some sort of identification with men who customarily exerted moral, social, and political suasion in the Commonwealth. No matter where he stood in the community's social and political rankings, he esteemed his "betters," his "elders," his "forebears," and, whether from self-interest, long custom, or anxiety, set great store by the dependability of fixed relationships.

Men of this stamp were to be found everywhere throughout the state—in almost every hamlet, in every section, within every occupational and economic division, and among the communicants of every religion. Identifying them poses the usual problems of dealing with obscure people. Moreover, every generalization about the patterns of Federalist strength must be qualified by those hundreds of people who defy categorization. Yet the distribution of Massachusetts Federalists was by no means entirely random.

A glance at the political map of Massachusetts reveals, for example, that Federalism flourished best along the coast from Boston north through Essex County and in the Connecticut River Valley. These areas could claim a vintage history stretching back into the 1630's. But the towns of Plymouth and Barnstable counties along the south shore, which showed greater affinity for Republicanism than the north shore and valley regions, also possessed this link with the oldest regions of the state. The political differences stemmed not from age but from tradition: Federalism took firmest root among those first-settled regions of the Commonwealth which had been associated with the old Massachusetts Bay enterprise and its non-Separatist Congregationalism. Republicanism was strongest in those areas of early settlement which possessed bonds with the Plymouth Colony, which had long felt estranged from the dominion of Massachusetts Bay, and which had been founded in Separatism or Baptism.

Federalists were also more likely to be found in slow-growing downstate Massachusetts than in the burgeoning District of Maine.[1] Even within Massachusetts proper, they tended to congregate within those counties—Hampshire, Franklin, Worcester, and Essex—which were the most static. Yet the population pattern provides only the roughest index to party identification: too many exceptions and too low a correlation between rising and falling population growth rates and party affiliation existed.[2] A more precise explanation of the varying partisan loyalties of different areas—and one which accommodates the factor of population growth rates—lies in the different character of the Maine and downstate populations.

At the beginning of the nineteenth century, the District of Maine was a frontier, not only for Massachusetts but for all New England. Except for the coastal towns and a few small inland villages, its lands were vacant, its few inhabitants scattered. Religious dissenters, escapees from economic and social bondage, and seekers after a new start began to swarm to these vast untenanted tracts after 1790, lured by promotional schemes, impelled from the state's long-settled regions by slackening opportunity for economic advance and by the mounting unavailability of good land, and chafing under the fetters of established ways and entrenched elites. How many arrived from Massachusetts proper and how many from elsewhere is

---

[1]Figures which relate the population growth rate of Massachusetts to that of the rest of the nation and reveal the sharp differences between the growth of downstate and Maine counties can be found in Percy W. Bidwell, "Population Growth in Southern New England, 1810-1860," *American Statistical Association Publications*, XV (Dec. 1917), 813-39, and U.S. Bureau of the Census, *Historical Statistics of the United States, Colonial Times to 1957* (Washington, 1960), p. 13. Between 1790 and 1820, new settlers trebled Maine's population while the population of Massachusetts proper rose only about 40 per cent. Maine was the fastest-growing region of New England.

On the problems and dangers of equating the properties of groups and regions with those of individuals—dangers which I have tried to avoid—see W. S. Robinson, "Ecological Correlations and the Behavior of Individuals," *American Sociological Review*, XV (June 1950), 351-57.

[2]For example, Maine's Washington County, whose growth rate fell in the middle range of other Maine counties, was Federalist. Slow-growing downstate Berkshire County was strongly Republican, and fast-growing Suffolk and Essex counties were Federalist.

impossible to ascertain. Many of the new Maine settlers had left the other New England states, especially Connecticut and Rhode Island. But a large number came from downstate. Salem's perceptive William Bentley attributed the relatively static population of Essex County not to low birth rate but to the high rate of emigration, and all evidence corroborates his belief.[3]

Many of the new settlers in Maine were bona fide purchasers of land, but probably as many were poachers and squatters, holding and working unsurveyed and ungranted lands and then, after the tracts were apportioned—often to speculators—battling to retain possession by force of arms and in the courts. Not a little of their Republicanism sprang from their treatment at the hands of attorneys and state officials, most of them representatives of the Commonwealth's standing Federalist order.[4] Even such prostration as the Embargo and war brought in their train could not move the bulk of the small landholders of the District from their Republicanism. By 1805, Maine was as far away in space and tradition from Boston and Essex County as Massachusetts Bay had been, almost two centuries before, from London.

The immigrants into Maine were not simply the dissatis-

---

[3]William Willis, *History of Portland* (2 vols., 2nd ed. rev., Portland, Me., 1865), II, 281; Harry C. Cochrane, *History of Monmouth and Wales* (2 vols., E. Winthrop, Me., 1894), I, 95-96, 118-19, 122-24; and William Bentley, *The Diary of William Bentley, D.D.* (4 vols., Salem, Mass., 1905-14), II, 370. Much of the emigration to the frontier from inland Massachusetts, supplemented but probably not matched by the movement of opportunity seekers into the maritime towns, originated in the more purely agricultural areas which lacked markets and prosperity. Percy W. Bidwell, *Rural Economy in New England at the Beginning of the Nineteenth Century* (New Haven, Conn., 1916), pp. 387-91.

[4]Information about the land problems in Maine will be found in Paul Goodman, *The Democratic-Republicans of Massachusetts: Politics in a Young Republic* (Cambridge, 1964), pp. 125-27, 155-62; William A. Robinson, *Jeffersonian Democracy in New England* (New Haven, 1916), pp. 42-46; *William Bingham's Maine Lands, 1790-1820,* ed. Frederick S. Allis, Jr., in *Publications of the Colonial Society of Massachusetts*, XXXVI and XXXVII *passim*; and William Allen, "Bingham Land," *Collections of the Maine Historical Society*, VII (1876), 353-60.

fied, the ambitious, or the dissenters. A large proportion of them, whether from downstate Massachusetts or other parts of New England, were young adults. The Commonwealth's entire population and, more specifically, that portion of the population legally qualified to vote, was disproportionately youthful: in the whole of Massachusetts during the first two decades of the new century, fully 69 per cent of the males who met the minimum voting age of twenty-one were under forty-five. More important, however, were the pronounced differences between the age distribution of downstate and Maine voters. In downstate Massachusetts, 65 per cent of the male voting-age population in 1800 was under forty-five, but in Maine the figure jumped to 79 per cent. In far greater proportion than their elders, the young were leaving downstate Massachusetts for Maine and other frontiers.[5]

That the Maine population was both more youthful and more Republican than the downstate citizenry did not escape the eye of contemporaries, many of whom worried that Jeffersonian principles disproportionately attracted all youth. "To those who pay attention to the political state of this country," noted one Federalist in alarm, "it has been a matter of astonishment and inquiry, Why so many young men should have been led to imbibe the dangerous and destructive principles of Democracy."[6] In the case of the young Maine inhabitants, the

---

[5]Bentley, *Diary*, II, 370. See Francis Jackson, *History of the Early Settlement of Newton* (Boston, 1854), p. 223, for the observation that emigrants from Newton in the 1780's and 1790's were "generally young married persons." See also Lee N. Newcomer, *The Embattled Farmers: A Massachusetts Countryside in the American Revolution* (New York, 1953), p. 153.

[6]Quoted in William A. Robinson, "Party Organization and Campaign Methods in New England in the Jeffersonian Era," *Washington University Studies*, Vol. III, part ii (Apr. 1916), 204. Benjamin Labaree has suggested that young artisans were disproportionately Republican, and Samuel Eliot Morison believes that sailors—probably a majority of whom were Republican—tended to be younger men. Benjamin W. Labaree, *Patriots and Partisans: The Merchants of Newburyport, 1764-1815* (Cambridge, 1962), p. 141; and Samuel Eliot Morison, *The Maritime History of Massachusetts, 1783-1860* (Cambridge, 1921), p. 73.

answer was that both Republican politics and emigration from Massachusetts proper were part of the same pattern of protest against the older society. The young men who went north and west were a special sort, in retreat from the closed professional establishments and political elites of the older towns and in pursuit of new opportunity elsewhere. Moreover, political identifications which developed under such circumstances during youth tended to be durable. For even as the gap between age groups in Maine and Massachusetts diminished after 1800, the established partisan pattern remained: Maine's political allegiance remained decidedly Republican until statehood was achieved in 1820.

In contrast to the youthful Maine inhabitants, those left behind in the older communities, with their more rigid stratifications and their limited opportunities for innovation, manifested a strong affinity for Federalism. The Federalist ideology appealed most strongly to older residents of the most long-settled and slow-growing areas of the state; it was most deeply entrenched in those communities which were the most homogeneous, the most static, and the most isolated from the outside world. As the exodus of the discontented continued, such towns became even more politically conservative. One Federalist compared the Federalism of the people of undynamic "Old Hampshire" with the Republicanism of the Berkshire inhabitants, which he attributed to the high proportion there of those whom he called "rovers." "We keep more to our old habits," he observed, "being composed chiefly of the descendents of old settlers." The valley town of Deerfield, another observed, lived in total harmony with "scarcely a dissenting individual." The same might have been said of the interior of Essex County, which was far more homogeneous and Federalist than the dynamic and Republican Essex maritime communities.[7]

---

[7]Jabez Cotton to Simeon Baldwin, Dec. 31, 1804, Baldwin MSS, Yale. Of course, a town or region like Baptist Cheshire in Berkshire County or the island of Nantucket, which had been founded in dissent and had remained homogeneous and static, could be as fiercely Republican as communities of a similar homogeneity could be Fed-

Fisher Ames, the most perceptive Federalist student of political sociology, saw these homogeneous interior settlements as citadels of Federalism. He was convinced that Republicanism took form in the highly differentiated society of the coastal towns—which the examples of Boston and Salem confirmed—and then moved outward into the countryside, which was slowly becoming integrated into the larger state- and nation-wide community by turnpike roads, newspapers, and party organizations. "On the whole," Ames wrote in 1799, "the *rabies canina* of Jacobinism has gradually spread, of late years, from the cities, where it was confined to docks and mobs, to the country."[8] The growth of party organization from the coastal regions outward explained this pattern in part. So too did the emigration of dissenters and discontented men from the coast into the interior. But an equally important source of party differentiation in the interior was the spread of the partisan press.

Much of the early unity of sentiment in Federalist towns had arisen from the uniformity of Federalist newspapers. After 1800, partisan attitudes changed with the growth of a diverse press. Young William Cullen Bryant, on a trip to the Old Colony town of Bridgewater, explained why the political sentiments of Plymouth and "Old Hampshire" counties differed so widely. "Let the 'Hampshire Gazette' only give the word," he wrote, "which, by the by, it copies from some leading Federal paper, and every Federalist in the county has his cue, every-

---

eralist. On the effects of emigration upon the Connecticut Valley counties after the Revolution, see Anson E. Morse, *The Federalist Party in Massachusetts to the Year 1800* (Princeton, N.J., 1909), pp. 181-85. Timothy Dwight implied a reason for Charlestown's Republicanism: after having been burned by the British during the Revolution, it lost roughly half its population. The remainder was composed of strangers "from many places, and of almost every description." *Travels in New-England and New York* (4 vols., London, 1823), I, 427.

[8]Ames to Gore, Nov. 10, 1799, *Works of Fisher Ames*, ed. Seth Ames (2 vols., Boston, 1854), I, 262; and [Boston] *Columbian Centinel* (hereafter *Centinel*), Jan. 10, 1810. See also Ames to Wolcott, Jan. 12, 1800, Wolcott MSS, Connecticut Historical Society; and Ames to Thomas Dwight, Aug. 8, [1794], Sept. 25, 1798, Ames, *Works*, I, 147, 239.

body knows what to think. Here [in Bridgewater] the case is different; one takes the 'Centinel,' one the 'Messenger,' and one the 'Boston Gazette,' while by far the greater part take no paper at all. The consequence is that one is very warm, another very moderate, and another is in doubt how to be."

Federalist cleric Samuel Worcester seconded Bryant. He almost invariably found, he observed, that men who were in the habit of reading the *Chronicle* or a similar paper were Republican and that those who took the *Centinel* turned out to be Federalist. "This you may say," he wrote to a friend, "is nothing remarkable. A man would doubtless choose the paper, which best accords with his own feelings and views. Be it so. It is a fact, however, which I have found none disposed to deny, that, as a general case, people have not first formed their political opinions, and of course, *taken their sides*, and afterwards chosen their paper accordingly; but have formed their opinions and *derived their feelings* from their papers in the first instance." The *Centinel* and *Chronicle* especially had gained wide circulation before the rise of the party spirit, "at least, before it had taken the direction which it now holds. After they declared in opposition to each other, they were still received and read, within their respective established circles, and from them the people imbibed their political notions and party spirit."[9]

In a society in which domestic newspapers were beginning to replace the clergyman and sea captain as the chief sources of information, there came to be an increasing correlation between newspapers read and party joined. Even in the absence of circulation figures, the link which Bryant and Worcester detected between one-newspaper regions and political unity on the one hand and many-newspaper regions and political competition on the other can be substantiated. In most

---

[9]William Cullen Bryant to Peter Bryant, Oct. 10, 1814, in Parke Godwin, *A Biography of William Cullen Bryant* (2 vols., New York, 1883), I, 128; and Samuel Worcester to Luther Jewitt, July 1798, in Samuel Worcester, *The Life and Labors of Rev. Samuel Worcester, D.D.* (2 vols., Boston, 1852), I, 220-21.

instances, the establishment of an opposition press led to a rapid growth in partisan warfare and a significant rise in electoral activity. For example, the Portland *Eastern Argus,* founded early in 1804, immediately exploited the widespread unrest over Maine land titles, completely reversed the political balance in York County, and inspired a sharp rise in voter participation throughout the District, particularly among Republicans. Similar occurrences were repeated elsewhere.[1]

Still another determinant of political affiliation was the local sense of community identity. Many regions and towns assumed their political complexion in reaction to the politics of a dominant neighboring community. Berkshire County, for instance, though slow growing and isolated, was Republican principally because it offered land to the disaffected of the nearby conservative valley towns, welcomed religious dissenters, and developed a strong local pride. Yet, in striking contrast, because the mainstream of Berkshire political life was Republican, many of the county's small towns and those isolated in the hills inclined toward Federalism.

Much of this negative affiliation infused populous Salem. It was a stronghold of Jefferson's party in Federalist Essex County largely because its leading men, with strong commercial ties to China and the Far East, competed with the Indies trade of Boston to the south and the European and Caribbean trade of Federalist Newburyport to the north. Similarly, Cambridge and Charlestown were Republican, in part because dominant Boston was Federalist. Marblehead remained a fiercely Republican island in a hostile Federalist environment despite repeated injury to its fishing interests by embargo and war—a circumstance which many have ascribed to the independent spirit of its original Jersey and Guernsey settlers,

---

[1] On the *Eastern Argus*, see Frederick G. Fassett, Jr., *A History of the Newspapers in the District of Maine, 1785-1820,* in *University of Maine Studies,* 2nd Ser., no. 25 (Orono, Me., 1932), 199-200. On the connection between the outbreak of party war and newspaper competition in Salem, see James Duncan Phillips, "Political Fights and Local Squabbles in Salem, 1800-1806," *Essex Institute Historical Collections,* LXXXII (Jan. 1946), 3.

"those ungovernable men." Washington County, Maine, a strongly Federalist territory in the otherwise overwhelmingly Republican region, exhibited a similarly divergent affiliation because it was close to the commercial orbit of Halifax, because its settlements were comparatively old, and because religious dissent was almost nonexistent.[2]

Underlying all these patterns of affiliation was the sequential and selective awakening to politics of the Massachusetts population. Men who had reached political maturity in the 1780's and 1790's did so at a time when politics were factionalized and factions not yet disciplined into parties. Given the ancient traditions of elitist government, becoming politically aware in that era more often than not meant associating publicly and actively with the ruling circles rather than making a partisan choice. Thus while the indifferent remained apathetic, the interested few aligned themselves with the dominant Federalists.

But after 1800, as young men reached voting age and developed a political consciousness, and as older men identified

---

[2]On Berkshire County, see Morse, *Federalist Party in Mass.*, p. 180*n*, and Richard D. Birdsall, *Berkshire County: A Cultural History* (New Haven, 1959), pp. 1-5, 235*n*. On Salem and Newburyport, see James Duncan Phillips, *Salem and the Indies* (Boston, 1947), pp. 9, 302, & *passim*; Labaree, *Patriots and Partisans*, pp. 131-32; and Morison, *Maritime History of Mass.*, pp. 84, 121-22. On Marblehead, see Samuel Roads, Jr., *The History and Traditions of Marblehead* (Boston, 1880), pp. 7, 15, 230 ff.; Morison, *Maritime History of Mass.*, pp. 137-40, and, by the same author, *By Land and By Sea* (New York, 1953), p. 183; Manasseh Cutler to Pickering, Dec. 28, 1808, Pickering MSS, Massachusetts Historical Society; and Benjamin Goodhue to Stephen Goodhue, Mar. 6, 1792, Goodhue MSS, Essex Institute. In 1808, Marblehead was ready to march on Beverly when the latter town threatened to hang Jefferson in effigy. Bentley, *Diary*, III, 404-05. Many of the small seaports—such as Marblehead, Dorchester, Weymouth, Fairhaven, and Dighton—with large rival towns nearby tended to be Republican. Morison, *Maritime History of Mass.*, p. 190. What is more, intracommunity political divisions often assumed this arbitrary form. For instance, Republicanism in the Berkshire community of Williamstown gained strength from the strong Federalist coloration of the college: "town-gown" relations were politically consequential. Arthur Lapham Perry, *Williamstown and Williams College* (New York, 1899), pp. 228-33, 278-79.

themselves for the first time with party politics, there developed two sharply defined political alternatives where one had existed before. As a result, an increasing number of men—gradually at first and then with increasing incidence by 1807—joined the ranks of Republicanism. As long as an older generation of voters remained in the majority of politically active citizens, the Federalists remained dominant. But when the more recently politicized generation outnumbered those voters whose first party identification had dated from the 1790's, the prospects of Federalism were imperiled.

II

FEDERALISTS THOUGHT OF THEMSELVES as well finished and well placed. "Nine-tenths of the wealth of *New-England*," a writer in the *Palladium* ventured, "nineteen-twentieths of its sense and ninety-nine hundredths of its honesty are federal." John Quincy Adams recalled with as much nostalgia as regret how firmly entrenched had been the party of his youth among the better elements of Massachusetts society. "With a few exceptions, the great mass of the talents of New England were Federal. The colleges, the clergy, the principal lawyers (including the judges), the wealthy merchants, were almost universally of that denomination."[3] Taken together, these descriptions, and many others like them, composed the self-portrait of an oligarchy built upon the foundations of family, occupation, and means and claiming for itself a solid record of achievement, experience, and usefulness to the community. Bearing in

---

[3][Boston] *New England Palladium* (hereafter *Palladium*), Mar. 10, 1801; and *Documents Relating to New England Federalism, 1800-1815*, ed. Henry Adams (Boston, 1905), p. 192. See also *Centinel*, Jan. 14 & Feb. 7, 1801; Henry Adams, *History of the United States of America During the Administrations of Jefferson and Madison* (9 vols., New York, 1889-98), I, 108; and Ames, *Works*, II, 116-17, 388, for similar views. Adams quotes the statement of an unnamed Boston lady to the effect that "there was no exclusiveness [in Federalist circles], but I should as soon have expected to see a cow in a drawing-room as a Jacobin." Henry Adams, *History*, I, 92.

mind that it excluded the average party adherent, the likeness which these well-placed Federalists outlined was strikingly close to the truth.

This reigning elite arose from a foundation of marriage and kinship bonds which knew few parallels in the nation. The tenacity and breadth of Federalist political and social power owed much to the intricate network of relationships which had become consolidated before the start of partisan politics. While in the space of about two decades after 1800 the Federalist establishment witnessed the steady erosion of its hegemony in the state, there was little cause to fear that the insistent cannonades of egalitarianism would breach the wall of blood ties and shared histories which bound most of the Federalist families of Massachusetts together. In a time of change, there still remained a refuge that could be entered only by invitation.

In an important sense, the Federalist Party of Massachusetts was an extended family. Take, for example, the famous Cabot-Higginson-Jackson-Lee-Lowell clan of Essex County and Boston, which one student has called a kinship group "second to none" in the region. That quintessential old-school Federalist, George Cabot, gained not a little of his eminence as the embodiment of the genealogical history of post-Revolutionary Massachusetts. Genealogists tell us that he married his double first cousin, daughter of the marriage of a Higginson to a Cabot aunt. Through this useful marriage he gained as brother-in-law Stephen Higginson, another cousin and wealthy pillar of Federalism's mercantile wing. Cabot's own sisters added conveniently to his circle by marriages to Joseph Lee, an influential merchant of Beverly with whom Cabot was allied in commerce until 1803, and to John Lowell, Sr., illustrious member of the bench of the United States District Court. One of Cabot's brothers married a Pickering. It is hardly a surprise that Cabot's nephews included Francis Cabot Lowell, the cofounder of the famous cotton manufactory in the town which bears his name, and John Lowell, Jr., the publicist of maritime Federalism. One of Cabot's daughters brought a healthy expansion to the family's occupational base by going outside the mercantile-legal community to marry John Thornton Kirkland, Unitarian cleric and president of Harvard but scarcely a political risk. And, to top it off, Cabot's nieces and nephews married into the high-stationed families of Jonathan Jackson and Thomas Handasyd Perkins.[4]

Such Federalist dynasties dotted the state. In Hampshire and Berkshire, the Sedgwicks, Dwights, Worthingtons, and Van Schaacks formed a regional clan with a slight Tory taint, to whose ranks marriages attracted men of power and impeccable patriotism. A daughter of the Worthington-Hooker branch wed Governor Caleb Strong, sedate exemplar of orthodox western Federalism, and the same Worthington side reached across the state to Dedham to give Strong a cousin by marriage in Fisher Ames. Josiah Quincy, descendant of Sewalls, Adamses, and Hulls, was nephew to wealthy merchant and Lieutenant Governor William Phillips, through whom he was also related to old-school Federalist leader Jonathan Mason. With unimpeachable good taste, the children of Harrison Gray Otis married Lymans, Boardmans, Thorndikes, and Ritchies. In Salem, Pickmans married Derbys, and farther north in Newburyport, after Tracys, Jacksons, Lees, Hoopers, and Daltons had concluded their matches, there were sons and daughters remaining to bring together Theophilus Parsons with an offspring of the estimable Judge Benjamin Greenleaf.[5]

This is not to deny that some Republicans shared the advantages of blood ties. In the matter of family origins, patriotism, and wealth, Republicans were often indistinguishable from Federalists. The ancestral roots of both parties stretched back into the seventeenth century and often to the days of

---

[4]Robert K. Lamb, "The Entrepreneur and the Community," in *Men in Business: Essays in the History of Entrepreneurship*, ed. William Miller (Cambridge, 1952), p. 97. For the Cabot family maze, see *ibid.*, pp. 117-19; L. Vernon Briggs, *History and Genealogy of the Cabot Family, 1475-1927* (2 vols., Boston, 1927), *passim*; and Kenneth Wiggins Porter, *The Jacksons and the Lees: Two Generations of Massachusetts Merchants, 1765-1844* (2 vols., Cambridge, 1937), I, 88-98.

[5]Labaree, *Patriots and Partisans*, p. 11.

Winthrop and Dudley. Among Republican ranks one found
Austins, Townsends, Lincolns, Devenses, and even the Win-
throps of Boston. But the greatest Republican families had for
one reason or another lost out in the contest for social and economic respectability. In society, in the professions, on the tax
rolls, they were outpaced by men of the same pedigree who
had managed to secure a higher place in the social rankings of
the new nation and called themselves Federalists. What family
ties had helped to win, few Federalists were going to risk by
political apostasy.

As with family, so with education: a formal exposure to
the day's higher learning and to the faculty strongholds of
Federalist orthodoxy almost invariably implanted a lifelong
affinity for the party of the wise and good. The Federalist
partisans who tried to neutralize the democratic solvent with
lessons from history, religion, and criticism monopolized the
faculties of New England colleges. And that most college
graduates were Federalists is suggested by the fact that over
three times as many university men represented the Federalist
Party in the General Court between 1800 and 1815 as sat for
the opposition.[6]

If Federalism was the drawing room orthodoxy of most
of the state's illustrious and educated families, it was also the
companion of wealth. Opulence and eminence of blood did not
necessarily go hand in hand, but more often than not, wealth
was extra insurance against deviations from Federalism where
family ties failed to serve. In 1807 Newburyport, for instance,
sixteen of the town's twenty-five wealthiest citizens were Federalist, and only two were Republican. In areas of economic
stability, where the fortunes of all fluctuated in unison and no
unusual or diverse patterns of religion, ethnic origins, or local
tradition obtruded to mar the general social homogeneity, the

---

[6]Of course, since few men of that day held college diplomas,
few political activists held them. Yet 9 per cent of the Federalist representatives in the General Court between 1800 and 1815 were degree-
holders compared to 4 per cent for Republican deputies. See Chap.
VII, Sec. iii, and Table VII (Appendix II).

link between old family, old wealth, and old creeds held with exceptional regularity. But where the economic and occupational pattern was highly differentiated and fortunes were constantly being made or lost, old, genteel money—not excluding great fortunes—was drawn to Federalism and the new money to Republicanism.[7]

Jefferson's party attracted "rich men not high in reputation," thought William Bentley. "Those who inherited wealth," Samuel Eliot Morison has written of the mercantile families of the coast, "or had begun business before the Revolution were more highly regarded than the self-made man who had traced new trade routes." Those who had acquired their wealth on account of the Revolution and in tandem with the consolidation of local and national political leadership were also considered respectable. Many of them, like the Tracys and Jacksons of Newburyport, lost much of their inherited fortunes in the 1780's but retained their social and political prominence.[8]

But the "new men," whose fortunes were even more recent and who, despite their economic leverage, could approach but not enter the circles of those who had arrived first, went into the political opposition. The foremost example of this pattern was the Republican Crowninshield family of Salem which, denied access to power for a decade by the Derbys, constructed a formidable local interest on the foundations of their fortune and finally overthrew the Derby group and took over the town's affairs. Crowninshield wealth was recent, amassed in the French trade of the 1790's. So too was the wealth of William Gray, Baltic merchant and reputedly the wealthiest American of his day. Harassed by the inner circle of the Essex leadership for ten years, Gray took the opportu-

---

[7]Labaree, *Patriots and Partisans*, pp. 139-40. One should add here that inasmuch as the dissenting sects tended to recruit from the less prosperous members of the community, the poor who were dissenters tended to be Republican. See Sec. iv of this chapter.

[8]Bentley, *Diary*, III, 350; Morison, *Maritime History of Mass.*, p. 129; and James Jackson, *Hon. Jonathan Jackson . . . Notes and Reminiscences* (Boston, 1866), pp. 10-11.

nity of the Embargo to bolt the party and give Massachusetts Republicanism its biggest prize of the era.[9]

Lower in the scale of wealth, it becomes increasingly difficult to discern any correspondence between relative affluence and party affiliation. On a regional basis, there was none. The Federalist river counties of western Massachusetts, judged by the state land tax and other valuations per capita, were among the poorest in the Commonwealth, but so were the farther northern and eastern Maine counties—and they were Republican. Indeed, the wealthiest downstate counties such as Essex, Suffolk, and Middlesex revealed a higher incidence of Republicanism than many of the poorer ones. Many Federalists like Ames were captive of the idea that the mean and poor were almost uniformly of the political opposition, but others disputed the argument. "The Republicans are the middle class," noted Bentley of Salem, adding, "and the Federalists in wealth, the top and bottom."[1]

Poverty and low social rank increased the likelihood that men dependent by experience and disposition upon the dominant powers would follow the bidding of their "betters." For example, many of the subsistence farmers of Worcester and "Old Hampshire" were Federalists, while similarly circumstanced men in Maine exhibited a tenacious Republicanism. In the end, regional history, social tradition, occupation, and religion were far better indices of political identification than wealth.

III

JUST AS THEY ARROGATED the top economic ranks, so the Federalists of Massachusetts were better placed professionally

---

[9]On the Crowninshields, see William T. Whitney, Jr., "The Crowninshields of Salem, 1800-1808: A Study in the Politics of Commercial Growth," *Essex Institute Historical Collections*, VCIV (Jan. 1958), 1-36; (Apr. 1958), 79-118. On Gray, see Edward Gray, *William Gray of Salem, Merchant* (Boston, 1914).

[1]Bentley, *Diary*, IV, 17.

than their opponents. Among the members of the learned and skilled professions—law, belles-lettres and education, and the Congregational, Presbyterian, and Episcopalian ministry—they composed an overwhelming majority. Only in the medical profession did they divide the field almost equally with the Republicans. In all these callings, education and experience provided and reinforced the convictions associated with the Federalist ideology.

In the case of the law, for instance, social origins and training, as well as the structure and ethic of the profession, powerfully disposed the legal practitioner toward Federalism. So irresistible was the trend, that around the turn of the century there were few Republicans at the bench and bar. "At the time of my admission to the bar," Joseph Story later recalled of 1801, "I was the only lawyer within its pale, who was either openly or secretly a *democrat*. . . . I scarcely remember more than four or five lawyers in the whole state, who *dared* avow themselves republicans."[2] Of the 178 lawyer-members of the Massachusetts House between 1800 and 1815 whose party affiliation is determinable, 144 (or almost 81 per cent) were Federalists and only 34 (or about 19 per cent) Republican, a gap unique among the principal occupations represented in the General Court's lower house.[3]

As a result of the erosion in the relative power of the Congregational clergy after the Revolution—largely because of the lawyers' own pivotal contribution to that event and to the Constitution making which followed—men of legal learning and talents had stepped forward to play a significant role in

---

[2]William W. Story, *Life and Letters of Joseph Story* (2 vols., Boston, 1851), I, 95-96, 129.

[3]I do not mean to suggest that the Massachusetts House was a microcosm of Massachusetts society, reflecting in its composition the occupational division of the greater population. On the contrary, in the case of lawyer-representatives, Republicans were certainly over-represented in comparison with the proportion of Republican attorneys in the society at large. For an explanation of the method used to determine the occupation of members of the General Court and for a fuller discussion of the composition of the lower chamber, see Chap. VII, Sec. iii, and Table VII (Appendix II).

state affairs. Prosperity, the growth of commerce and manufacturing, increasing population, the opening of new territory to the north and west, and the surge of land speculation brought a steep rise in the demand for men versed in the intricacies of realty, contract, finance, insurance, and admiralty. Indeed, by the early nineteenth century, law was overtaking the mercantile trades as the most reliable avenue to power and prestige—and the Federalists had secured it first. The profession was particularly attractive to the middle-class gentry of the community—both to the families of high standing, comfortable means, but little inherited wealth, and to those somewhat lower in distinction, who aspired from a position within the establishment to attain the higher reaches of society. The lives of such men as Harrison Gray Otis and old-school gentleman Theophilus Parsons attest to the opportunities and affluence which awaited the young man of moderate beginnings who persevered and heeded the dominant political ethos of the craft.[4] There was a good chance that aspirants to the law were already Federalists, but the politically uncommitted had no difficulty discerning that if he valued professional achievement or political office, he would do best to cast his lot with the majority party of his colleagues.

Legal education in Massachusetts confirmed the Federalism of young aspirants to the bar. Until the establishment of the first professorship of law at Harvard in 1817, the young legal trainee read law in the office of a judge or a member of

---

[4]Otis wrote late in life, "We have been ever since I was born an unfortunate family as to worldly concerns root and branch. I am the only individual I believe of the male line (to say nothing of the female) who has been moderately prosperous." Otis to Mary Otis, Feb. 13, 1834, Gay-Otis MSS, Columbia. On the collapse of Otis's father's fortunes after the Revolution and Otis's later affluence, see Samuel Eliot Morison, *The Life and Letters of Harrison Gray Otis, Federalist, 1765-1848* (2 vols., Boston, 1913), I, Chap. II and pp. 229-34. Parsons taught for three years while reading law in order to make ends meet. On his respectable but moderate origins and the utility of following legal training as a means to prosperity, see Theophilus Parsons, [Jr.], *Memoir of Theophilus Parsons* (Boston, 1859), Chap. I and pp. 135, 141-42.

the bar, an education sufficiently expensive that only the reasonably affluent or those fortunate enough to have a patron could afford the two or three years of the typical course.[5] Preparation for practice consisted largely of carrying out the detailed work of the mentor and reading the great historical and legal commentaries of Gibbons, Hume, Vattel, Blackstone, Justinian and Coke. From these texts and from experience in association with established attorneys, the apprentice imbibed a respect for precedent and tradition and for the maintenance of precise relationships among men and institutions. In addition, the young lawyer-in-training had direct access through his teacher-employer to men of power in the immediate community and in the state at large. Since more often than not these older lawyers were Federalists, the trainee was unlikely to imagine his future in Republican hues.

The structure of the bar itself perfectly served the purposes of the professional elite. At the top of the state's legal hierarchy was the Supreme Judicial Court, led in Jefferson's time by the renowned and learned Theophilus Parsons, the scourge of Republicans and poor advocates. By means of their power to establish requirements for admission to the bar of the Court, these Federalist jurists set standards for legal education throughout the whole of Massachusetts. In 1806, they set down, in some of the nation's stiffest rules, that admission to the bar would henceforth require a "good school education," at least seven years devoted to "literary acquisitions," and three years under the instruction of a member of the Court's bar.[6] Ostensibly designed to insure high standards of learning and pleading, the new regulations served notice that the men who

---

[5]Much of the material in this and the succeeding paragraph is taken from James Willard Hurst, *The Growth of American Law: The Law Makers* (Boston, 1950), Chaps. XII & XIII; Alfred Zantzinger Reed, *Training for the Public Profession of the Law* (New York, 1921), Part II; and Anton-Hermann Chroust, *The Rise of the Legal Profession in America* (2 vols., Norman, Okla., 1965), II, 35-36, 130-40, 230-31. See also Charles Warren, *A History of the American Bar* (Boston, 1911), pp. 199, 308.

[6]*Reports of the Supreme Judicial Court of Massachusetts* (hereafter *Mass. Reports*), II, 74; IV, 382-85.

charged themselves with guarding property, established religion, and the entire public interest were not about to permit democracy to enter the judicial chambers. Once these requirements were satisfied, moreover, an applicant for admission to the bar had to win his preceptor's character reference, an added incentive to political regularity, before the Court would accept his qualifications.

Centered in Boston, the Supreme Judicial Court worked closely with the conservative Suffolk County bar, probably the most highly organized and prestigious legal guild in the nation at the time. In 1810, the Suffolk Bar ruled that its members charge students $500 for a three-year reading term. The lower orders were not encouraged to apply. Local courts and bar associations could set their own standards of practice, but most looked to Boston for guidance. All in all, the legal community in Massachusetts was able to enforce appreciable conformity upon its members and, until 1836, to prevent a democratization of its standards and procedures. Any who were excluded from the guild by inability to meet its various requirements or who resented the hegemony of the Suffolk bar were likely to become opponents of the standing order—if they were not already so. Men such as the dyspeptic Nathaniel Ames drew upon a venerable tradition of hostility to the profession and exploited the same spirit of defiance of the Boston-centered court system which had nourished the Shaysites when they assailed the "pettifoggers" and the "prigarchy" which held the state in thrall.[7]

The situation of the practicing physician in Massachusetts varied enough from that of the lawyer to incline him somewhat more frequently toward Republicanism. Attorneys had their bar societies and their precedents; they practiced before instrumentalities of the state; and they applied a conservative social logic which had the sanction of immemorial usage. In contrast, the medical profession was relatively unorganized, medical science was still in its infancy, the doctor's practice

---

[7]Charles Warren, *Jacobin and Junto* (Cambridge, 1931), *passim*.

brought with it no easy introduction to the Commonwealth's leadership, and medical work was considerably less lucrative than the law.[8] Moreover, the status of the medical practitioner, already suffering from the profession's legacy of Toryism, was not raised by the era's hostile and conservative reaction against natural science.[9]

To be sure, as professional men, physicians were associates of the local elites. They enjoyed the esteem which still accrued to men of learning, and they played an essential role in many communities. But among other professionals their standing was at a discount. Lawyers and merchants, more closely related to political and economic affairs, overshadowed them in public life. And thus, in part out of resentment against their comparatively low estate and against the political elite recruited from the other callings, doctors frequently found themselves drawn to Republicanism.

Furthermore, in contrast to the legal profession, no hierarchical system of courts or committees existed to give organization and security to medical practice. The Massachusetts Medical Society, chartered in 1781, was the state's sole medical association and, as might be expected, had fallen early under the direction of Harvard-educated doctors who, like the esteemed John Warren and his son John Collins Warren, numbered themselves among the Federalists. But the Society was little more than the establishment of Boston medicine. Because

---

[8]Many of my comments on the Massachusetts medical profession are derived from the following sources: Francis Randolph Packard, *History of Medicine in the United States* (2 vols., Philadelphia, 1901); Henry Burnell Shafer, *The American Medical Profession, 1783 to 1850* (New York, 1936); Walter L. Burrage, *A History of the Massachusetts Medical Society* (Norwood, Mass., 1923), esp. Chaps. II, III, VIII, X & XIV; and Samuel Abbot Green, *History of Medicine in Massachusetts. A Centennial Address Delivered Before the Massachusetts Medical Society at Cambridge, June 7, 1881* (Boston, 1881).

[9]For a survey of the conservative "counter-revolution" against the spirit of the Enlightenment, especially where new inquiries challenged the established order of religion and the state, see Merle Curti, *The Growth of American Thought* (2nd ed., New York, 1951), pp. 204-06.

of its proximity to the seat of government, it attracted the patronage of the state and made use of the facilities of the thriving capital town; it supported some notable medical research and education and established commendable licensing procedures and standards of practice. But since it lacked the support of effective regional medical societies until well after 1815, its jurisdiction never reached much beyond the vicinity of Boston.

This meant first that, among the learned professions, the structure of Massachusetts medicine was least centralized and offered the greatest opportunities for advancement to rural outlanders and those not born into the ruling elite. It meant too that doctors, unlike lawyers, were usually on their own, independent of the centers of learning and power of the maritime towns. And this was not always to their advantage. What they gained in independence they lost in training, prestige, and fortune. Except on the coast, where a fee system developed and an elitist *esprit* bound physicians together, medicine was unprofitable, and the doctor had often to supplement his practice through farming. His lack of training was often a scandal.

Yet the rural practitioner, though frequently the scourge of the sick, resisted most efforts to better his preparation and looked upon apprenticeship costs and standards, admission requirements, and licensing terms recommended by the Massachusetts Medical Society as little more than attempts to close the profession to outsiders and to solidify eastern control.[1] When rural doctors interested themselves in medical standards, they characteristically—and unsuccessfully—tried to circumvent the entrenched leadership of the Society by establishing

---

[1]Under the rules of the Massachusetts Medical Society, a candidate for admission to the Society—and hence to respectable practice—had to know Greek, Latin, geometry, and experimental philosophy and had to study and practice for at least three years with a fellow or honorary member of the Society. The Essex South District of the Society, one of the few active regional groups, required its members to charge $200 for a three-year apprenticeship. Packard, *History of Medicine*, I, 400, and Shafer, *American Medical Profession*, p. 33. On the economics of the profession in its early years, little has been written, but see Bidwell, *Rural Economy in New England*, pp. 254-56.

a rival Massachusetts College of Physicians.[2] Thus, their horizons limited to the local region, their training and sense of professional membership low, their links to power weak, their resentment of the greater esteem and prosperity of lawyers and merchants keen, they drifted more easily into the ranks of the opposition party.

The roster of the medical profession contained the distinguished names of such Republicans as William Eustis, Charles Jarvis, Nathaniel Ames, and William Aspinwall. Moreover, a higher proportion of Republicans in the General Court were doctors than lawyers. Aspiring Republicans used achievement within the profession as a steppingstone to careers in the public service. In contrast, most of the state's great practitioners who avoided public affairs were Federalists. Chief among them were the two Warrens and young James Jackson, husband to a niece of George Cabot and brother both to the distinguished lawyer and young Federalist leader Charles Jackson and to wealthy merchant and early cotton manufacturer Patrick Tracy Jackson. Men of outstanding ability, unassailable pedigree, and wealth, their positions were beyond challenge, and they risked little by pursuing a calling whose status was still open to question. But for others whose standing was less exalted and who had to work harder to preserve their position in a profession less esteemed than others, the openness of membership in the medical community represented a potential danger not simply to standards of practice but to their place in professional circles as well. Behind the movement for more rigorous training of doctors and greater guild oversight of its members through the Massachusetts Medical Society was the

---

[2]For a history of the unavailing attempt by some Republicans in 1811 to charter a rival medical association, see Green, *History of Medicine in Mass.*, pp. 111-17; Edward Warren, *The Life of John Collins Warren, M.D.* (2 vols., Boston, 1850), I, 103-07; and Goodman, *Democratic-Republicans of Mass.*, pp. 167-68. Despite the lack of evidence for so broad a claim regarding Massachusetts physicians, Massachusetts Republicans argued that most doctors adhered to Jefferson's party. [Portland] *Eastern Argus*, Dec. 2, 1803, quoted in Robinson, *Jeffersonian Democracy in New England*, p. 113.

impulse to keep out the ambitious and undeserving leveler and to make sure that even in this least Federalist of professions, the highest rewards went to the well-placed gentlemen who had risen from within the establishment.

Despite the frequent charge that merchants, bankers, and manufacturers neglected the Federalist cause, the world of business affairs contained as many Federalists as the medical profession, and perhaps more. The political patterns of businessmen were more complex. Given the variety of business enterprise, there was bound to be considerable political diversity within business ranks not observable among lawyers and men of letters. Moreover, the business callings lacked the canons, the training, and the cohesion of the professions. Anyone who wished to try his hand and who could raise the capital might set up a mercantile house or a manufactory.

Men whose businesses were old, who traded principally within the orbit of the British mercantile system, and who depended upon established patterns of supply and finance placed themselves more frequently with the party which championed the cause of England than men of more recent and less-established interests who worked the French, Baltic, and Asian trade routes outside the purview of English dominion and whose prospects depended in part upon dislodging the dealer in English dry goods. Like the line which separated old and new wealth, the line between Federalist and Republican businessmen, Benjamin Labaree has written of Newburyport, was drawn "between established merchants, lawyers, and their associates, and those still working their way up from the quarterdeck to the countinghouse. This is not to say that all of the Republican candidates were younger but only that the Federalists had generally 'arrived' first."

In addition, political allegiance often depended upon the businessman's position in the new economic order of the 1790's. Most merchants, whose opportunities after the Revolution had been based on durable English connections, had become Federalists. They had periodically allowed some new and ambitious men to gain entrance to their standing commercial order. But by the 1790's, the equilibrium of the post-Revolutionary era was shattered. The accelerated growth of broad-based prosperity, the accumulation of new capital often unable to find outlets in commerce alone, and the opening of new trade routes in the wake of the European wars created new ambitions and new opportunities which placed the Derbys, the Perkinses, Higginson, and many other Federalist merchants in an unexampled domestic competitive position where old foundations might be as much of a hindrance as help. The triumph of the Crowninshield interest in Salem, the emergence of the Dearborn, Cutts, and King connections in Maine, the political apostasy of William Gray, and the proliferation of new banks, many of them under Republican domination, signaled the breakup of the relatively stable and secure commercial system of the 1780's.[3]

On top of these general dislocations, the crises of the Embargo and the War of 1812 precipitated even greater confusion in the business community. Credit became unsettled, the cost of maritime insurance fluctuated widely, the risks of search and capture at sea soared, inventory conditions became chaotic. But even more significant, as Gray's case testifies, an increasing number of men found the Republican commercial and diplomatic policies, which sought some accommodation with France as well as England, to their advantage. If they did not, like Gray, desert the Federalist Party, they could not bring themselves to agitate for an end to policies which benefited them. These were the "lukewarm" Federalists whom other party stalwarts so often assailed.

Similar partisan patterns existed for bankers and manufacturers, many of whom were also merchants. In Massachusetts, banking money often originated in commercial money. Funds for new factory enterprises frequently came from old commercial capital diverted into more immediately profitable chan-

[3]Whitney, "Crowninshields of Salem," *passim*; Goodman, *Democratic-Republicans of Mass.*, pp. 116-18, 121-24; Phillips, "Political Squabbles in Salem"; Porter, *Jacksons and Lees*, p. 6 and *passim*; and Labaree, *Patriots and Partisans*, p. 140.

nels because of disruptions in trade. Indeed, the most renowned and successful manufacturing venture of the age—the cotton manufactory at Waltham founded in 1813 by Patrick Tracy Jackson and Francis Cabot Lowell—resulted from a combination of old mercantile wealth and the partnership of powerful and prosperous blood-relations from the Commonwealth's greatest Federalist clan.

In the maritime trades, circumstances were different. Those men who commanded the ships of the Massachusetts mercantile fleet had close links with the large and wealthy merchant community of the port towns. Yet, contrary to common observation, the shipmaster was not generally a Federalist. The habit of shipboard command may have inclined him to embrace the party which stood for order and subordination, but the employer with whom he identified was as likely to be a Republican as a Federalist. Moreover, the shipmaster was typically a self-made man, and after 1800 this kind of individual was more and more drawn to Republicanism. The captain's calling held the respect of the community, but hardly to the same degree as the law or the church, and it rarely attracted members of the old families. The master could obtain substantial wealth only by leaving the quarterdeck for the countinghouse where, as a newcomer to business, he was an outsider, especially to the older circles.[4] When at sea, he was as much subject to the attacks of the French naval commander as to those of the British captain and as readily detested the one as the other. The most reliable indicator of party preference among these men is their representation in the General Court, and here they were well represented in both parties. In fact, in proportion to Republican strength in the lower house, ship captains formed a larger bloc among the minority party than among the Federalists (Table VII, Appendix II).

The record is more obscure regarding members of the lesser maritime trades. The sailors' and fishermen's lower level of education and information, their participation in occupa-

---

[4]Morison, *Maritime History of Mass.*, pp. 107, 113.

tions which, while rich in popular lore, lacked social respectability, and their general isolation from the larger community rendered them more politically apathetic than others. Like single-crop farmers, their livelihood depended upon a single variable; both were at the mercy of economic change and political crisis which, overnight, could close their ports and destroy what little prosperity they enjoyed. Sailors and fishermen were dependent to an extreme degree upon an environment over which they had little control.

Most sailors were young men imbued with the habit of subordination, and they thus tended to follow their captains' wills. An entire ship's company was known to march to the polls together on election day and scurry to the political commands, as the case might be, of a Federalist or Republican captain. Yet, since the shipmaster and his crew often came from the same town, the political identification of the sailor probably reflected more the dominant politics of the community than the success of a domineering captain in making him vote "right."[5]

Among men of the fishing fleets, however, there was a consistently high incidence of Republicanism. But this, too, resulted as often from community tradition and religious dissent as from the nature of the calling. In Marblehead, for example, with its abundance of fishermen, the Channel Island ethnic heritage of the town played as large a part in its hostility to the Federalist order as did its dominant occupation. And in the fishing and whaling towns of Nantucket and New Bedford, the tradition of dissenting Quakerism inclined most people from birth to Republicanism. Yet, with fishermen as with lumbermen, miners, and trappers, the poverty, insecurity, and isolation of their work probably would have inclined them to dissent in politics even in the absence of dissent in religion.[6]

---

[5]Regarding the youthfulness of sailors, see *ibid.*, p. 73.

[6]On the lot of lumbermen in Maine, see Edward Augustus Kendall, *Travels Through the Northern Parts of the United States in the Years 1807 and 1808* (3 vols., New York, 1809), III, 70-84. Seymour Martin Lipset has commented on the political radicalism—which in

V: *Social Sources of Massachusetts Federalism*

The partisan divisions among Massachusetts farmers owed even less to the nature of their occupation. Farmers composed the bulk of the state's population—certainly no less than 70 per cent—and in town after town, as Timothy Dwight said of Shrewsbury, the inhabitants were "almost all farmers." Moreover, most of the state's produce was grown for subsistence or the limited local market, and most farms exhibited none of the specialization necessary for participation in the larger national market. Except for the farmers who inhabited the coastal towns or their shallow hinterlands, there were few foreign or even home markets, for the markets on the coast obtained most of their wheat and corn from the middle states. Thus, despite Dwight's boast that "we have in New-England no such class of men as on the eastern side of the Atlantic are denominated peasantry," living standards among farmers were low, emigration to the maritime towns and the frontier was higher than elsewhere, the economy was stagnant, improvements in farming methods were few, and self-sufficiency was the rule.

Even the commercial paralyses of 1808 and 1812 did little injury to the majority of farmers, who were distant from ports and transportation. For them, economic perspectives were narrow and profit almost nonexistent. What is more, the agrarian calling generated no rapport among far-flung farmers. They were not bound by a common ethic or education. Their experiences and identifications were local.[7]

---

early nineteenth-century Massachusetts would have been Republicanism—of groups such as fishermen, lumbermen, and miners isolated naturally from contact with people who possess different sentiments. *Political Man: The Social Basis of Politics* (New York, 1960), p. 76. For a unique and challenging analysis of the sailor population, see Jesse Lemish, "Jack Tar in the Streets: Merchant Seamen in the Politics of Revolutionary America," *William and Mary Quarterly* (hereafter *WMQ*), 3rd Ser., XXV (July 1968), 371-407.

[7]Bidwell, *Rural Economy in New England*, pp. 318, 352, 387-93; and "The Agricultural Revolution in New England," *American Historical Review*, XXVI (July 1921), 683-702; Dwight, *Travels*, IV, 335; [John Lowell, Jr.], *Peace Without Dishonour—War Without Hope* . . . (Boston, 1807), p. 38; *Palladium*, Jan. 1, 1808, Jan. 13, 1809; and Thomas Boylston Adams to John Quincy Adams, Apr. 10,

Thus, among farmers as among fishermen and sailors, the variable influences of religion, economic condition, and local tradition asserted themselves with far greater consequence than among the well circumstanced. There was no connection between soil type and party nor between subsistence and commercial farming and political persuasion. Subsistence farmers of the Connecticut River Valley voted overwhelmingly Federalist, those of Maine, Republican. The Essex towns of Hamilton and Wenham, homes of Manasseh Cutler and Timothy Pickering and reported to be "merely collections of farms," were also mere collections of Federalists. But Berkshire's Cheshire, a haven for Baptists and thoroughly agricultural, was Republican.[8] Farmers were not to be categorized by party.

The other occupations and trades are equally difficult to characterize politically. Skilled artisans and semiskilled laborers had no more sense of solidarity than farmers and sailors and were equally dependent upon local conditions. To sort out their politics would require more refined data than we will ever have, and even then it is unlikely that sharp political differentiations would emerge.[9] Beneath the top levels of wealth, occupation, education, and family, a kaleidoscope of political patterns existed—diverse, unpredictable, complex. Yet there was,

---

1808, reel 406, Adams Family Papers microfilm (hereafter Adams microfilm). In 1810, the early statistician Samuel Blodget, Jr., calculated that 80 per cent of the population of the United States was engaged in agriculture. *Economica: Statistical Manuel for the United States of America* (Washington, 1810), p. 89. The Census of 1820 credits Maine with an agrarian population of about 82 per cent, Massachusetts proper with roughly 58 per cent. See also Birdsall, *Berkshire*, pp. 27-30.

[8]Dwight, *Travels*, I, 332, 406.

[9]Benjamin Labaree has speculated that in the Newburyport area at least, the skilled, well-off, and self-employed artisans were Federalist; the marginal laborers, younger artisans, and shipyard workers, Republican. *Patriots and Partisans*, p. 141. On the aspirations—or the contemporary belief in the aspirations—of the common seamen and common laborers, see Dwight, *Travels*, IV, 335, 341, 347. In Boston, the Mechanics' Association was headed by Federalists, all of them successful men such as Benjamin Russell, editor of the *Centinel*. *Centinel*, Dec. 18, 1802.

in fact, one variable—religious association—which had a universal influence on political affiliation in Massachusetts.

IV

RELIGION, LIKE OCCUPATION, made itself felt in the political affairs of the Commonwealth in a manner considerably more complex and variable than most observers have remarked. Broadly conceived, the Massachusetts religious community was divided by 1800 into two sectors, one incorporating the established Congregational church, the other the dissenting "sects"— a word which in the Federalist-Congregational lexicon embraced all religious and political nonconformists. In the roughest sense, political alignments expressed this central division among the denominations. As defenders of a preferred position, seekers after an ancient exclusiveness, and opponents of all sectarianism, Congregationalists and their Calvinist allies, the Presbyterians, were naturally inclined to identify themselves with the party of stability and tradition.[1] In contrast, members of the dissenting sects generally joined the party which championed an end to all limitations upon the free exercise of religion.

Yet, in a state where the vast majority of citizens were practicing or professed Congregationalists, the Republican Party could hardly have won a single election without having attracted thousands of Congregational votes. In other words, had the Federalists managed to hold the entire Congregational vote, they ought never to have lost a statewide contest. Thus, while the existence of a strong bond of interest between Re-

---

[1]Unlike the Presbyterians outside New England, who joined the party which claimed to have been responsible for disestablishing the Anglican Church, traditional enemy of Presbyterians and the Scotch-Irish, the Presbyterians of New England inclined toward the same party as the majority of Congregationalists because of their theological kinship with the established religion, the spread of the consociation principle among the Congregationalists, and a joint interest in limiting the spread of radical dissent.

publican and dissenter cannot be gainsaid, neither should the size of the dissenting bodies nor their influence upon the politics of the day be overrated. Efforts should be directed instead toward understanding the role of the Congregationalists in both political parties.

In the absence of verifiable church membership figures, the strength of the dissenting sects can only be approximated. Yet even by a liberal estimate, their numbers fell short of constituting a large and dependable majority of the party with which they are usually associated. In 1810, when the total population of Massachusetts proper and the District of Maine stood at about 700,000 and the number of potential voters at 151,000, on the basis of sketchy official membership tallies the state contained not many more than 15,000 Baptists, no more (and probably considerably less) than 7,000 Methodists, and an unrecorded number of Quakers, Shakers, and Universalists, but probably no more than 3,000—a sum equal to less than 5 per cent of the population.[2] Thus the theoretical voting

---

[2]On the basis of a conservative allowance, about 40 per cent, or 10,000, of these were denied the suffrage because of their sex and youth. But the loss of these voters was no doubt fully compensated by adult males not tabulated in the early church censuses and by those who for many reasons worshipped with, but did not care to identify themselves formally as, dissenters.

No two sources agree on these early church census figures. If the 25,000 figure for dissenters underplays the actual following of dissent, so does any figure for Congregationalists, thus keeping the relative proportions in line. For estimates of the Baptist populations of Massachusetts and Maine in 1810, see A. H. Newman, *A History of the Baptist Churches in the United States* (New York, 1894), p. 271, which suggests a total of 13,398; Henry S. Burrage, *A History of the Baptists in New England* (Philadelphia, 1894), p. 310, which offers a figure of 15,337; and David Benedict, *A General History of the Baptist Denomination in America, and Other Parts of the World* (2 vols., Boston, 1813), II, 497-508, 549-50, from all three of which I have derived an approximate figure for 1810 of 15,000. By a process of extrapolation from the following sources, it appears that Massachusetts and Maine Methodists numbered about 5,500 at a minimum and 8,500 at a maximum in 1810. I have chosen to rely on a compromise figure of 7,000. See Abel Stevens, *History of the Methodist Episcopal Church in the United States of America* (4 vols., New York, 1867), IV, 325; Jesse Lee, *A Short History of the Methodists, in the United States of America* (Baltimore, 1810), pp. 264, 281; C. C. Goss, *Statistical History*

strength of the dissenters fell somewhere in the neighborhood of 25,000, or 28 per cent of the statewide gubernatorial vote in 1810—enough to carry many elections for the Republicans and to disrupt the religious peace of many communities, but hardly enough to explain the source of the total Republican vote in any year. In fact, even in the unlikely case that all these dissenters had balloted for the Republican candidate for governor in 1810, they would have constituted only about 53 per cent of the party's vote. Without the dissenting vote, it is true, the Republicans would have won no state offices; with it alone, the party would have ceased to exist. Somehow, somewhere, Congregationalists were voting Republican.

That the Congregationalists failed to vote as a bloc, though not in itself surprising, attests to the presence of forces which were gradually eroding the solidarity of the "church of the saints" and of the entire middle class of Massachusetts, where it found its firmest support. As elsewhere, religious differences in the Commonwealth expressed significant social and economic distinctions. As the economy and politics of the state were transformed under the successive stimulants of prosperity, the Embargo, and war, religion could hardly remain untouched. While the dissenting and evangelical sects were making inroads on the New England frontier and among the rural and metropolitan poor, the first religion of the Commonwealth was barely able to hold its own. Indeed, the rate of Congregational growth between 1790 and 1820 was the slowest of any denomination in Massachusetts. Among an increasingly differentiated population, Congregationalism was becoming isolated within the powerful but smaller elite of the community. In the commercial communities, it was in danger of losing the allegiance of the prosperous and cosmopolitan men of affairs

---

of the First Century of Methodism (New York, 1866), p. 157; and *Minutes of the Annual Conferences of the Methodist Episcopal Church for the Years 1773-1828* (2 vols., New York, 1840), I, 183. The last source gives a figure of approximately 6,200. For a review of the reliability of church membership figures, see Seymour Martin Lipset, *The First New Nation: The United States in Historical and Comparative Perspective* (New York, 1963), pp. 141-50.

who were being attracted away by Unitarianism and Episcopalianism.[3]

Many of the defections from the religious establishment originated in a doctrinal dispute between orthodox Calvinists and a loose grouping of Arians, Arminians, Universalists, and Unitarians. What began as a serious debate over vexing theological questions had by 1800 developed into an irreversible schism within the old Puritan church and a major contest for mastery over the minds of the state's Congregational population. In reality, Congregationalism had splintered into many schools; but in the bitter public controversies of the day, the old church was in effect divided into two wings. On one side were the Hopkinsians and Edwardeans, concentrated in central and southern Massachusetts and resisting the trend toward wider church association, and, joined to them, the orthodox Calvinists of the western counties, who customarily supported the movement for ministerial consociations along Presbyterian lines. On the other side were the liberals of the coastal counties who rejected a major part of the conservative theology and were largely indifferent to matters of organization.

Both groups fought spiritedly for parishes and grappled over the succession to Harvard's Hollis chair. Ministers of the different persuasions refused to swap pulpits in the old manner, and conservative-controlled ministerial associations began to read more liberal members from their ranks. Until the end of the eighteenth century, differences of view in the conservative camp prevented a concerted effort to rout the liberals. But by 1800, spurred on by the likes of Jedidiah Morse and Yale's Timothy Dwight, the conservatives pulled together against Illuminism, French infidelity, and deism, and by 1808 reconciled their differences in order to unite their separate magazines and establish the Andover Theological Seminary

---

[3]H. Richard Niebuhr, *The Social Sources of Denominationalism* (New York, 1929), pp. 152-53; and Joseph S. Clark, *A Historical Sketch of the Congregational Churches in Massachusetts, from 1620 to 1858* (Boston, 1858), pp. 218, 224, 226, 232, 244-45.

for the purpose of countering the lukewarm Calvinism of Harvard.[4]

Behind this schism were the subtle differences of age and experience.[5] A group of clerics who had been born no later than the early 1760's and had been educated at Yale spearheaded the orthodox counterattack centered in the Second Great Awakening. Among them were leading and outspoken members of the Federalist clergy—some Hopkinsians, others orthodox—such as Abiel Holmes, Samuel Austin, Jedidiah Morse, Nathaniel Emmons, Samuel Spring, Elijah Parish, Joseph Lyman, and David Osgood.[6] Since the 1770's, Congregationalists of their stripe had gradually expanded their hold upon the churches of Massachusetts proper and brought close to fruition their resolve to regain a commanding voice in church and state. Their following resided for the most part in the placid towns of the interior, and their parishioners came from the less-prosperous and less-informed segment of the population.

From their Connecticut River Valley base, they penetrated to within twenty or thirty miles of Boston, but at that perimeter—except for a few like Holmes in Cambridge and Morse in Charlestown—they had been halted. Around the cap-

---

[4]For a general outline of the widening schism, see Joseph Henry Allen and Richard Eddy, *A History of the Unitarians and the Universalists in the United States* (New York, 1894), pp. 170-221; Williston Walker, *A History of the Congregational Churches in the United States* (New York, 1894), pp. 313-23; George Willis Cooke, *Unitarianism in America: A History of its Origins and Development* (Boston, 1916), Chaps. IV & V; James King Morse, *Jedidiah Morse: A Champion of New England Orthodoxy* (New York, 1939), pp. 40-116 *passim*; and Birdsall, *Berkshire*, pp. 44-45, 53-63.

[5]For a brief but suggestive discussion of the social and geographic distinctions between the liberals and conservatives, see Conrad Wright, *The Beginnings of Unitarianism* (Boston, 1955), pp. 251-59.

[6]Their birth dates, the average of which was 1754, were as follows: Emmons, 1745; Spring, 1746; Osgood, 1747; Lyman, 1749; Austin, 1760; Morse, 1761; Parish, 1762; and Holmes, 1763. All but Osgood, Parish, and Spring, who trained at Harvard, Dartmouth, and Princeton respectively, were Yale educated. This data, and that for the liberals, is derived from William B. Sprague, *Annals of the American Pulpit* (9 vols., New York, 1857), I, II, VIII, *passim*.

ital, the Unitarians were in control. All but one Boston church was in the hands of the liberals, and three of Salem's five Congregational churches had fallen to them. The liberal ministers, among whom were William Bentley, Joseph Tuckerman, James Freeman, Joseph Stevens Buckminster, William Emerson, and William Ellery Channing, were of a younger generation, and most were Harvard trained.[7] In the large towns where they were concentrated, they drew a wealthier and more influential body of worshippers than their orthodox opponents.[8]

Of the two groups, conservatives showed a decidedly stronger tendency toward Federalism. In the Connecticut Valley, high seat of Massachusetts orthodoxy, Federalism was the ruling persuasion; and throughout the state the most vocal and uncompromising defenders of the old religious canons were almost invariably the champions of the clerical legions of the Federalist Party. Where they led, the isolated people of simple means, dependent for recognition and information upon their social superiors and habituated to a deferential regard for authority, followed obediently along.

That conservative Congregationalists were Federalists is not surprising. The two ideologies, one political, the other religious, contained great similarities: they extolled stability and uniformity, and they both assumed the imminent ruin of western institutions. Moreover, religious conservatives viewed the new religion with as much distaste as the political conservatives viewed the new politics. Yet the cleric's keen anxieties were due even more to the apostasy of political friends. It was easy enough to locate the source of democracy in defects of moral character, but how explain the apostasy from true religion of the better sort? How make sense of the actions of those

---

[7]Their birth dates, the average of which was 1772, or eighteen years less than the conservatives cited, were as follows: Bentley, 1759; Freeman, 1759; Emerson, 1769; Tuckerman, 1778; Channing, 1780; and Buckminster, 1784. All were educated at Harvard. The affiliations of the Boston ministers are noted in Cooke, *Unitarianism in America,* p. 75.

[8]Wright, *Beginnings of Unitarianism,* pp. 259-63; and Allen and Eddy, *Unitarians and Universalists,* pp. 183-84.

who professed an attachment to the principles of Washington and at the same time allied themselves with newfangled religion? The conservatives felt betrayed. The more they tightened their hold upon rural and interior Massachusetts, the stronger became the forces of Unitarianism on the coast. The more frequently they established missionary societies and ministerial associations, the more rapidly fell to the liberals the eastern command posts of government, finance, education, and religion. The moderate and decorous politics of the eastern Federalists-turned-Unitarian only intensified their disappointment. Conservative outlanders, who detested with unrivaled bitterness all that Thomas Jefferson lent his name to, found incomprehensible the failure of the Boston-based Federalist Party leaders to smite Republicanism a mortal blow. That Jacobinism and infidelity had not been rooted out of the Commonwealth could only be the fault of the backsliding easterners whose latitudinarian religion was the counterpart of Jefferson's unprincipled politics. There was no sanctuary, it seemed, not even in religion, from the Jacobin cancer.

For their part, the liberals who bore the brunt of the Puritan counter-reformation were as little sympathetic to an orthodox and rigid political stance as to orthodox religion. To a large degree, a milder religion inspired a milder politics and sometimes, as in the case of William Bentley, outright Republicanism. Yet this is not to say that a majority of the religious liberals became Republicans. Most of them, nominally at least, were Federalists, and most could be called upon to support the party in moments of crisis. Their social ideals differed little from those of their orthodox opponents. Liberal ministers like Thaddeus Mason Harris and John Thornton Kirkland, for example, struck out at the idle hope of equalizing the conditions of mankind. The rich and poor, said Harris, should "contribute to each other's accommodation and comfort." Kirkland remarked that American equality is "an equality which secures the rich from rapacity, no less than the poor from oppression; the high from envy, no less than the low from contempt; an equality, which proclaims peace alike to the mansions of the affluent, and the humble dwellings of the poor."⁹ Nevertheless, although most liberal pastors hewed to the Federalist line, religious liberalism among the rank and file weakened the force of the old social imperatives. The most significant Republican gains after 1800 and the most enduring centers of Republican strength were in those areas where orthodoxy was weakest, especially in Norfolk and Middlesex counties near Boston.

One of the main bonds which united men like Cabot, Pickering, and Otis, despite differences in their age and their diversity of views on other matters, was their decorous and urbane religion. All things considered, they were far closer in spirit to Jefferson's religious principles than to those of Morse and Parish. Yet, in order to safeguard what was left of their standing in the eyes of the pious, they felt it necessary to inveigh against irreligion and to pay lip service to the ideal of maintaining the old denominational uniformity of the state. Most of them genuinely welcomed the stabilizing effects of all religion, but few any longer found personal satisfaction in the exacting creed of the conservative churches. Thus it was not mere hatred of Jefferson which impelled the orthodox, clerics and laity alike, to denounce him with unremitting ferocity and to urge upon the party leaders the most extreme forms of political protest. They were also trying to avenge themselves against the religious liberals. By the time of the War of 1812, they were in a position seriously to jeopardize the political claims of the ruling—and liberal—party leaders.

At the same time that these doctrinal disputes were eroding what was left of the unity of the established church and the Federalist clergy, the politicization of community life was causing more Congregationalists to become Republican. An examination of the political loyalties of the state's predominantly Congregational communities—those towns which contained few dissenters and no organized dissenting church societies—illuminates the fallacy of equating Congregationalism with Federalism. In 1806, when the parties were more closely

---

⁹Quoted in Wright, *Beginnings of Unitarianism*, p. 250.

balanced than anytime before 1815, the predominantly Congregational towns were divided almost equally between the two parties.[1] Their politics conformed not to religion but to the general political alignments of surrounding towns.

In Federalist Essex County, for example, five of its eight Congregational towns were strongly or overwhelmingly Federalist (one by 96 per cent), two divided their votes, and only one was strongly Republican. Yet, in sharp contrast, twenty-two of the thirty Congregational towns in Republican Middlesex County were strongly or overwhelmingly Republican (one by 97 per cent), four were divided, and four Federalist. In the state as a whole, where the margin of the Federalist victory in 1806 was less than 1 per cent, the Federalists could only claim a correspondingly small 2 per cent majority of the Congregational towns (Table I, Appendix II).

No doubt, the impression that Congregationalists were always Federalists is an over-generalization from the unique political situation which existed in years of national crisis, when even dissenters were swept along in the Federalist surge and Congregationalists returned to Federalism in large numbers. If we compare Congregational political loyalties in 1806 and 1813, when the Federalist Party carried the state by the largest margin ever obtained by either party, we find a marked intensification of Federalism in Congregational towns. Lest we lose sight, however, of continuing Republican strength throughout all the denominations, it is important to note that there remained in 1813 a large number of Republican-Congregational towns—the Republicanism of four of which sharply increased—and that the rough parallel between regional and Congregational-town patterns persisted (Table II, Appendix II). That

---

[1] I have chosen to use the year 1806 because by then an enduring political stability had at last been established in the state, because the parties were never again in such close equilibrium (only .84 per cent of the vote separated them), and because, unlike most of the years which followed, there was no major national crisis to disturb the close balance. It is, of course, necessary to point out that in 1806 the Federalist towns were more strongly Federalist on the whole than the Republican towns were Republican.

even in a Federalist landslide a large number of Congregationalists were able to resist the general current attests to the durability of community tradition and the frequent precedence of non-religious forces in the political life of the Commonwealth.

How partisan division and religious division corresponded and which preceded the other are questions of considerable importance. Yet so many other factors—such as the mounting heterogeneity and mobility of the population, the declining estate of the clergy, the sharpened denominational rifts, and the establishment of regional, class, and occupational patterns—played their parts in weakening the solidarity of the old Puritan church and undermining a united political front, that all generalizations are perilous. Just how complex the interrelated processes of partisan and denominational schism were—and how risky are any assumptions about the political alignments of Congregationalists—becomes clear in the light of what seem to be some innocent matters of parish administration and town government.

In the old town of Cambridge, for example, inhabitants of the First and Second (Congregational) Parishes had fought for decades over the payment of clerical salaries. The First Parish, home of the town's original church, had long sought to force the Second Parish, which had a newer church society, to finance the administration of the original and central Cambridge church. This the Second Parish had stoutly refused to do, attempting all the while to win incorporation by the General Court as a separate town. After more than seventy-five years, the religious antagonisms between the two parishes had affected other local affairs, and what had begun as a relatively minor rift in the Congregational community divided the town's entire population into hostile factions. Even in the 1790's, nevertheless, the conflict was confined to town precincts; it was articulated principally in religious terms and was "political" only in the sense that the parishes vied for local office and preferment. The emergence of political parties scarcely affected the fundamental schism, but partisanship did transform its meaning. The larger First Parish—seat of Harvard College and still overwhelmingly Congregational—became Federalist; the Second, equally Congregational, became Republican in reaction to the First. After the two parishes finally separated into two towns in 1807, the old First Parish, now a new and smaller Cambridge, sent a Federalist to the legislature with 60 per cent of the vote. West Cambridge, formerly the Second Parish, sent a Republican with 79 per cent.[2]

The experience of Cambridge was common but not typical. Dracut, a town without dissenters, was long rent by a disagreement over the location of the local church, but even after the offended side of town set up its own church, the town was consistently 95 per cent Federalist. Similarly, Bath, Maine, was the scene of a bitter clash between Arminians and Hopkinsians; yet in the aftermath of a formal division of the Congregational community, Bath remained 95 per cent Federalist. Still another instance of a liberal-conservative dispute had a different ending. When Worcester's First Congregational Parish placed Hopkinsian Samuel Austin in the pulpit, high-placed political leaders of both parties seceded to form a liberal Second Parish and to demonstrate that whom parties had put asunder, religious conviction could still join together.

On the other hand, political rivalries often served as abrupt catalysts of religious dissent. In Pittsfield, a long-standing rift between Federalist and Republican members of the same congregation eventuated in the incorporation of a new parish by the Federalists. And in Dedham's First (Congregational) Parish, where the fight over a new minister pitted Federalists, led by Fisher Ames, against Republicans, led by his brother Nathaniel, a Federalist victory in the matter precipitated a sizable Republican exodus to the local Episcopalian con-

---

[2]For the outlines of these hostilities, see Lucius R. Paige, *History of Cambridge* (Boston, 1877), p. 188; and Charles S. Parker, *Town of Arlington* [West Cambridge], *Past and Present* (Arlington, Mass., 1907), pp. 34-60.

gregation, demonstrating the frequent irrelevance to politics of denominational creeds and practices.[3]

Not surprisingly, while a large share of Congregational energies were taken up by the establishment's internal crisis, the dissenters were going zealously about the business of making converts. How much of their rapid increase after 1800 can be ascribed to genuine religious conversion and how much to the fact that the sects offered an asylum from the disrupting contests within the establishment is not altogether clear. No doubt both factors played their part, but informed contemporaries emphasized the secular rather than the spiritual grounds of sectarian growth and looked upon the evangelical denominations as the passive recipients of the disaffected. At a time when the old forms of religion were under mounting attack, people were as much repelled by Congregationalism as attracted by Methodism and Baptism. The shrewd William Bentley, himself no admirer of adult baptism or itinerant preaching, watched the rise of dissent and discounted its religious origins: "A wish to restrain the Congregational Clergy who have been uniformly of a political party against the present spirit of the administration is the principal cause." And Republican Congregationalists, he added, were failing to defend their church against the new religious temper: "Many of the republicans unfriendly to the sects have beheld at least with indifference their growing strength, as a balance to the influence which some men had obtained."[4] The dissenting sects were reaping rather than sow-

[3]On Dracut, Bath, Worcester, and Pittsfield, see: Silas R. Coburn, *History of Dracut, Massachusetts* (Lowell, Mass., 1922), pp. 188-98, 203-04; Henry Wilson Owen, *History of Bath, Maine* (Bath, Me., 1936), pp. 414-17; William Lincoln, *History of Worcester* . . . (Worcester, Mass., 1862), pp. 155-59, 167; and Birdsall, *Berkshire*, pp. 89-91. On Dedham, see Ames to Thomas Dwight, Dec. 7, 1798, Ames, *Works*, I, 244; Charles Warren, *Jacobin and Junto*, pp. 289-99; and Winfred E. A. Bernhard, *Fisher Ames: Federalist and Statesman, 1758-1808* (Chapel Hill, N.C., 1965), pp. 330-31.

[4]Bentley, *Diary*, III, 82, 235. See also *ibid.*, II, 419. There is abundant evidence that, just as the crisis within Congregationalism was precipitated by nondoctrinal as well as doctrinal controversy, dissenters often had little interest in creedal matters but severed themselves from the established church out of dismay with local condi-

ing the harvest of discontent. Politics were helping to create new religions.

Dissatisfaction with the policies of the established clergy was not, however, the sole catalyst to dissent. Religious dissent was also rooted in secular discontent. Most sectarians belonged to the lower ranks of society and had only a fleeting—and negative—relationship with the establishment. Most were unconcerned with doctrinal niceties and had a low regard for the style of mind appropriate to theological disputation. Such matters as clerical politics and religious creeds were secondary to their larger concern with privilege and intolerance. Long before they turned on Congregationalism, they were dissatisfied with the conventional order of things. Most dissenters were rebelling not against the religious canon of the old church but against its special status, its overbearing clergy, and its well-placed communicants—all of which highlighted their misfortune and made a mockery of their hopes.[5]

The rapid growth of sectarianism in New England was of course inconceivable without the vivid preaching and active proselytizing of such men as Jesse Lee and Isaac Backus. But what they said meant less than what they signified to those who saw them. Much as the orthodox appealed to the fears

---

tions. The birth of Massachusetts Methodism in 1791 in the town of Lynn, after a visit by the great itinerant preacher Jesse Lee, coincided with a typical schism within the local Congregational society over the incumbent minister. For a chronicle of the foundations of Massachusetts Methodism, see: Wade Crawford Barclay, *Early American Methodism, 1769-1844* (2 vols., New York, 1949), I, 132-40, and Parsons Cooke, *A Century of Puritanism* . . . (Boston, 1855), pp. 212-50, 346-49 *passim*.

[5]There is general agreement that the dissenters were people of simple means, little education, and no standing in society. See, e.g., Benjamin W. Hathorne to William Plumer, Feb. 22, 1804, Plumer MSS, Library of Congress; George Claude Baker, Jr., *An Introduction to the History of Early New England Methodism, 1789-1839* (Durham, N.C., 1941), pp. 16-18; Barclay, *Early American Methodism*, I, 136; Robinson, *Jeffersonian Democracy in New England*, pp. 140-41; Niebuhr, *Social Sources of Denominationalism*, p. 175; Charles J. Taylor, *History of Great Barrington* (Great Barrington, Mass., 1882), pp. 339-40, 393-94; and Bentley, *Diary*, III, 106, 134, 170, 515.

and frustrations of the potentially dispossessed, Baptist and Methodist preachers spoke to the frustrations of the unpossessing. Among people who were outside the powerful centers of Massachusetts life, these dissenting ministers created a veritable revolution in religion. In New England as elsewhere, the Baptist and Methodist sects flourished among the newcomers to the rural frontier and among the poorer inhabitants of the coastal towns. In areas such as the Connecticut River Valley, where an isolated and stable population, little differentiated by class or occupation, was under the diligent watch of the orthodox clergy, sectarianism was almost unknown.

The spoken and unspoken aims of dissenters coincided with those of the Republican Party. The explicit concern of each was to remove the artificial disabilities which stood in the way of their full participation in the life of the Commonwealth, and both groups welcomed the chance to replace an entrenched leadership and alter the rules of government. Thus the sects' poor and ill-placed members flocked to Jefferson's party, not out of approval of its budgetary policy or its diplomacy, but because of the willingness of local Republican leaders to champion their demands for relief from parish taxes and from obstructions placed in the way of their itinerant and irregular clergy and because the Republicans vigorously besieged the citadels of Federalist strength in government, the professions, and the church.

Yet the union of political and religious dissenter was inherently unstable. In Massachusetts, where the church-state controversy still raged, ensnared in politics, the union of Republican and dissenter may have been crucial to the life of each, but it was a triumph, as Bentley knew, of expediency over principle.[6] As few were willing to admit, Jefferson's party and the evangelical sects were making common cause against the common enemy for different reasons. There were potent grounds for friction between them. The true Jeffersonians in the coalition were mounting an attack upon all dogma, the

---

[6]Bentley, *Diary*, III, 91.

non-doctrinaire Republicans who sought their own power and preferment were uninterested in any dogma, the Congregational Republicans preferred their own dogma, and the dissenters were defending the rights of every dogma. The Republican coalition in Massachusetts was secure as long as these contradictory impulses were minimized and as long as the local issue of disestablishment was not displaced in the public mind by more momentous national issues.

In this context of denominational relations, the Republican Party's task was to attract and hold both dissenters and Congregationalists. Federalists had only to split the Republican coalition to destroy all hopes of Republican victory. During the first decade of the nineteenth century, Federalist efforts to lure back the Congregationalists-turned-Republican and to exploit the latent instability of the Republican-dissenter alliance by appealing to the conservative pietism of the sects and playing up Jefferson's irreligion were unavailing.[7] The Embargo crisis, though interrupting a period of steady Republican growth and revealing the vulnerability of Republicanism in Massachusetts, did not profoundly alter the relationships between the sects and the parties. Rather, it was the war which, coming on the heels of the Republican-sponsored Religious Freedom Bill of 1811 and the infamous Gerrymander, served to divide Republican from dissenter and Congregationalist as no political rhetoric could and which hastened the dissolution of this uneasy union.[8]

---

[7]The relationship between pietism and politics deserves far greater study than it has yet received. The Federalist line of attack failed primarily because Federalists would not take the additional—and crucial—step of relaxing or repealing the legal restrictions under which they forced the dissenting sects to labor. Had they done so before the Republicans got around to it in 1811, they might well have had ample time to attract pietists and evangelicals to their side in the great struggle with infidelity and Jacobinism. In sheer instrumental terms, their failure to do so remains one of the significant lost opportunities in American politics.

[8]Details of dissenter attempts to lift their religious disabilities and of the Federalist reaction to them, which ranged from a gradual but reluctant liberalization of the laws by Federalist-controlled legislatures to an apparently outright hostility toward the sects by the

The Massachusetts Federalist Party greatly benefited from the Republican-directed war with Britain. But it benefited equally from the Religious Freedom Bill of 1811, which the Republicans sponsored in the state legislature. This act of 1811, which, by allowing public taxes to be paid for the support of any religion, stopped just short of total disestablishment, handed the dissenters their long-sought victory.[9] But more important, it destroyed the central pretext for cooperation between Republicans and the evangelical and pietistic sects. Recognizing this, the Federalist leadership made no effort to repeal the act but tried instead to capitalize upon the mounting disarray in Republican and dissenting circles. To woo the many sectarians who by conviction found all wars repugnant, the Federalists adopted a Peace Party label in 1812 and appealed to the pacifist strains within Quakerism and Methodism. To

---

Federalist courts, may be found, e.g., in Jacob C. Meyer, *Church and State in Massachusetts from 1740 to 1833* (Cleveland, Ohio, 1930), pp. 134, 143-49, 155-57; Samuel Eliot Morison, "The Struggle Over the Adoption of the Constitution of Massachusetts, 1780," *Massachusetts Historical Society Proceedings*, L (May 1917), 368-74; Benedict, *General History of the Baptist Denomination*, I, 445-51; *Acts and Laws Passed by the General Court of Massachusetts* (hereafter *Mass. Acts and Laws*), 1786, Chap. 10 (June 28, 1786); 1797, Chap. 23 (June 23, 1797); 1799, Chap. 87 (Mar. 4, 1800); 1802, Chap. 129 (Mar. 8, 1803); and 1811, Chap. 6 (June 18, 1811); and *Mass. Reports*, esp. Ebenezer Washburn v. 4th Parish of West Springfield (Sept. 1804), I, 335, William Montague v. Inhabitants of the First Parish in Dedham (Mar. 1808), IV, 271, Kendall v. Inhabitants of Kingston (Oct. 1809), V, 524, Thomas Barnes v. Inhabitants of the First Parish of Falmouth (May 1810), VI, 401-18, Edward Turner v. Inhabitants of the Second Precinct in Brookfield (Sept. 1810), VII, 60-62, and Shubael Lowell v. Inhabitants of the Parish of Byfield (Nov. 1810), VII, 320-32.

[9]The Religious Freedom Bill will be found in *Mass. Acts and Laws*, 1811, Chap. 6 (June 18, 1811). In effect, the act permitted taxes allocated to the support of religion to be paid to any minister considered ordained by the usages of any denomination in either an incorporated or unincorporated religious society as long as the taxpayers were certified by members of such a society as "usually" worshipping there. The act undercut the effect of nearly all previous legislative enactments and judicial decisions. On the entire problem of disestablishment, see John D. Cushing, "Notes on Disestablishment in Massachusetts," *WMQ*, 3rd Ser., XXVI (April 1969), 169-190.

win away the pietists, they intensified their attacks upon deism and irreligion in general.

It was not long before the natural cleavages within the dissenting camp were exposed. Most Quakers moved into the Federalist ranks.[1] Methodists too began slowly to drift away. They had always been less-dedicated Republicans than the Baptists. Methodists were generally better off than Baptist communicants. Moreover, the hierarchical organization of their church accustomed them to respect superior authority and undoubtedly immunized them somewhat against the excessive distrust of official power which characterized the Baptists.

Because of an unintended unevenness in the application of the discriminatory laws against dissenters, Methodists also had less reason than Baptists to attack the establishment. Under Massachusetts law before 1811, one could escape the payment of parish taxes by proving membership in, and regular worship at, the church of a legally incorporated dissenting society. Strongest in the larger towns and more accessible than the frontier Baptists to the incorporated church societies there, Methodists found it reasonably simple to win exemption from parish taxes. But the Baptists, scattered more widely in the rural hinterlands, were distant from incorporated societies. Hence they experienced more sharply the oppressive weight of the Congregational establishment. Moreover, the residence and occupational patterns of the Methodist population weakened their links to Republicanism and inhibited them less from crossing to Federalism in times of political turmoil. In the seaport towns where they were concentrated, the vicissitudes of foreign war and commercial policy affected them more directly than rural inhabitants, and they were often directly dependent

---

[1]Obed Macy, *The History of Nantucket* (2nd ed., Mansfield, Mass., 1880), pp. 173 ff.; Phillips, *Salem and the Indies,* p. 378; Morison, *Maritime History of Mass.,* p. 199; and Bentley, *Diary,* IV, 102. Since 1797, Quakers had been exempted from paying parish taxes, a dispensation which no doubt reduced somewhat their hostility toward the same Federalist establishment which enforced these taxes against other dissenters. See *Mass. Acts and Laws,* 1797, Chap. 23 (June 23, 1797).

for their livelihood upon the Federalist gentry, practiced in the subtle arts of social and economic persuasion.[2] Finally, though Methodist attitudes on the war varied, a large percentage opposed it as destructive of religion and contrary to the gospel of peace.

Because most Baptists lived in isolated interior and frontier villages and had to make do on subsistence farming and marginal occupations such as fishing and lumbering, of all the dissenters they were probably least under the thumb of their social and economic betters and least affected by economic crisis. Unlike the Methodists, whose conversion was often linked to the disruption of parish affairs, the fast-growing Massachusetts Baptist sect had much deeper roots in the conditions of the lower class and had been connected since the seventeenth century with efforts to sever church and state. Whereas a Methodist, whose protest against the establishment often had a local origin, might not change his party with his religion, a Baptist's conversion was more total and involved a protest against all manifestations of officialdom and "respectability." Hence neither economic disaster nor war nor appeals to their piety against irreligion had any effect upon their Republicanism. During the war years, for example, the twenty-two voters in the little Baptist hamlet of Hull in Plymouth County gave the Federalists only two votes each year. And surely nothing can equal the record of Baptist Cheshire in Berkshire County, whose 241 voters deposited only seven Federalist ballots in 1812.

Historians have not been wrong in pointing to the Baptists' undeviating loyalty to the Republican Party in New England. They have been in error only in concluding from this that the Baptist experience was representative of all the denom-

---

[2]Some suggestive comments on New England Methodism in this period are to be found in Baker, *Early New England Methodism*, esp. pp. 16-18, 58 ff. Bentley was quick to note that old and "respectable" families were unaffected by Methodism and Baptism. *Diary*, III, 388. See also *ibid.*, II, 409; III, 4.

inations. Although all religions were identified with one party or another, the political affiliations of probably a majority of their followers were fluid. Had it not been so, there would have been no two-party system in Massachusetts.

VI

The Genesis of
Party Organization

I

I<small>T</small> was not until the late 1790's—well after the Federalist ideology had taken shape—that Massachusetts Federalists began to construct a formal party organization. Once, however, that it was in operation and once it was fueled by the Federalists' determination to reclaim the republican experiment from its corrupt Republican foes, its leaders were quickly inspired to move beyond the restraints of the old-style elite methods and to achieve within a few years that most un-Federalist of results: political democracy. Yet ideology was not alone responsible for the timing of party development nor for the form which the party assumed. Party growth was the outcome of many forces—among them the actions of the opposition, the legal context of voting and representation, and the flow of foreign and domestic events.

Nor did ideological restraints alone impede the formation of a party organization before 1800. More important was the simple factor of political success: in the government they administered, the Federalists already possessed a party mechanism. The Constitution was its table of organization, the executive and legislative branches its structure, the civil service its cadre. It was not simply because they found themselves in the opposition after 1801 that Federalists began to organize against the Jeffersonians, nor that Thomas Jefferson, the anti-republican Anti-Christ, had assumed the Presidency, but also because they were abruptly bereft of the governmental machinery which for so long served as a surrogate for the party apparatus. To redeem the nation now called for new organization.

But in defeat the national party was bitterly divided into Hamilton and Adams wings. Its political base had eroded in the Northern cities and the South. And few national leaders displayed an interest in assuming the task of uniting the party. So demoralized, for instance, was outgoing president John Adams and so reduced was his political influence that even in his home state of Massachusetts he refused to have much to do with the party again. In the end, it was left almost exclusively to Federalists on the state level, their efforts little coordinated with party colleagues elsewhere, to pick up the fragments of defeat and keep alive the party's fortunes.

In Massachusetts, the highly factionalized Federalist Party began to take shape only toward the close of the eighteenth century. Not until 1797 did Sam Adams retire from the governor's chair, and not until then was a long era of Revolutionary leadership at last closed out and the remaining obstacle to a thorough realignment of factions removed. For the continuation in office of popular and prestigious figures from the momentous days of Independence had long inhibited the birth of a two-party system. In the last years of the century in Massachusetts, these notables had generally been Federalists, and their resignations raised the prospect of strong Republican challenges in hitherto "safe" Federalist elections. Voter apathy and lopsided election results had been common; now electoral interest was intensified and spirited two-party contests became the rule. On the gubernatorial level, for instance, voter participation jumped 84 per cent between Sam Adams's retirement and the critical election of 1800, as men outside the old ruling circles made their bids for power.

In most cases, Federalists from the Revolutionary generation or their direct political legatees proved unable to bequeath their own majorities to their intended Federalist successors, and long periods of Republican rule often followed equally long years of Federalist domination. In Berkshire County, where House Speaker Theodore Sedgwick relinquished his seat in 1800 after a decade as elder statesman of an increasingly Republican constituency, the Republicans defeated his party successor and then held the seat into 1813. In Boston, where Harrison Gray Otis sought to escape the ravages of the gathering storm by refusing to run again in 1800, young Josiah Quincy succumbed to Republican William Eustis. In situations such as these, there was no alternative to rallying and campaigning for the Federalist candidates. Only organization and action could save the day.[1]

The general circumstance of Federalist politics throughout the nation around 1800 goes far to explain the Federalists' mounting interest in organization. The party was deeply split into factions led by John Adams and Alexander Hamilton, and it had lost much popular support for its sponsorship of the Alien and Sedition Acts. But the chief precipitant of party development in Massachusetts, rather than the schism on the national level, was a crisis of leadership which beset the state party. For a time after Sam Adams's retirement, Federalist leaders were able to hold together a coalition around the gubernatorial standard of Increase Sumner. A moderate and well-liked old-school Bostonian whom Sam Adams had defeated in 1796, Sumner was elected handily to fill Adams's vacated seat a year later, and control of the General Court and the state's congressional delegation passed into Federalist hands. Had Sumner not died suddenly in 1799, he would have continued, perhaps indefinitely, to be the party's standard-bearer. Even more, the lieutenant governor could have been expected under normal conditions to assume the deceased governor's place within the party or at least to make a serious bid for the chief magistracy of the state. But because Moses Gill, who filled out the governor's term until the spring of 1800, had

---

[1]Henry Van Schaack to Sedgwick, Dec. 7, 1800, Daniel Dewey to Sedgwick, Dec. 8, 1800, Sedgwick MSS, Massachusetts Historical Society (hereafter MHS); Sedgwick to Rufus King, May 24, 1801, King MSS, New York Historical Society (hereafter NYHS); Richard E. Welch, Jr., *Theodore Sedgwick, Federalist: A Political Portrait* (Middletown, Conn., 1965), pp. 218-19; Dwight Foster to Jonathan Dayton, Oct. 11, 1800, Gratz Coll., Pennsylvania Historical Society; and James Duncan Phillips, "Political Fights and Local Squabbles in Salem, 1800-1806," *Essex Institute Historical Collections*, LXXXII (Jan. 1946), 6.

few supporters within the party, Sumner's death precipitated a scramble for the succession.[2]

Sumner himself had been the approved candidate of that small group of old-school leaders who, in the absence of formal party machinery, had served as the party's governing board. Though known to American folklore as the Essex Junto, they neither lived in Essex County nor remotely resembled a cabal. Their political roots struck as deeply into Boston as the North Shore; their views and loyalties often diverged on important matters of policy; and by the century-turn most of the active survivors among them, including George Cabot, Stephen Higginson, Jonathan Jackson, and John Lowell, had moved to the capital.[3] But Essex Junto or not, they were in fact the most eminent embodiments of a large congregation of old-school notables across the state. It was they who most successfully turned the widespread political apathy and the prevailing canons of elite leadership to their own account in order to govern the party and much of the state in their own image for the last few years of the century.

Their direct authority began to wane after 1799. But in spite of their thinning ranks, they managed until then to retain much of their influence and stature. Their most important

---

[2]A brief survey of Massachusetts Federalist politics at the end of the century is to be found in Anson E. Morse, *The Federalist Party in Massachusetts to the Year 1800* (Princeton, N.J., 1909), pp. 174-88. Larger studies of the Federalist Party at the national level in the 1790's are Manning J. Dauer, *The Adams Federalists* (Baltimore, 1953), and Stephen G. Kurtz, *The Presidency of John Adams: The Collapse of Federalism, 1795-1800* (Philadelphia, 1957). See also Paul Goodman, *The Democratic-Republicans of Massachusetts: Politics in a Young Republic* (Cambridge, 1964), pp. 60-61. I have been greatly stimulated in thinking about the problems of Federalist organization by Maurice Duverger, *Political Parties* (rev. ed., New York, 1963); Richard P. McCormick, *The Second American Party System: Party Formation in the Jacksonian Era* (Chapel Hill, N.C., 1966); and Paul Goodman, "The First American Party System," in *The American Party Systems: Stages of Political Development*, eds. William Nisbet Chambers and Walter Dean Burnham (New York, 1967), pp. 56-89.

[3]David Hackett Fischer, "The Myth of the Essex Junto," *William and Mary Quarterly* (hereafter *WMQ*), 3rd Ser., XXI (Apr. 1964), 191-235.

legacy was preserving for maritime Massachusetts a predominating voice in the affairs of the far-flung Commonwealth. From some time before 1797 and for at least two years after, they set in motion most nominations for statewide office, had a say in drawing up legislation, and represented Massachusetts Federalism to the country at large. Critics they always had, but few real challengers. Their preeminence discouraged revolts against their leadership, and, until the careers of the new generation of political stalwarts were well under way, they enjoyed the deference of much of the state. Jonathan Mason, Jr., betraying the regard in which young party initiates held the older gentlemen, admitted to Otis in 1798 that he showed Otis's letters to "the Cabot, Lowell & Higginson *crew* for without their approbation, Where will the *fat* be?"[4]

Yet political power turned out to be elusive. For in 1799, only two years after the party had captured control of the state, it was faced with a succession crisis. The settlement of 1797 in which Sumner had assumed the governorship, as it rapidly became all too clear, was not yet universally accepted; and for those who had no liking for Gill there were no precedents to go by in choosing Sumner's successor. To make matters worse, Sumner's death coincided with the rift between Adams and the Hamiltonians in the national administration. Even under normal circumstances, a sharp factional dispute would have been difficult to resolve; but now that local intramural hostilities had taken on the coloration of battles raging at the highest echelons of the party, solutions under the old procedures were not to be found. At least half the party was in no mood to heed the preferences of the old-school leaders in Boston. The old nominating system had broken down—

---

[4]Jonathan Mason, Jr., to Otis, Mar. 26, 1798, Samuel Eliot Morison, *The Life and Letters of Harrison Gray Otis, Federalist, 1765-1848* (2 vols., Boston, 1913), I, 92. Though we may dismiss the reality of a Junto, there is no dismissing the widespread belief, even in Federalist circles, of its existence. See Francis Dana to Rufus King, Jan. 30, 1802, King MSS, NYHS, and Gore to Wolcott, Sept. 30, 1808, Wolcott MSS, Connecticut Historical Society (hereafter CHS).

not out of a desire to replace it but because of its inability to resolve the crisis and remove the antagonism between different cliques.

The party reconstruction which began in 1799 was thus more the work of accident than design. Except for a nudge here and there from figures serving at the national level, it was wholly the affair of Federalists on the state scene. On the heels of Sumner's death, no less than half a dozen gubernatorial hopefuls were pushed forward by their friends. Acting-Governor Gill, whose unacceptability was the main pretext for discarding the old system, was nevertheless in contention. North Shore Federalists, most of them Hamiltonians, urged the nomination of old-school jurists Francis Dana and the elder John Lowell. John Adams's friends countered by pressing the claims of Elbridge Gerry. Even Fisher Ames had his champions for a time. Finally, the Connecticut River Valley, long chafing under the overlordship of the eastern counties, stood by the candidacy of Northampton's Caleb Strong.[5] So sharp were the hostilities between the Adams and Hamilton camps and so unyielding the holdouts for Strong and Gill that the summer session of the General Court passed without a nomination.

In the midst of this paralysis, and in hopes of hitting upon a more regularized and less cliquish nominating method, a few Federalists who had never approved the old system, under which mercantile elements in the eastern towns controlled the party, saw a chance to change the rules along with the candidate. It was House Speaker Theodore Sedgwick from the western town of Stockbridge, known then and later for his sharp resentment toward the party chieftains of the east, who

---

[5]Morse, *Federalist Party in Mass.*, p. 178. Dana, for one, was finally dismissed as a candidate because, among other reasons, he was neither popular enough nor known as a "party man," a revealing commentary on the changing standards of availability. See Abigail Adams to Mary Smith Cranch, June 3, 1797, Dec. 4, 1799, in *New Letters of Abigail Adams, 1788-1801*, ed. Stewart Mitchell (Boston, 1947), pp. 94, 219. See also Joseph Hale to Rufus King, Sept. 30, 1799, King MSS, NYHS.

first proposed that a legislative caucus designate the party's choice for governor.[6] The idea of the legislative caucus was not novel; since the 1790's congressional parties had caucused in Philadelphia, and the Maryland legislature had caucused as early as 1788. Yet despite the derivative nature of Sedgwick's plan, what is striking is that the initial pressures for a new departure were coming from men who were keenly suspicious of Boston politics, who had gained some experience with the caucus system at the national capital, and who were acquainted with the desperate state of party affairs on the national scene.

It was one thing, however, to trim the power of the old Boston leadership and another to substitute a workable nominating system. To entrust the nomination to a caucus was to run the risk of deadlock among the competing factions and the paralysis of the party; not to do so was to capitulate publicly to the old and tainted backroom methods. The solution was a legislative caucus held in Boston on February 5, 1800.[7]

This caucus had little more than a legitimizing function. So short and unanimous were its proceedings, so readily accepted its decision, that, given the state of Federalist opinion only a short time before, a compromise between the principal competing factions must already have been hammered out.[8] Western Federalists in particular must by the time of the

---

[6]Sedgwick to Rufus King, July 26, 1799, King MSS, NYHS. On Sedgwick's hostility toward maritime Federalists, see Richard E. Welch, Jr., "The Parsons-Sedgwick Feud and the Reform of the Massachusetts Judiciary," *Essex Institute Historical Collections*, XCII (Apr. 1956), 171-87; Thomas Dawes, Jr., to Francis Dana, June 21, 1800, Dana to Strong, June 25, 1800, Strong MSS, Forbes Lib., Northampton; Samuel Sewall to Sedgwick, Aug. 27, 1800, Strong to Sedgwick, Nov. 13, 1800, Sedgwick to Henry Van Schaack, May 23, 1806, Sedgwick to Theodore Sedgwick, Jr., Dec. 9, 1806, Sedgwick MSS, MHS; and Dawes to Otis, Jan. 22, 1801[?], Sedgwick to Otis, May 16, 1806, Otis MSS, MHS.

[7]Caucuses of the state's Federalist leadership had, of course, met long before 1800, but the 1800 caucus was the first of the party's legislative caucuses. See, e.g., Morse, *Federalist Party in Mass.*, pp. 42*n*, 58*n*, 141*n*.

[8][Boston] *Columbian Centinel* (hereafter *Centinel*), Feb. 12, 1800. The first national nominating caucus, a Republican one, did not meet until 1804.

caucus meeting have been satisfied that their interests were already protected, for resistance to the whole idea of a caucus and the early return home of many Federalist representatives kept caucus attendance to below half the size of the Federalist delegation, a situation which left maritime Federalists in command.[9] Old-school Bostonian John Lowell, himself considered for the nomination, placed Strong's name before the seventy-two-man caucus in a gesture of party harmony, and the reluctant favorite of western Massachusetts was nominated effortlessly by written ballot.[1]

This is not to say that Strong's selection was everywhere greeted with pleasure, nor that there was not a good deal of trading between the factions. To balance the ticket, Gill was permitted to retain the lieutenant governorship. Regarding Strong, Ames reported that some easterners objected to "a man who lives a hundred miles from salt water, whose wife wears blue stockings, and who, with his household, calls hasty pudding luxury."[2] But compelling arguments overcame such resistance. Identified with neither Adams nor Hamilton factions, Strong was, a western Federalist observed, "the only Man in whom our Friends at the Eastward can unite."[3] He was, moreover, a Federalist from the valley, whose yeomanry, notoriously touchy on the subject of Boston rule, were said to be "not only united but spirited—if anything, forward of the

---

[9]According to my calculations from the roster of the General Court, the Federalist caucus in 1800 numbered between 130 and 155 men. Breaking down its membership, slightly less than half its members came from towns east of Worcester County, slightly more than half from towns in Worcester, "Old Hampshire," and Berkshire counties and the counties of Maine. In the caucus, Essex County's twenty-three-man delegation was the largest, "Old Hampshire's" twenty the next largest.

[1]Thomas C. Amory, *Life of James Sullivan* (2 vols., Boston, 1859), II, 65. See also Sedgwick to Henry Van Schaack, Feb. 9, 1800, Sedgwick MSS, MHS; and Strong to Ezra Starkweather, Feb. 4, 1808, Strong MSS, Forbes Lib., Northampton.

[2]Ames to Gore, Mar. 5, 1800, *Works of Fisher Ames*, ed. Seth Ames (2 vols., Boston, 1854), I, 277. See also Strong to Sedgwick, Feb. 12 & Apr. 5, 1800, Sedgwick MSS, MHS.

[3]Samuel Henshaw to Henry Van Schaack, Mar. 24, 1800, Van Schaack MSS, Columbia University.

Seaports."[4] Because the caucus system could reward those regions which sent the largest number of party members to the General Court and because in full caucus western Massachusetts and Maine representatives could at least equal and usually outnumber those from east of Worcester, the caucus system itself placed the eastern leaders in a position where they could not risk disregarding Strong's claims. He was a Revolutionary patriot, first Massachusetts senator to the general government, and widely respected for his old-school virtues. A link to the past and a new and much-needed symbol of party unity, he would be governor for eleven of the next sixteen years.

As the election results showed, the party had acted none too soon in adopting the caucus system. The Republicans, concentrating on capturing the statehouse, shrewdly nominated Elbridge Gerry and ran him as a friend of peace and John Adams. And as if Gerry's candidacy was not threat enough, residual though unsolicited support of Acting-Governor Gill, passed over by the caucus, endangered the Federalist plurality.[5] Even in the face of these perils, however, the party as a whole did nothing about the campaign. Few viewed Gerry as a serious threat.

As before, it was left to individual Federalists, like Berk-

---

[4]Jonathan Mason, Jr., to Otis, May 28, 1798, Morison, *Otis,* I, 96.

[5]Joseph Hale to Rufus King, Sept. 30, 1799, Sedgwick to King, May 1, 1800, King MSS, NYHS; Thomas Dwight to Sedgwick, Apr. 11, 1800, Otis to Sedgwick, Apr. 18, 1800, Sedgwick MSS, MHS; Parsons to John Jay, May 5, 1800, Jay MSS, Columbia; and Goodman, *Democratic-Republicans of Mass.,* pp. 104-05. As the Republicans realized, until they developed a following of their own on their own merits, they had to put up moderate candidates who had a somewhat Federalist and establishment tint. They carried Boston with Gerry in 1800 and 1801 and elected William Eustis over Josiah Quincy and John Quincy Adams to the "Boston seat" in Congress in 1800 and 1802. In 1801, Republicans talked of putting up ex-President John Adams for governor. But once Massachusetts Republicanism began to acquire a more outspokenly partisan character, moderate Federalists dropped away. In 1802, Boston returned a Federalist slate to the General Court and remained in the Federalist fold until the party's demise in the 1820's.

VI: *The Genesis of Party Organization*

shire County's Henry Van Schaack, to get out the vote. Unaided in his efforts, young Van Schaack took upon himself the burden of drumming up support for Federalist candidates in his county. He hurried from town to town, distributing handbills with the aid of "faithful agents" in a vain attempt to arouse the voters. Nothing but inertia greeted him. Not surprisingly, the Federalist vote in Berkshire remained low despite his efforts, unity was not restored, and Gill ran ahead of Strong in many places.[6] When the party finally called for new-style leadership in a few years, it would turn to men like Van Schaack; but in the meantime, such well-meant but isolated efforts went unsolicited and unrewarded.

In the end, because the caucus proved powerless to do more than commit the party to a single candidate, the party's vote was down 13 per cent from the 1799 level throughout Massachusetts, while Gerry attracted enough Adams Federalists to boost the Republican vote almost 100 per cent. Had not the Federalist caucus healed the breach within the party's top echelons, Gerry would have triumphed. As it was, Strong carried the state by only slightly over 50 per cent of the 39,059 votes cast. Gerry came within 2,600 votes of equaling Strong. With Gill's vote added to Gerry's, Strong had a majority of only 201 votes.[7]

---

[6]Henry Van Schaack to Sedgwick, Apr. 7, 1800, Sedgwick MSS, MHS. Before the spring elections of 1801, Van Schaack even went so far as to suggest that Berkshire Federalists and Republicans face each other in a public debate. Daniel Dewey to Van Schaack, Mar. 13, 1801, Van Schaack MSS, Columbia. By the autumn of 1800, Van Schaack had set up a rudimentary Federalist organization of his own in Berkshire by employing agents in the towns and preparing a handbill for them to distribute. Such efforts not only anticipated the founding of a formal statewide Federalist organization by about four years but alleviated the problems facing its leaders when they began to set up the committee system; instead of constructing a Berkshire County committee from the bottom up, they had only to assert their authority over the one that existed. Van Schaack to Sedgwick, Oct. 20, 1800, Sedgwick MSS, MHS.

[7]These figures and calculations, like all the rest in this chapter, are based upon the official manuscript "Returns of Votes for Governor and Lieutenant Governor" deposited in the Massachusetts State Archives, State House, Boston.

Measured by local election results, this election was a "deviant" election, a temporary dislocation of the normal party balance.[8] Gerry's abnormally high vote barely ruffled the two-party equilibrium in the state and made no dent in basic Federalist strength during the separate contests for state senators and representatives. In some regions, Federalist candidates for senator attracted 80 per cent of the vote. Equally important, because they had easily retained control of both houses of the General Court, Federalists were in a position to choose the method of selecting presidential electors and, in effect, to decide the outcome of the presidential balloting long before November. The question was simply how to go about doing so.

Under a mixed electoral system in 1796, some presidential electors had been chosen in special electoral districts, others by the legislature. Now, in the face of mounting Republican strength, especially in Middlesex, Norfolk, and Bristol counties in the central and southern portions of the state, the district system no longer recommended itself: not only might two electoral votes be lost, but district-chosen electors might be inclined to throw away their votes for Pinckney in order to insure Adams's chances, a prospect not welcomed by the Hamiltonians.[9] Another alternative was the general ticket system, under which the party that received the most popular

---

[8]I have been particularly influenced in my understanding of elections by the following works: V. O. Key, Jr., "A Theory of Critical Elections," *Journal of Politics*, XVII (Feb. 1955), 3-18, and "Secular Realignment and the Party System," *ibid.*, XXI (May 1959), 198-210; Donald E. Stokes and Gudmund R. Iversen, "Party Loyalty and the Likelihood of Deviating Elections," *ibid.*, XXIV (Nov. 1962), 689-702, and Stokes, "On the Existence of Forces Restoring Party Competition," *Public Opinion Quarterly*, XXVI (Summer 1962), 159-71; and Angus Campbell, "Surge and Decline: A Study of Electoral Change," *ibid.*, XXIV (Fall 1960), 397-418, the last three of which have been reprinted along with other related essays in Angus Campbell *et al.*, *Elections and the Political Order* (New York, 1966).

[9]On this point, see Benjamin W. Labaree, *Patriots and Partisans: The Merchants of Newburyport, 1764-1815* (Cambridge, 1962), p. 123, and Cabot to Rutledge, Oct. 22, 1800, Rutledge MSS, University of North Carolina (hereafter UNC).

votes in the state at large would take all sixteen electoral votes. After the narrow spring election triumph, this method had little to recommend it. Legislative choice of electors, an increasingly unpopular but safe method in use in other states, seemed to be the best option.

The state's Federalist congressional delegation, which had begun by the summer to sense the drift of national opinion toward Jefferson, favored this method. Fearing that district and general ticket elections would imperil the whole national ticket, the entire delegation privately circulated a letter to leading state figures urging that the caucus see to it that the General Court make the choice. "In this critical state of things we feel that it is very important to guard against one anti-federal vote from Massachusetts; for one vote may turn the election," the circular read. "We presume not to point out the mode, but only to suggest the danger which we apprehend and which we in this place, and in our present employment, are perhaps better circumstanced to observe than our friends of Massachusetts can be. Excuse us for suggesting our ideas; our anxiety for the event of the election must be our apology."[1] During the summer session, the caucus took the hint and committed its members to adopt the legislative method.

These details suggest that the origins of the Massachusetts Federalist Party structure are to be found in issues peculiar to Massachusetts Federalism and not outside. The party received no significant assistance or encouragement from Federalists in other states or in Congress. The stirrings of interest in new methods of party administration were little related to events in Philadelphia or elsewhere. Indeed, the party organization came into being around the gubernatorial, not the presidential, contest. If Massachusetts caucus development signifies anything more than the search for more effective party management, it signals the Federalists' jealous regard for quarantining state party affairs from the ills of national politics.

---

[1] Samuel Lyman *et al.* to ?, Jan. 31, 1800, printed in *Massachusetts Historical Society Proceedings*, XLIII (May 1910), 652-54.

Furthermore, the caucus was not an after-the-fact reaction to Republican efforts. It was the Federalists who set the pace of party growth in the Commonwealth and laid out the ground rules of representative and centralized party management. That the Republican Party soon seized the initiative from them should not diminish their place in the history of American political development.

Nor should it cause surprise that the Federalists themselves minimized the caucus. They wished to avoid the imputation of adopting "jacobinic" measures; they hoped to conceal the party schism; and above all they could not foresee how large a role the caucus was to play in the future. In a public statement, caucus members justified their action as an improvement upon tradition rather than a departure from it. They emphasized that caucus members had met in their private rather than legislative capacities to "discuss the merits of certain persons." Disavowing any desire to dictate a choice to the people, they nevertheless offered no more than the barest information of what had taken place. As before, the rank and file were to be informed without being consulted; they were not to have a role in party affairs.[2] Yet nothing could obscure the fact that, in committing itself to the caucus system, the party had broadened and reapportioned its base of leadership. By giving a greater voice to Federalists outside Boston, it had diluted the power of the old-guard eastern oligarchy and opened the way for a new type of nominating system. And it had created a mechanism through which the force of public opinion could make itself felt in the party's innermost circles.

For a quarter-century after 1800, the legislative caucus was the supreme council of the Massachusetts Federalist Party, a board of trustees to which every committee and every member had to defer. It nominated candidates, made policy, appointed committees, dispensed patronage, issued propaganda, and drew up legislative programs. And as the legislative caucus,

---

[2]*Centinel,* Feb. 1, 5, & 12, 1800. See also [Worcester] *Massachusetts Spy,* Mar. 26, 1800, quoted in William A. Robinson, *Jeffersonian Democracy in New England* (New Haven, 1916), p. 57.

limited exclusively to General Court members, became a mixed caucus—a more inclusive body of state senators, representatives, and influential men from outside the legislature—and expanded by 1808 to roughly 300 members, it developed an internal executive machinery of officers and committees.

Its chairman, or "moderator," was elected by the whole caucus to brief but often successive terms of single legislative sessions. He was often Speaker of the House, President of the Senate, or, when the party was in the minority, floor leader of one or the other branch.[3] The chairmanship carried with it not only the responsibility of calling and running caucus meetings but also the strategic duty of appointing committees, subject to caucus approval. Composed in large part of minor political figures serving only briefly in the House, the caucus not surprisingly turned for its chairman to the long-tenured and most prestigious members in its ranks. When Otis moderated the caucus in 1808, for instance, he was also Senate President and Chairman of the Federalist Central Committee. Through the kind of plural office-holding which combined both official and unofficial positions, one man could run the party and hold sway over the whole state government at the same time.

The burden of executive leadership in the caucus fell to a series of ad hoc committees, appointed anew at each session and responsible for bringing in the names of possible nominees for state office, preparing public caucus addresses, drawing up caucus agendas, and proposing legislative programs.[4] In effect,

---

[3]In 1808, Senate President Otis headed one session of the caucus. Two years later, House Speaker Timothy Bigelow chaired it. But in 1806 and again in 1811, Elijah Brigham of Worcester County, and in 1808 Ezra Starkweather of Worthington, neither of them Speaker nor Senate President, were moderators for various sessions. James Lloyd, Jr., to Otis, June 1, 1808, Otis MSS, MHS; Benjamin Whitman to Samuel Dexter *et al.*, Aug. 1, 1812, Misc. MSS Colls., Columbia; untitled caucus meeting records, dtd. Feb. 12, 1806, William Smith Shaw MSS, Boston Athenaeum (hereafter BA); and *Centinel*, Mar. 26, 1808, Feb. 20, 1811.

[4]See, e.g., MSS caucus resolves sent to the Central Committee, Feb. 12, 1806, Shaw Papers, BA. For an example of a Federalist cau-

this system resulted in control by a group of senior House and Senate members from which the powerful moderator inevitably selected his appointees. The committees were themselves accountable to the whole caucus, and the chairman could not set up a committee, nor charge it with specific tasks, unless authorized by the caucus itself.[5]

Committees usually included one representative from each county—a membership policy which acknowledged the claims of Federalists outside the powerful maritime and Connecticut River Valley towns.[6] Yet no arrangement could in fact reduce the dominance of the eastern towns. They were by all indices the wealthiest and most powerful communities and regularly returned the state's leading political figures. In addition, House members tended to drift back home as sessions wore on, in order to attend to their own business and to avoid antagonizing the constituents whose taxes paid for their attendance at the General Court.[7] Those who remained were generally the eastern Federalists who were close to home and who could turn out for caucus business without much difficulty. Therefore, soon after the opening of each legislative session, the caucus was often little more than a rump controlled by eastern Federalists.

Whatever the composition of the caucus and its committees at any one moment, it always remained the director, the voice, and the disciplinarian of the party. Rather than following the lead of its offshoot, the Central Committee, it continually "enjoined," "directed," and "instructed" the Com-

---

cus report, see *Dissent, Offered in the House of Representatives of the Commonwealth of Massachusetts*, dtd. Jan. 31, 1807. Confusion regarding caucus committees has resulted from a misreading of Morison, *Otis*, I, 288-89. Morison's evidence, like that which I have discovered, suggests nothing more than that there were successive caucus committees for different purposes, each made up of one caucus member from each county. There was no single and powerful caucus committee which ran the caucus from session to session.

[5]Untitled caucus meeting record, Feb. 7, 1806, Shaw MSS, BA.
[6]Gore to Rufus King, Feb. 22, 1809, King MSS, NYHS.
[7]See the illuminating instructions in MSS caucus resolves sent to the Central Committee for action, Feb. 12, 1806, Shaw MSS, BA.

mittee to fulfill specific responsibilities.[8] The caucus alone had the authority after 1800 to nominate candidates for governor, lieutenant governor, United States senator, and governor's councillor. It resolved contests for the House speakership and the Senate presidency. On the recommendation of one of its committees, the caucus selected Christopher Gore over Otis to succeed Strong as gubernatorial candidate in 1808, and it was the caucus which called Strong back into the party's service in 1812.[9] The caucus of 1803 resolved the divisive question of electing a successor to Jonathan Mason in the United States Senate by choosing John Quincy Adams over fellow-Federalist Timothy Pickering in a series of complicated maneuvers.[1] In 1808, the caucus decided that presidential electors would be chosen by the Federalist-controlled General Court, directed the Central Committee to send out a circular written by Pickering under caucus auspices, and appointed its own special committee of correspondence to communicate with Federalists in other states about the Embargo.[2] It was this committee

----

[8]Gore to Rufus King, May 28, 1808, King MSS, NYHS; and John Quincy Adams, *Diary*, entry for May 27, 1802, reel 27, Adams Family Papers microfilm (hereafter Adams microfilm). For cases of revolt against a caucus nomination, see William H. Sumner, *A History of East Boston* (Boston, 1858), pp. 742-43*n*; and John Quincy Adams to Louisa Adams, May 9 & 14, 1804, reel 403, Adams microfilm.

[9]Ezra Starkweather to Strong, Feb. 1, 1808, Strong MSS, Forbes Lib., Northampton; Gore to Rufus King, Feb. 7, 1812, King MSS, NYHS; Helen Reisinger Pinckney, "Christopher Gore, A Federalist of Massachusetts, 1758-1827" (unpub. Ph.D. dissertation, Radcliffe, 1942), pp. 339-40; and Morison, *Otis*, I, 327.

[1]Bigelow to Plumer, Feb. 11, 1803, Plumer MSS, New Hampshire State Library; and John Quincy Adams, *Diary*, entry for Feb. 3, 1803, reel 30, Adams microfilm.

[2]Gore to Rufus King, May 28, 1808, June 4, 9, & 16, 1808, King MSS, NYHS; and Thomas Boylston Adams to John Quincy Adams, Mar. 15, 1808, reel 405, Adams microfilm. For other evidence of the caucus's policy-making role, see untitled caucus meeting records, Feb. 12, 1806, Shaw MSS, BA. The caucus organized and led the protest against the Gerrymander in 1812. *Protest in the House of Representatives of the Commonwealth of Massachusetts*, dtd. Feb. 20, 1812, and *Address to the Free and Independent People of Massachusetts*, dtd. Feb. 21, 1812.

which set in motion the events which led up to the party's dalliance with DeWitt Clinton that year and to the first national nominating convention in American history.[3] And soon after the declaration of war in June 1812, it was the caucus which moved to organize and consolidate a massive grass-roots protest against the administration.[4]

Not the least of caucus powers was its ability to discipline the party and, through it, the whole political system. By committing the party to single candidates for each position, it eliminated irregular candidacies, forced voters to take one of two sides, and, after 1800, reduced the "scattering" vote and multiple candidacies to a fraction of what they had been before. The caucus system also eliminated run-off elections, a frequent necessity in former years to satisfy the state constitutional rule that elections be won by simple majorities. By bringing some order to the electoral process, the nominating caucus enabled party leaders to shift their attention from party unity to campaign and electoral matters, no small event in the growth of a two-party system.[5]

After the 1800 elections the caucus system became a permanent feature of Federalist—and Republican—politics at all levels of government. As early as the autumn of 1800, William Bentley noted that "for the first time the zeal of Caucusing has been introduced into Salem."[6] Within a few years, from the

---

[3]For a general survey of this convention, see Samuel Eliot Morison, "The First National Nominating Convention, 1808," *American Historical Review* (hereafter *AHR*), XVII (July 1912), 744-63.

[4]Unsigned printed circular letter to ?, June 1812, Broadside (hereafter Bdse.) Coll., Library of Congress (hereafter LC); Thomas Dawes to Noah Webster, June 25, 1812, Webster MSS, New York Public Library (hereafter NYPL); *Protest in the House of Representatives of the Commonwealth of Mass.*, dtd. Feb. 20, 1812; *Address to the Free and Independent People of Mass.*, dtd. Feb. 21, 1812; and [Boston] *New England Palladium* (hereafter *Palladium*), Mar. 20, 1807.

[5]George D. Luetscher, *Early Political Machinery in the United States* (Philadelphia, 1903), p. 121; and MSS "Votes for Governor and Lieutenant Governor," 1800-1815, Massachusetts State Archives.

[6]William Bentley, *The Diary of William Bentley, D.D.* (4 vols., Salem, Mass., 1905-14), II, 354. For the spread of the caucus system as far as the ward level, see, e.g., William T. Whitney, "The

state down to the county, town, and even ward levels, party members met before each election to select their candidates and issue those addresses which were the forerunners of the modern party platform. Rarely did the legislative caucus interfere in local caucus affairs.[7] The local bodies were autonomous and elected from the bottom up. The caucus system took a federal form, its supporters as jealous of local initiative as the best of Virginia's Old Republicans. At all echelons, private cliques relinquished to the caucuses the power to make nominations in the party's name for the lowliest of local offices. Everywhere the caucus choice became the party choice, and dissident party members could not easily contest a caucus selection or defy caucus policy without taking on the entire party apparatus.

It is difficult to assess with precision how representative the caucuses were. In the day's parlance, there were two sorts: the "grand" caucus or rally pitched to the level of the rank and file, a speech-filled spectacle which usually ratified by acclamation decisions made by the local elite, and the small meetings or "communications" which were the true nominating and policy-making caucuses. What remains something of a mystery is how members of the representative caucuses were selected. In the largest towns such as Boston, Salem, and Newburyport, the Federalist ward caucuses sent up representatives to the town caucus. In the smaller communities, where the well placed

---

Crowninshields of Salem, 1800-1808: A Study in the Politics of Commercial Growth," *Essex Institute Historical Coll.*, XCIV (Jan. 1958), 20-22, 34-35; Bentley, *Diary*, III, 17, 79, 286; [Portland] *Eastern Argus*, Apr. 4, 1804; and *Centinel*, Oct. 25 & 29, 1800, Feb. 11 & Oct. 28, 1801, Feb. 25, 1802, Apr. 2, 1803, Feb. 26 & Mar. 26, 1806, May 13, 1807, Mar. 29, 1809, Mar. 10, 1810, Mar. 6, 1811, May 12, 1812. Local caucuses had, of course, met since the colonial era. On the Boston caucus, see G. B. Warden, "The Caucus and Democracy in Colonial Boston," *New England Quarterly* (hereafter *NEQ*) (forthcoming), which the author graciously allowed me to read in manuscript. On the structure of the Massachusetts Republican Party, see Noble E. Cunningham, Jr., *The Jeffersonian Republicans in Power: Party Operations, 1801-1809* (Chapel Hill, N.C., 1963), pp. 133-42.

[7]See, e.g., the disclaimer in Gore to the Bristol County Committee, Mar 25, 1807, Misc. Colls., MHS.

could more easily exert control, caucuses tended either to be little more than the old cliques in a new guise or, at the other extreme, "grand" caucuses to which everyone was invited to applaud decisions made by the restricted ruling circle. In either case, the ruling elite usually remained in control of the meetings, imposed policy upon them, and won caucus approval of its choices for every post from state representative to hog reeve.[8]

For example, the Salem Federalist caucus in March 1806 named a nine-man committee of the town's most eminent Federalists to select a list of nominations for town and regional offices. With a speed which suggests that the list had been predetermined, the committee returned with nominations and the whole caucus approved them unanimously. The caucus then chose twenty men from each of the town's four wards to distribute votes on election day, four men to challenge illegal voters at the polls, and a three-man committee to examine the town's expenditures and to publish the results.[9]

Considered as a whole, however, the caucus system marked a revolution in state and local politics. It republicanized Federalist Party affairs. Its establishment marked the opening round of an arduous contest to displace the cliques which had monopolized leadership for so long. For the first time, rank-and-file party members could participate to some degree in party decisions and deliberations. And as the public learned to vote, the caucus system became a defense against the illusion that the party could ignore its following. Indeed, from the

---

[8]Bentley, *Diary*, III, 421. An example of a congressional district caucus address is the printed circular letter, Nicholas Tillinghast *et al.* to ?, Nov. 7, 1812, Bdse. Coll., LC.

[9]Printed bdse., *Federal Meeting*, Salem, Mar. 7, 1806, Bdse. Coll., NYPL. See also printed bdse., *Federal Meeting*, Salem, Mar. 6, 1807, Misc. Bdse. Coll., Boston Public Library; untitled bdse., Salem, Mar. 30, 1810, Bdse. Coll., LC; and *Federal Meeting*, Salem, May 12, 1809, Misc. Bdse. Coll., American Antiquarian Society (hereafter AAS). For evidence of the old Federalist controlling group in Salem, see William Prescott to Nathan Read, Jan. 25, 1802, Read MSS, Essex Institute.

early 1800's on, no American party was ever again immune from public sentiment expressed through the local caucuses.

II

FOR ABOUT FOUR YEARS after the advent of caucus politics, there were few additional innovations in the Commonwealth's political life. By solving the crisis in leadership, the caucus system neutralized rather than intensified the forces of change. And the Republicans' failure to offer a sustained and statewide challenge to the Federalist ascendancy discouraged still further any interest in altering the party's way of doing things. Almost everywhere, Federalist majorities were large, the Republicans confused and leaderless, and the imbalance between the two parties consequently undisturbed. Only here and there, as in Boston where the two parties were evenly matched, were Federalists impelled to go beyond the polite and informal practices of the past, and even then modifications in the style and operations of Federalist politics were few. Control of party affairs remained diffused, campaigns low keyed, and the voters apathetic. What developments there were had the earmarks of sudden improvisation, or else they were gradual and unheralded and their implications not fully realized.

Among these developments, a significant but little-noticed one was the entrance into the party's leadership ranks of the new generation of political captains. This substitution of new leaders for old was neither abrupt, conscious, nor unambiguous. Rather it was cumulative, largely the result of the natural process of generational change, and everywhere full of complication. Young Federalists were more the natural legatees of change than its instigators, its exploiters rather than its authors.

The caucus always controlled the manner and pace of political evolution, and the caucus remained in the hands of the older men. The more youthful leaders were given new and central responsibilities, but no young "Turks" suddenly took over and revolutionized the party. Too much emphasis can be placed upon the likes of Cabot and Higginson, living comfortably as gentlemen, out of touch, as they liked to assert, with the world. But in fact, their opinions continued to be sought, their weight felt. Many gentlemen of the older generation, themselves reluctant to undertake new responsibilities, nevertheless, as I have already suggested, lent support to new-style efforts and helped elevate into positions of responsibility a young and more contemporary breed.[1] And if the caucus representation be taken as a cross section of Federalist Massachusetts, it is then clear that Federalists both young and old gradually realized that circumstances demanded changes in the old ways of politics. New-school Federalism was a state of mind as much as a concomitant of youth.

Yet, until 1804, party leadership remained unconsolidated and in a state of flux. Largely because Massachusetts Federalism was flourishing, the younger men were prevented from coming into their own much before Jefferson's re-election. The Republicans made only minor gains in the Commonwealth before 1802; and when internal schism and indecision sharply reduced the Republican vote in the spring of 1803, most Federalists believed that further changes in party structure and further concessions to popular politics were unnecessary.[2]

Little did they count on the Republicans. Chastened by defeat, Jefferson's followers set in motion a root-and-branch reform of their own party and made extraordinary efforts to reunify their support and recoup their losses. Coming on top of the increasingly popular Louisiana Purchase of 1803, these developments enabled the Republicans to make a stunning recovery in the spring elections of 1804. Thoughtful Federalists now saw that the party was in great difficulty. The Republicans had gotten the jump on them, the Federalist rank and file were as apathetic as ever, and, moreover, Boston Federalism

---

[1] Thomas Handasyd Perkins to Noah Webster, May 18, 1811, Webster MSS, NYPL; and Sedgwick to Theodore Sedgwick, Jr., Mar. 17, 1804, Sedgwick MSS, MHS.

[2] Goodman, *Democratic-Republicans of Mass.*, p. 129.

was on the verge of rupture. Prospects for the fall presidential election were not good.

Under these conditions, the party's spring caucus proved crucial. Like its predecessor in 1800, its chief task was to settle on a method of choosing presidential electors. The Republicans repeated their call for district tickets, hoping to capture some scattered electoral votes in the state. The Federalist caucus, heedless of the changed political mood of the nation, confidently rejected this alternative on the assumption that both legislative election and a general ticket would guarantee nineteen Federalist votes. Recalling the chorus of criticism which had greeted the legislative election in 1800, acting in the belief that they were making a concession to popular feeling, and responding to pressures, noted Cabot, "chiefly from the western parts of the State," caucus members decided on the general ticket.[3]

Once again, a change in election procedures, this time in a presidential contest, was the catalyst of new structural developments. Having made the decision for a general ticket, the caucus could not long overlook its implications for party administration. Some sort of centralized administrative structure would no doubt have recommended itself sooner or later, if only because the caucus was a clumsy instrument for overseeing electoral details, and because centralization coincided with Federalist ideals of elite leadership. But by forcing the party to mobilize for a statewide presidential campaign, the general ticket system, more than anything else, necessitated the formation of centralized electoral machinery and hastened the reconstruction of party leadership. And thus, what the popular election of the governor on a statewide basis had failed to gain, the popular election of presidential electors now achieved.

The major energies for the new party system originated in two groups which were also its chief beneficiaries: the younger men throughout the state whose political careers were

---

[3]Cabot to Pickering, Nov. 30, 1804, Henry Cabot Lodge, *Life and Letters of George Cabot* (Boston, 1878), p. 349; and *Resolves of the General Court of Massachusetts*, June 15, 1804.

in the balance and who were more willing than their elders to apply democratic techniques in the defense of elitism, and eastern Federalists, many of them of the old school, seeking to reduce the recent outlander influence in the party caucus. The younger men came into their own more by default than by design. Many Federalists had complained after their reverses in the spring of 1804 that the legislative caucus lacked an organization to apply the policies which it developed and that it ignored the problems of coordination with the local caucuses. The summer caucus of 1804 moved to rectify these weaknesses by naming some of its leading members to take command of election activities in each county. The caucus also designated a special committee, the first of its kind, to watch over and coordinate the actions of these men.[4] Within a year, what was originally intended as an ad hoc electoral committee became a standing Central Committee in command of a permanent and highly centralized committee system, descending downward through county to town and ward committees.

The caucus intended the Central Committee, like others subordinate to it, to supplement, not to supplant, it. Yet from the beginning, because of its permanence and its crucial role as electoral manager of the whole party, the Central Committee came to overshadow the other ad hoc committees. The responsibility of the caucus ended at the close of each legislative session. Here the Central Committee's responsibility began, and here lay the roots of its influence. Since the General Court was rarely in session more than three months out of twelve, the Central Committee directed the whole party without limitation for about nine months, assumed many of the day-to-day func-

---

[4] I have deduced this order of events from a mass of circumstantial evidence for the years 1804 and 1805, of which the most significant single item is the unsigned circular letter of September 1804 in the Misc. Bdse. Coll., AAS. An undated copy of this letter is in the Bdse. Coll., LC; it was also printed in the [Boston] *Independent Chronicle* (hereafter *Chronicle*), Sept. 20, 1804. I discuss it in more detail below. For further evidence that the caucus elected the Central Committee, see *Centinel*, Apr. 21, 1810, and Otis *et al.* to Samuel Crocker *et al.*, Feb. 19, 1811, Morison, *Otis*, I, 292 (facing).

tions of party leadership, and seemed at times to eclipse the caucus itself.

In view of the obvious deficiencies in caucus administration, the striking growth in the size of the electorate, and the rise in General Court representation, it is difficult to see how the further centralization of party affairs could have been avoided. Rather than being the product of some revolutionary movement within the party, the new committee structure was a logical outgrowth of a party reform movement in evidence as early as 1797. The new reform continued the broadening of participation in party affairs, gave a greater voice to local community leaders, yet, paradoxically, quickened the pace of centralization already in evidence within the caucus. Equally important, party centralization also restored effective power to the eastern Federalists after a period of irresolution in party control.

To run the party efficiently, party leaders had to be available to each other at all times; and therefore the caucus saw to it from the start that all Central Committeemen were Bostonians, long-time friends and associates in business, politics, and society in the state capital. In common with the old-school clique which had run the party before 1800, the Central Committee—which first numbered five and then finally seven men—was in effect never adjourned; it could convene at a few hours' notice in some Boston meeting place. Committee membership was not limited to the General Court, but so rigid was the residence rule that major party figures in the legislature were excluded from the Committee if they did not live in the capital. As the Republicans were fond of pointing out, in the Central Committee the Federalists had a Boston Junto equal to the best ever produced in Essex County.[5]

Besides reestablishing and consolidating the authority of eastern Massachusetts in party circles, the creation of the Cen-

---

[5]Conclusions regarding the size and membership of the Central Committee are based upon a whole series of circular letters, committee correspondence, and private letters which are cited throughout this chapter.

tral Committee marked the emergence to power, though by no means the triumph, of the new generation of political leaders. Of the sixteen men who are known to have served on the Committee between 1800 and 1815, only three were born before 1761. Nearly half were not yet fifteen when the nation's independence was won in 1783; most were not yet twenty. In 1805, the average age of the six principal Committee members was thirty-eight.

Six out of the fifteen identified Committee members served four or more annual terms, thus re-creating the stability and continuity of party leadership enjoyed under the old informal system of guidance. The average term of Committee service was slightly over three years and, if we can assume that many served for at least ten years, probably considerably longer. Younger members enjoyed long Committee tenure; older members served more briefly. Otis, Thomas Handasyd Perkins, Daniel Sargent, and William Sullivan, young members of the 1805 Committee, apparently served continuously until at least 1815. Of the three oldest men in the list of fifteen, Christopher Gore was forty-nine when he served the last of his two known terms, Theophilus Parsons and Israel Thorndike fifty-six during their single terms.[6] Yet, while the representation of the older leaders was low, the fact remains that they were admitted into the Committee directorate and that, more

---

[6]The known Committee members and their known terms of service are as follows: Harrison Gray Otis (b. 1765), 1804, 1805, 1809-1814; Daniel Sargent (b. 1764), 1805, 1808-1813; Thomas Handasyd Perkins (b. 1764), 1805, 1808-1811, 1813; John Phillips (b. 1770), 1808-1813; John Welles (b. 1764), 1809-1813; William Sullivan (b. 1774), 1804, 1810-1814; Christopher Gore (b. 1758), 1805-1807; Samuel Dexter (b. 1761), 1805, 1812; James Lloyd, Jr. (b. 1769), 1808, 1809; Francis Dana Channing (b. 1775), 1810; Thomas Danforth (b. 1774), 1807; Charles Jackson (b. 1775), 1805; Theophilus Parsons (b. 1750), 1804; Josiah Quincy (b. 1772), 1805; Israel Thorndike (b. 1755), 1811; and Artemas Ward, Jr. (b. 1762), 1811.

On the composition of the initial Central Committee, see Benjamin Whitwell to Theophilus Parsons, Aug. 13, 1804, to William Sullivan, Aug. 24, 1804, Misc. MSS Colls., Columbia; and Bigelow to Sullivan, Aug. 9, 1804, Misc. MSS Colls., NYPL.

important, it was only at the level of the state Committee that they were in the small minority.

The Central Committee was preeminent not simply because it headed the system, but because its members were leading members of the Boston elite, because they were welcome in the drawing rooms of the wealthy and well placed throughout the Northeast, and because of their strategic position in a wide-ranging circle of endeavors throughout New England. Committee appointments did not bestow prominence; members were selected because of prominence already achieved. In Otis alone, the Committee had legislative leader, bank director, Maine landholder, Boston developer, general factotum to the Massachusetts upper class, lion of Boston society, and beau ideal of the younger Federalist generation. "He is everything of himself to the party," wrote a friend of Otis, "and it is expected he does everything."[7] Rare was the occasion after 1805 that at least one member was not an elected leader of partisan and nonpartisan organizations such as the Washington Benevolent Society, the Masonic lodge, or the state militia, did not serve on special General Court committees, or was not called upon to lead the proceedings of the Boston town meeting.[8]

Additional influence and leverage, of course, accrued to Committee members as a result of their party role. They frequently visited other states to sound out sentiment, make plans,

---

[7]Perkins to Lloyd, Feb. 16, [1809], Misc. MSS Colls., Harvard. A detailed description of Otis's role as party leader and a pioneering study of state political machinery, which additional evidence has led me to amend and enlarge, is in Morison, *Otis*, I, Chap. XVI.

[8]Central Committeemen John Welles and William Sullivan were treasurer and secretary, respectively, of the Washington Benevolent Society of Massachusetts, located in Boston. *A Directory . . . of the Members of the Washington Benevolent Society of Massachusetts* (Boston, 1813). See also *Boston Town Records, 1796-1813* (Boston, 1905), pp. 237, 240, 316-21; *Palladium*, Aug. 11, 1812; and [Lucius Manlius Sargent], *Reminiscences of Samuel Dexter* (Boston, 1857), pp. 80-83. Central Committeemen were often members of select committees of the caucus; cf. untitled caucus meeting record, Feb. 7, 1806, Shaw MSS, BA, and *Centinel*, July 23, 1808.

and coordinate policies. They played an indispensable role in organizing the first two presidential nominating conventions in New York City.[9] Committee members solicited the views of congressmen and proposed courses of action to them.[1] In their managerial capacities, they recommended party policies to the caucus, drew up addresses which went out over the caucus's name, kept watch over the entire committee system, sought patronage for the party's electioneering newspapers, served as party whip during legislative sessions, and raised money.[2]

To assist its work, the Committee had a staff of its own. In early 1805, it named as its administrative secretary young

---

[9]For full details on the conventions, see Morison, "The First National Nominating Convention, 1808," 744-63; John S. Murdock, "The First National Nominating Convention," *AHR*, I (July 1896), 680-83; and David Hackett Fischer, *The Revolution of American Conservatism: The Federalist Party in the Era of Jeffersonian Democracy* (New York, 1965), pp. 83-90.

[1]Morison, *Otis*, II, 29-30; draft MSS circular letter in Noah Webster's hand, dtd. May 1, 1811, with a notation that a copy was sent to Cabot and Perkins in Boston, Webster MSS, NYPL; James A. Mason to Otis, July 11, 1808, Otis MSS, MHS; Daniel Webster to William Sullivan, Oct. 17, 1814, Norcross Papers, MHS; Otis to Josiah Quincy, Nov. 29, 1807, Dec. 15, 1808, Edmund Quincy, *Life of Josiah Quincy* (Boston, 1868), pp. 115, 164-65; and Quincy to Otis, Nov. 8, 1811, Nov. 25, 1811, Otis MSS, MHS. John Henry, the notorious double agent, accurately reported the role of the Federalist Central Committee in Boston. See E. A. Cruikshank, *The Political Adventures of John Henry: The Record of an International Imbroglio* (Toronto, 1936), pp. 34, 58; and Douglas Brymmer, *Report of Canadian Archives . . . 1896* (Ottawa, 1897), pp. 42-43.

[2]Perkins to Woodbury Storer, May 7, 1808, Sullivan to Otis, May 3, 1811, Washburn Papers, MHS; *Palladium*, May 13, 1808; John Phillips *et al.* to ?, Apr. 19, 1808, Misc. MSS Colls., AAS; Benjamin Whitman to Samuel Dexter *et al.*, Aug. 1, 1812, Henry Dwight Sedgwick to William Sullivan, Apr. 26 & 29, 1811, Misc. MSS Colls., Columbia; two MSS caucus resolutions, dtd. Feb. 1806 and Feb. 12, 1806, MSS bill rendered by John Park, publisher of the [Boston] *Repertory*, to the Central Committee, Mar. 10, 1807, and "Subjects for the Consideration of the Central Committee," [1806?], Shaw MSS, BA; and Gore to Bristol County Committee, Mar. 25, 1807, Misc. MSS Colls., MHS. The Federalists, it should be added, did not publicly confess the existence of the Central Committee nor publish its circular letters in newspapers until 1810. *Centinel*, Mar. 31 & Apr. 21, 1810, and *Palladium*, Apr. 24, 1810.

VI: *The Genesis of Party Organization*

William Smith Shaw, John Adams's nephew and a valuable link to the independent-minded Adams wing of the party. For about two years, until he was lured away by the life of letters and put off by the machine's dalliance with democracy, Shaw was an invaluable aid, keeping records, distributing party literature, and accounting for the funds which began to flow through Boston headquarters.[3]

The Central Committee did not, however, achieve its full measure of organization and influence for some years. The first Committee of 1804 was a makeshift arrangement. Its membership mixed, its mandate uncertain, fearful of stirring up too much old-guard resistance, it moved cautiously, seeking on the one hand to bring some system to party affairs and on the other to assure the sponsoring caucus of its respect for party traditions. Its early efforts were clearly adapted to the tone of polite exhortation and designed to test the workability of the existing organization.

In early August 1804, for example, the Committee drew up and distributed a pamphlet to county leaders for circulation throughout the state.[4] The reaction to this first effort, though encouraging, revealed, as Otis expected, how deep was party complacency. Young Federalist Timothy Bigelow, for instance, still trusting in the natural correctness of public opinion, was satisfied that the pamphlet alone would call forth the dormant patriotism of New England. Otis's reaction, on the contrary, was to urge that the organization be further refined, extended, and financed.[5] Out of such impulses came the first official party circular, inspired and penned by a Central Committee member but printed and distributed by county leaders in deference to

---

[3]Joseph B. Felt, *Memorials of William Smith Shaw* (Boston, 1852), pp. 180 ff., 240. A complete record of Shaw's role is to be found in the William Smith Shaw MSS, BA.

[4]Benjamin Whitwell to Sullivan, Aug. 24, 1804, Misc. MSS Colls., Columbia; Timothy Bigelow to Sullivan, Aug. 9, 1804, Misc. MSS Colls., NYPL; and *Chronicle*, Oct. 4, 1804.

[5]Bigelow to Sullivan, Aug. 9, 1804, Misc. MSS Colls., NYPL; and Otis to Woodbury Storer, Aug. 29, 1804, Misc. Bound Colls., MHS.

local sensibilities and out of a desire to spread evenly the initial costs of the new system.

The only extant copy of this circular was printed in Worcester County for distribution by county leaders to leading Federalists in each town. The summer caucus, it reported, "a large number of respectable characters, from all parts of the Commonwealth," had consulted together out of a conviction that "systematic exertions" had been made to oust the Federalist state administration and to "introduce measures destructive of the habits, institutions, and independence of the citizens." The caucus had decided that the best way to counteract these efforts, incited by "venal presses," was through "the diffusion of correct information among the people." To this end, "good citizens" had been chosen to correspond with each other, to distribute literature, and "to suggest such expedients as you may deem useful to be adopted" in preserving for the New England character "a just weight and influence in all public concerns." Such measures, noted the circular, were meant to keep Massachusetts from "abandoning the men and measures whose wisdom has been tested by a long and uniform course of public prosperity, for new men, and new measures." Finally, explained its authors, recipients were to do their utmost to elect the nineteen electors and two congressional candidates, one for each district in Worcester, who had been agreed upon at the caucus. Their names were listed at the end.

Noteworthy as this first party directive was, it illustrates how far even the young party managers were from comprehending the rapidly changing character of state politics. In words reminiscent of their private correspondence, they reemphasized the age-old aims of Federalist policy. They said nothing about new measures or a new party structure: "The diffusion of correct information" was the best of old-style methods.

Thus Massachusetts Federalists remained in 1804 at a serious disadvantage to the Republicans who had strengthened their committee structure and who, through direct appeals to the average elector, were revolutionizing the conduct of campaigns. For an all-out program to woo the common voter, management by broadside was no substitute, particularly when it began so late. To the surprise and shock of the Federalists, Jefferson's party carried the general ticket and took the state in November. In the space of little more than six months, and in spite of important new efforts, the Federalist tide had ebbed away.[6]

This unexpected setback sealed the fate of the old politics and helped consolidate the new. Changes in election rules had called the new organization into existence just six months before. Now defeat and the superiority of the Republican system brought it to maturity. "A degree of organization has been effected in the opposite party," wrote Josiah Quincy, "unexampled, I suspect, in this country, since the revolutionary committees of 1775." Clearly, the Federalists had something to learn from their opponents. The party's humiliation might after all "give such a spring to our exertions as the security resulting from our interrupted majorities made necessary."

To others as well, the task ahead was obvious: organize for victory. "It has been found," remarked Thomas Boylston Adams, "that *organization* is your only weapon of defense against organization." "Everywhere in New England democracy is making rapid strides towards the accomplishment of its object," party elder Theodore Sedgwick wrote darkly. "On the other hand the federalists are not only torpid & indifferent but their principles of defense are of a nature to be eternally attended with disgrace and defeat. It is merely a system of

---

[6]There was much recrimination regarding the adoption of the general ticket scheme. Otis to Rutledge, Dec. 2, 1804, Rutledge MSS, UNC; Benjamin Russell to Charles Prentiss, Apr. 16, 1805, Prentiss MSS, AAS; Jedidiah Morse to his father, Nov. 10, 1804, Morse MSS, Yale; John Adams to John Quincy Adams, Nov. 9 & 16, 1804, Quincy to John Quincy Adams, Nov. 23, 1804, Dec. 15, 1804, and John Quincy Adams to Thomas Boylston Adams, Nov. 26, 1804, reel 403, Adams microfilm; John Quincy Adams to Quincy, Dec. 4, 1804, Edmund Quincy, *Josiah Quincy*, pp. 63-65; and Cabot to Pickering, Nov. 30, 1804, Lodge, *Cabot*, p. 349. In 1808, the Federalists, then in control of the General Court, not surprisingly committed the legislature once again to elect the nineteen electors itself.

defense against the attacks of their adversaries." "Despite the desirability of preserving the consistency & dignity of our party," wrote Otis later, reflecting on his own actions, "it is of more *consequence* to *save the country*."[7] In this spirit, the winter caucus of 1805 voted plans for a thorough reorganization of party structure and operations. Caucus members strengthened the 1804 Committee, clarified its mandate, and authorized it to create and direct a hierarchical system of local party committees throughout the state. Within a few weeks, the committee system was in full operation.

It is remarkable how easily the Committee was able to stamp its will upon Federalists everywhere in Massachusetts. Rather than resenting the assertion of authority from the top, most local leaders, including those in the western towns, welcomed the new dispensation as a sign, however belated, that Boston and the party as a whole had at last recognized the straitened condition of party affairs in the hinterlands.[8] Moreover, any fears which they initially may have had about the Committee were blunted by its close links to the representative caucus which, the Committee itself was always careful to explain, had commissioned it to lead the party.[9]

[7]Quincy to John Quincy Adams, Nov. 23, 1804, John Adams to John Quincy Adams, Nov. 9, 1804, Thomas Boylston Adams to John Quincy Adams, Apr. 9, 1806, reel 403, Adams microfilm; Otis to Sedgwick, June 23, 1808, Welch, *Sedgwick*, p. 245*n*; and Sedgwick to Theodore Sedgwick, Jr., May 17, 1804, Sedgwick MSS, MHS.

[8]For an indication of pressure brought to bear on Boston Federalists to take the lead in party reorganization, see Benjamin Whitwell to Theophilus Parsons, Aug. 13, 1804, Misc. MSS Colls., Columbia; and Cyrus Hamlin to Samuel Dexter, Dec. 10, 1804, Shaw MSS, BA.

[9]The degree to which the caucus could in fact enforce its will on the Central Committee is revealed by its action in rebuking John Quincy Adams in 1808 for his support of the Embargo, electing a successor, and then, by issuing unacceptable instructions to Adams, forcing his early resignation—all of which left Central Committee Chairman Otis "mortified" but powerless to do anything. Gore to Rufus King, June 4, [1808], King MSS, NYHS; John Quincy Adams to the Massachusetts Senate and House, June 8, 1808, to Orchard Cook, Aug. ? 1808, to William Branch Giles, Nov. 15, 1808, reel 135, Adams microfilm; John Quincy Adams, *Diary*, entries for June 7, 27, & 28, 1808, reel 30, Adams microfilm; Morison, *Otis*, I, 328-29; Benja-

Yet just because the Committee's place was rapidly accepted does not mean that all Federalists were waiting for some signal from the top before taking the initiative themselves. There already existed a number of locally inspired party organizations over which the Central Committee had to assert its supremacy. Particularly in the populous eastern towns, local committees had long antedated the formal committee structure, and in the smaller towns lonely Federalists like Henry Van Schaack had long awaited the day that they should be integrated into a larger system. In addition to the early nominating caucuses in Boston, Salem, and Newburyport, for instance, committees of correspondence, like that established in 1804 by Kennebec County Federalists in Maine, sought locally to coordinate party activities.[1]

At about the same time, problems connected with local party discipline and election procedures called into being many town committees. A successful campaign required that the voters be fully apprised of the names and affiliations of each candidate. This could become a staggering task when the party's ticket contained many names and offices, as it did, for example, during the presidential campaign of 1804, when nineteen names had to be balloted for. The difficulties of the long ballot were compounded, especially in the large towns, by short polling hours and an expanding electorate. Sometimes, not everyone could be accommodated at the polls; or, as often happened, supporters of one party might monopolize the polling place and prevent their opponents from depositing their ballots. For these reasons, both parties took to printing and

---

min Whitman to Samuel Dexter *et al.*, Aug. 1, 1812, Misc. MSS Colls., Columbia; and George Wallingford to Cyrus King, Feb. 1, 1814, Cyrus King MSS, Columbia. For an account of John Quincy Adams's treatment in 1808, with which I disagree in part, see Worthington C. Ford, "The Recall of John Quincy Adams in 1808," *Massachusetts Historical Society Proceedings*, XLV (Jan. 1912), 354-75.

[1]Bentley, *Diary*, II, 354; III, 17; *Centinel*, Oct. 25 & 29, 1800, Mar. 25, 1801; Whitney, "Crowninshields of Salem," pp. 20-22; *Chronicle*, Oct. 4, 1804; Benjamin Whitwell to Parsons, Aug. 13, 1804, Misc. MSS Colls., Columbia; and Whitwell to Otis, July 31, 1804, Otis MSS, MHS.

distributing tickets of their candidates, which could be deposited with the vote takers on election day. To distribute the lists, both Federalists and Republicans appointed vote-distributing committees, which handed out party tickets at each residence before election day. By 1803, Salem and Boston Federalists had organized ward committees of thirty men each to do the task.[2]

When a year later the state court ruled that each ballot had to be handwritten, the problem was immeasurably magnified. In consequence, each party turned to employing local youths, a source of both cheap labor and potential voters, to prepare handwritten tickets for distribution. These pools of young party workers formed the nucleus of what rapidly became permanent organizations of Young Federalists and Young Republicans who, besides writing up tickets, performed ceremonial functions, provided forums for party speechmakers, and became just one more source from which future party leaders were recruited.[3]

None of these early committees—whether Central Committee or otherwise—were meant to be permanent. In the main, their purposes were limited by the old politics; at first they sought only more effective discipline and unity. They possessed little formal structure. Yet, they offered valuable experience to the emerging party leaders and provided a cadre of local managers to whom the Central Committee could turn when in 1805 it set up a full-fledged party system. In fact, the Committee minimized resistance to its initiatives by turning to these practiced local leaders for support. In the end, then, although the mature Federalist organization in Massachusetts was operated from the top, it grew neither from the top down nor from the bottom up. The party apparatus developed and reached maturity at all levels at about the same time.

---

[2]*Centinel*, May 3, 1801, Apr. 1, 1802, Apr. 2, 1803.

[3]Goodman, *Democratic-Republicans of Mass.*, p. 141; William King *et al.* to John Quincy Adams, July 3, 1807, reel 405, Adams microfilm; "Address of the Young [Federal Republican] Men of Boston, May 1807," Strong MSS, Forbes Lib., Northampton; *Palladium*, Oct. 12, 1804, July 4, 1806, July 7, 1807, July 16, 1811; and *Centinel*, Oct. 6, 1804, July 9, 1806, Mar. 16, 1807.

III

THE CAUCUS AND COMMITTEE SYSTEMS were meant to be distinct: to parallel one another, to work together, but not to merge. From the outset, the committees were considered to be the administrative and electoral arms of the caucuses. Reduced to essentials, their function was to get out the vote. The caucus made policy, and the committees carried it out. Caucuses nominated candidates, committees got them elected.

The role envisaged for the committees is most vividly revealed in the circular letters frequently drawn up by the Central Committee. The second of these, with minor changes and additions, served as the party's organizational guide for over two decades. Drawn up by the Committee "at the request of a large meeting of Federalists, composed of Members of both Houses of the Legislature and others," the circular went out to all county committee chairmen after the decisive winter caucus of 1805. It indicated that the committeemen had been appointed by the caucus upon the recommendation of the county delegations to the House, and it called upon the chairmen to convene early meetings of the full county committees. It directed county committeemen to designate three-man town committees which, in their own turn, were to divide each town into districts, to secure a list of the towns' voters, and to draw up a roster of "all doubtful characters . . . that the men may be known who may be influenced, by correct information." Moreover, each district was to have its own subcommittee.

Members of these district committees were expected to do the party's work: they, rather than the town committeemen, were told to get out the vote, and they were expected to make special efforts to win the support of the inactive, undecided, or independent voters by "disseminating such information, as they may possess, and also such as may, from time to time, be sent to them . . . and in general to take all fair means to convince them of the justice of the federal cause. This is highly important," noted the circular's authors, "as it is only from the class of honest and mistaken men, that we can hope to increase the numbers of Federalists." In the interests of control and coordination, committee membership lists were to be passed up the line to county committeemen. Strict secrecy was enjoined upon the whole machine in a vain attempt to camouflage its existence, and town committees were directed to conceal their connection with the county committees "in order that the exertions in every Town may appear to originate in said Town. This is thought to be necessary, in order to prevent jealousies and unfounded prejudices."

The Central Committee went out of its way to foster the view that its function was to succor the party rather than to direct it. County committeemen were told to request pamphlets and papers from Boston headquarters and were assured that the Committee stood ready to assume the cost of expenses not defrayed by local fund-raising drives. The Committee even went so far as to send along a draft circular which the county committees were urged to print and to send to town committee appointees. In such a manner, the Committee hoped to deflect fears about its power.[4]

The organization which this first detailed administrative circular propelled into being had its intended effect. The Federalist vote leaped sharply in the spring elections of 1805, just in time to avert defeat in the governor's contest and to retain control of the state House of Representatives in the face of a mounting Republican campaign to capture it. After this show-

---

[4]Unsigned printed circular letter to Daniel Waldo, Jr., Feb. 25, 1805, Misc. Bdse. Coll., AAS. The draft circular for distribution by county to town committees eventuated in circulars which repeated almost word for word the Central Committee circular of Feb. 25. For the four-man Barnstable County Committee's directive to the Yarmouth town committee, see Ebenezer Bacon *et al.* to Silvanus Crowell, [1805], Bdse. Coll., MHS. This circular, incorrectly dated 1807 in the MHS collections, was also printed in the *Chronicle*, Mar. 28, 1805. The Hampshire Committee's directive is printed in the *Centinel*, Mar. 30, 1805, the Cumberland County Committee's in the *Eastern Argus*, Mar. 21, 1806.

ing, there was to be no turning back. Rather than listening to counsels of caution, the caucus continued to refine the committee system to make it more efficient and responsive to local option. Caucus members enlarged the already hard-pressed Central and county committees, persuaded local committees to call more frequent meetings of the rank and file, charged them all with new tasks, permitted inferior committees to elect their own chairmen, and generally gave more autonomy to the local organizations.[5] Within two years, the system had reached full growth, a testimony to the rapid adaptation of the political system to the federalization and democratization of American life and government.

Beneath the Central Committee, the county committees directed regional affairs. Their membership differed with the extent and population of their counties and fell somewhere between five and nine. Their principal task was to carry out Central Committee directives, oversee the town committees below, distribute party literature, and organize county caucuses and conventions.[6] Their members, most of them locally prominent, were chosen upon recommendation of county delegations in the caucus. Their membership was reasonably stable and geographically representative and included a much larger proportion of older Federalists than the Central Committee.

For example, old-schoolmen Fisher Ames and Stephen

---

[5]See, e.g., Josiah Dwight to Otis, Nov. 18, 1805, Morison, *Otis*, I, 312-13; Cyrus Hamlin, Secretary of the Oxford County Committee, to Samuel Dexter, Dec. 10, 1805, Shaw MSS, BA; and Dexter *et al.* to Dwight Foster, June 13, 1805, Misc. Bdse. Coll., AAS. Other circulars from the Central Committee include: Otis *et al.* to Bigelow, Feb. 9, 1810, Misc. Colls., MHS; Otis *et al.* to John Holmes, Mar. 8, 1809, James Lloyd, Jr., *et al.* to Holmes, Apr. 14, 1809, Perkins *et al.* to Holmes, Apr. 19, 1811, John Holmes MSS, NYPL; Otis *et al.* to Ebenezer Childs, Apr. 13, 1810, Misc. Bdse. Colls., NYHS; and ? to Daniel Waldo, Jr., Feb. 1806, Waldo MSS, AAS; ? to Oliver Fiske *et al.*, Mar. 1, 1808, Otis *et al.* to Thomas W. Ward, Feb. 22, 1812, Otis *et al.* to Oliver Fiske, Feb. 26, 1813, Misc. Bdse Coll., AAS.

[6]Nathaniel Wells *et al.* to Cyrus King, Jan. 12, 1809, Cyrus King MSS, Columbia; and Otis to John Holmes, Apr. 15, 1811, Holmes MSS, NYPL.

Codman, both born in 1758, were the initial chairmen of the Norfolk and Suffolk County (Boston) committees.[7] At one end of the spectrum of county committees was the elderly four-man York County Committee of 1809, two members of which were born in the early 1740's and a third in 1761. At the other end was the youthful four-man Hampshire County directorate of 1815, one of whose members was born in 1767 and the rest in the 1770's. Occupying a middle position in the age distribution of their memberships were the Essex and Worcester committees. The ages of the former's 1812 members ranged from sixty-one to thirty-seven, the latter's 1805 members from sixty-two to thirty-nine.

Town committee membership was similarly spread among the two political generations. The 1811 committee of the Plymouth County town of Bridgewater was composed of six men whose ages ranged from sixty-two to forty-one. Two members of Amherst's four-man 1815 committee were born in the 1750's, a third in the 1770's. Only one member of Shrewsbury's 1810 committee was born later than 1760. And finally, the nearby town of Brookfield was the home of a Federalist ruling group most of whose members in 1812 were born in the 1760's. There was, in other words, no pattern to be found in the generational distribution of regional and town committee membership. When it came to arousing the local community to political action, older Federalists were no less disposed to enter the political lists than their younger colleagues.[8]

---

[7]Ames's and Codman's chairmanships are noted in "Copy of a Letter to Stephen Codman, Chairman &c, 25 Mar 1807" and "The C[entral] C[ommittee]" to Ames, Apr. 1805, Shaw MSS, BA. For another analysis of the committee structure, which, however, emphasizes the state rather than the local committees, see Fischer, *Revolution of American Conservatism*, Chaps. III and IV.

[8]I have gathered evidence of committee membership from the following: Nathaniel Wells *et al.* to Cyrus King, Jan. 12, 1809, Cyrus King MSS, Columbia; Eli P. Ashmun *et al.* to Ebenezer Mattoon *et al.*, Mar. 10, 1815, Misc. Bdse. Coll., NYPL; Jacob Ashton *et al.* to ?, Mar. 25, 1812, Misc. Bdse. Coll., MHS; Samuel Dexter *et al.* to Daniel Waldo, Jr., Feb. 25, 1805, Waldo to Thomas W. Ward, Mar. 1, 1810,

VI: *The Genesis of Party Organization*

Theoretically, county committees were the pivots of the organization, interpreting Central Committee policies to the towns and collating local sentiment for the Central Committee.[9] But, in reality, the county committees were victims of a governmental structure which reduced the county jurisdiction to minor importance. Compared to the towns, counties were unimportant. There were few elected county officials, and, of these, only state senators were annually elected. Some counties served bienially as congressional or presidential electoral districts, but just as often they were cut in half or grouped together for these purposes. Some appointive county posts, such as justices of the peace and county attorneys, were patronage positions, but there is little evidence that under a Federalist governor the county committees played a significant role in the distribution of political favors. What functions besides town committee oversight the county committees possessed were few and peripheral.

Considered in isolation, the town committees also appear relatively insignificant. Yet the town was the Commonwealth's primary political unit, and some of the towns were more powerful than whole counties. Boston, Salem, and Newburyport together made up one tenth of the state's population in 1800. In many particulars, the town was the legal agent of the state government. In electoral matters, town selectmen administered the drawing-up of accurate voting lists, oversaw

Joseph Allen *et al.* to Ward, Mar. 9, 1812, to Dwight Foster *et al.*, Oct. 23, 1812, Misc. Bdse. Colls., AAS; and Perkins to Sullivan, May 10, 1811, Misc. MSS Colls., NYPL. I have gathered members' ages from a number of sources, including the biographical file of the members of the Massachusetts General Court, Mass. State Library, Boston, and Andrew H. Ward, *History of the Town of Shrewsbury* (Boston, 1847).

[9]See, e.g., Henry Dwight Sedgwick to Sullivan, Apr. 26 & 29, 1811, Misc. MSS Colls., Columbia. County committee circulars include Jacob Ashton *et al.* to ?, Mar. 25, 1812, Misc. Bdse. Coll., MHS; Daniel Waldo, Jr., *et al.* to Thomas W. Ward, Mar. 1, 1810, Ward MSS, AAS; and Joseph Allen *et al.* to Dwight Foster *et al.*, Oct. 23, 1812, to ?, Mar. 8, 1813, William Orne *et al.* to ?, Mar. 24, 1813, Misc. Bdse. Coll., AAS.

the balloting, and applied voting and residency requirements for the state.

The relationship between state and town committees reflected the direct line between state and town governments. Central committeemen never hesitated to bypass county committees in the interest of efficiency, especially since some of the town committees outweighed most county committees.[1] The most powerful was certainly the Suffolk County Central Committee in Boston. Close behind came the Salem and Newburyport committees. The Boston committee's position was so critical not only because the capital was a Federalist stronghold and had the largest single bloc of votes, but also because it sent the largest delegation of representatives to the General Court. The size of the vote there, as well as the town's willingness to send a full slate of representatives, often made the difference between a Federalist majority and minority in the General Court and between victory and defeat in gubernatorial elections.

Like most of the committees in the large towns, the Boston committee was in charge of twelve inferior ward committees. As in Salem, the ward caucuses chose the ward committees, a rare instance of local initiative within the committee hierarchy. Approximately two weeks before each election, the Suffolk Committee convened a "primary caucus" composed of committee members, Boston ward committeemen, and select outsiders, to nominate candidates for local, state, and congressional offices. Then, on the Sunday before election day, a "general caucus" of all Federalists in the county met in Faneuil Hall. The general caucus, like similar gatherings elsewhere, was no more than a party rally, called to ratify nominations already agreed upon in the primary caucus and to drum up the enthusiasm of the ordinary voter. But expressed through such large meetings, local sentiment might exercise a powerful

---

[1]Perkins to Sullivan, May 10, 1811, Misc. MSS Colls., NYPL. For an unflattering analysis of the actions of town officials in electoral and other affairs, see David Syrett, "Town-Meeting Politics in Massachusetts, 1776-1786," *WMQ*, 3rd Ser., XXI (July 1964), 352-66.

influence upon local committees and the Central Committee itself.[2]

Because of the multitude of offices to be filled by election in Massachusetts and because of the continuity of the town caucus which, unlike the county caucus, could easily assemble the Federalist townspeople, town caucuses and committees worked in close harmony. Here, as nowhere else in the Federalist system, public sentiment was transmitted immediately from the rank and file into the committee hierarchy. In many cases, town committeemen were members of the town caucus.[3] What this meant was that the Central Committee was exposed to shifts in public opinion not only from the caucus above but, through the intermediation of the county committees, from the town committees below.

When functioning at its best, the committee system was a well-drilled electoral machine turning out as many Federalist votes as possible. All energies concentrated on achieving maximum Federalist voter participation. "As we value our liberties," declared the Salem town committee, "it behoves us to see that every qualified voter in our town gives in his vote." Circular after circular brought home the point that "your increased exertions may possibly procure one additional vote; and that single vote may save the Commonwealth." "You must embolden the confident, awaken the inert, encourage the desponding, *conciliate the doubtful,* and *support the feeble,*" was a common admonition of party literature.[4]

---

[2]Morison, *Otis*, I, 293-94, and, e.g., Stephen Codman to John Quincy Adams, Apr. 4, 1807, reel 405, Adams microfilm; *Centinel*, May 13, 1801, Apr. 3 & 7, 1802, May 5 & Nov. 3, 1804, Nov. 5, 1808; and *Palladium*, Apr. 3 & May 10, 1807, Mar. 10 & 25, Apr. 2 & 5, 1808.

[3]For the overlapping membership of town caucuses and town committees, see, e.g., the example of Salem in Jacob Ashton *et al.* to ?, Mar. 25, 1812, Misc. Bdse. Coll., MHS; "Circular letter from the Committee of Arrangements of Salem for the April election 1813," *Federal Proceedings in Salem*, dtd. Mar. 30, 1810, and *Federal Meeting*, dtd. May 12, 1809, Misc. Bdse. Colls., AAS; and untitled bdse., Salem, Mar. 25, 1808, Bdse. Coll., LC.

[4]William Orne *et al.* to ?, Mar. 24, 1813, Joseph Allen *et al.* to Thomas W. Ward, Mar. 23, 1813, Misc. Bdse. Coll., AAS; and Perkins *et al.* to John Holmes, Apr. 19, 1811, Holmes MSS, NYPL.

Surviving voter lists show how committee members tallied up firm and doubtful Federalists and unregenerate Republicans before each election and then went after the apathetic, the undecided, the absent, and the infirm.[5] Despite Central Committee urgings to adopt only "fair and honourable measures," methods which earlier would have appalled the "better" sort became commonplace. Federalist employers threatened with dismissal those employees who voted Republican.[6] Food and wine were liberally dispensed before polling hours.[7] Federalists attempted illegally to enroll aliens and minors, took property vouchers from men who lived in distant towns, falsified vouchers for some who owned no property at all, and, in desperation, even summarily struck voters from the rolls and resorted to outright bribery.[8] They loaned money to indigents to satisfy voting requirements, and, in order to learn who voted for whom, printed their tickets on special-colored paper.[9] In the maritime towns, they stacked their vote-canvassing committees with shipmasters who exercised their renowned talents for persuasion at sailors' doors and aboard ship.[1] During the 1808 congressional campaign in Beverly, fully one seventh of

[5]Manuscript voter lists, [1806?], Misc. Bound Coll., MHS; [1804?], Sedgwick MSS, MHS. See also bdse. entitled "Ward No. 1, List of Qualified Voters . . . 1810," Misc. Bdse. Coll., MHS, and *Centinel*, Mar. 27, 1802.

[6]Bentley, *Diary*, II, 458, 459; IV, 14-15, 227-28, 504; and Whitney, "Crowninshields of Salem," p. 31. See also Chilton Williamson, *American Suffrage from Property to Democracy, 1760-1860* (Princeton, N.J., 1960), p. 176. Ballots were not sealed.

[7]"Extracts from the Ames Diary," *Dedham Historical Register*, XIII (1902), 114; and Luther S. Cushing *et al.*, *Reports of Controverted Elections in the House of Representatives, of the Commonwealth of Massachusetts, from 1780 to 1852* (Boston, 1853), pp. 55-56.

[8]Bentley, *Diary*, II, 249; IV, 91-92, 162; and Cushing, *Controverted Elections*, pp. 48-49, 90-96. Under a law of 1802, town assessors and selectmen made up and revised the voting lists and, in so doing, often introduced partisan considerations. *Acts and Laws Passed by the General Court of Massachusetts*, 1802, Chap. 16.

[9]*Autobiography of Amos Kendall*, ed. William Stickney (New York, 1949), pp. 78-79; Robinson, *Jeffersonian Democracy in New England*, pp. 72-73; Cushing, *Controverted Elections*, pp. 137-38; and Bentley, *Diary*, III, 359.

[1]Labaree, *Patriots and Partisans*, pp. 130-31.

the town's vote, or one sixth of the Federalist electorate, was honored with appointment to vote-distributing committees, and in 1804 Salem's canvassing committee numbered 193.[2]

The party often laid plans to enter the polling place en masse when it opened, take every seat in the room, then ballot as slowly as possible so that opponents could not get to the ballot box before the polls closed at an arbitrary hour. It was also customary among Federalists to hire carriages for free transportation to the polls and to prepare workers for being called away from their labor if their votes were needed. "Not a single person is left unnoticed, not a single hamlet unexplored," noted one newspaper. "If they are sick they are conveyed to the meeting house almost upon their beds. . . . Property, loaned expressly for the occasion, is put in the hands of indigent brothers." In Boston, a special committee visited the wharves in 1812 and brought up all the qualified voters who could be found. "Carriage loads of seamen and others belonging to Plymouth and Salem," reported one observer, "were sent last night to those towns to vote, and to be brought back immediately to their vessels."[3]

Such chicanery, however, was only a part of Federalist electoral efforts. Federalists relied equally on newspaper and pamphlet propaganda. In an era of high printing costs and poor transportation, newspapers and broadsides were efficient and economical. Carried in bulk into the countryside and passed about from hand to hand, they brought politics into the home.[4] Besides their concern with cost, Federalists had

---

[2]"List of Committee for Distributing votes Novemb 7th 1808," Robert Rantoul MSS, Beverly Hist. Soc.

[3]Bentley, *Diary*, III, 422; IV, 11, 162; Robinson, *Jeffersonian Democracy in New England*, p. 72; Eliza S. M. Quincy, *Memoir of the Life of Eliza S. M. Quincy* (Boston, 1861), pp. 150-51; *Centinel*, May 11, 1805; William Orne *et al.* to ?, Mar. 24, 1813, Misc. Bdse. Colls., AAS; and Whitney, "Crowninshields of Salem," pp. 35-36.

[4]For an early example, see Higginson to Pickering, Mar. 25, 1797, Pickering MSS, MHS, in which Higginson reveals that the Federalists have "scattered" more than 200 copies of a pamphlet in Massachusetts and nearby states. Also Higginson to Pickering, Feb. 13, 1798, *ibid.*

discovered long before 1800 how powerful an influence on public sentiment the brief and vivid published argument could exert. None could ignore the lessons of the *Federalist Papers* and Tom Paine's *Common Sense*. The question now was to modernize their old-school belief that the aloof essay, widely circulated among the common people, could recreate good political sense. A more popular form of propaganda was needed.

The first efforts at newspaper propaganda coincided with the first stirrings of party organization: the crisis of 1800 proved as creative in the field of publishing as in the area of political discipline. Sometime between the spring and autumn elections of that year, a group of Connecticut and Massachusetts old-school Federalists, of whom Fisher Ames was the leader, decided to revive Federalism's flagging spirit with a new newspaper. *The New England Anti-Jacobin*, Cabot reported, it was to be called.[5] What marked this venture from other New England papers of the time was its avowedly partisan purpose. It was to be underwritten by Federalists, edited by a Federalist, filled with Federalism, and "circulated as extremely as possible especially thro New England."[6] When problems of finance and literary patronage, however, eventually led proponents to abandon the scheme for a new paper, they instead took over the old *Massachusetts Mercury*, re-christened it the *Palladium*, and appointed Warren Dutton, a young lawyer just

---

[5]Cabot to Alexander Hamilton, Oct. 11, 1800, Hamilton MSS, LC.

[6]Cabot to Alexander Hamilton, Oct. 11, 1800, Hamilton MSS, LC. See also Ames to Rutledge, July 30, 1801, Rutledge MSS, UNC; Henry Van Schaack to Peter Van Schaack, Mar. 13, 1801, Van Schaack MSS, Columbia; and Ames to Wolcott, Dec. 2, 1802, Wolcott MSS, CHS. One of the chief impulses behind the project was dislike of Benjamin Russell, whom one detractor called a "vain half witted Federalist," who edited the *Centinel*, probably the most heavily subscribed paper in the nation, with a circulation of roughly 4,000. Frank Luther Mott, *American Journalism* (rev. ed., New York, 1950), p. 159; Benjamin Goodhue to Stephen Goodhue, May 26, 1798, Goodhue MSS, Essex Institute; and Ames to ?, Feb. 4, 1797, Ames MSS, Dedham, Mass., Historical Society.

out of Yale, as its new editor. They began publishing in time for the state elections in 1801.[7]

The paper's promoters were divided, however, over the nature of their project. Was the paper to be a vehicle for polite partisan essays which explored the party's national role and provided a rallying point for all the divided factions, as the Connecticut Federalists wanted, or was it to be an appealing electioneering sheet? Ames and the Massachusetts sponsors wanted to make a bold play for the public mind, but they still believed that old-school canons of journalism should be followed. No matter the political stakes, contended Ames, any paper should be "fastidiously polite and well bred. It should whip Jacobins as a gentleman would a chimney-sweeper, at arm's length, and keeping aloof from his soot."[8] This kind of eighteenth-century decorum was not to editor Dutton's taste. He wanted not to correct opinion but to activate it, not to teach but to arouse. As the contents of Dutton's paper began to outstrip Ames's sense of the appropriate, Ames began to divert his patronage to other publications.[9]

The subversion of Ames's early hopes was not due merely to his editor's attitudes. Rather, by 1805 unabashed electioneer-

---

[7]Robert Edson Lee, "Timothy Dwight and the *Boston Palladium*," *NEQ*, XXXV (June 1962), 229-39. I am unable to agree with Lee's argument that Dwight was the prime force behind the *Palladium* scheme. He may have originated the idea of a party paper, but Ames did more than anyone to get it under way.

[8]Jedidiah Morse to Wolcott, Oct. 27 & Dec. 10, 1800, Wolcott MSS, CHS; Timothy Dwight to Morse, Dec. 19, 1800, Misc. MSS Colls., MHS; Ames to Rutledge, Dec. 15, 1800, Jan. 26, 1801, Rutledge MSS, UNC; Ames to Wolcott, Mar. 18, 1801, to Thomas Dwight, Apr. 28, 1801, Ames MSS, Dedham; Ames to Jeremiah Smith, Dec. 14, 1802, to Pickering, Mar. 10, 1806, Ames, *Works*, I, 314, 370; Cabot to Alexander Hamilton, Oct. 11, 1800, Hamilton MSS, LC; and Cabot to Gore, Oct. 11, 1800, Lodge, *Cabot*, p. 292.

[9]Winfred E. A. Bernhard, *Fisher Ames: Federalist and Statesman, 1758-1808* (Chapel Hill, N.C., 1965), p. 339. Many New England Federalists were repelled by the *Palladium*'s tone. Connecticut Federalist John Cotton Smith hoped that "the press of the Palladium can be silenced & its types scattered to the four winds." John Cotton Smith to David Daggett, Mar. 17, 1803, Smith MSS, Yale.

ing and a new hortatory style had everywhere replaced the dignified style of eighteenth-century journalism. Old journals which had been independent became partisan sheets; new ones started their careers in the service of party. In Massachusetts, because of the narrow margin between the two parties between 1805 and 1812, the development of the Federalist electioneering press was more complete and its techniques more refined than the Federalist press in most other states.[1] In addition, the Massachusetts Federalist electioneering papers owed their existence far less to the autonomous efforts of risk-taking editors and publishers than to the party apparatus which underwrote their costs. Their mailing lists were fattened by committee subscriptions, their accounts met by party subvention, their news columns lengthened by partisan squibs, and their libel suits handled by partisan attorneys.[2] As part of the larger effort to get out the vote, the Federalist press had become an adjunct of the party organization.

In addition to the press, the most striking manifestation of the party's interest in propaganda were the conventions and mass meetings which by 1810 had become common features of Federalist politics. Although Federalists had long disparaged large public gatherings as the hallmark of "Jacobinism" and democracy, once the party had embarked upon its new political course the convention idea quickly recommended itself.[3]

---

[1]Fischer, *Revolution of American Conservatism*, Chap. VII.

[2]See, e.g., Benjamin Whitwell to Theophilus Parsons, Aug. 13, 1804, Misc. MSS Colls., Columbia; itemized account of payment due John Park, editor of the *Repertory*, for sending various volumes of his paper into the countryside on behalf of the Central Committee, Mar. 10, 1807, Shaw MSS, BA; and Oliver Fiske *et al.* to Dwight Foster *et al.*, Apr. 14, 1806, Misc. Bdse. Colls., AAS.

[3]See, e.g., the sarcastic attack upon a Republican convention in the *Centinel*, Oct. 27, 1804. Cabot's 1795 reaction to as innocuous an affair as a meeting of merchants expressing support for the Jay Treaty was typical of early old-school attitudes which later changed: "After all," he asked, "where is the boasted advantage of a representative system over the turbulent mobocracy of Athens, if the resort to popular meetings is necessary?" Cabot to Rufus King, Aug. 14, 1805, Lodge, *Cabot*, p. 85.

These public meetings served many purposes. They were forums for propaganda; they were occasions for coordinating regional party efforts; and they conveyed a sense of that broad participation in party affairs which the Federalist public was beginning to demand.

Generally speaking, there were two types of conventions: the delegate meeting and the public rally or mass meeting. Both were more truly representative of regional and local power than the caucus. They were more visible to the public, and in many cases they were elective.[4] Drawing upon the precedent of county protest conventions in the 1780's, county delegate conventions were being convened as early as 1807 to regularize and broaden the nominating procedures. At first, they were representative caucuses called to nominate candidates for state senator and congressman, to debate party issues, and to draw up public addresses. It is difficult to determine just who attended these meetings and how they were chosen, but in 1812 the Northampton town meeting went on record with the election of four delegates to a county convention. County and district committees charged with running the county and congressional elections seem to have called the conventions; town caucuses or committees probably selected the delegates.[5]

---

[4]Historians seem to have been misled by the early Federalist tirades against conventions. Morison denies that Federalist conventions made nominations. Noble Cunningham flatly states that Federalists never held mass meetings or conventions of delegates. Morison, *Otis*, I, 287*n*; and Cunningham, *Jeffersonian-Republicans in Power*, p. 141. See also McCormick, *Second American Party System*, p. 39. But in 1897, Frederick W. Dallinger called attention to Massachusetts delegate conventions which made nominations to district offices as early as 1802. Dallinger, *Nominations for Elective Office in the United States* (New York, 1897), p. 24.

[5]*Proceedings of the Town of Northampton*, dtd. July 1, 1812, Misc. Bdse. Coll., Forbes Lib., Northampton; *Palladium*, Mar. 31, 1807, Mar. 13, 1810; *Centinel*, Mar. 16, 1814; Benjamin Pickman *et al.* to Israel Thorndike, May 13, 1808, Rantoul MSS, Beverly Hist. Soc.; *Essex Resolutions*, dtd. Oct. 6, 1808 (Newburyport, Mass., 1808); printed untitled bdse., Salem, Mar. 25, 1808, Bdse. Coll., LC; Henry Dwight Sedgwick to William Sullivan, Apr. 26, 1811, Misc. MSS Colls.,

For example, in February 1809, delegates from fifty-one towns met in Northampton to settle on county Federalist candidates and issued a stinging rebuke, authored by the county committee, of the administration's embargo policy.[6] When the Worcester County Committee in 1810 sent out a convention call, it did its best to play down its part in the proceedings. The purpose of the meeting, said the Worcester leaders, was to nominate state senators and consider "any other matters that may promote the true interest of our common country. It would ill become us," added the Committee, "to impose upon the County the names of any persons for their choice to that important station."[7] Partly by choice, partly by necessity, sometimes sincerely, sometimes cynically, the Federalists made efforts to consult public sentiment as well as to control it.

Although Massachusetts Federalists never went so far as to meet in a state convention, there was considerable agitation for convening one in the critical summer of war in 1812, and a call was issued. The movement began when the legislative caucus and the state House circularized each town meeting to elect delegates to July county conventions. The county meetings would protest the war and reveal to the administration the breadth of popular opposition against it. But as so often happened, matters quickly got out of hand in the Connecticut River Valley. There in mid-July, representatives chosen by fifty-two town meetings and four town caucuses met as directed in Northampton to memorialize President Madison. The meeting, however, went beyond its directives and, under the leadership of Lewis Strong, the governor's son, chose four delegates from each of the three counties to meet in a state convention.

Columbia; *Bristol County Resolutions*, dtd. Mar. 12, 1812, Bdse. Coll., Rhode Island Historical Society; and *Proceedings of a Convention of Federal Republicans from the South Senatorial District in the County of Worcester, March 11, 1812.*

[6]*An Address to the People of the County of Hampshire* (Northampton, Mass., 1809).

[7]Daniel Waldo, Jr., *et al.* to Thomas W. Ward, Mar. 1, 1810, Ward MSS, AAS. See also *Centinel*, Mar. 16, 1811.

Soon after, Essex, Plymouth, and Worcester Federalist conventions voted to support the state convention idea, and even Suffolk Federalists chose twelve delegates, headed by Otis. But moderate Federalists behind Samuel Dexter, who scathingly attacked the plan in the Boston town meeting, worked successfully to postpone a Suffolk gathering, and successive meetings in the other counties failed to respond to the original Hampshire call.[8] For the time being at least, the state convention was averted. When the scheme was taken up again two years later, it eventuated not in a state meeting but in the interstate Hartford Convention.

These delegate conventions had much of the aspect of the caucuses and committees, whose political management they supplemented. The genuine departure in party style arose with the "grand conventions" or "grand caucuses" which more directly served the propagandizing and vote-getting interests

---

[8]*Palladium*, July 14 & 24, Aug. 1 & 25, 1812; *Centinel*, Aug. 8, 1812; Morison, *Otis*, II, 59-61; Labaree, *Patriots and Partisans*, pp. 183-84; Josiah Gilbert Holland, *History of Western Massachusetts* (2 vols., Springfield, Mass., 1855), I, 323; *Boston Town Records, 1796-1813* (Boston, 1905), p. 325; and Pickering to Lowell, Nov. 7, 1814, Lodge, *Cabot*, pp. 539-40. The call of the caucus is to be found in *Address of the House of Representatives to the People of Mass.*, dtd. June 25, 1812. The state convention recommended itself at this juncture because the state senate was still in Republican hands, making it impossible for the Federalists to put the entire state government on record in opposition to the war. The idea of some sort of public protest was implanted by the Boston town meeting of June 11, 1812, whose address was sent by the Boston Selectmen to the Selectmen in all other towns. *Boston Town Records, 1796-1813*, pp. 316-20; Charles Bulfinch *et al.* to the Selectmen of Waldoborough, June 15, 1812, Bdse. Coll., LC; and Bulfinch *et al.* to the Selectmen of Northampton, Misc. Bdse. Coll., Forbes Lib., Northampton. Documents revealing the progress of the convention scheme include: unsigned circular letter to the Worcester County Committee, [June 1812], Ward MSS, AAS, another copy of which is in Bdse. Coll., LC; *Proceedings of a Convention of Delegates from the Counties of Hampshire, Franklin, and Hampden, Holden at Northampton, the 14th and 15th of July, 1812* (Northampton, Mass., 1812); *An Address to the Citizens of the County of Plymouth* [1812]; *Proceedings of a Convention of Delegates from Eighteen Towns in the County of Cumberland, Holden at Gray, August 31, 1812*; and *Proceedings of A Convention of Delegates from Forty One Towns in the County of Worcester . . .* (1812).

of the party leaders. The party leadership in Boston took a direct hand in organizing these affairs. In 1811, the Central Committee directed its district subcommittees to "immediately notify, or collect, as many citizens as can be easily assembled. . . . At these preparatory meetings, *some popular addresses should be read and distributed,* and the most animating sentiments expressed; a solemn resolution should be then made to support and promote the ensuing election, and to request all persons of like politics to attend.[9] Typical of such gatherings was the "Federal Grand Caucus," a giant election eve rally held in Boston to whip up popular enthusiasm for the party's candidates and to popularize the party line.

It was in periods of crisis, such as the years of Embargo and war, that the mass public rally came into its own. This kind of "caucus," starting out as a delegate convention, climaxed with a gigantic public meeting at which speeches were offered, bonfires lit, fireworks set off, and food served. "Upwards of seven hundred people," reported one source, rallied upon the call of the "Friends of Peace" at a Middlesex County convention in Concord during the summer of 1812, and 900 gathered in Kennebunk to "nominate" Cyrus King for Congress.[1] In that one summer alone, public antiwar rallies were held in every county in Massachusetts proper and Maine and in tens of towns throughout the state. Their function was not to nominate but to arouse and mobilize public opinion behind the party leaders' anxious protests to the national government.

Probably the most ambitious of the Federalist propaganda efforts was the Washington Benevolent Society, ostensibly a charitable organization but in reality an arm of the party leadership. In Massachusetts, the first society was founded in 1811, after the example of those in New York, Baltimore, and Rhode

---

[9]Perkins *et al.* to John Holmes, Apr. 19, 1811, Holmes MSS, NYPL.

[1]*Address to the Friends of Independence, Peace, and Union in the County of Middlesex* (n.p., 1812); and Daniel Remich, *History of Kennebunk* (Portland, Me., 1911), p. 226. See also *Palladium*, Apr. 26, 1811; and James W. North, *The History of Augusta* (Augusta, Me., 1910), p. 410.

Island. By 1815 there were no less than fifty-two auxiliaries in the state. In the interest of attracting large numbers, the membership fee of one dollar was usually waived. At its height, the Boston society had branches in each ward and numbered 1,500 members, about half the town's Federalist vote, and the Berkshire society claimed 2,300.

Members met together annually on February 22nd to bear witness to their faith. Local worthies praised the first President, recounted the iniquities of his Republican successors, and paraded the virtues of latter-day Federalism. During the remainder of the year, apart from an occasional benevolence, the societies sponsored the distribution of countless tracts carrying texts of the Constitution, the Farewell Address, and, with misplaced political charity, Jefferson's own Declaration of Independence. How effective were its efforts to arouse Federalist constituencies is difficult to measure, but according to one Republican, Berkshire County went Federalist in 1812 for the first time in twelve years due to the Society's activities there in support of Caleb Strong.[2]

In conjunction with the annual Fourth of July celebrations, the fast day and election sermons, and the periodic harangues of the Federalist clergy, these newspapers, pam-

---

[2] Fischer, *Revolution of American Conservatism*, pp. 110-28; Harlan H. Ballard, "A Forgotten Fraternity," *Collections of the Berkshire Historical and Scientific Society*, III (1913), 279-98; William A. Robinson, "The Washington Benevolent Society in New England: A Phase of Politics During the War of 1812," *Massachusetts Historical Society Proceedings*, XLIX (1915-16), 280; Morison, *Otis*, I, 302; Labaree, *Patriots and Partisans*, p. 137; Perkins to Noah Webster, May 18, 1811, Webster MSS, NYPL; Robinson, *Jeffersonian Democracy in New England*, p. 91*n*, quoting the [New Hampshire] *Patriot*, May 4, 1813; James Truslow Adams, *New England in the Republic, 1776-1850* (Boston, 1926), p. 278; and *Centinel*, Feb. 26, 1812. For an example of the kind of rhetorical fare served up at these meetings, see e.g., Richard Henry Dana, *An Oration, Delivered Before the Washington Benevolent Society at Cambridge, July 4, 1814* (Cambridge, 1814), and [Josiah Quincy], *An Oration Delivered Before the Washington Benevolent Society of Massachusetts, on the Thirtieth Day of April, 1813* (Boston, 1813). Berkshire's swing to Federalism in 1812 undoubtedly owed much also to the reaction against the Republicans' 1811 Religious Freedom Bill and the Gerrymander.

phlets, broadsides, and public rallies made up one of the most formidable concentrations of political propaganda in American political history. Rarely has a population been subjected in the same degree to such emotion-laden and insistent pressures upon its loyalties as were the people of Massachusetts in Jefferson's time. Few escaped its effects, few were unmoved. The party's efforts to excite the public mind succeeded. Did they not perhaps succeed too well?

One of the central dilemmas of Federalism lay in the fact that the party never had any alternative but to accommodate itself to the ascendent democratic political mode. Old-school Federalists had warned of the cost of stimulating the popular mind and encouraging widespread participation in the political arena; but they had also recognized that not to do so only meant defeat.[3] Young party leaders knew of the perils, too: they had had a foretaste of them in Shays's Rebellion and the Democratic-Republican Societies of the 1790's; they were scarcely unmindful of the lessons of the French Revolution. Yet they were always encouraged by the elitist belief that once public opinion were aroused it could ultimately be controlled.

Nevertheless, the committee system remained, through the caucus, highly vulnerable to the same public sentiment which it was called upon to excite. Rather than satisfying de-

---

[3]George Cabot was always apprehensive that "the people will run mad." Reporting on Cabot's reluctance to serve on a committee of merchants, Ames noted that "he hates hypocrisy, and respects principles, and he dreads lest the popular feeling should impel the committee to deny what he believes to be true, or to ask for what he knows to be mischievous." Cabot to Pickering, Dec. 31, 1807, Lodge, *Cabot*, p. 374; and Ames to Pickering, Dec. 2, 1805, Ames, *Works*, I, 342. Ames himself seems briefly to have glimpsed the peril of propaganda. "The newspapers," he wrote in a statement which served equally well for all types of propaganda, "are an overmatch for any government. They will first overawe and then usurp it." Ames to Theodore Dwight, Mar. 19, 1801, *ibid.*, I, 294. His fears led him once to urge, after the force of propaganda had been revealed, that the party lessen its public appeals and rely more on leading figures in each town to exert their influence privately. Ames to Benjamin Goodhue, July 30, 1806, Goodhue MSS, New York Society Library.

mands from the Massachusetts interior for greater participation in the political process, it often seemed resistant to them, especially because, in the eyes of conservatives from the western counties, it appeared to have fallen into the hands of eastern latitudinarians. Moreover, it invited and intensified the frustrations of those who, like the Federalist clergy on its fringes, had always been suspicious of the Boston elite, who distrusted politicians, and who had little patience with an opposition which seemed the personification of evil.

Once political instrumentalism triumphed over the old elitist ideology, once the committee system began to fuel the popular mind with all the themes of the Federalist ideology, the demise of deference politics was assured. Yet, once deference politics became a thing of the past, there was no immunizing party leaders from the force of public sentiment. The exposure of the party leaders to the caucus above and to the committees below—channels in which public opinion could be brought directly to bear upon party managers—diminished the resistance of the Central Committee and of the entire maritime elite for which it spoke to the very type of popular agitation which Federalists feared but which they had done so much to arouse. It is not too much to say that without the committee system Massachusetts Federalism would hardly have survived the pre-Embargo years. But with it, the Hartford Convention seems in retrospect to have been inescapable.

VII

The Fruits of Organization: Democracy and Republicanism

I

T HE artificers of the first party system faced difficulties which have beset American party managers ever since. And, in the larger perspective of American political history, they solved these problems about as well as most of their successors. Their performance is particularly impressive when we consider that, unlike those who came after them, they were first obliged to politicize a whole people. From vague preferences they had to create lasting political affiliations. They had to mobilize the votes of those who had seen little purpose in going to the polls. And perhaps most important, they had to make it appear as if voting yielded some sort of reward and as if neutrality toward the great partisan issues of the day was a disservice to the larger community. To do all of this, they were obliged to overcome an unquestioning acquiescence in elitist government so old and so profound that in destroying it they put an end to elitist rule itself. The passions and "phrenzies" of these years become more intelligible if we take into account the magnitude of these tasks.

It is surely the supreme irony of Federalist history that political victory could be purchased only at the cost of the end in view. The demise of elitist politics did not, of course, have any single cause. The gradual erosion of the elitist canon, the ideological attack from the Jeffersonian left, and the emergence of the presidential contest as the transcendent national political event all played their part. Yet, in retrospect, nothing was more important in undermining the habits of elitism than the thousands of individual decisions to participate once and then again in the political process. Once these decisions had been made, voters began to gain a new perspective on the importance of their own vote and to see in a new light their own role in the wider society. The great increase in the size of the electorate, brought on chiefly by the efforts of rival party organizations, thus implied more than the creation of party identifications. It prefigured a rising demand for participation in all areas of American life—in religion, in enterprise, in government, and in the community—which gradually altered the character of the national experience and strengthened the foundations of a democratic society.

Electoral democracy in Massachusetts was achieved without major constitutional revision or legal reform. According to the provisions of the state constitution of 1780, voting in state elections was open to any adult male who had been a resident of the town in which he voted for at least one year prior to elections and who possessed a freehold estate which yielded either £3 annually in the new silver currency or any kind of property, real or personal, valued at a minimum of £60.[1] Envisaged originally as restrictive limits, these requirements were nullified by the mid-1790's through increased prosperity and the pronounced tendency of town officials to ignore property qualifications, construe the £3 requirement to mean an income of £3 from any source, and take one year's residency to mean one's presence in town on two successive election days. In effect, all adult males who paid a poll tax and claimed a settled residence—even the propertyless laborers who managed to earn £3 in annual wages—could vote. Only paupers, shiftless migrant laborers, and young men still living with their families had trouble gaining the ballot, but often enough even they were transformed into prosperous independent citizens by the election-day shenanigans of the party captains. This did not mean that everyone voted, nor that

---

[1]Massachusetts Constitution of 1780, Part II, Chap. I, Sec. 3, Art. iv, in Francis Newton Thorpe, *The Federal and State Constitutions . . .* (7 vols., Washington, 1909), III, 1888-1923.

universal suffrage existed in 1800. But it did mean that in a prosperous economy nearly everyone who wished to vote could do so. It was up to the parties to convince him that he should.[2]

Over a period of about a decade, the two party organizations went far toward achieving this goal. After 1800, election turnouts in Massachusetts and Maine began to approach the census estimate of adult white males.[3] In the 1790's, roughly 20 per cent of the state's adult white males had voted in gubernatorial elections.[4] By the turn of the century, this pro-

---

[2]Chilton Williamson, *American Suffrage from Property to Democracy, 1760-1860* (Princeton, N.J., 1960), pp. 176-77. For similar conclusions for an earlier period, see Robert E. Brown, *Middle-Class Democracy and the Revolution in Massachusetts, 1691-1780* (Ithaca, N.Y., 1955). The most complete review of the history of the suffrage in Massachusetts is J. R. Pole, "Suffrage and Representation in Massachusetts: A Statistical Note," *William and Mary Quarterly*, 3rd Ser., XIV (Oct. 1957), 560-92, as corrected in "Letters to the Editor," *ibid.*, XV (July 1958), 412-16. A recent and insightful amplification of Pole's earlier studies—devoid, however, of some useful details—will be found in his *Political Representation in England and the Origins of the American Republic* (New York, 1966), esp. pp. 169-249. Voting statistics are found in *ibid.*, pp. 544-52. See also Paul Goodman, *The Democratic-Republicans of Massachusetts: Politics in a Young Republic* (Cambridge, 1964), pp. 137-39.

[3]I have based my figures upon census returns for adult white males rather than for all adult males because the addition of an interpolated sum from the catch-all census category of "all other persons except Indians not taxed" would have needlessly introduced another untrustworthy factor into an already questionable sum. In any case, figures for voting participation based upon the census of adult males after 1810, if they reveal any difference from my figures, are lower by only 1 per cent.

[4]Aside from the elections for presidential electors in 1804 and 1812, the April elections for governor and lieutenant governor were the sole occasions in which the voters at large balloted on a statewide basis.

Regarding my reliance upon gubernatorial election statistics, they are not only the most complete, but they are also the most dependable. Tallies for state senatorial districts exist, but the districts themselves, like congressional districts, frequently failed to conform to either political or geographic boundaries and just as frequently were subjected to Gerrymandering—and not by Republicans alone. Long before Gerry's administration had tried its hand at the business, the Federalists had revealed themselves to be capable practitioners of the art. As for the popular vote in presidential elections, statis-

portion had risen to about 32 per cent, and during the next four years it swelled spasmodically to 41 per cent. Then, after 1804, electoral interest shot up dramatically, until in the governor's race of 1812 it reached the unprecedented height of 68 per cent, a level unsurpassed before the Civil War. In that same year, Hampshire County turned out 81 per cent of its adult white male population.[5] If the year 1800 be taken as a starting point, the contest between rival political machines almost doubled the proportion of voters who turned out at the polls and did so at a rate considerably higher than the rate of population growth. After 1805, the total vote in any single gubernatorial election never fell below a majority of the state's adult white males.

On the surface, this record is remarkable enough. But it is even more so in the light of the post-Embargo economic depression which made meeting the legal qualifications for voting in state elections increasingly difficult. In Newburyport, for example, the proportion of the town's adult males which could meet these standards dropped from 92 per cent to 76 per cent in the eight years after 1807.[6] In the state as a whole, the decline in the number of legally qualified voters due to economic adversity after 1807 was probably in the neighbor-

---

tics exist only for the elections of 1804 and 1812; in 1800 and 1808, the General Court named the electors. Election tallies for town representatives were not centrally collected by the state; their collection would have been a massive task, if possible at all, and probably unrewarding, given the frequent changes in town boundaries and hence of voting population and legislative entitlement.

[5]This figure represents the turnout for the "new" Hampshire County, from which Hampden and Franklin counties were separated in 1812. In 1810, "new" Hampshire's voting turnout was 83 per cent.

[6]This decline was matched by a slide in actual voting participation from 66 per cent to 42 per cent between 1807 and 1815. Benjamin W. Labaree, *Patriots and Partisans: The Merchants of Newburyport, 1764-1815* (Cambridge, 1962), pp. 133, 203. Newburyport's experience was not typical, inasmuch as a disastrous fire in 1811 obliterated the economic gains of two decades and contributed heavily to the reduction in the size of the electorate. The figures on participation have been taken from the town's votes for the years cited. See also Stephan Thernstrom, *Poverty and Progress: Social Mobility in a Nineteenth Century City* (Cambridge, 1964), p. 10.

hood of 10 per cent. Yet in the face of the contraction in the number of people who, in a weakening economy, were able to meet the legal property requirements, the size of the actual electorate continued to rise. That is to say, a 68 per cent turnout of the total adult white male population in 1812 was equivalent to a significantly higher percentage, say 75 or 80 per cent, of the then-qualified adult white males. And taking account of the fishermen, sailors, farmers, lumbermen, and others who were far from the polling places but who would have voted if given the chance, the potential electorate in 1812 may well have approached 85 per cent of the qualified males, something close to full participation.[7] Electoral democracy, mass voting, and the political emergence of the common man long antedated the advent of Andrew Jackson, the hero of New Orleans, and William Henry Harrison, the hero of Tippecanoe.

Many voices were raised against these developments and, by implication, against those who encouraged them. Newspaper attacks on "the principles of universal suffrage uncontrolled by such restraints as are imposed by the spirit of the constitution" were typical. Ames was of the belief that "a reform in our elections ought to exclude those who have nothing, or almost nothing, from control of everything." Cabot dallied briefly with the idea of restricting the vote to those who owned $2,000 in land free and clear. Otis deplored "the effects of universal suffrage."[8] But the fact was that uni-

---

[7]William Bentley reported that "hundreds" of Boston sailors were at sea during the gubernatorial election of 1812. *The Diary of William Bentley, D.D.* (4 vols., Salem, Mass., 1905-14), IV, 93. See also Parker Cleaveland to Josiah Quincy, Apr. 2, 1811, Edmund Quincy, *Life of Josiah Quincy* (Boston, 1868), p. 225; and [Boston] *Columbian Centinel* (hereafter *Centinel*), Apr. 4, 1810. At the time of the British Reform Bill of 1832, only one seventh of the British adult males voted. Norman Gash, *Politics in the Age of Peel: A Study in the Technique of Parliamentary Representation* (London, 1953), p. 89.

[8]*Centinel*, July 13, 1811; *Works of Fisher Ames*, ed. Seth Ames (2 vols., Boston, 1854), II, 207; Cabot to Pickering, Feb. 14, 1804, Henry Cabot Lodge, *Life and Letters of George Cabot* (Boston, 1878), p. 344; and Otis to Rutledge, May 4, 1814, Rutledge MSS,

versal manhood suffrage was indispensable to the Federalist cause. It brought to the polls the propertyless laborers in the populous maritime towns and the small farmers from the Federalist strongholds in the western counties—voters who kept the party's hopes alive. Realizing this, most Federalists rejected all thoughts of suffrage reform.[9]

The stages of electoral change closely reflected the parties' efforts to get out the vote (Tables III and IV, Appendix II). Before 1803, Massachusetts politics were in a state of disequilibrium. Federalists won gubernatorial elections by at least 10 per cent of the total vote and, at the nadir of Republican fortunes in 1803, by 35 per cent. But rather than reflecting an increase in Federalist strength, the wide margins of victory reflected a deep crisis within Massachusetts Republicanism which was largely responsible for the sharp decline in the Republican vote in 1803.[1] The next year's rehabilitation of Republican fortunes, signaled by the recovery of the lost votes of 1803 and the addition of almost 5,000 more, was accomplished behind a new party organization. It presaged the Republican victory in the autumn presidential race. A disturbing

---

Univ. of North Carolina. These restrictive notions should be compared with the somewhat more latitudinarian ideals which many of the old-school Federalists held in the 1770's and 1780's and then discarded. See, e.g., [Jonathan Jackson], *Thoughts Upon the Political Situation of the United States of America* . . . (Worcester, Mass., 1788), p. 114; [Theophilus Parsons], *Result of the Convention of Delegates Holden at Ipswich in the County of Essex* . . . (Newburyport, Mass., 1778), pp. 28-29, 50, 57-58; and *A Defence of the Legislature of Massachusetts, or the Rights of Newengland Vindicated* (Boston, 1804), p. 10.

[9]For the fate of a short-lived Federalist movement to increase suffrage requirements for state elections by indirection, see Williamson, *American Suffrage*, pp. 177-78. One sign of the Federalists' early capitulation to the democratic imperative in the matter of the suffrage is Abijah Bigelow, *The Voters' Guide* . . . (Leominster, Mass., 1807), whose stated purpose it was to emphasize the importance of voting—and voting correctly. Bigelow, a Federalist, struck out against loose interpretations of the suffrage requirements. *Ibid.*, pp. 26-27.

[1]The Republican schism, which pitted eastern against western Republicans, can be followed in the [Boston] *Independent Chronicle, Centinel*, and [Pittsfield] *Sun*, Feb.-Apr., 1803.

feature of the presidential vote itself was the sharp drop in Federalist ballots and the steep rise in Republican rolls.[2] If the Federalists needed any sign that their statewide majority was in permanent jeopardy, this was it. All signs pointed toward a Republican governor in 1805.

What enabled the party to break its three-year voting pattern and avert defeat in 1805 was its own fledgling organization. Had the Federalist voting tally remained unchanged for one more election, Republican James Sullivan would have been governor in 1805. As it was, both parties organized large campaigns to gain the statehouse and drove the total vote up almost 10 per cent in that one year alone—witness to the relationship between party organization and electoral democracy and a vivid reminder that conflict is crucial to democracy. With some variations, the same sharp rise in participation occurred in every county that same year. Thereafter, and

---

[2]The appreciable differential between turnouts for gubernatorial and presidential elections, of which the 1804 election is a striking exception, has been noted by many students of Massachusetts history. See, e.g., Richard P. McCormick, *The Second American Party System: Party Formation in the Jacksonian Era* (Chapel Hill, N.C., 1966), p. 41. The explanation, I believe, is that the election day for town officials, which by law could be held on any date in March or April, was customarily scheduled to coincide with the gubernatorial election which, along with the balloting for state senators, was called by law for the first Monday in April. Given the traditional importance of town affairs in Massachusetts and everyone's interest in reducing the multiplicity of elections, the townspeople's reluctance to be called away from their pursuits any more often than necessary, and party managers intent on turning out the largest vote, voting participation in gubernatorial elections benefited. Statewide figures for electoral interest in the May House elections are unavailable, but it is likely that, like the figures for presidential and congressional races in the fall, they were lower than those for the April contest. The year 1804 proved an exception to autumn election apathy because the Republicans were highly mobilized and made unusual efforts to capture the general ticket. The next time the general public had an opportunity to vote for electors was 1812; but then the disruptions of war intervened, Republicanism was shattered, and electors were chosen by districts rather than on a statewide basis. The result was a presidential vote of 78,250, or 25 per cent lower than the previous spring's peak. Most of the loss was sustained by the Republicans.

until the election of 1813, the margin of one party's victory over the other rarely exceeded 3 per cent of the total vote. A new political equilibrium, a close two-party race, and mounting voter interest, which aided the Federalists but helped the Republicans more, were the early fruits of organization.

After 1805, the level of voting participation began to reflect the currents of state and national politics as much as the activities of the party organization. From the Embargo on, national events intervened regularly in the state political arena, not so much because national issues suddenly assumed pre-dominance over local affairs, but because party organizations now existed to exploit their relevance to local politics. In 1809, for instance, the precipitous jump in voting stemmed in part from passions aroused on both sides by the Embargo and En-forcement Acts and in part from the fight over the sucessor to the popular and moderate James Sullivan, who had died in office. Mounting its most concerted campaign to date, the Federalist Party was the chief beneficiary of this electoral tide. Over twice as many of the 12,175 new voters in 1809 balloted for Christopher Gore as for Levi Lincoln, Jr., enabling the Federalists to recapture control of the executive mansion after two years' exclusion.

The sharpest rise in the vote in any one year occurred, however, in April 1812—not after, it must be noted, but two months before the declaration of hostilities with Britain. Over 11,000 voters who had never before voted turned out to send a Federalist to the statehouse for the first time since Gore's election in 1809. The chief cause of the sudden deluge of new voters was not this time to be found within the realm of national politics, but in the furor created by the unalloyed partisanship of the Gerry administration and in changes in the state's religious and election laws. The Gerrymander, the un-disguised one-sided reapportionment of the state senate, was only one, and probably not the principal, source of the popular revulsion against the Republican Party.[3] Equally if not more

[3]On the Gerrymander, see Elmer C. Griffith, *The Rise and Development of the Gerrymander* (Chicago, 1907).

important, as I have already been at some pains to suggest, was the Religious Freedom Bill of 1811, which guaranteed almost total freedom of worship to dissenters and for all practical purposes disestablished the Congregational church. Their religious sensitivities aroused to high emotional pitch by a flood of political and pulpit jeremiads, many normally apathetic Federalists rushed to the polls to register their disapproval of Gerry's course.

Voting in 1812 received an additional stimulus from an act passed by the Gerry forces in 1811, which opened the vote for town officers to all adult males except paupers with one year's residence in town and qualified for the vote in other town affairs all persons who paid a poll tax. Because town and gubernatorial elections tended to be simultaneous and because under the informal system of applying legal requirements almost anyone who voted in town elections was permitted to vote for governor, the act encouraged most of the newly enfranchised town electors to participate in the gubernatorial canvass. The result was suddenly and sharply inflated voting rolls. The vote would have been still higher had so many not been at sea and had town officers, such as the Federalist selectmen of Salem, not intimidated the town's "humble and timid" into staying away from the polls.[4]

The Republicans hoped to benefit from an enlarged local suffrage. But they failed to foresee the differential effects of the Gerrymander and the Religious Freedom Bill. And in the process, by ignoring Federalist drawing power among poorer citizens in the larger coastal towns, they miscalculated the growth in Federalist support throughout the population. Thus, while both parties augmented their voting rolls, the Federalists added 4,500 more of the new votes than their adversaries and

---

[4]*Acts and Laws Passed by the General Court of Massachusetts* (hereafter *Mass. Acts and Laws*), 1811, Chap. 5 (June 18, 1811); and Bentley, *Diary*, IV, 91-93. In Salem, the Federalists exploited the act to vote poor Negro laborers in 1812 and thus captured control of the town meeting for the first time in years. *Ibid.*, IV, 90. Not surprisingly, the Federalists made no attempt to repeal the act when they regained control of the General Court.

regained the governorship. The Federalist surge was the product of two factors: one, the majority status of the Congregationalists who, in any test of strength involving religion, could easily outnumber the dissenters, and, two, the return to Federalism of many Congregationalists who, for one reason or another, had supported the Republican Party up to this point but were repelled by Gerry's actions.

It was not the war, then, but matters of state politics which renewed the political lease of Massachusetts Federalism and established the Federalists as the majority party in a two-party setting for the first time. Once the war began, it did of course have an appreciable influence on the Commonwealth's politics, causing a greater dislocation in the electoral equilibrium than any event to that point—and by far a more permanent one. But its principal effect was not so much to swell the ranks of Federalism as to deplete those of Republicanism. Between the spring gubernatorial canvass of 1812 and the autumn ballot for president, the Republican rolls plummeted almost 50 per cent. And then, while the Federalists added about 4,000 votes in 1813, the Republican total dropped by almost 9,000—figures which reveal that only a small part of the Republican losses can be ascribed to defections to the Federalist camp. The remainder were due to abstention.

Such contrary motion in party votes was unusual. The votes of both parties tended to rise and fall in unison, one party's gain rarely meaning a commensurate loss for the other. This resulted from the absence of what we would today call the independent voter. In the state as a whole, there existed no large body of unaffiliated voters who changed sides as a bloc and were thus capable of swinging close elections from one party to the other. Elections were won by activating already committed voters rather than creating new affiliations. Moreover, as the Republican gubernatorial tally for 1813 and the presidential vote for 1812 so dramatically illustrate, protest voting was more likely to take the form of abstention than party switching. Indifference rather than revolt was the price of a politically unpopular course.

Had voting participation in Massachusetts been as consistently high as, say, 85 per cent, the Republican Party would have had small chance for statewide victory at any time. For, as the votes in 1809, 1812, and 1813 most graphically show, the Federalists had greater residual voting support among the general public than their adversaries and could bring out a majority of these latent votes in moments of crisis far more successfully than the Republicans. If a majority of the voting-age population of Massachusetts was of the Federalist persuasion, it is equally true—looking at the wider range of fluctuation in the Federalist vote than the Republican—that the average Federalist voter was less dependable and less well motivated than his Republican counterpart and on the whole more apathetic. While Republicanism was rooted in a posture of opposition to the established procedures of political life, Federalism was set in a mold of deference and passivity which party managers had to struggle to shatter. Only when this was accomplished could Federalism move beyond being the majority persuasion to become the majority party of Massachusetts.

The massive surge of Federalist votes between 1811 and 1813 signaled the formation of a durable majority coalition, centered on the state's dominant Congregational population, where none had existed before. Measured against the symmetrical voting patterns and the narrow victory margins of the previous eight years, the election of 1813 stands out as a unique event, where the party's margin of victory again approached 10 per cent and did so not only because of a steep decline in the opposition vote but in company with an impressive accumulation of new votes which it was able to hold for another year and was not to lose for a decade. This clear Federalist majority—originating in the events of Gerry's final term, consolidated by the war, and held together by a memory of both—shattered the Republican coalition and was able to endure into the 1820's. Its survival was aided by the party's successful exploitation of the slavery issue toward the end of the decade, by the Federalist leaders' demonstrable willingness to get along

with the national administration during the "era of good feelings," and by the separation of Maine, with its large Republican vote, in 1820. Not until 1823 did the party relinquish
the governor's mansion, and only in 1827 did it put forth its
final gubernatorial candidate.[5] Democracy had helped preserve
the Federalist Party.

II

IN ADDITION TO ADVANCING the cause of political democracy, organized politics richly enhanced the prospects of
representative government in Massachusetts. And once the
party chieftains began to give as much attention to the town-
centered races for the General Court as they did to the guber-

---

[5]When Maine was separated from Massachusetts in 1820, the
Federalist vote dropped 11,803 from the previous year and the Republican vote 13,343. On the final years of the Federalist Party
in Massachusetts, see Shaw Livermore, Jr., *The Twilight of Federalism: The Disintegration of the Federalist Party, 1815-1830* (Princeton, N.J., 1962), pp. 117-19; and McCormick, *Second American
Party System*, pp. 41-43. The demise of Massachusetts Federalism in
the 1820's must be ascribed not to the party's irrelevance to the day's
concerns, not to the appreciably greater popularity of state Republican leaders, and not to the triumph of some lingering and slow-
growing reaction against the Hartford Convention, but rather to the
disruptive effects of John Quincy Adams's presidential candidacy
and the mounting disarray of national politics. Adams's popularity
attracted to his National Republican Party the votes of some thousands of Federalists who meant to be loyal to a native son and
who rejoiced in the rehabilitation of Massachusetts influence on the
national scene. His candidacy also split the Federalist Party into
two wings: those who recognized in Adams the only remaining
executor of the Federalist estate and those, like Theodore Lyman,
who could not forgive Adams's apostasy nor his more recent
aspersions against the Hartford Convention and who, on these accounts and from considerations of opportunism, voted for Jackson
in 1828. In other words, Federalism remained strong in the state
only in the absence of presidential politics between 1816 and 1824. If,
as Richard McCormick has argued, Adams's contest for the Presidency was "the most important single factor bearing upon party
formation in Massachusetts" after 1824, it was also the executioner
of the Federalist Party in Massachusetts and, by extension, of
the first party system in the Commonwealth. *Ibid.*, p. 41.

natorial elections, a party organization capable of arousing voters in the smallest hamlet became inescapable.

Before the development of the first party system, one of the persistent features of Massachusetts government had been the under-representation of towns in the General Court. Under the constitution of 1780, a community, in order to gain incorporation and, as a consequence, representation in the legislature, had to possess at least 150 ratable polls, defined, with a few exceptions, as males sixteen and over. For each additional deputy, a town needed 225 additional polls. Thus the ancient principle of representation by towns as corporate units— championed by the small interior communities—became reconciled with the more recent principle of the representation of individuals—urged by the maritime towns, which benefited by a calculus which tied representation to population.[6]

Because of population growth and redistribution, neither these constitutional prescriptions nor those which regulated voting for General Court representation were restrictive. Yet actual representation in the General Court remained far below that countenanced by law. In the last half-decade of the eighteenth century, the level of representation averaged only about 46 per cent of those towns eligible to send deputies to Boston and by 1800 had barely surpassed 50 per cent.[7] Although denied as a legal principle, what English political science recognized as "virtual representation" was a practical reality in Massachusetts.

One reason for this circumstance was the unwillingness of the poor interior towns to bear the costs of representation as required by law, even though they risked fines for their recalcitrance. Some towns reduced their representation below the legal level; others simply sent no deputies at all. Towns

---

[6]Constitution of 1780, Part II, Chap. I, Sec. 3, Art. ii; Pole, *Political Representation,* pp. 213-14.

[7]See Table V (Appendix II). The first attempt to calculate the level of town representation in Massachusetts was made by Oscar and Mary F. Handlin, *Commonwealth: A Study of the Role of Government in the American Economy, Massachusetts, 1774-1861* (New York, 1947), Appendix II.

were known to elect representatives in order to satisfy the legal requirements and then to prohibit them from going to Boston. Many men elected to the lower house failed to take up their posts due to the exigencies of travel, the risks of being absent from their livelihood, and an intangible but widespread dislike of life in Boston. Faced with what often bordered on mass resistance, the House by and large refrained from fining the derelict towns and the reluctant deputies.[8] In addition, the small, relatively impoverished frontier communities often found it difficult to recruit as deputies men who could meet the constitutional requirements for representative: possession of a £100 freehold in town or "any rateable estate" valued at £200, and residence in town for at least one year. Moreover, hard times only increased resistance to representation. Thus, not surprisingly, the wealthy and populous towns of the coast long dominated the lower chamber.[9]

What has been called a "crisis in participation" was ended only with the birth of party organization. And as in the history of Massachusetts democracy, the years 1804 and 1805 marked a turning point in the larger history of Massachusetts republicanism. Until 1804, both parties more or less conceded Federalist control of the House and directed their efforts toward gubernatorial and congressional elections.[1] Only the birth of a Republican organization in 1804 and its immediate call for full representation from Republican towns began to erode Federalist apathy toward House elections. Not surprisingly, one of the first steps of the Federalist Central Committee in 1805 was to issue a similar call. The origins of organized

---

[8]Constitution of 1780, Part II, Chap. I, Sec. 3, Art. ii. The Federalist-controlled General Court of 1813 enacted that towns which sent more than their legislative entitlement be fined. *Mass. Acts and Laws*, 1812, Chap. 85. On the remission of fines, see, e.g., *Resolves of the General Court of Massachusetts* (hereafter *Mass. Resolves*), Feb. 24, 1801. On the underrepresentation of towns, see Pole, *Political Representation*, pp. 234-36.

[9]Constitution of 1780, Part II, Chap. I, Sec. 3, Art. iii; Pole, *Political Representation*, p. 234.

[1]See, e.g., Samuel Phillips to Eliphalet Pearson, May 4, 1801, Park Family Papers, Yale; and *Centinel*, May 30, 1804.

party politics were not unrelated to the struggle for the General Court.

A few weeks before the spring elections of 1805, Central Committee Secretary William Smith Shaw sent to the county committees a circular letter which pointedly examined the opposition's year-old campaign to gain a House majority. "The singular success which attended this plan, and the consequent federal weakness which the last year's House of Representatives exhibited, was one and no inconsiderable cause of the disgrace which it has this spring hardly escaped," noted the circular in reference to the close gubernatorial race. Out of the one hundred towns which failed to elect even one deputy in 1804, the circular went on, only fifteen were Republican. The rest were Federalist. As to the Republican scheme, "the whole of this plan, it is, perhaps, unworthy of the Federalists to copy; but a part, it is certainly their duty not to neglect." All Federalist towns must send at least one representative and "the great federal towns . . . as many representatives as they conveniently can, without giving offense to their own party." A list of all Federalist towns in each county accompanied the circular.[2]

Like so many of the early actions of the organization, this directive was too late to have an appreciable effect upon the 1805 elections. The party kept hold of the lower house, but more by the failure of the Republicans to fully exploit their initiative than by the efforts of the Federalists themselves. Where the party was already well drilled, however, the Com-

---

[2]A copy is in the William Smith Shaw MSS, Boston Athenaeum (hereafter BA). See, in addition, "Subjects for Consideration of the Central Committee," [1806?], Shaw MSS, BA; John Phillips *et al.* to ?, Apr. 19, 1808, Misc. MSS Colls., American Antiquarian Society (hereafter AAS); James Lloyd, Jr., *et al.* to John Holmes, Apr. 14, 1809, and Thomas Handasyd Perkins *et al.* to Holmes, Apr. 19, 1811, Holmes MSS, New York Public Library (hereafter NYPL); Otis *et al.* to Thomas W. Ward, Feb. 22, 1812, Ward MSS, AAS; and Otis *et al.* to Ebenezer Childs, Apr. 13, 1810, Broadside Coll., New York Historical Society (hereafter NYHS).

mittee action brought an immediate response. The Boston Federalist caucus, for instance, broke with the long-standing custom which had limited the town to seven deputies and exercised its power over the Federalist capital by committing the town to a full slate of twenty-six. A year later, Boston augmented its delegation by five more and thereafter sent the full complement permitted under law.[3] Where the tables were turned and, as in Salem, the well-organized Federalist apparatus found itself in the minority, it fought against full representation rather than pushing for it.[4] But whether the party found itself in the majority or minority, the burden of regulating the representation of each town fell directly upon the town committees and further enhanced their influence in the party hierarchy.

Soon, both parties were locked in a battle to turn out their last party representative. At times, the Federalist leaders appealed to principle and duty. "The expense of sending a full number of Representatives," read one circular, "is not to be regarded. Should we lose a majority in the House, their attendance would seldom be required. If we obtain a majority, the expense and trouble, would be but as dust in the balance, compared with the beneficial consequence, resulting from possessing the power to restrain the headstrong course of the adversaries of the public welfare." At other times, the party captains were more solicitous of local fears of too much taxation for representation and tried only to get deputies to Boston for the organizing session of the General Court. "The attendance of many of the members," declared another party flyer, "need not be extended beyond a week in May for the purpose of electing Counsellors and other publick Officers, and not

---

[3]Gore to Rufus King, Apr. 22 & 30, 1805, Mar. 26, 1806, King MSS, NYHS; John Quincy Adams, *Diary*, entry for May 13, 1806, reel 30, Adams Family Papers microfilm (hereafter Adams microfilm); and *Centinel*, Apr. 24, May 1 & 4, 1805. Republicans accused Federalists of increasing their representation simply by having the tax assessors count as ratable polls the poor people who paid no taxes.
[4]Bentley, *Diary*, III, 157-58.

above half that time in November for making the choice of electors."[5]

As the parties drew abreast of each other and the stakes of legislative control became higher than ever, the rival forces began to reduce the cost of representation and to increase the number of incorporations. The Republicans proved far more accomplished at both than the Federalists. The Republican-controlled General Court of 1811 made the first twenty days of representation chargeable to the state and admitted new towns to corporate status with an unmatched abandon.[6] Even if such actions were not strictly within the realm of fair play, representative government benefited in the process.

How effective the partisan campaign turned out to be is revealed by the records of representation. In the first session of the 1800 General Court, only about 53 per cent of the incorporated towns were represented by at least one member in the lower house. In the 1811 General Court's first session, that figure had risen to slightly over 82 per cent. Such growth far exceeded in extent and pace the increase in the number of incorporated towns and in the state's population. At the same time that the number of incorporated towns increased 14 per cent between 1800 and 1811, the number of towns represented rose 70 per cent and the number of representatives 163 per cent (Table V, Appendix II).

The Republican campaign to recruit new representatives

---

[5]John Phillips *et al.* to ?, Apr. 19, 1808, Misc. MSS Colls., AAS; and Otis to John Holmes, Apr. 6 & 19, 1811, Holmes MSS, NYPL. See also Perkins to Woodbury Storer, May 7, 1808, Washburn Coll., Massachusetts Historical Society; and Gore to Rufus King, Feb. 22, 1809, King MSS, NYHS.

[6]*Mass. Resolves*, June 7, 1811. A year later, the Federalists repealed the act. *Ibid.*, Jan. 21, 1812. Most of the new incorporations were in Maine. On new downstate towns, see John Fairfield Sly, *Town Government in Massachusetts (1620-1930)* (Cambridge, 1930), p. 108*n*. An additional stimulus to representation after 1811 was a court decision that aliens who were ratable for taxes be considered ratable polls for the purpose of apportionment of legislators. *Reports of the Supreme Judicial Court of Massachusetts*, VII, 523-30.

which got under way in 1804 yielded only insignificant results until the Federalists joined battle the next year. And it was not until the first session of the 1806 legislature that the consequences of party organization were felt directly in the legislative chambers. Town representation leaped by 23 per cent and membership by 39 per cent. Throughout the Commonwealth, the estate of representative government assumed a new prosperity. In Essex County, representation was up over 40 per cent, in Barnstable 75 per cent, in many of the Maine counties almost 100 per cent, and in Oxford County, Maine, whose Federalist organization was born in 1806, almost 300 per cent. The rise in representation enabled the Republicans for the first time to organize the House.[7]

After a temporary decline in representation in 1807, the embargo laws spurred both parties to return to battle early in 1808. The effects upon representation were striking. From a cyclical low of almost 57 per cent in the spring of 1807, town representation climbed steadily to its peak of 82 per cent in 1811 and House membership to 739 in the autumn of 1812. That the membership of the U.S. House of Representatives was only 142 at the time—less than a fifth the size of the General Court—scarcely increased confidence in the power and effectiveness of the government in Washington.

Moreover, this rise ran counter to the general economic depression of the larger community, the paralysis of its commerce, the disruption of its markets and fisheries, and the reduction of its agricultural prosperity. In the past, such conditions would have caused a severe reduction in representation. But now, because the party organizations gave to each event the deep coloration of partisan significance, no one was spared from appeals to party duty. Failure to send a full representation began to have the aspect of a crime against the party and

---

[7]For the breakdown in representation by counties, see "Representation in the General Court, 1780-1856," *Massachusetts Senate Documents*, 1854, Doc. 56.

the state. It was because of, rather than in spite of, the economic crisis that representative government prospered.

While House membership grew, so did the number of towns represented, although the magnitude of change was not so large as the near doubling of membership in the same period. The General Courts of 1811 and 1812—the legislatures of the Religious Freedom Bill, the Gerrymander, and the war protests—were particularly noteworthy. Governor Gerry and his floor managers succeeded in the first session of 1811 alone in incorporating a total of ninety new towns, compared with a total of fifty-seven incorporations since 1800. Deputies from the newly incorporated towns could not sit in the House until after the elections of 1812. But when they did take their seats, they not only ran House membership to its peak but enabled the Federalists to capture control of the lower chamber. Like the town election law of 1811, which added hundreds of names to the voting lists, the Republican movement for new incorporations failed to stem a resurgence of Federalism.

The General Court elected in 1812 reached a peak in both membership and towns represented after a hectic Federalist campaign to blame the opposition for the Gerrymander and for increasing the prospects of war. Membership rose to a record in the second and special autumn session, called by the Federalists not only to place the House on record against the war which had at last broken out but to settle on a method of choosing presidential electors. After 1812, membership and town representation declined rapidly in the face of economic stagnation and the disruptions due to war. During the second and special session of the 1814-1815 General Court—the session which issued the call for the Hartford Convention and chose the Commonwealth's nine delegates—both membership and the number of towns represented fell to pre-Embargo levels.

One of the unintended consequences of increased representation was a significant advance toward legislative reapportionment and a shift away from the domination of the House by maritime Massachusetts and maritime Federalists. As part of their efforts to secure full House delegations from towns under their control, both parties began to emphasize this malapportionment and to claim that, by sending their legal entitlement of representatives, all towns would win for themselves their fair weight in the legislature. "Is it just," asked a Federalist commentator defending Boston's decision to send a full legislative complement instead of its customary seven, "to impose it upon an inhabitant of Boston, that his political weight should be less, than that of an inhabitant of any other town?" Analysts in Federalist newspapers argued that while twenty-six Republican towns in the interior with a total population of 14,481 sent twenty-six deputies to the House, Boston's 24,937 inhabitants sent the same number. Republican writers advanced similar statistics to support their calls for full representation from Republican towns. Both parties invoked the principle of republican equality in support of partisan purposes.[8]

Ideals and principles were often obscured in these charges and countercharges, but the fact remains that party development brought about the reapportionment of the General Court. Roughly estimated, the total possible representation in 1800 was in the neighborhood of 650, in 1810 roughly 825.[9] This means that from early 1800, when about 30 per cent of the potential representation was claimed, representation swelled to around 85 per cent of potential in the first year of the second war with Britain. In the light of the early figures, this was no small achievement for the first party system and for republicanism.

Like all legislative reapportionments, this one had an important effect upon factional relationships within the parties. Until about 1806, populous eastern Massachusetts—comprising the counties east of Worcester—was able to maintain a near parity with the western and Maine counties, largely because of the failure of the inland towns to claim their full legislative entitlement. But upon the establishment of two party organi-

---

[8]*Centinel*, Apr. 24, May 1 & 11, 1805; and *Chronicle*, May 30, 1808.

[9]This estimate is based on the 1800 and 1810 census returns for adult males sixteen and over.

zations, there occurred a reconstruction of the sectional balance within the lower house (Table VI, Appendix II).

The most striking change in the composition of the lower chamber was the doubling of Maine's proportion of the representation between 1800 and 1812. But the relative decline in the membership of the western counties signaled the most politically significant development. While population growth spurred a steep rise in the representation of maritime and Maine towns, and while Boston's membership in the party caucus rose from seven to forty-four, the static population and low incidence of new town incorporations decreased the western representation from a third to roughly a quarter of the lower house.

More important, the decline in western influence in the party caucus occurred at the very time that the Federalist western counties had the highest voting levels in the state. Western Federalists, whose votes often provided the margin of victory to winning gubernatorial tickets, were failing to gain the power within party circles which their vote-getting achievements warranted. Indeed, what influence the west possessed bore little relationship to its voting strength. Northampton's Caleb Strong repeatedly headed the party ticket less because he was a power in his own right than because, in John Adams's view, he was "so good and unexceptionable a Man" that he did not threaten eastern control of the party machinery.[1] Moreover, pressure from the eastern wing of the party continually frustrated Strong's own efforts to correct the party imbalance: behind his decision to appoint Theophilus Parsons chief justice of the Supreme Judicial Court, for instance, lay considerable eastern efforts to prevent the appointment of Berkshire's Theodore Sedgwick.[2] The most heavily Federalist region of the state was being denied its share of party influence.

---

[1] John Adams to John Quincy Adams, Dec. 14, 1804, reel 403, Adams microfilm.
[2] Richard E. Welch, Jr., "The Parsons-Sedgwick Feud and the Reform of the Massachusetts Judiciary," *Essex Institute Historical Collections*, XCII (Apr. 1956), 171-87.

III

THE BIOGRAPHICAL AND OCCUPATIONAL PROFILE of the membership of the Massachusetts House of Representatives provides additional evidence of the strains within the state's Federalist Party (Table VII, Appendix II).[3] The average legislator was born around 1762. He was too young to have participated actively in the events of the Revolution but old enough to recall them. In his mid-twenties by the time of Shays's Rebellion, he was likely to have entered into the debates over the national Constitution, and he had lived through the stormy years of the new government when he received his partisan baptism. By 1812, he was fifty.

There was, however, a significant difference in the ages of the deputies from Maine and the downstate counties: the typical House member from Massachusetts proper was over three years older than his counterpart from Maine. In addition, although Federalist and Republican representatives were of the same age on a statewide basis, Maine Federalists were over two years younger than Maine Republicans and almost five years younger than their downstate party colleagues. What occasioned this age differential is unclear. But as the young men who by 1805 left downstate Massachusetts for Maine

---

[3]I have derived all the information in this section, except for party affiliation, from the biographical card file of General Court members in the Massachusetts State Library. For party membership, I have depended upon sources too numerous to list in entirety, among which the most important were the *Centinel, Palladium,* and *Chronicle,* 1800-15; signed party literature; and miscellaneous town histories, manuscript collections, and fugitive private tallies of legislative strength. Of the 2,283 men who sat in the House during the period, I have ascertained the party affiliation of roughly 85 per cent. I have accepted as evidence of affiliation only positive information; and by double-checking the allegiance of about one half the membership, I have found less than 1 per cent whose affiliation was in dispute. No two sources agree precisely on membership for any single year. I have relied upon the membership list published annually with the *Mass. Resolves.*

found most positions of power and influence arrogated by older dissenter-Republicans who had migrated earlier, they were inclined to join the political opposition—which in Maine was the Federalist Party. In addition, many of the later emigrants to Maine were younger men of Federalist origins who left downstate out of no profound dissatisfaction with the established religious or political elite but rather with an eye to new opportunity. They were young Federalists whose Federalist elders had gotten in their way.

Turning to the occupations of the deputies, almost half were farmers.[4] Furthermore, not only were 55 per cent of the farmer-members with ascertainable political loyalties Federalists, but over 42 per cent of the Federalist delegations in the fifteen years after 1800—more than double the proportion of merchants—were farmers. Thus the Massachusetts Federalist Party was by no means under foregone mercantile control. Federalist farmers, most of them from the interior, had the numbers and the latent power to take command of the party. They had only to be mobilized.

For even though the merchants or men representing mercantile interests customarily wielded greatest influence in the legislature, in Federalist circles they equaled less than half the number of farmers and only about one fifth of the average Federalist delegation. Not surprisingly, among Republican delegations this ratio was appreciably smaller. About two thirds of those identifiable as merchants were Federalists, and of these over one hundred came from the four maritime counties of Suffolk, Essex, Plymouth, and Bristol, thirty-eight from Boston alone. When a conflict between agrarian and commercial interests arose, the merchants were vastly outnumbered, especially when the House membership approached full strength. Such was the case in the waning months of the Embargo crisis and the early months of the War of 1812.

---

[4]Cf. Robert E. Brown's statement that before 1780, the farmers had "complete control" of the General Court. *Middle-Class Democracy*, p. 402.

In education and professional training and experience, the Federalists clearly outranked their adversaries. Although only 6 per cent of the legislative members possessed college degrees—which was higher than the figure for the population in general—nearly three fourths of these were Federalists. This figure represents almost one tenth of the Federalist delegations and about three times the proportion of Republican degree-holders. Among the major occupational groups represented in the lower house, lawyers ranked fourth, with roughly one tenth of the membership. And though they made up only about 10 per cent of all Federalist deputies, they numbered almost three times the proportion of Republican lawyer-representatives. As for doctors, they were distributed, as I have indicated before, in roughly equal proportion between the two parties, witness to their domination of the ranks of Republican professionals.

Few clerics sat for either party but, like the physicians, men of the cloth received greater political responsibility from Jefferson's party, and most of them were dissenting clergymen articulating the grievances of the sects. Partly for similar reasons of recruitment but also because of a more closely balanced division among men of the maritime trades, an almost equal number of sea captains and ship masters served each party in the House, and a proportionately higher number were Republican. Finally, the Republicans recruited a relatively higher proportion of artisans than their opponents, attesting not only to the greater drawing power of Jefferson's party among the lower-ranking callings but also to its inability to develop leaders from among the better stationed.

As for general public service and prior political activity, the legislators of both parties had about equally good records. Their participation in state and national constitutional conventions, their military service during the Revolution, and their occupation of government posts as public attorneys, justices of the peace, and judges substantiate the accepted view that public service of this sort was considered a prime qualification for further public service. But, in this case, the parity between the two parties suggests that Revolutionary service and membership in the great conventions of the day did not differentially predispose the public servant more toward one party than toward the other.

Finally, information about party affiliation permits an analysis of legislative stability and also suggests the legislative consequences of party organization. Measured by levels of incumbency, the General Courts during which party organization first occurred—those of 1804, 1805, and 1806—and the General Courts of the Embargo years and of 1812 were those in which a high proportion of the membership had not sat during the previous year (Table VIII, Appendix II).[5] In 1805, for instance, after the Federalist Party's initial attempt to recruit full legislative complements from Federalist towns, enough first-time Federalist deputies were elected to diminish the number of that year's delegation veterans to one half the total delegation strength. The first Federalist delegation chosen after the Embargo was a small army of raw recruits and non-veterans of the year before, testimony to the success of party operations but also a harbinger of the perils of republicanism. The demands of this large freshman caucus delegation for concerted action against the administration were so insistent and ungovernable that veteran party leaders, Otis foremost among them, felt constrained, in self-defense, to try to organize a New England-wide conclave of Federalist notables.

Once again in 1812, when a sharp climb in Federalist House strength eventuated in a drop in delegation incumbency, it was all that party managers could do to restrain the Federalist caucus. As it turned out, the caucus call for separate county protest conventions against the war developed into a movement for a statewide convention, which moderate Federalists halted only with the greatest difficulty. A rise in party

---

[5]I have defined "incumbency" strictly to mean the return to office of a representative who had served in the lower house during the immediately preceding year.

strength in the legislature was purchased only by a loss in the stability of party management and the continuity of party policy. Organized politics solved some problems only to create new ones.

VIII

To the Hartford Convention

I

THE political crisis of 1814 was not unprecedented. In the fifteen years after 1800, the aroused forces of ideology and politics converged three times—and three times occasioned a movement for a convention of New England Federalists.

The first emergency to foretoken the circumstances of the Hartford Convention broke over the heads of the captains of Massachusetts Federalism in 1808. In an attempt to substitute economic coercion for war in retaliation against the continuing maritime depredations of England and France, Jefferson and Congress had imposed the drastic Embargo in late December 1807. Within a few months, American trade was at a standstill, the national economy had collapsed, ships stood idle—and New England Federalism was up in arms. By the middle of the next year, it seemed more essential than ever for the Federalists to regain the White House: in order to end the Republicans' coercive program, to unshackle the New England economy, and to preserve the republic. In the thinking of well-placed party figures, moreover, it appeared crucial that they recapture the Presidency to maintain their own influence with the party's rank and file.

The task of organizing the autumn campaign fell to Massachusetts Federalists. By the early summer of 1808, party members throughout the country who hoped to coordinate a national campaign awaited a sign of Massachusetts Federalists' intentions. Philadelphia Federalist Charles Willing Hare wrote Central Committee Chairman Otis that "it is generally expected here that the first movement will be with you. And your advice would have decisive influence with us."[1] Characteristically, Otis quickly assumed the responsibility pressed upon him by Hare. Within a week, an ad hoc twenty-man committee, which an early caucus of the new legislature had appointed, named a smaller council of five men to correspond with Federalists in the other states and to establish a united effort to secure the Presidency in November. Five high-placed party activists—Otis, George Cabot, Christopher Gore, James Lloyd, and Timothy Bigelow—made up this special committee.[2]

Within a few days of its appointment, the group met and decided to propose a general meeting of Federalists from all the states—in effect, the first presidential nominating convention at the national level—in order to agree upon a national party policy for the election and to fix on a party standard-bearer.[3]

---

[1]Charles Willing Hare to Otis, June 2, 1808, Otis MSS, Massachusetts Historical Society (hereafter MHS).

[2]Gore to Rufus King, June 9 & 16, 1808, King MSS, New York Historical Society (hereafter NYHS). Gore's letter of June 16 indicates that Hare's letter "hastened" but did not originate plans for a national party meeting, and it also reveals how swiftly the Massachusetts organization swung into action. Within a week of the first letter, Bigelow was off to Vermont, Otis to Rhode Island, and Edward St. Loe Livermore, a special emissary of the extraordinary committee, to New Hampshire. Of the five, Otis was then Senate President, Bigelow House Speaker, Gore an ex-governor and now a member of the state's lower house, and Lloyd, John Quincy Adams's recent replacement in the national Senate. Gore would be the next Federalist governor. Otis and Lloyd were also Central committeemen and Gore probably so. On earlier thinking about some sort of unified effort see, e.g., Gore to King, Mar. 10, 1808, Pickering to King, Jan. 19, 1808, King MSS, NYHS; Pickering to Charles Willing Hare, Jan. 16, 1808, Pickering MSS, MHS; Noah Webster to Wolcott, May 13, 1808, Wolcott MSS, Connecticut Historical Society (hereafter CHS); and [Boston] *New England Palladium* (hereafter *Palladium*), Feb. 23, 1808.

[3]Gore to King, June 16, 1808, King MSS, NYHS. For the central role of the Massachusetts figures, see Charles Willing Hare to Otis, June 19 & July 12, 1808, Egbert Benson to Otis, July 13, 1808, Abraham Van Vechten to Otis, July 21, 1808, Rutledge to Otis, Sept. 18, 1808, Jacob Radcliff *et al.* to Otis, Oct. 9, 1808, and Thomas Fitzsimons to Otis, Gore, & Lloyd, Oct. 4, 1808, Otis, MSS, MHS; and Otis to Rutledge, July 3, 1808, Rutledge MSS, Univ. of North Carolina (hereafter UNC). Other accounts of the convention, with

Then, for the next two months, it bent its every effort to secure
a full representation of the states at the convention and labored
to commit the convention beforehand to the antiadministration
candidacy of Republican George Clinton. The Clinton scheme
recommended itself for two reasons: it might in the first place
most effectively raise the political heat on the Jeffersonian Republicans, and in the second it would allow the Federalists
either to assume credit for an unlikely Clinton victory or to
blame the Republicans for his defeat. The burden of drumming
up support for the elder Clinton fell upon Otis, Gore, and
Lloyd, who journeyed to New York for the meeting.[4] The
durable and practical-minded Cabot, though reluctant to travel,
proved no less warm a partisan of the Clinton scheme and no
less concerned to promote the New Yorker's candidacy.[5]

The Clinton movement was a project of the Central
Committee and of the small circle surrounding it. What opposition to the plan existed developed from outside eastern
party circles. Berkshire's Theodore Sedgwick, for one, was unable to endure "the humiliating idea that those who alone
from education, fortune, character and principle are entitled
to command should voluntarily arrange themselves under the
banners of a party in all respects inferior, and in many odious,

---

which mine differs in emphasis, include Samuel Eliot Morison, "The
First National Nominating Convention, 1808," *American Historical
Review* (hereafter *AHR*), XVII (July 1912), 744-63; Morison, *The
Life and Letters of Harrison Gray Otis, Federalist, 1765-1848* (2 vols.,
Boston 1913), I, 303-308; and David Hackett Fischer, *The Revolution
of American Conservatism: The Federalist Party in the Era of Jeffersonian Democracy* (New York, 1965), pp. 84-87. The 1808 convention
took the place of the Federalist congressional caucus, which in that
year, because of the small size of the party delegation in Washington,
would have been unrepresentative of the party.
    [4]The composition of the Massachusetts delegation to New York
is revealed in Cabot to Pickering, Aug. 10, 1808, Henry Cabot Lodge,
Life and Letters of George Cabot (Boston, 1878), p. 397.
    [5]Cabot to Otis, Aug. 14, 1808 (two letters), Otis MSS, MHS.
See also Cabot to Rutledge, Aug. 15, 1808, Rutledge MSS, UNC, and
Cabot to Pickering, Aug. 10, 1808, Pickering MSS, MHS. Otis reported that Ames, then on his deathbed, also supported the Clinton
plan. Otis to Rutledge, July 3, 1808, Rutledge MSS, UNC.

to them." There were others who believed with Sedgwick that principles, and principles alone, should govern the party's stance.[6]

When the convention met, the members decided, after intensive deliberation and a close scouting of Clinton's prospects in New York and Pennsylvania, to offer a straight party ticket of Charles Cotesworth Pinckney and Rufus King. The old-style politicians had gained their way.[7] Yet, while conditions extraneous to New England forced the abandonment of the Massachusetts delegation's scheme, they did not change the minds of those Massachusetts party figures who had been the principal champions of a Clinton nomination. Otis was never reconciled to the party's choice, and, until the eve of the meeting of the state's presidential electors, he flirted with the idea of throwing New England's Federalist votes behind the New York Republican. But the resistance of other New England Federalists and the apparent futility of such a last-minute act were decisive in the end. Massachusetts went down to defeat with Pinckney and awaited four more years of Republican rule.[8]

The ardor of the Massachusetts party leaders for a separate Clinton ticket arose from their own special predicament. When put to the test, their effectiveness as political directors had recently been found wanting: by the summer of 1808 they had twice lost the governorship, twice the General Court, and once, amidst considerable recrimination, the presidential elec-

---

[6]Sedgwick to Otis, June 6, 1808, Otis MSS, MHS. See also Sedgwick to Otis, June 18, 1808, *ibid.*, and Otis to Sedgwick, June 23, 1808, Sedgwick MSS, MHS.

[7]See, e.g., Wolcott to Cabot, Sept. 7, 1808, Wolcott MSS, CHS; and Thomas Fitzsimons to Sedgwick, July 10, 1808, Sedgwick MSS, MHS. The official convention report is found in [Jacob Radcliff *et al.*] to [Otis?], [Sept. 1808], Otis MSS, MHS.

[8]Cabot & Otis to Christopher Champlin, Oct. 24, 1808, and Otis to [Champlin?], Dec. 5, 1808, bound with C. G. Mason, "Reminiscences of Newport," MSS Colls., Rhode Island Historical Society; King to Gore, Sept. 24, 1808, King MSS, NYHS; and James B. Mason to Otis, Nov. 21, 1808, Otis MSS, MHS.

toral slate. Now, caught up in the unprecedented Embargo crisis, they were more than ever expected to deliver the political goods. To make matters worse, in September, District Judge John Davis—a Massachusetts Federalist consistently dedicated to loose construction and nationalist principles—had upheld the constitutionality of the embargo acts.[9]

From outside the organization, the Federalist clergy was urging resistance to the government, and grass-roots pressures for some dramatic protest against the administration's commercial policies were rising. In mid-winter, the irrepressible Pickering, whom Cabot unsuccessfully sought to tranquilize, had written Republican governor James Sullivan a public letter which, distributed by the thousands, called upon all good New Englanders to condemn the administration and urged "that those States, whose farms are on the ocean, and whose harvests are gathered in every sea, should immediately and seriously consider how to preserve them. . . . Nothing but the sense of the commercial states, clearly and emphatically expressed, will save them from ruin."[1] "The scene we are witnessing," Josiah Quincy was led to reflect, "is altogether unparalleled in history. . . . A new writ is executed upon a whole people. Not, indeed, the old monarchial writ *ne exeat regum*, but a new republican writ, *ne exeat republican*." By late March, the western town of Northampton led the way in memorializing Congress to repeal the Embargo, and by late September roughly seventy other towns in the state had joined it. From those

---

[9]For some details on this decision, see John Quincy Adams to William Branch Giles, Dec. 10, 1808, reel 135, Adams Family Papers microfilm (hereafter Adams microfilm); *Documents Relating to New England Federalism, 1800-1815*, ed. Henry Adams (Boston, 1905), p. 223; and John Quincy Adams, *Parties in the United States* (New York, 1941), p. 100.

[1]David Osgood, *A Discourse, Delivered Before the Lieutenant Governor . . . May 31, 1809* [Boston? 1809], p. 25; and Timothy Pickering, *A Letter from the Hon. Timothy Pickering . . . Addressed to his Excellency James Sullivan* (Boston, 1808). The letter was printed in its entirety in the [Boston] *Columbian Centinel* (hereafter *Centinel*), Mar. 12, 1808. Pickering's own copy is dated Feb. 16, 1808. On Cabot's attempts to rein in Pickering, see Cabot to Pickering, Oct. 5, 1808, Lodge, *Cabot*, p. 308.

barred from electoral and judicial redress, the party leaders faced a growing rebellion in their own ranks.[2]

To compound the leadership's troubles with radical sentiment on one side, conservative concern about New England's real intentions was beginning to swell on the other. Rumors of secessionist plots, once again abroad, were driving middle-state Federalists to urge that their New England colleagues issue an unequivocal declaration of loyalty to the union.[3] Under these confusing circumstances, the fate of the entire party, state and national, seemed to ride with the Massachusetts strategists. They needed a winning ticket, not simply for their party's sake, but to dampen the mounting dissatisfaction with their own leadership. The plan to nominate Clinton was imperfect, but it did not seem unreasonable in a critical political setting. Long before Andrew Jackson's time, the presidential election was looming as the central consideration of American party politics, and party captains were seeking in the general nominating convention a national solution to local party ills.

Though anticipated, Madison's victory proved a heavy blow to the party captains. And as if to compound their embarrassment, the Republican leadership proceeded in early January 1809 to enact the Draconian Enforcement Act, which allowed for the seizure of goods on the mere suspicion that they were intended for export and authorized the use of army and naval forces to enforce the Embargo. The party leaders'

---

[2]Quincy in *The Debates and Proceedings in the Congress of the United States* (Washington, 1834-1856), usually cited as *Annals of Congress*, 10th Cong., House, 1st Sess., p. 2202; *Centinel*, Mar. 30, 1808; and Morison, *Otis*, I, 330-37. Many of these petitions can be found in the *Centinel* and *Palladium*, Apr.-Sept., 1808. An important sidelight on the discipline and efficiency of the Federalist organization is revealed in the petition campaign of 1808. Blank petitions were printed in large quantities by the county committees, then circulated in town and party meetings at which time they were filled in and signed. See the blank Memorial to Congress, Nov. 7, 1808, in the Rantoul MSS, Beverly, Mass., Historical Society.

[3]William H. Sumner to William Smith Shaw, Jan. 25, 1808, in Joseph B. Felt, *Memorials of William Smith Shaw* (Boston, 1852), pp. 251-52.

demoralization was complete. Political initiative in Massachusetts began to pass to the more radical voices.

People's patience with Washington had worn thin. Now they began to demand redress through the state government. "Having respectfully and earnestly petitioned the President of the United States and the Congress for relief," Newburyport Federalists declared, "We will address ourselves to the Legislature of our Commonwealth, as the more immediate guardians of our rights." "If the spirit of '76 was that of opposition to tyranny," exclaimed one Federalist, "so is that of the present moment. If that was a spirit of defiance to foreign tyranny, this is a spirit of opposition to domestick usurpation." "Submission," warned Theodore Sedgwick, "is not, then, to be expected."[4]

From town and county meetings, from farm and coastal communities, arose the call for overt and concerted protest. Petitions and remonstrances inundated the General Court. A Newburyport town meeting, "the most numerous ever witnessed in the town," declared all Embargo backers to be "violators of the Constitution of the United States" and called upon the General Court "as our last resort . . . to interpose in our behalf, and to adopt such measures for our relief, for the

[4]*Newburyport Resolutions*, dtd. Jan. 12, 1809 (Newburyport, Mass., 1809); *The Patriotick Proceedings of the Legislature of Massachusetts, During their Session from Jan. 26, to March 4, 1809* (Boston, 1809), p. 98; and Theodore Sedgwick to Theodore Sedgwick, Jr., Feb. 6, 1809, Sedgwick MSS, MHS. Before the Newburyport town meeting adopted these resolutions, 803 Newburyport Federalists had petitioned Congress for repeal. They received no response. Benjamin W. Labaree, *Patriots and Partisans: The Merchants of Newburyport, 1764-1815* (Cambridge, 1962), p. 164. The November special session of the General Court, called to settle on a mode of choosing presidential electors, stayed in session long enough to make a final appeal to Washington to rescind the Embargo. The legislative resolves are printed in the *Palladium*, Nov. 15, 1808. See also *Essex Resolutions*, dtd. Oct. 6, 1808 (Newburyport, Mass., 1808); *The Ordeal: A Critical Journal of Politicks and Literature*, ed. Joseph T. Buckingham (Boston, 1809), Feb. 18, 1809; Matthew Carey, *The Olive Branch, or Faults on Both Sides* (3rd ed., Boston, 1815), pp. 135-38; and Tufts, *An Address to the People of the County of Hampshire* (Northampton, 1809).

restoration of our rights and privileges, and the removal of the recent distressing evils, as may be compatible with the honor and dignity of the Commonwealth, and with the Constitution of the United States."[5] Local gatherings hinted that Federalists would use force to prevent compliance with the commercial laws, and some towns formed local armed committees of safety. "If *force* to *force* must be the dreadful result," wrote "Old Whig," ". . . [may] our hands possess a nerve, and our hearts be inspired with a spirit that shall not shrink, so long as the last vestige of tyranny defiles our land." Calls for secession, usually rare in the public press, now appeared in small but rising volume. Because, it was said, the Constitution was "a Treaty of Alliance and Confederation" and the government an association of states, then it followed "that whenever its provisions are violated, or its original principles departed from by a majority of the states or of their people, it is no longer an effective instrument, but that any state is at liberty by the *spirit of that contract* to withdraw itself from the union."[6]

George Cabot had earlier predicted that "the people will run mad," and now alarm overtook the men who just a short time before had been baffled by the torpor of their constituents. Had not the excitement aroused by the party organization itself perhaps gone too far? "The mass of the People of this

---

[5] *Newburyport Resolutions*, p. 13; and Labaree, *Patriots and Partisans*, pp. 166-67. The Boston town meeting itself, under the leadership of Otis, Daniel Sargent, and Samuel Dexter (the first two Central committeemen) echoed the appeals of the rest of the state Federalists, appealed to the General Court for aid, swore off all cooperation with the Embargo, and stigmatized those abiding by it as enemies of the Constitution. The party leaders not only went this far in genuine anger and protest; they had to go this far in order to keep up with public sentiment. *Boston Town Records, 1796-1813* (Boston, 1905), pp. 240-45.

[6] Labaree, *Patriots and Partisans*, pp. 166-68; and *Centinel*, Sept. 10, 1808, Jan. 14, Feb. 25, 1809. In New England, the Embargo was openly flouted and convictions for violating it could not be gotten in court. John Quincy Adams reported over forty cases in which juries would not convict. John Quincy Adams to William Branch Giles, Jan. 16, 1809, reel 135, Adams microfilm.

state," observed Christopher Gore, "are much more daring in their means, and measures of Opposition . . . than the Persons, whom they are pleased to style their leaders." The danger, he reasoned, was not so much violent protest against the administration as the possibility that the public frustration would spill over into disdain for all established leadership. And "this will rather take place in the outposts and in Boston, where the Merchants are too rich to hazard much on uncertain projects & in Defiance of Law." The public's loss of patience with moderate measures could be expected to assume political form when the General Court convened. "You may be assured," wrote Gore, "We shall have no easy task, to temper the zeal of our Representatives, when they assemble." Moreover, Massachusetts could not get out ahead of the other New England states, whose calls for redress had not reached fever pitch. "To run counter to them would destroy our own Majority & occasion a dreadful Revulsion."[7] How then stay in line with the rest of Federalist New England, satisfy the local expectation of action, and at the same time hold a lid on the radicalism of the general populace?

The leaders' plan to deal with their predicament began to take shape in mid-December. Although their deliberations eventually encompassed the Federalists of all New England, the party leaders tailored them at the start, like the Clinton scheme, to the needs of the Massachusetts cadremen. That the governor was still a Republican actually increased what little flexibility they possessed: because of the executive veto, the General Court could remonstrate and publicize its grievances without threat of committing the state government to some immoderate course. Frustrations could be vented and Republican follies exposed. In the meantime, the party captains could search for the middle ground.

What form the leaders' solution to their predicament would have taken is revealed in two letters from Otis, one to

---

[7]Cabot to Pickering, Dec. 31, 1807, Lodge, *Cabot*, p. 374; Gore to Pickering, Dec. 20, 1808, Pickering MSS, MHS; and Gore to Rufus King, Dec. 26, 1808, King MSS, NYHS.

Josiah Quincy in Washington, the other—recently identified—
to Roger Griswold in Hartford.[8] With Congress bent on
enforcing the Embargo, wrote the Central Committee Chairman, the principal hope of stemming the Republicans' headlong
rush to disaster lay with the states. To be sure, when the General Court meets, "the majority will require the bridle rather
than the spur. . . . This temper, you are sensible, must not be
extinguished for want of sympathy, nor permitted to burst
forth into imprudent excess." But, Otis wrote confidently, the
representatives would respect any course of action "deliberately
recommended by the leading members," although "it is a very
embarrassing question to determine the precise extent, to which
their measures of disapprobation shall be carried. Unless measures of an explicit and energetic character shall be adopted,
our people are enslaved and our country ruined. And on the
other hand the assumption of ground, on which the people
upon due reflection will not sustain their legislatures, would be
equally fatal to our cause and to the public interest." That is,
to do too little would risk the republican experiment and the
anger of the rank and file; to do too much would incur the
recriminatory wrath of Republicanism and a reaction against
the party throughout New England.

But, Otis continued, Massachusetts Federalism itself was
in an unusually delicate position, for the rest of the nation
considered the Commonwealth to be the home of secession,
neo-Toryism, and obstructionism. "The eternal nonsense, that
an Essex or a Boston Junto give the cue to the Eastern States,
and that the Federalists in those States are our Dupes and tools,
has been propagated with studious care, & with too much
success." Could not Connecticut Federalists, through their Central Committee, formulate a plan for a general meeting of New
England Federalist leaders either in Hartford or New York

---

[8]Otis to Quincy, Dec. 15, 1808, Edmund Quincy, *Life of
Josiah Quincy* (Boston, 1868), pp. 164-65; and [Otis] to [Roger
Griswold], Jan. 4, 1809, William Griswold Lane MSS, Yale. A copy
of the first letter has recently become available in the Quincy MSS,
MHS. The second letter is reproduced in Appendix I.

"for the purpose of more efficient remonstrance and more certain amendment to the Constitution" and to "prevent insurrection, civil commotion, fruitless opposition, or a convulsive severance of the union?" Here was a plan well fitted to the leadership's needs. A convention would appear the product of popular agitation, but party moderates could easily control it and, while offering a conservative attack on the administration, dampen the fires of radical protest.

By early January 1809, general approval of the convention proposal was near. Otis announced to Rutledge that the legislatures of New England would recommend that a convention to amend the Constitution be held after the spring elections. Gore wrote to Pickering of the need for sectional unity and requested the senator to scout out opinion in Congress regarding interstate cooperation. The chief concern was always the same: to control the public and to focus the protests, for, wrote Otis, the yeomanry were on the move. The people are in "a very feverish state," believed Sedgwick.[9] In no case among the party directors was there a thought of secession.[1]

---

[9]Otis to Rutledge, Dec. 15, 1808, Jan. 8, 1809, Rutledge MSS, UNC; Gore to Pickering, Dec. 20, 1808, Samuel Blanchard to Pickering, Jan. 16, 1809, Pickering MSS, MHS; and Sedgwick to Theodore Sedgwick, Jr., Feb. 6, 1809, Sedgwick MSS, MHS. Otis made clear in his letter to Rutledge of December 15 his belief that if the Federalists had followed his plan, Clinton might have been elected and the crisis of expectations avoided. John Quincy Adams refused to lend credence to Otis's efforts to extinguish the agitation, and Henry Adams followed him in believing that Otis was trying to keep the public fever up. John Quincy Adams to William Branch Giles, Jan. 16, 1809, reel 135, Adams microfilm; Henry Adams, *History of the United States of America During the Administrations of Jefferson and Madison* (9 vols., New York, 1889-98), IV, 280 ff.

[1]One of the foremost purposes of these men, on the contrary, was to prevent disunion. "The men who lead to the adoption of the [General Court] resolutions which you see do not direct their conduct merely to electioneering purposes," wrote Sedgwick to his son. "Everyone wishes to preserve the union if it can be done without ruin; but opinion is becoming more and more prevalent, that it will probably become impossible." Sedgwick to Theodore Sedgwick, Jr., Feb. 6, 1809, Sedgwick MSS, MHS. Pickering, it should be noted, had lost interest in disunion for the moment and was an exponent,

During the winter meeting of the General Court, Federalist Party leaders won the approval of three moderate resolutions. Only the first, which denounced the Enforcement Act as "unjust, oppressive, and unconstitutional, and not legally binding on the citizens of this state" could be considered a reward of the radicals, yet it also "earnestly recommended" that forcible resistance be eschewed. The second resolve stated the legislature's desire to "co-operate with any of the other states, in all legal and constitutional measures, for procuring such amendments to the constitution of the United States, as shall be judged necessary . . . to give to the commercial states their fair and just consideration in the government of the union." A final resolution directed Senate President Otis and House Speaker Timothy Bigelow to seek the cooperation of other states wishing "to preserve inviolate the Union of the States." Massachusetts Federalists awaited a convention call from another state.[2]

No New England state government responded. Even

---

like many of his fellow Massachusetts Federalists, of interposition. He was, of course, in favor of interposition without delay: "Some *cautious* men here of the Federal party discovered an inclination to wait patiently till the first of June the promised repeal of the embargo," he wrote early in 1809. From an outsider's viewpoint, the organization looked timid. Pickering to Gore, Jan. 8, 1809, Pickering MSS, MHS; and Pickering to Samuel P. Gardner, n.d., Adams, *New England Federalism*, p. 379. It was John Quincy Adams who linked rumors of a convention with fugitive threats of secession and concluded that a convention to propose disunion was in the offing. John Quincy Adams to Nahum Parker, Dec. 5, 1808, reel 135, Adams microfilm.

[2]The *Address*, resolutions, and various other speeches and proceedings of this session were published for wide public consumption as *The Patriotick Proceedings of the Legislature of Massachusetts, During their Session from Jan. 26, to March 4, 1809* (Boston, 1809). See also Israel Thorndike to Pickering, Feb. 2, 1809, Pickering MSS, MHS. On the unsuccessful attempts of the party leadership to keep the General Court in session until after Madison's inauguration speech revealed what might be in store, see Gore to Rufus King, Feb. 22, 1809, King MSS, NYHS: "The wish of many has been to sit until the 11th March, but the Federalists are constantly returning home, either called by their own affairs, or from Fear of giving Discontent to their townsmen, by imposing the additional expence, which is incurred by so large a Representation."

before the General Court had concluded its work, Congress, acting under the spur of Northern Republicans and shaken by the uproar from New England, rescued the Federalist leaders from their plight by going on record for the Embargo's repeal.[3] Without meeting, the convention had done its work— or so New England Federalists might well have believed. If hopes of permanent constitutional reform had to be shelved, it was a sacrifice worth suffering for cooled tempers and the restoration of trade.

II

FOUR YEARS LATER, events appeared to relive themselves. The outbreak of war in 1812 and the demands of another presidential election, coming upon the heels of Gerry's tumultuous administration, catapulted the party directorate into the thick of a second political crisis. With the news of Madison's war message in late June, Federalist Massachusetts was once again aflame. When, as much to appease as to consolidate public sentiment, Governor Caleb Strong issued a call for a public fast to decry the war "against the nation from which we are descended, and which for many generations has been

---

[3]New Hampshire and Vermont were in Republican hands. Plans for the Connecticut response merely echoing the Massachusetts resolves are to be found in Elizur Goodrich to Simeon Baldwin, Feb. 26, 1809, Baldwin MSS, Yale. On the reaction outside Massachusetts and the effect of the Embargo repeal on these maneuverings, see Morison, *Otis*, II, 13-14; Adams, *History*, IV, Chaps. XVIII & XIX; Carey, *Olive Branch*, Chap. XXVI; and *Documents Respecting the Resolutions of the Legislature of Massachusetts, Passed February 15, 1812: Containing a Refutation of Certain Insinuations Against the Hon. Messrs. H. G. Otis and Timothy Bigelow, Esqrs.* [Boston? 1812]. The last was printed by order of the House after the Republican-controlled Senate in the wake of the John Henry letters fiasco had required Otis and Bigelow to submit all papers relating to the 1809 proceedings for scrutiny. The pamphlet contains the tepid responses of Connecticut and Rhode Island. Jefferson never forgave Congressmen Joseph Story and Ezekial Bacon for throwing their influence behind repeal, and he candidly admitted the role played by the New England protests in bringing it about.

the bulwark of the religion we profess," the Federalist clergy unlimbered their heaviest rhetorical weapons. In one of the most inflammatory productions of the era, Elijah Parish of Byfield told his parishioners to "proclaim an honourable neutrality; let the southern *Heroes* fight their own battles, and guard . . . against the just vengeance of their lacerated slaves. . . . Break those chains, under which you have sullenly murmured, during the long, long reign of democracy; . . . and once more breathe that free, commercial air of New England which your fathers always enjoyed. . . . Protest did I say, protest? *Forbid this war to proceed in New-England.*"

Others joined their voices to his. War, Samuel Worcester warned, is "one of God's expressly appointed judgments, for the punishment of guilty nations." Offer no aid to the effort, admonished John Sylvester John Gardiner, the Boston Episcopal cleric. Either "cut the connexion" with the Southern states "or so far alter the national constitution, as to ensure yourselves a due share in the government." Since the union had long been virtually dissolved, it was time that "this portion of the *disunited* states should take care of itself. . . . The time has arrived when common prudence is pusillanimity, and moderation has ceased to be a virtue."[4]

The clerics correctly gauged the public temper. By mid-July, all signs pointed to a mounting violence of mood and action. Public protest meetings took place spontaneously. For the first time in over three years, the public heard calls for disunion, men disclaimed an obligation voluntarily to aid the war, and newspapers, themselves unable to risk censure, printed the most extreme statements of disaffection and frustration. "Our common interests, liberties, and safety," Essex County

---

[4]Elijah Parish, *A Protest Against the War. A Discourse Delivered at Byfield, Fast Day, July 23, 1812* (Newburyport, Mass., 1812), pp. 16-17; Samuel Worcester, *Calamity, Danger, and Hope. A Sermon . . . July 23, 1812* (Salem, Mass., 1812), p. 10; and John S. J. Gardiner, *A Discourse Delivered at Trinity Church, Boston, July 23, 1812 . . .* (Boston, 1812), pp. 15-19. See also David Osgood, *A Solemn Protest Against the Late Declaration of War . . .* (Cambridge, 1812), pp. 9-10.

Federalists declared, "are now more injured, oppressed and endangered, by the doings of our own National Government, than they were when in 1775 we took arms to protect and defend them against the measures of the government of Great-Britain." As if to repay a Republican attack upon a Federalist press in Baltimore, a Boston crowd seized Republican congressman Charles Turner of Plymouth on an August evening and kicked him through town. Even the old-school conservatives lost their reserve. "There is but one way left to save us from the yoke of Bonaparte and Virginia," Thomas Dawes wrote to his friend Noah Webster, *"the rising of the New England people. I mean nothing illegal or unconstitutional; I do not mean a Whiskey rebellion or any thing like it. You know what I mean,"* he hinted darkly. "And tho' *late,* I think with you, it is not *too* late."[5]

What Dawes and Webster had in mind was an old plan, a convention of New England Federalists. Reviving the project of 1808, Webster had just urged such a convention upon Governor Strong, who had brought Webster's written recommendation to the attention of his Federalist-controlled council. There it met with disfavor, and the council decided to postpone its consideration until the party had had the opportunity to try a milder expedient. In the meantime, the caucus called on the party committees to hold county conventions and local party meetings to condemn the war and send memorials to Congress and the President.[6] It was at this moment that a

---

[5]*Centinel,* June 27, July 4 & 18, 1812; *Palladium,* July 24, 1812; and Thomas Dawes to Noah Webster, June 25, 1812, Webster MSS, New York Public Library (hereafter NYPL). Pickering, not unexpectedly, was quickly drawn to thoughts of disunion, but, as I have pointed out, when he wrote, "I would not be deluded by a *word.* To my ears there is no magic in the sound of Union," he had in mind a division between East and West. Pickering to Edward Pennington, July 12, 1812, Pickering MSS, MHS.

[6]Thomas Dawes to Noah Webster, June 25, July 24, 1812, Webster MSS, NYPL. Printed circular letter, ? to Worcester County Federalist Committee, [June 1812], Ward MSS, American Antiquarian Society (hereafter AAS). Another unaddressed copy is in Misc. Broadside (hereafter Bdse.) Coll., Library of Congress (hereafter LC). See also *Address of the House of Representatives to the People of*

gathering of Northampton men closely associated with Webster tried to broaden the scheme for separate county conventions into a movement for a statewide conclave of Federalists.[7] Had such a convention met, its momentum would undoubtedly have resulted then and there in a call for a Hartford Convention.

Yet these simultaneous programs for state and New England conventions were both abortive. Organizational confusion was not to blame nor, except for Samuel Dexter's able attack on the state convention plan in the Boston town meeting, was outright opposition. Rather, party leaders knew that the

---

Mass., dtd. June 25, 1812. Webster, who had recently moved from New Haven to Amherst, had long been drawn to the convention idea. See Webster to Wolcott, May 13, 1808, in Emily E. F. Ford and Emily E. F. Skeel, *Notes on the Life of Noah Webster* (2 vols., New York, 1912), II, 36.

[7] See Chap. VI, Sec. ii. The Northampton meeting led the way in calling for a statewide convention and was followed by similar meetings in Essex, Worcester, Middlesex, Plymouth, Cumberland, and other counties. The governor's son, Lewis Strong, was not only appointed by the Hampshire meeting to attend the proposed state convention, but he wrote the memorial which issued at Northampton. Joseph Lyman, later a Hartford Convention member, was also present and was chosen to attend the state convention. *Proceedings of a Convention of Delegates From the Counties of Hampshire, Franklin, and Hampden, Holden at Northampton, the 14th and 15th of July 1812* (Northampton, 1812); and Josiah Gilbert Holland, *History of Western Massachusetts* (2 vols., Springfield, Mass., 1855), I, 323.

The declaration of the Essex County meeting, written by Pickering, justified such a gathering because the state senate was in the hands of "usurpers," that is, of supporters of the Gerrymander. Pickering, rarely to be outdone in demagoguery, wrote that "the remedy is in the People's own hands" and won concurrence in the statement that "our common interests, liberties and safety, are now more injured, oppressed, and endangered, by the doings of our own National Government, than they were when in 1775 we took arms to protect and defend them against the measures of the government of Great-Britain." Once universally believed, such revolutionary logic would be irresistible. *Declaration of the County of Essex in the Commonwealth of Massachusetts, by the Delegates assembled in Convention at Ipswich, on Tuesday, the 21st of July, 1812* (Salem, Mass., 1812). The attribution to Pickering is by his son John on the copy in the MHS. Henry Adams is wrong in making this meeting out to be the earliest response to the Central Committee's call. The Hampshire convention met on the 14th. Adams, *History*, VI, 401-02.

Massachusetts senate, still in Republican hands due to the Gerrymander, would kill every official call for a convention. Even more important, if the party could take the presidential election in the fall, a convention would be unnecessary.[8]

Indeed, it was with the fall election in mind that many Massachusetts Federalists, especially those who had always opposed a general convention of New England Federalists, undertook to unite their efforts behind a "peace" Republican, to establish a "peace party," and to put up "peace candidates."[9] Connecticut and Massachusetts Federalists, with the aid of their Pennsylvania party colleagues, revived the old plan to support a Clinton—this time, DeWitt Clinton, who had answered discreet Federalist inquiries with a pledge to seek peace if elected. And, as before, these men set in motion a movement for a party convention in New York.[1]

---

[8]Later on, Pickering reflected that had a convention of New England states been held in 1812, the war would have ended. "But timidity in the garb of *prudence* defeated that salutary proposal." Pickering to Lowell, Oct. 15, 1814, Pickering MSS, MHS. Dexter's part in weakening the state convention movement is noted in Morison, *Otis*, II, 60-61. In a letter which quite clearly reflected the views of the Central Committee of which he was a leading member, William Sullivan wrote in late August 1812 that a convention at that time could only recommend constitutional amendments and "this will perhaps be done by the circumstances of the war and the activity of the Clintonians. . . . I am inclined to wait for events." Despite what ideas others may have had for a general meeting of Federalists, the organization heads right from the start limited its goals to remonstrance and amendment. Sullivan to George Bliss, Aug. 29, 1812, Gratz Coll., Pennsylvania Historical Society (hereafter PHS).

[9]On the Massachusetts Federalist attempt to exploit the peace issue, see, e.g., *Address of the House of Representatives to the People of Mass.*, dtd. June 25, 1812; and William Orne *et al.* to ?, Mar. 24, 1813, Misc. Bdse. Coll., AAS.

[1]For accounts of the convention, with which I differ in some details, see John S. Murdock, "The First National Nominating Convention," *AHR*, I (July 1896), 680-83; Morison, *Otis*, I, 309-19; and Fischer, *Revolution of American Conservatism*, pp. 87-90. On Connecticut's central role in reactivating convention maneuvers, see Theodore Dwight to Sullivan, Aug. 7, 1812, Dwight Family MSS, NYPL; and Peter Augustus Jay to John Jay, Sept. 17, 1812, Jay MSS, Columbia. Josiah Quincy conferred personally with Clinton at an early date. Charles R. King, *The Life and Correspondence of Rufus King* (6 vols., New York, 1894-1900), V, 266. See also Josiah O. Hoff-

VIII: *To the Hartford Convention*

Central committeeman William Sullivan and some Connecticut party notables initiated the convention plans at a meeting in Saratoga Springs shortly after the declaration of war.[2] Within a few weeks, procedures like those of 1808 resulted in the appointment by the Massachusetts Federalist caucus of a special committee, a number of whose members were Central committeemen, which voted that Clinton be supported, and named delegates to the New York meeting.[3]

---

man to Otis, July 17, 1812, Otis MSS, MHS. There is considerable information on the activities of the Pennsylvania Federalists in the Daggett MSS, Yale, in the Daniel Webster MSS, LC & New Hampshire Hist. Soc., and in Jabez D. Hammond, *The History of Political Parties in the State of New York* (4th ed., 2 vols., Buffalo, N.Y., 1850), I, 319-89 *passim*. A full account of the convention remains to be written. A revealing letter, showing the link between the fear of violence and the planning for a convention, is Otis to Rutledge, July 31, 1812, Rutledge MSS, UNC.

[2] On what was not altogether convincingly reported to be the accidental meeting in Saratoga Springs of Sullivan, Calvin Goddard, Jonathan Dwight, and Roger Griswold, see Sullivan's own account in *The Public Men of the Revolution* (Philadelphia, 1847), pp. 350-51. Theodore Dwight seems also to have been present. Dwight to Sullivan, Aug. 7, 1812, Dwight Family MSS, NYPL. Warren Dutton and Israel Thorndike may have been in Hartford as early as July to promote joint support for Clinton. See Charles Warren, *Jacobin and Junto* (Cambridge, 1931), p. 255. Sullivan kept in close touch throughout the autumn with the Pennsylvania steering committee deputized to follow up the convention action. See, e.g., Sullivan to William Meredith, Oct. 5, 1812, Meredith MSS, PHS.

[3] Otis to Sullivan, Aug. 17, 1812, Misc. MSS Colls., NYPL, also printed in Morison, *Otis*, I, 318-19. This letter is a revealing commentary on the secondary role of western Massachusetts in these proceedings, for, almost as an afterthought, Otis suggests that the "Hampshire people" be informed that they "may" send someone to New York; and from notations on the letter it appears that the Hampshire man was not decided upon until long after the committee had chosen the other delegates. I conclude from the accounts in Murdock, "The First National Nominating Convention," that Theodore Sedgwick attended the convention as western Massachusetts' representative. Gore, Cabot, and Sullivan were at the center of these activities, and Otis refused to go to New York unless the entire Massachusetts delegation backed Clinton. Gore to Rufus King, Oct. 5, 1812, King MSS, NYHS. Otis was confident enough to declare on many occasions that "it is unequivocally the sentiment of the Federalists of this State that Mr C must be the man." Otis to Samuel Breck, Sept. 5, 1812, Library Co. of Philadelphia. See also Peter Augustus Jay to John

Better organization this time resulted in a well-attended, secret, presidential nominating convention of roughly seventy Federalists in September 1812. After a series of complex maneuvers throughout the autumn, Federalists everywhere finally lined up behind Clinton. And this time the Federalists came close to success: at the final count, Clinton needed only a scant nineteen electoral votes—the votes of Pennsylvania would have sufficed—to have defeated James Madison and carried the nation.[4]

But in Massachusetts, this fourth successive Federalist failure in the presidential stakes invited only dark forebodings. Prospects for a moderate Federalist politics in Massachusetts diminished swiftly. From this time on, any opposition to administration policies, in order to be effective, would have to take form outside the government. And for those who hoped that 1813 would bring some improvement in the nation's posture, only bad tidings were in store. The military situation worsened, the likelihood of peace lessened, and the administra-

Jay, Sept. 17, 1812, Jay MSS, Columbia, and Otis to Rutledge, July 31, 1812, Rutledge MSS, UNC. The *Centinel* had been calling for Clinton's nomination since July. *Centinel*, July 22, 1812.

[4] According to Gore's account, Cabot, Strong, and Parsons favored Clinton's nomination. Gore himself opposed it. Gore to Rufus King, Oct. 15, 1812, King MSS, NYHS. On the central role which Otis once again played in developing what support there was for Clinton, see, e.g., Sullivan, *Public Men of the Revolution*, pp. 350-51, Otis to Rutledge, July 31, 1812, Rutledge MSS, UNC; and James Milnor *et al.* to Otis, July 27, 1812, George Tibbits to Otis, Oct. 22, 1812, Otis MSS, MHS. A copy of the convention's resolves, along with a partial membership list, is in the Washburn Papers, MHS. The convention had every intention of keeping its proceedings secret until a final post-convention scouting of Federalist opinion revealed an overwhelming sentiment one way or the other regarding Clinton. So when news of the convention broke prematurely in the papers of both parties, the anger and embarrassment of the party leaders knew no bounds. See Otis to ?, Oct. 23, 1812, Misc. MSS Colls., NYPL; Sullivan to William Meredith, Oct. 23, 1812, Meredith MSS, PHS; Murdock, "First National Nominating Convention," p. 683; and *Centinel*, Oct. 21, 1812. For an anti-Clintonian tract by a Massachusetts Federalist, see *Washington to the People of the United States on the Choice of a President* (Boston, 1812).

tion steadfastly refused to modify its policy of conscripting state militia forces into national service. Culminating these successive Federalist reverses was the imposition of an embargo, as total and restrictive as the measures of Jefferson's presidency, in the final weeks of the year.

To Federalists, these developments signaled the improbability of peace. And with every dashed peace hope, despair deepened until customary modes of redress—petitions, memorials, remonstrances—seemed no longer worth the effort. The government was deaf to protest, and the rights and needs of a political minority were only ignored and scoffed at. "Petitions, memorials, and remonstrances from individuals, corporations and States, have already often been tried in vain," exclaimed Timothy Bigelow, "and to repeat them, under existing circumstances, would be but to invite contempt." "Instead of wishing to withdraw from the Union," Middlesex County Federalists argued, "we fear that Government has withdrawn from us." Other views were even more ominous: "The determination that was necessary in 1776," declared a newspaper writer, "is necessary now."[5]

It was the embargo of December 1813—which prohibited the coasting trade and which the administration enforced with a rigor disastrous to the flourishing smuggling enterprises of New England's borders and to the people of Nantucket—which put an end to Federalist patience. With the General Court once again due to convene, Federalists throughout the Commonwealth began to press their demands upon the party leadership. Town meetings and hastily called party caucuses drafted remonstrances and petitioned the legislature for relief.

The most insistent and intensive pressures for state action

---

[5]Timothy Bigelow, *An Address, Delivered on the Third Anniversary of the Washington Benevolent Society, April 30, 1814* (Boston, 1814), p. 16; *Address to the Friends of Independence, Peace and Union in the County of Middlesex* (n.p., 1812), p. 61; and *Centinel,* May 26, 1813. See also the New Bedford memorial, *ibid.,* Feb. 9, 1814.

originated outside the capital. Throughout 1813, Federalists in the interior grew convinced that the Bostonians were temporizing, and by early 1814 even so sedate and cautious a gentleman as Beverly's Nathan Dane was reported to have remarked that he had learned from "long experience" that "it will not do to trust the Boston lead."[6] Coupled with concerns for defense and survival, the long-rankling distrust of the Boston-centered party captains was producing a political rebellion to the west.

What finally blossomed into the Hartford Convention originated with the party committees of Hampshire County. In late December 1813, the Federalist-controlled town meeting of South Hadley instructed the town's representative to the General Court to propose a convention of New Englanders to consider what action could be taken in the "awful crisis." By the very first days of January, a group of men, including county committeeman Joseph Lyman, called a meeting of "some of the most discreet and intelligent inhabitants of the old County of Hampshire" for "a free and dispassionate discussion touching our public concerns," in time to make known its views for the early sessions of the General Court. At this meeting, Noah Webster revived his 1812 plan for a "Convention of Delegates from the Northern States to agree upon & urge certain amendments to the Constitution." And the gathering chose Webster to draft a circular letter on the subject to the towns of Old Hampshire. Soon, petitions which

---

[6]The agitation for action by the state government followed close on the heels of Clinton's defeat. "Epaminondas," *ibid.*, Dec. 28, 1812, lay the responsibility at the door of the General Court: "At your hands . . . we demand deliverance." On contemporary manifestations of anti-Boston sentiment, see Alexander H. Everett to John Quincy Adams, June 25, 1813, reel 415, Adams microfilm, and Samuel Putnam to Pickering, Feb. 11, 1814, Pickering MSS, MHS. Pickering blamed "the Headquarters of Good Principles," i.e., the Boston leadership, for having quashed plans for the 1812 convention. Pickering to Lowell, Oct. 15, Nov. 7, 1814, *ibid.* New pressures for a New England convention and concerted measures of the New England states are found in *Centinel* and *Palladium*, Jan. & Feb., 1814.

had their origin in Webster's circular began to flood the legislature from western Massachusetts.[7]

Webster's letter reviewed the standing grievances of Massachusetts Federalism. New England's influence was at an end: "The southern states have an influence in our national councils altogether disproportionate to their wealth, strength, and resources." Much of their excessive weight arose from the unjust and unconstitutional admission of new states not contemplated by the Founding Fathers. The compromise whereby "the northern states acceded to the representation of slaves . . . upon the express stipulation in the constitution, that they should be protected in the enjoyment of their commercial rights" has been "repeatedly violated." The Northern states "whose active foreign trade is so necessarily connected with the interest of the farmer and mechanic" had been prostrated by a series of embargoes the most recent of which, in its enforcement provisions and its proscription of the coasting trade, was arbitrary and unconstitutional.

All of these evils might well be removed by peace, wrote Webster, but "our hopes of a speedy peace are not very sanguine." Moreover, peace would be but a temporary remedy to permanent evils growing out of a "perverse construction" of the Constitution; only constitutional amendment would guarantee the Northern states "their due weight and influence in our national councils." Therefore, Webster's letter argued, town meetings should memorialize the General Court to pro-

---

[7]MSS memorial from South Hadley, Dec. 20, 1813, Senate Doc. 4820/28, Mass. Archives. The original meeting of Hampshire Federalists is reported in Joseph Lyman to Noah Webster, Jan. 5, 1814, Webster MSS, NYPL. Webster later marked this letter, "Origin of Hartford Convention, Paper No. 1." The full text of this and Webster's circular letter, signed by Lyman, are most conveniently found in Noah Webster, *A Collection of Papers on Political, Literary and Moral Subjects* (New York, 1843), pp. 311-14. Details of the January 19 meeting are contained in Webster's hand on his copy of the printed circular letter in the Webster MSS, NYPL, which he marked, "This is the germ of the celebrated Hartford Convention, NW. paper No. 2." The presence at these meetings of the governor's son suggests the governor's knowledge and approval of them.

pose "a convention of all the northern and commercial states, by delegates to be appointed by their respective legislatures, to consult upon measures in concert, for procuring such alterations in the federal constitution, as will give to the northern states a due proportion of representation, and secure them from the future exercise of powers injurious to their commercial interests."

By the time the General Court met in late January, agitation for a convention had become all but universal among Commonwealth Federalists. Yet, as Otis later conceded, it was the Hampshire leadership alone which initiated the scheme. To Webster, he wrote a "direct negative" when asked if Boston had anything to do with the project's origins. "We at Boston played only second fiddle to our country friends. . . . My impression [is] that the County of Hampshire was always foremost in these matters, and that if I had been hanged as a ringleader, you & your friends would have been bound in honor to maintain my family." Webster's assertions were no less unequivocal: "Citizens of Boston had no concern in originating the proposal for a convention," he wrote around 1843; "it was wholly the project of the people in old Hampshire County."[8]

As soon as it met, the General Court came under irresistible pressure to act for New England's relief. At least forty memorials, all imbued with revolutionary fervor, demanded redress for the people's grievances. "There was a time," wrote petitioners from Hadley, "when our country, under the protecting providence of the Almighty, and guided by Washington . . . presented to the eyes of an admiring world

---

[8]Otis's statements are in a letter to Webster, May 6, 1840, Webster MSS, NYPL. Webster's are in his essay, "Origin of the Hartford Convention of 1814," in *Collection of Papers*, p. 314. See also "A Letter of Noah Webster to Daniel Webster, 1834," ed. Worthington C. Ford, *AHR*, IX (Oct. 1903), 96-104, for a letter of Sept. 6, 1834, in which Noah Webster wrote of the Hartford Convention that he was "personally concerned in the origination of it," that the plan was originated by the "people in their primary assemblies," and that "not one person in Boston had any concern in these proposals."

the most perfect specimen of national happiness and the nearest approximation to the felicity of Paradise which since the fall of man this great globe ever exhibited." But now the nation had degenerated into "a gigantic system of despotism." "The history of the late administration of the National Government," wrote the memorialists of Wendell in the manner of the Declaration of Independence, is "a history of repeated injuries and usurpations, having a direct tendency to the Establishment of an Absolute tyranny over these States. Let a few facts be submitted to a Candid World."

To Hatfield Federalists, the war guaranteed "the certain destruction of our moral virtues, the basis of our republican institutions." Brookfield memorialists in the center of the state would no longer tolerate their plight: "We cannot, we will not be slaves. We have not submitted, we will not submit to be the willing Dupes of wanton Oppression, foreign or domestick." New Bedford agreed: "The time has arrived in which it is incumbent on the people of this state, to prepare themselves for the great duty, of protecting, by their own vigor, their unalienable rights."[9]

So high was the popular fever that the state party captains had great difficulty in controlling the public demands for radical action. Unlike 1809, the entire state government was in Federalist hands: the caucus might defy discipline, and no Republican governor could be counted upon to rescue the party leadership by vetoing a convention bill. This time, the party leaders alone could deflate the popular excitement.

Although they differed in their assessment of the session's work, observers had no difficulty agreeing that the organization's leaders were hard pressed to maintain order in the General Court. Radical speeches, loudly applauded by galleries out of sympathy with moderation, hailed Britain, excoriated

---

[9]These MSS memorials, numbered Senate Docs. 4820/36, 4820/39, 4820/47, 4820/45, and 4820/19, are preserved, along with many others, in the Mass. Archives. Tallies of the petitions rolling in upon the General Court are contained in the *Centinel*, Jan. & Feb., 1814. Many of the petitions are printed there.

the administration, and proposed some drastic measures. Many urged that the state set up an autonomous customs house, that all persons—including, by implication, federal officials—be prohibited from restraining any vessels in their chosen voyages, and that the state government organize a force of 30,000 men to "protect the citizens of this commonwealth in the enjoyment of their constitutional rights." It was time, thundered Samuel Fessenden of New Gloucester, Maine, "to take our rights into our own hands. . . . The sooner we come at issue with the general government the better."

As usual, the task of smothering the agitation fell upon Otis. He did not enjoy his responsibility, being, reported an observer, "without the slightest taste for political martyrdom." But before galleries silent because "he was not up to their mark," Otis uncharacteristically argued the right of secession in order to allay the popular uproar. He was reported, however, to have added that "we were not yet ready to proceed to those extremities."[1] Although his efforts and those of his fellow moderates resulted in the postponement of the convention, Otis had found himself dangerously exposed. He was not likely to let public sentiment get so far ahead of him again.

Part of Otis's difficulty was that as the convention appeared more imminent it aroused national concern. As a result, conflicting counsel flowed in from everywhere. From Philadelphia, Charles Willing Hare, like others a man of caution grown desperate, urged Otis to avoid threats of disunion but to declare the new embargo "absolutely void," to prohibit its enforcement, and to carry through Fessenden's plan for a state customs establishment. From men in Congress, counsel was in a different vein: "All the advice from this place," wrote Jeremiah Mason of New Hampshire, "disuaded from violent measures." Pickering, who judged Otis "timid" and who once again urged a convention independently of the Old Hampshire

---

[1] These events are reported in Francis Baylies to William Baylies, Jan. 24, 1814, Misc. Bound Colls., MHS; [Lucius Manlius Sargent], *Reminiscences of Samuel Dexter* (Boston, 1857), pp. 78-79; and Morison, *Otis*, II, 89.

inspiration, was disgusted when his confidant, Samuel Putnam, reported that a convention would not be proposed. "You cannot sufficiently realize," wrote Putnam, "the embarrassments which the Politicks of the Boston Stamp have occasioned." The party leadership, by his report, was indecisive and confused. For the first time, it appeared, it had lost control of the party.[2]

Yet, by early February, a workable consensus, which put the meeting off to allow further consultation, had developed. It conceded to the radicals their position on the embargo and acknowledged the utility of a convention. The agreement was embodied in a report on the town memorials. Drafted by a special caucus committee composed of one member from each county, the report explicitly rejected the idea of another remonstrance to Congress "again and again resorted to . . . with no other effect than to increase the evils complained of." It opposed the nullification of the embargo on the ground that it was already void. It approved the plan for an interstate convention to amend the Constitution. But in an attempt to provide not only more time for planning but also an opportunity to cloak the convention with popular legitimacy, it recommended first seeking public approval at the spring elections. The Federalist Party of Massachusetts was going to the people.[3]

---

[2]Charles Willing Hare to Otis, Feb. 10, 1814, Morison, *Otis*, II, 174-75; Jeremiah Mason to Jesse Appleton, Mar. 27, 1814, in [George S. Hilliard], *Memoir and Correspondence of Jeremiah Mason* (Cambridge, 1873), pp. 89-91; and Samuel Putnam to Pickering, Feb. 12, 1814, Pickering to Putnam, Feb. 3 & 4, 1814, Pickering MSS, MHS. Years later, Pickering, reflecting that he had never held Otis in his confidence, approvingly related the observation of an acquaintance of the machine leader: "Otis was bold as a lion; but in a different situation, timid as a hare." Pickering to William Coleman, Apr. 30, 1827, *ibid.* Even the usually prudent George Thacher and Thomas Dawes were at their wits' end, writing that the tyranny that Massachusetts was now forced to bear was worse than Lord North's oppression. Thacher to Cyrus King, Feb. 14, 1814, Cyrus King MSS, Columbia; and Dawes to Noah Webster, Feb. 17, 1814, Webster MSS, NYPL. See also Labaree, *Patriots and Partisans*, p. 192.

[3]On maneuverings behind this report, see George Wallingford to Cyrus King, Feb. 1, 1814, Cyrus King MSS, Columbia, and Putnam

The state elections of 1814 offered a good chance to test public sentiment on the convention. After the resounding defeat in 1813, the Republicans nominated the moderate Federalist Samuel Dexter for governor. Dexter deplored the administration's war policy, but he also found intolerable the Federalists' convention plans and their "indiscriminate opposition" to the war. By appealing to the war's moderate opponents, Dexter hoped to make the election a clear referendum on the convention. The results could only be viewed as a vote of confidence in the Federalists: roughly fifty-five per cent of the vote went to Caleb Strong. And in the legislative canvass soon after, the Federalists, campaigning on the theme that "the hand of despotism has prepared *fetters of iron* to succeed their icy chains," gained control of the lower house by a margin of 204. Not only were the old stalwarts of the moderate and radical wings of the party returned to this General Court, but western Massachusetts' proportion of the House membership rose appreciably. It was going to be more difficult than ever to avert a New England convention.[4]

Yet, again as in 1809, the repeal of the 1813 embargo and the fall of Bonaparte reduced public agitation, and, by the early summer of 1814, a convention suddenly seemed less urgent. With Otis arguing that precipitous action might impede the

---

to Pickering, Feb. 11 & 12, 1814, Pickering MSS, MHS. The final report, known as "Lloyd's Report" after its author, James Lloyd, Jr., appeared as the *Report on the Memorial of Deerfield, and Several Other Towns, Against the Existing War and Embargo* [Boston, 1814]; was printed in the *Centinel*, Feb. 23, 1814; and is retained in the Mass. Archives as Senate Doc. 4820/1. Long after the Hartford Convention, Otis noted that the meeting had been "postponed for twelve months, by the influence of those who now sustain the odium of the measures." Otis to Mrs. Willard, in Emma H. Willard, *History of the United States* (Philadelphia, 1843), p. 351n.

[4]Joseph Allen *et al.* to "The Friends of Peace & Union," March 8, 1814, Misc. Bdse. Coll., AAS. Dexter's position was made clear in *Mr. Dexter's Address to the Electors of Mass.* It was rebutted by [Lowell], *A Temperate Examination of Mr. Dexter's Address, by a Citizen of Massachusetts* (Boston, 1814). (These two pieces were first published separately and, later, together.) In this General Court, western Massachusetts' proportion of the lower house representation jumped sharply at the expense of Maine's. (Table VII, Appendix II.)

peace negotiations then in progress, the party leadership took advantage of the rapid improvement in the public temper to ward off once again demands for an early meeting of New England Federalists. The summer passed, the General Court met, no action was taken.

But events conspired to provide only a short breathing spell. By midsummer, the war had vastly expanded. July witnessed the first military engagements on the New England coast. By August, the English had carried war to the entire nation: New York was invaded, Washington burned, and Maine invested south to the Penobscot. Demands for a separate peace, for secession, for Madison's resignation, were heard once again. And to these demands Federalists once again added complaints about the inaction of the state government. The proceedings of two years, announced one outspoken diatribe, had led Federalists to expect "that if the General Government did not immediately make peace, that then New-England would secede from the Union and make a separate peace for themselves." But neither peace nor secession had occurred. Therefore, wrote the anonymous author, "I believe that I am not alone in thinking that the leading Federalists have (not in a direct, but) in an indirect way promised what they dare not perform." Under such converging threats of internal rebellion, foreign invasion, and conquest, the Federalist state administration had to go ahead with convention plans at last. In early September, reasoning that there existed "hardly any chance" of peace within three months, Strong ordered the General Court back into special session to adopt such measures as "the present dangerous state of public affairs may render expedient."[5]

---

[5]Don Quixote [pseud.], *The Ichneumon. Being an Essay on Politics, Written in the District of Maine, July, 1814* (n.p., n.d.). A copy is in the Yale Library. Also Caleb Strong to Clarissa (Strong) Dwight, Oct. 19, 1814, Dwight Family MSS, Yale. Otis's arguments against a convention during the summer session are indicated in Noah Webster's notes on Joseph Lyman's circular letter, Jan. 19, 1814, Webster MSS, NYPL. Otis reasoned that it might impede peace negotiations then taking place. See also Strong's mild speech before the General Court in the summer and the General Court's mild responses. *Centinel*, June 1, 8, & 11, 1814.

Strong issued his summons at a time, Otis was later to recollect, when "all hope of stopping hostilities was at an end." Blockaded and invaded, the New England coast was without protection. Two years of sophistic constitutional debate between national and state governments over the command and payment of local defense had at last to be suspended. A special Federalist meeting of August 30th pressed Strong for the defense of Boston—inexcusably left without protection until then—and four days later, in a special town meeting which witnessed an acrimonious exchange between Otis and Samuel Dexter, the capital's inhabitants finally agreed, though half-heartedly, to preparations for defense. News that the British, much to the surprise of trusting Massachusetts Federalists, were not respecting private property along the Southern coast and that the Maine town of Castine had fallen to the invaders then forced Strong on September 6th to waive the last of his constitutional scruples and to call up the state militia for the defense of Maine. It was on the following day that he ordered the General Court back into session.[6]

In the month before the special session met, the party leaders in intensive consultations had evolved a general plan. Their position was exceedingly difficult. The language of the public, according to Otis, was "high toned and menacing." The only way the legislature could satisfy the radical public demands was to adopt nullification, a step for which the legislators were neither "prepared or desirous." Of the public proposals, only the convention scheme was "constitutional & peaceable." In order that "the Session might not on the one

---

[6]Otis's comment is in Otis to Noah Webster, May 6, 1840, Webster MSS, NYPL. The report of the August 30 Federalist meeting and the Sept. 14 town meeting is in [Sargent], *Reminiscences of Dexter,* pp. 80-83, and *Boston Town Records, 1814-1822* (Boston, 1906), pp. 17-19. Strong's order to the legislators is in *Centinel,* Sept. 10, 1814. On the halting and feeble gestures toward coastal defense before this date, see Morison, *Otis,* II, 63-65, 97-101. On the degree to which the war was tearing at the unity of the party, see [Sargent], *Dexter,* p. 82.

hand end in abortion nor on the other produce violent measures," leading members of the caucus and the Central Committee decided to support "the sentiments of our country friends" in favor of a "convention of the New England States, and *upon the faith of that persuasion* it was determined to cooperate with them in promoting it, and to use it as a medium for obtaining from the General Government if possible security against Conscription, taxes & the danger of invasion by being allowed to take care of ourselves, & in any event, for restraining the tendency to excess manifested in some of the petitions, by a 'declaration of rights' coupled with a declaration of duties."[7] The convention was to be the affair of the party managers.

Even before Strong delivered his speech before the special session in early October, the radicals were demanding action. Representative John Low of the York County town of Lyman offered a resolution calling for an early deputation of Massachusetts notables to Washington to inform Madison of New England's feelings and to urge him to resign. Low withdrew his motion the following day, but only after firm exertions on

---

[7]Otis's observations are in his letter to Noah Webster, May 6, 1840, Webster MSS, NYPL. Indications of Strong's intimate connection with the planning for the session are contained in James Walker, "Memoir of Hon. Daniel Appleton White," *Massachusetts Historical Society Proceedings*, VI (1862-63), 288-89. In 1829, Rufus G. Amory recalled a conversation with Otis in 1814 in which the party leader had expressed the opinion that a convention would be unwise. After Otis accepted membership in the delegation, Amory expressed surprise. Otis—somewhat disingenuously—said that the convention proposal had been agreed to against his judgment, "but the members from the Westward, seemed to be highly inflamed, and required that some such measure should take place." Otis had come to conclude that a convention might pacify some caucus members dissatisfied with the state's efforts to date. Finally, he thought it "most proper not to abandon those, with whom he had been accustomed to act in concurrence and that he might thus mitigate any evil, which would arise from the violence of passion." Legally attested document signed by Rufus G. Amory, Dec. 3, 1829, Otis MSS, MHS. Few documents illustrate more nicely the internal divisions within the party or Otis's attempts to hold onto the party leadership.

the part of the party management and a cautious, low-keyed address by the governor.[8] The General Court swiftly referred Strong's speech to a joint committee of moderates from both houses which, by careful prearrangement, fell under the chairmanship of Otis, who was now to become the chief marplot of the extremist cause. Quickly, and probably as planned, the committee issued its findings—"Otis's Report," it was always called—and offered them for debate.[9] The report rehearsed the administration's abandonment of New England's defense, New England's historic grievances with the rest of the nation, and the need for constitutional amendment to preserve for the Eastern states their "equal rights and benefits." The committee proposed a conference "between those States the affinity of whose interests is closest." A meeting of New England representatives was not to limit its concern, wrote Otis, to defense matters but would "enable delegates from those States, should they deem it expedient, to lay the foundation for a radical reform in the national compact, by inviting to a future convention a deputation from all the States of the Union." As proposed to the General Court, the Hartford Convention was to be no halfway measure; it was to hold out the fullest hopes of constitutional and national reform.

The resolutions did not escape attack from party radicals. Francis Blake of Worcester proposed a scheme which would have prohibited the collection of the internal duties of the national government in Massachusetts, but Otis, who feared its effects upon peace negotiations, personally beat down the plan.

---

[8]Charles Jared Ingersoll, *Historical Sketch of the Second War Between the United States of America, and Great Britain* (2 vols., Philadelphia, 1849), II, 225; and *Centinel*, Oct. 8, 1814. Strong's message was printed, among other places, in *ibid.*, Oct. 8, 1814.

[9]The Report appeared in *ibid.*, Oct. 12, 1814. The committee which produced it was composed of two Republicans and five Federalists, of whom William Sullivan, along with Otis, was a Central committeeman and Leverett Saltonstall a young pillar of the Salem and Essex organizations. The invitation to the convention was limited to the New England states because New York, which had traditionally been encompassed in all plans for concerted Eastern state action, was now firmly in Republican hands.

VIII: *To the Hartford Convention*

John Lowell spoke against a convention because it "would not go far enough," for which he was attacked "with great asperity" by Benjamin Pickman, Jr., of the Salem organization. Just prior to the adoption of the report, House members were able to commit the Massachusetts delegation to take action at Hartford on amending the slave representation and limiting congressional power to lay embargoes. And Otis promised that the convention would draft a circular letter to the other states.[1]

In mid-October, a depleted lower chamber resoundingly approved Otis's Report by a vote of 260 to 90.[2] Swiftly there-

---

[1]Portions of the debate will be found in *Synopsis of Debates, in the Massachusetts Legislature* [Boston? 1814], published by Republicans to expose the Federalist role in the proceedings. Lowell's feelings are revealed in Lowell to Pickering, Dec. 3, 1814, Pickering MSS, MHS. According to the *Centinel*, Oct. 15, 1814, Joseph Lyman and Stephen Longfellow (both to be Hartford Convention members), Noah Webster, Leverett Saltonstall, William Sullivan, and Nicholas Tillinghast (all members of various party committees), and others actively backed the report. Webster, in his notes on Joseph Lyman's Jan. 19, 1814 circular letter, Webster MSS, NYPL, later noted that he supported the resolutions although they did not fully meet his views. The origin of the proposal that a national convention be called to amend the Constitution was probably suggested to Otis, as Morison has concluded, by Charles Willing Hare of Philadelphia in a letter to Otis of Oct. 1, 1814, Otis MSS, MHS. The letter is printed in Morison, *Otis*, II, 176-78.

[2]The Senate vote was 22-12. The effects of war on the Maine coast and the reluctance of Republicans, knowing their efforts would have no effect, to legitimize the proceedings by their presence, account for the poor attendance on the day the vote was taken. The House's elected membership stood at 512, of whom 350 voted. The attrition was greatest among the representatives of Republican and war-torn Maine; only 57 of 120 Maine deputies voted, of whom a majority surprisingly favored the convention. The Maine vote was 34 in favor, 23 opposed. Out of 392 representatives from downstate Massachusetts, 293 were present, 226 of these voting for the convention, only 67 against. Only Norfolk County, among the downstate counties, was opposed, 11-5. Even with full attendance, Republican opponents of the convention would have been outnumbered. The breakdown of the vote will be found in Morison, *Otis*, II, 104*n*, and [Theodore Lyman], *A Short Account of the Hartford Convention . . .* (Boston, 1823), pp. 6-7. Lyman concluded without excessive exaggeration that 75 per cent of the Massachusetts citizenry at that point in time favored the convention. The resolution approving the convention is in *Resolves of the General Court of Massachusetts* (hereafter *Mass. Resolves*), Oct. 15, 1814.

after, both houses rejected a minority report on the convention proposal, voted that Otis's Report and letters of invitation to the convention be dispatched to the other New England governments, and got down to the business of electing convention delegates.[3] While the Republican members absented themselves, the Federalists of both houses unanimously chose the twelve delegates.[4]

In granting to the convention members broad permissive power to "advise and suggest" a course of action to the states without limiting the range of subjects to be debated, the General Court assured that the character of the convention would be determined by the character of the delegates themselves. And the Massachusetts delegation, from which the party management studiously excluded men of "impetuous temperament and fiery earnestness," represented moderate, established, practical Federalism.[5] Although younger men predominated, its members came from both political generations; all were, or previously had been, political activists. Ten were lawyers, two merchants. Three of the twelve represented the western coun-

---

[3]The letter from the General Court, although sent out over the names of Senate President John Phillips, a former Central committeeman, and House Speaker Timothy Bigelow, was drafted, like most of the other documents at this time, by Otis. It closely echoed Otis's Report. A MSS copy of the letter, dtd. Oct. 17, 1814, is in the Otis MSS, MHS. An official copy, John Phillips and Timothy Bigelow to the Governor of Connecticut, Oct. 17, 1814, is in the Connecticut State Archives, Conn. State Library.

[4]A record of the votes is reported in the *Centinel,* Oct. 19, 1814.

[5]Josiah Quincy was reported to have reflected that when the General Court came to select convention members it was "very careful to choose men of known moderation of views and tried discretion of conduct. It was for this reason . . . that he was passed by on that occasion. The prudent Federalists, when called upon to face this emergency, were afraid of [Quincy's] impetuous temperament and fiery earnestness. They dreaded lest he might express too well the spirit of those whose urgency exhorted the Convention." Edmund Quincy in *Josiah Quincy,* pp. 357-58. Henry Adams is in error in concluding, "The Massachusetts delegation to Hartford was in sympathy with Cabot, while the Massachusetts legislature seemed to sympathize with Pickering." The situation was more complex. Adams, *History,* VIII, 292.

ties; three were Boston men, two from "down east." Among
the westerners was Joseph Lyman, the prime figure in reviving
the convention scheme in Northampton earlier in the year.
Boston could claim the representation of Otis and the party's
grand old figure, George Cabot. Essex County's Nathan Dane,
perhaps in order to palliate the gentlemen who, like him, distrusted the "Boston lead," was also included. Besides Central
Committee Chairman Otis, nine were intimately linked with
the party organization through high positions on county or regional committees. All could be depended upon to guard the
prerogatives and influence of the organization.[6]

Among Federalists everywhere, the Massachusetts delegation met wide approval. Timothy Pickering, who harbored
doubts as to their energy, nevertheless felt called upon to
defend them as men of "more wisdom, virtue and real patriotism than it would be easy to bring together elsewhere in the
United States." Virginia Federalist Archibald Lee welcomed
the appointment of those "grave and valuable members of
society . . . reflecting and prudent men." Indeed, their known
prudence is what attracted most comment—and was the source
of what criticism they met. To John Lowell, Cabot was too
much "a desponding man as to our public affairs," Otis "naturally timid, and frequently wavering,—to-day bold, and to-
morrow like a hare trembling at every breeze." Prescott could
be counted upon to be firm but also "extremely prudent, and
so modest that he will too readily yield his own opinions to
the counsels of others whom he respects." As for Dane: "im-
practicable. . . . It must be uncertain what course he will take."[7]

---

[6]For full information on the composition of the Massachusetts
delegation and further details on the membership from all the states,
see Morison, *Otis*, II, 130-37.

[7]Pickering to James Hillhouse, Jan. 14, 1815, Hillhouse MSS,
Yale; Archibald Lee to James McHenry, Dec. 20, 1814, McHenry
MSS, Clements Library, Univ. of Michigan; and Lowell to Picker-
ing, Dec. 3, 1814, Pickering MSS, MHS. See also Manasseh Cutler to
Pickering, Nov. 28, 1814, *ibid*. Regarding Cabot, Pickering was of
Lowell's opinion: "He is too moderate." Pickering to Lowell, Nov. 7,
1814, *ibid*. Lowell, in his December 3 letter to Pickering, wrote that

Although Federalists in the other New England states had long harbored the same grievances as their Massachusetts counterparts, it remained for Massachusetts Federalists to catalyze the movement for the convention. Connecticut party leaders, enthusiastic backers of the convention plan, nevertheless steadfastly refused, as Massachusetts Federalists had done before, to issue the initial call.[8] Once, however, Massachusetts had decided to proceed with the scheme, Connecticut Federalists eagerly followed along. Immediately upon the Connecticut Assembly's receipt of Otis's Report, a special legislative committee took up its consideration and urged compliance with the Massachusetts action. The lower house adopted the committee's recommendations by an overwhelming vote of 153 to 36, and selected a delegation of seven moderate figures—all lawyers and experienced public figures, all practiced in party affairs—to join the Commonwealth's representatives.

Soon after, the Rhode Island legislature took similar action by a vote of 39 to 28 and named four men to the Hartford delegation. In New Hampshire, a combination of the legislature's adjournment, Democratic control of the governor's council, and the disinclination of many leading Federalists—among them young Daniel Webster—to support the Hartford Convention rendered impossible that state's formal participation. In Vermont, the British invasion brought about a holiday in partisanship, and the Federalist legislative caucus, under the urgings of Governor Gilman, declined the opportunity to send

---

he would have preferred Daniel Sargent, William Sullivan, and Israel Thorndike—all Central committeemen—on the slate, but there is no reason to believe that these three would have acted differently than those named.

[8]Governor Smith's reluctance to convene a special session is indicated in Smith to David Daggett, Feb. 12, 1814, John Cotton Smith MSS, Yale. By early March, many towns were pressing the governor. See the petitions of Bridgeport and Kent, Jan. 28 and Mar. 16, 1814, Smith MSS, CHS, and Charles Denison to Daggett, Feb. 9, 1814, Daggett MSS, Yale. On the Connecticut deliberations, see also Smith to Daggett, Mar. 5, 1814, Smith MSS, Yale; Ebenezer Huntington to Smith, Apr. 12, 1813; David Humphreys to Smith, Apr. 10, 1814, Smith MSS, CHS; and Humphreys to Daggett, July 13, 1813, Mar. 31, 1814, Daggett MSS, Yale.

delegates to Hartford. Instead, Federalist delegate conventions in three counties which boasted Federalist majorities—two in New Hampshire, one in Vermont, and all bordering on the Connecticut River—took it upon themselves independently of official state action to elect convention representatives. The Federalists in a second Vermont county dispatched a delegate to Connecticut, but because he represented a minority of the county's voters, the convention rejected his credentials.[9]

Twenty-one of the twenty-six men at Hartford were lawyers; five were merchants. Nathan Dane and Connecticut's Zephaniah Swift had written learned legal treatises, and many of the others with legal training had long occupied positions on the bench. The cautious conservatism of their profession manifested itself in the convention results. Moreover, the leaders of New England extremism—Timothy Pickering, Francis Blake, Samuel Fessenden, and others—were absent at Hartford and had no stand-ins. As outside observers were not long in noting, this was not a delegation to cause anxiety among friends of the union and the Constitution. The besetting question was whether it would satisfy the expectations of the New England Federalist public at large.

Conflicting advice soon flooded in upon the convention members. Loudest was the counsel from the Federalist left. Gouverneur Morris, long an ardent proponent of a New England convention but now hopelessly out of touch with the

---

[9]Details regarding the circumstances in New Hampshire and what one newspaper report claimed to be Daniel Webster's strategic opposition to convention representation in an Exeter Federalist meeting are to be found in Claude M. Fuess, *Daniel Webster* (2 vols., Boston, 1930), I, 170*n*; Lynn W. Turner, *William Plumer of New Hampshire, 1759-1850* (Chapel Hill, N.C., 1962), pp. 231-32; and William Plumer to John Adams, Nov. 25, 1814, reel 420, Adams microfilm. Webster later averred that he had counseled Governor Gilman against appointing delegates but had interfered in preparations for the convention no further than this. [Sargent], *Dexter*, p. 86. The particulars under which the Federalist county conventions selected deputies to Hartford are outlined in Morison, *Otis*, II, 108*n*. On the parallels between the social and political structure of the Connecticut Valley regions of Vermont and Massachusetts, see David Ludlum, *Social Ferment in Vermont, 1791-1850* (New York, 1939), pp. 10-12.

party, argued in early November for an autonomous New England confederacy. Morris was not alone. An average Federalist who despaired deeply of peace called "for as many of the States as dislike the War to form themselves into a new Government and make peace for themselves, leaving the way open for the other states to join them whenever they become tired of the contest." Pickering, as was his custom every four years or so, spoke of disunion—by the Western states if they could be forced out, or by the Northeastern if not—and reminded his friends that *"obsta principiis* was the motto of the movers and leaders of our Revolution." John Lowell, Jr., no friend of disunion, had nevertheless become fatigued with "talk: talk of amendments, talk of militia, talk of defence, talk of being paid out of the national taxes what we advance, but nothing more." He would suspend the Constitution, that "mere paper," and declare New England neutral for the remainder of the war. Many newspaper essayists argued with less restraint the absolute sovereignty of each state and the legality of interposition. And the Federalist clergy, not uncharacteristically, was exhorting to extreme measures.[1]

These views did not, however, go unopposed. From both North and South came well-placed pleas for moderation. Baltimore's Robert Goodloe Harper read Central committeeman

---

[1]Morris's sentiments are found in Morris to Otis, Apr. 29, 1813, to Quincy, Aug. 18, 1813, to Rufus King, Oct. 18, 1814, to Lewis B. Sturgis, Nov. 1, 1814, to Otis, Nov. 8, 1814, and to Pickering, Dec. 22, 1814, in Jared Sparks, *The Life of Gouverneur Morris* (3 vols., Boston, 1832), III, 291-324 *passim.* Lowell's views are expressed in Lowell to Pickering, Dec. 3, 1814, Pickering MSS, MHS, and reviewed in Ferris Greenslet, *The Lowells and their Seven Worlds* (Boston, 1946), p. 150. Pickering's are in Pickering to Lowell, Nov. 7, 1814, Pickering MSS, MHS. See also Cabot to Pickering, June 11, 1813, Pickering to George Logan, July 4, 1813, to Lowell, Nov. 7, 1814, to James Hillhouse, Dec. 16, 1814, *ibid.*; Gore to Rufus King, Sept. 13, 1813, King MSS, NYHS; Otis to Rutledge, May 5, 1813, Rutledge MSS, UNC; and Ebenezer Huntington to John Treadwell, Jan. 10, 1811, Treadwell MSS, CHS. For a typical clerical outburst of the time, see Adams, *History,* VIII, 21-22. Newspaper radicalism is reviewed in Frank Maloy Anderson, "A Forgotten Phase of the New England Opposition to the War of 1812," *Mississippi Valley Historical Society Proceedings,* VI (1912-13), 176-88.

William Sullivan a harsh lesson in sectional politics, cautioning him against trying to dictate peace terms to the administration and warning that Southern Federalism was in no mood to endure New England obstructionism. Similar advice originated with Federalism's old antagonist, John Randolph of Roanoke. Since 1812, this Old Republican had found a growing rapport with Josiah Quincy in opposing the policies of Jefferson and Madison. In frequent correspondence, both men inveighed against the war, attacked the administration's expansionist policies, and lamented the decline of public morality. But Randolph the Virginian never failed to make clear to the hotheaded Quincy that their unity of views had limits. In 1813, Southern Quiddism played the cautious part: "Rash counsels," wrote Randolph, "are not always, *if ever*, wise. I trust we shall hold together." Middle-state Federalists were no less disuasive. Oliver Wolcott and Rufus King both arraigned the upcoming convention. Wolcott thought it unconstitutional. King, no devotee of the new political style, feared that it might, of all things, satisfy the public; talk, he advised, but do little.[2]

No less a figure than John Quincy Adams later charged that the Hartford Convention was intended by its organizers to incite moderate opinion to support radical, even secessionist, actions. But there is no evidence to sustain this judgment. As the leading convention participants expressed it at the time and later recalled, their sympathies resided with the moderates, and they considered it their most critical task to assuage the more extreme popular temper. Cabot journeyed to Hartford,

---

[2]Robert Goodloe Harper to Sullivan, Nov. 2, 1814, Harper-Pennington Coll., Maryland Historical Society; John Randolph to Quincy, Feb. 8, 1814, Edmund Quincy, *Josiah Quincy*, p. 349; Wolcott, "Remarks on the Proposal for a Convention at Hartford" (1814), Wolcott to George Gibbs, May 27, 1813, Wolcott MSS, CHS; Wolcott to Frederick Wolcott, Sept. 20, 1814, Wolcott MSS, Litchfield, Conn., Historical Society; Hammond, *Political Parties in New York*, I, 388; Rufus King, memorandum dtd. 1814, King, *King*, V, 444-48; and Morison, *Otis*, II, 129n. Massachusetts Federalists had difficulty in convincing other Federalists of their fidelity to the Union. See Samuel Taggart to Jedidiah Morse, Dec. 16, 1814, Misc. Bound Coll., MHS, and Daniel Gookin to Cyrus King, Oct. 28, 1814, King MSS, Columbia.

he said, "to allay the ferment and prevent a crisis. . . . We are going to keep you young hot-heads from getting into mischief." "The proceedings of the Convention," wrote Otis soon after leaving Hartford, "are adopted rather to appease than produce excitement." The convention call, he later recollected, "was the consequence, not the source of a popular sentiment; and it was intended, by those who voted for it, as a safety valve by which the steam arising from the fermentation of the time might escape, not as a boiler in which it should be generated."

Nathan Dane shared these views. "Somebody must go to prevent mischief," he confided on the way to Hartford. And, he wrote afterwards, "The fact was, moderate men saw the excitement was going too far and that it was leading to evils far greater than the war itself. . . . This convention, as intended, moderated and checked an inflamed, growing opposition to the then administration of federal affairs" which "might, in the then violence of party spirit, have in time embarrassed and shaken the Union." What is more, he added, "When multitudes are very much excited and highly dissatisfied with their rulers' conduct, often they can be moderated by their friends only when they know not their friends check them."[3]

---

[3]Adams's accusation is contained in his "Reply to the Appeal of the Massachusetts Federalists," in Henry Adams, *New England Federalism*, p. 322. For the expectations of the conventioneers, see Gore to Rufus King, Apr. 11, 1811, King MSS, NYHS; Otis to ?, Jan. 21, 1815, Otis MSS, MHS; Otis to Mrs. Willard in Willard, *History of the United States*, p. 351n; Robert C. Winthrop to Henry Cabot Lodge, Aug. 23, 1878, Lodge, *Cabot*, p. 602 (some printings of this work do not carry this letter); and Nathan Dane, *A General Abridgement and Digest of American Law* (9 vols., Boston, 1823-29), IX, 594-98. Cabot's comment, made to Dr. James Jackson, is recorded in Lodge, *Cabot*, p. 519. Otis's mission to Hartford, it was later reported, "was forced upon him by three-fourths of the Massachusetts Legislature against his most earnest remonstrances, and to the great sacrifice of his convenience." James S. Loring, *The Hundred Boston Orators* (2nd ed., Boston, 1853), p. 204. On Otis's fears, see also Otis to Gore, Dec. 3, 1814, in Samuel Eliot Morison, "Two Letters of Harrison Gray Otis on the Hartford Convention, 1814-15," *Massachusetts Historical Society Proceedings*, LX (1926-27), 27-28. Joshua Thomas also wrote of his "extreme repugnance" at undertaking his trip to Hartford. Thomas to Joshua Barker [Thomas], Dec. 17, 1814, Misc. MSS Colls., Conn. State Lib. See also Prescott to Dane, Sept. 30, 1829,

The dampening of popular fervor was not, of course, the sole object of the convention members. They also sought, as the original Massachusetts resolution charged them to do, to define plans to defend the war-torn New England coast and to lay the groundwork for a lasting alteration in the form and operations of the national government. Otis was unyielding on this point. When challenged beforehand to explain what the meeting was to be about, he brushed aside as "ridiculous" the suggestion that it would seek secession. The object, he affirmed, was "to take measures to defend ourselves against the enemy; as the General Government cannot do it." His inclination, Otis wrote, was "to treat the administration as having *abdicated* the Government."[4] There was nothing in the arrangements, the proceedings, or the report of the convention to suggest ulterior purpose, nor is there any reason to doubt Dane's assertion that "a vast majority of the members of the Convention were totally opposed to any measures tending to dissolve or impair the union of these states or in the least degree to cripple their defence in the war."[5]

Although many convention members denied that any plan had been arranged beforehand, the Massachusetts delegation in fact carried with it a scheme of convention proceedings.[6] On

Dane MSS, MHS; Benjamin Pickman [Jr.] to John Quincy Adams, Sept. 27, 1834 [photostat], Misc. MSS Colls., MHS; and Otis to Robert Goodloe Harper, Oct. 27, 1814, Harper MSS, LC.

[4]Joseph Hopkinson to Otis, Feb. 15, 1829 (typescript), Hopkinson Coll., PHS; and Otis to Gore, Dec. 3, 1814, Morison, "Two Letters of Otis," pp. 27-28.

[5]Dane to Theodore Dwight, Nov. 6, 1830, Dane MSS, MHS. See also Roger Minott Sherman to David Daggett, Feb. 4, 1815, Daggett MSS, Yale; and William Plumer, Jr., *Life of William Plumer* (Boston, 1857), p. 411. For Noah Webster's belief that the main issue facing New England and the Hartford Convention was defense, see Webster to ?, Nov. 23, 1814, Gratz Coll., PHS. Cabot thought disunion "the worst of evils." Gore to Rufus King, Apr. 11, 1815, King MSS, NYHS. See also Theodore Dwight, *History of the Hartford Convention* (New York, 1833), p. 405, and Francis Baylies's speech in the *Centinel*, Nov. 29, 1814.

[6]Christopher Gore later denied that an agreement among the delegates had been reached beforehand. But Gore, then in Washington as Senator from Massachusetts and neither on the convention slate

the day he left Boston for Hartford, Otis wrote Gouverneur Morris, "You must not think me wholly destitute of plan and concerted measures in consequence of my asking your advice." George Cabot, slated to be convention president, hinted at a plan to Josiah Quincy at about the same time. "What *do* you suppose will be the result of this Convention?" Quincy asked him. "I can tell you exactly," was Cabot's reply. Quincy was surprised. "Can you, indeed? Pray tell me what it will be." Cabot responded, "A GREAT PAMPHLET!"

The most direct testimony to a pre-existing plan and to the role of the Commonwealth's Federalist organization in formulating it occurred at the opening of the convention. Cabot, who, as president, possessed the authority to name all committees and recognize all speakers, immediately called on Otis. And the head of the Massachusetts party quickly seized the initiative to offer proposals which became the basis of debate for the following sessions.[7] The Hartford Convention

nor any longer a member of the committee system, was ignorant of the swift developments in his state. So, it appears, were the Connecticut delegates. Before the meeting opened, Calvin Goddard, Roger Minott Sherman, and Theodore Dwight, who was to be named Secretary of the Convention, all disclaimed knowledge of a convention agenda or of prearrangement among the delegates. Dwight's own unsatisfactory history of the meeting, if we are to believe his claim that it represented a full disclosure of events, is testimony only to the author's ignorance of what actually preceded the gathering. Whether by accident or design, the Connecticut figures were excluded from pre-convention planning. Gore to Rufus King, Apr. 24, 1815, King MSS, NYHS; Calvin Goddard to David Daggett, Nov. 24, Dec. 19, 1814, Roger Minott Sherman to Daggett, Daggett MSS, Yale; Theodore Dwight to Timothy Pitkin, Nov. 24, 1814, Pitkin MSS, Huntington Library, San Marino, Calif.; and Dwight, *History, passim.*

[7]Otis to Morris, Dec. 10, 1814, Morris Coll., Columbia; and Edmund Quincy, *Josiah Quincy,* p. 358. Unless otherwise noted, all information regarding convention proceedings will be found in the convention journal, printed in Dwight, *History,* pp. 383-99. Cabot named Otis to every important committee. Convention members, who refused throughout the proceedings to lift the ban of secrecy which they had imposed upon themselves after the example of the Philadelphia Convention of 1787, were on this account often accused thereafter of having maintained secrecy in order to conceal disloyal words and proposals. Even after Theodore Lyman, Jr., published the convention journal in 1823 and after Dwight reprinted it in his *History,*

was going to answer to the requirements of Massachusetts Federalism.

Unfortunately, little is known about the day-to-day sessions of the convention, the give-and-take of debate, or the character of the arguments. Pledged to secrecy, the members faithfully remained silent both during and after the gathering. When not accusing convention delegates of speaking treason, contemporary detractors liked to say that nothing happened during the sessions. Evidently, however, the debates were spirited, maneuverings were intensive, and all members took seriously their responsibilities. Besides the general outlines of the proceedings, this much—but not much more—can be gleaned from the convention documents, some fugitive contemporary reports, and a few surviving personal reminiscences.

Otis's opening remarks wholly concerned defense. He cautiously urged the convention to recommend that the New England legislatures "petition" Congress to allow the Northeastern states to unite in defending themselves against England and that the national revenues collected in New England be appropriated to cover the costs of defending them. He also suggested that these revenues be credited to the national treasury and that the federal government agree to reimburse the states for any expenses incurred in their defense beyond this amount. These proposals contained no mention of constitutional amendment—a striking omission, in view of Otis's own earlier pledges before the General Court.[8] Almost immediately, the convention referred Otis's plan to a five-man committee, which included Otis and Dane. And the next day, this com-

---

the claims of loyalty reiterated by convention members and their heirs were widely disbelieved. For the journal, see also Lyman, *Short Account*. Attestations to the journal's authenticity and disclaimers that anything but what was recorded therein passed before the convention will be found throughout the literature, especially Dwight, *History*, pp. 404-05; and [Harrison Gray Otis], *Letters Developing the Character and Views of the Hartford Convention: by "One of the Convention"* (Washington, 1820), pp. 22-25.

[8]The report of Otis's opening speech is that of Roger Minott Sherman, contained in Samuel G. Goodrich, *Recollections of a Lifetime* (2 vols., New York, 1856), II, 27.

mittee proposed formally that the convention take up the plan, now slightly enlarged: the constitutional issue of militia command, the question of reimbursing the mobilized militia not placed under national authority, the pending national conscription bill to lower the draft age to eighteen, the general expenses of the war, and the matter of state defense.[9]

Otis's limited agenda occasioned a heated debate, particularly on the part of those who favored a set of constitutional amendments; and the discussions revealed divisions within the membership which persisted for almost two weeks. Soon after Otis's opening speech, Connecticut's James Hillhouse, who both publicly and privately had long urged a full-scale alteration in the Constitution, was reported to be mortified by the "timid half way measures" contemplated so far and to have pressed for action of a "decided energetic character." George Bliss of Springfield later recalled that he had argued for a different course, which there is every reason to believe was less conciliatory than the final outcome. Bigelow was said to be "really bold in the present crisis."[1]

---

[9]The emotional controversy over the conscription bill is reviewed in Adams, *History*, VIII, Chap. X.

[1]Joshua Thomas to Joshua Barker [Thomas], Dec. 17, 1814, Misc. MSS Colls., Conn. State Lib.; James Hillhouse to Pickering, Feb. 7, 1815, Lowell to Pickering, Dec. 3, 1814, Pickering MSS, MHS; and George Bliss to Otis, Oct. 31, 1818, Otis MSS, MHS. For Hillhouse's early program of constitutional amendments, none of which were adopted by the convention in its report, see Hillhouse, *Propositions for Amending the Constitution of the United States* . . . (New Haven, 1808). The convention's attempts to collect information are revealed in Hillhouse to Timothy Pitkin, Dec. 17, 1814, Huntington Lib.; Hillhouse to John Cotton Smith, Dec. 17, 1814, Smith MSS, CHS; and Smith to David Daggett, Dec. 23, 1814, Smith MSS, Yale. The information, both printed and in manuscript, is in the possession of the Connecticut Historical Society and is marked "Documents relating to the late War between the United States and Great Britain, left at Hartford, at the time of the Hartford Convention, by a member of that body. Presented by a Friend, Feby 1842." All are endorsed by Nathan Dane and some prepared by him. For the contents of this small archive, see Morison, *Otis*, II, 147*n*. These documents were no doubt used in the preparation of the supporting and illustrative schedules which accompanies some of the printed versions of the convention report (such as the 2nd ed. corrected and im-

In any case, a more energetic spirit than that manifested by the principal Massachusetts leaders threatened from the start to upset the convention managers' plans. Soon after the initial skirmish, Cabot named a second committee, on which Otis also sat, to bring in a set of proposals for the convention to adopt. This committee, like all the others, excluded the convention's most outspoken members, such as Hillhouse and Bliss—no doubt due to Cabot's manipulations. It reported out a set of recommendations on December 20th which, it appears from the length of the debate which followed, once again ignored the subject of amendment. But when four days later the members finally approved a course of action, it included recommendations not only for defense and revenue matters but also, for the first time, a list of proposed constitutional amendments regarding the war power, the admission of new states, embargoes, presidential succession, and the three-fifths clause. Otis had been forced to yield the main point. This plan, with the addition of one more amendment, became the basis for the final convention report.

Shortly before, on December 21st, the delegates had appointed still another committee, this time chaired by Otis, to "prepare a report illustrative of the principles and reasons which have induced the Convention to adopt the results to which they have agreed." The working plan was now referred to this committee, which, after having been directed to add an amendment regarding restraints on the rights of naturalized citizens, issued its draft convention report on the 30th. After what seems to have been intensive discussions and the recommittal of early portions of the draft to the Otis committee, the convention adopted its final report on January 3rd and made it public two days later. The convention journal failed to record that the vote approving the report was unanimous.[2]

---

proved, Boston, 1815) and some of which are in the Otis MSS, MHS. Two of the schedules, not adopted by the convention, are reproduced in Morison, *Otis*, II, 193-95.

[2]It is probable that some members refused to vote their acquiescence in the report. Dane confided that danger had been only

Considering the disagreements within the convention, the report represented an unmistakable victory for the moderate forces and, if bearing an occasional note of irresolution and compromise, neatly conveyed two decades of Federalist thought. Generally conceded to be Otis's handiwork, it opened with a compassionate but firm rebuke of extremism. Warning that resistance to government was warranted only "after full deliberation," in times devoid of "the fervour of sudden excitement," and by necessity, the report pleaded a lack of "conclusive" evidence that resistance was justified at that time. "In the hope of reconciling all to a course of moderation and firmness," it also sought to convince the radicals of the self-defeating logic of revolution: "Precedents of resistance to the worst administration, are eagerly seized by those who are naturally hostile to the best."

Americans should recall, the report reminded its readers, that though all men had hoped that the infant nation would avoid "the embarrassments of old and rotten institutions," such evils as the lust for power, the abuse of executive patronage, exorbitant taxation, and "unjust and ruinous wars" were "the natural offspring of bad administration, in all ages and countries." Moreover, "when abuses, reduced to a system, and accumulated through a course of years, have pervaded every department of government, and spread corruption through every region of the state; when these are clothed with the forms of law, and enforced by an executive whose will is their source, no summary means of relief can be applied without recourse to direct and open resistance." Yet those resigned to these ancient republican truths would recognize the wisdom of prudence: "To attempt upon every abuse of power to change

---

narrowly averted: "If certain persons could have had their own way, and carried the measures which they proposed, I know not where we should have been." Robert C. Winthrop to Henry Cabot Lodge, Aug. 23, 1878, Lodge, *Cabot*, p. 602 (contained in only some printings of this work). Hillhouse in a letter to Pickering, Feb. 7, 1815, Pickering MSS, MHS, wrote of his acquiescing in unanimity but suggested by this that he refrained from issuing a minority report. The report is conveniently reprinted in Dwight, *History*, pp. 352-79.

the constitution, would be to perpetuate the evils of revolution."

The South, too, had to be considered. Studiously ignoring the West, the report extended a conciliatory hand to "the southern Atlantic states" whose political attitudes appeared on the verge of reformation. A reunion of sentiment between the Eastern sections might still be accomplished once the South rid itself of "visionary theorists." Why risk frustrating the reconciliation of the original parties to the union by threatening resistance without offering reunion? Moreover, if the union must dissolve, why not wait for peace? If the cause of the nation's plight was judged "radical and permanent," then a division of the union would of course be preferable to continued alliance between the states. But if so, all parties to the original compact would have to consent: "A severance of the Union by one or more states, against the will of the rest, and especially in a time of war, can be justified only by absolute necessity."

Over one third of the report dwelt upon the defense of New England and the constitutional prerogatives of the state. It assailed attempts to place national officers in command of state militia detachments, to conscript part of the militia into national service, and to enlist minors without the consent of their parents and guardians.[3] It decried the proposed apportionment of the conscripted militiamen on the basis of the white population alone, and arraigned the condition of the national finances and the inequitable burden of the war's costs. That the militia acts were "absolutely void," the convention had no doubt, nor, that in cases of emergency when the courts had proven irrelevant and speed of decision was essential, that the states must be their own judges. "In cases of deliberate, dangerous, and palpable infractions of the constitution, affecting the sovereignty of a state, and liberties of the people; it is not only the right but the duty of such a state to interpose its authority for their protection."

---

[3]These bills were dead in Congress by Dec. 28, 1814, though Federalists feared their resurrection. See Adams, *History*, VIII, 268-80.

Yet, as if frightened by the implications of thus national-izing the Virginia and Kentucky doctrines of 1798, the report swiftly withdrew into equivocation, deeming it unwise "to fly to open resistance upon every infraction of the constitution" and cautioning the states to await the final disposition of the militia legislation in Congress before taking further action. Instead, "solicitous for the continuance of the Union, as well as the sovereignty of the states" and "unwilling to furnish obstacles to peace," it went on to "suggest" an "arrangement" with the national government, whereby the administration would permit the states to assume their own defense and to defray the war's costs by paying a "reasonable portion" of their taxes into the state treasuries for credit against their na-tional accounts. Should this plan fail to meet with approval, only then would state legislatures, "or conventions of the whole people, or delegates appointed by them for the express purpose in another Convention," be justified in taking action which circumstances might then require.

The final and longest section of the report redeemed the convention's pledge to examine how the national harmony of interests might be restored, how a relapse into crisis might be averted, and how "the profligacy and folly of political theo-rists" might be reduced. It recited the many causes of the nation's ruin: Virginia had deliberately combined with the other states to secure "the controul of public affairs in per-petual succession"; "men of exceptionable merit" had been excluded from public office "for want of adherence to the executive creed"; judicial commissions had been withheld and judges impeached; taxes had been reduced to the peril of na-tional defense; public office had gone to the least worthy under "the influence of patronage in the distribution of offices"; the admission of new states in the West had destroyed the "balance of power" among the original states; "the easy admission of naturalized foreigners, to places of trust, honour or profit" had operated as an inducement "to the malcontent subjects of the old world" to immigrate "in quest of executive patronage, and to repay it by an abject devotion to executive measures";

hostility to Britain and partiality to France had stultified public policy; and "a visionary and superficial theory in regard to commerce" had eventuated in domestic coercion and foreign war.

To alleviate these evils, the convention proposed a list of seven constitutional amendments, judged "essential . . . to strengthen, and if possible perpetuate, the union of the states." The first and most important provided for the apportionment of representation and direct taxation among the states according to their free white population. The second, reflecting concern over the recent admission of Louisiana and deemed "indispensable" because "none of the old states can find an interest in creating prematurely an overwhelming western influence," called for a two-thirds vote of both houses of Congress to admit new states.[4] The third and fourth echoed older proposals to limit embargoes to sixty days and to require a two-thirds vote for their enactment, in order to preserve that commerce whose welfare "can never interfere with the other great interests of the state, but must promote and uphold them" and whose practitioners, because always in the minority, must be protected against "the sudden and injudicious decisions of bare majorities."[5]

The fifth—in order to protect the exposed maritime states and to reduce the influence of the Western states whose "im-

---

[4]Although this amendment, as offered in the report, had not been formally proposed before, it grew out of protests in 1812 and 1813 against the admission of Louisiana. See, e.g., Josiah Quincy's report on new states in *Mass. Resolves*, June 4-16, 1813, and the remonstrance drawn by a committee headed by Elijah Hunt Mills which derided the advantages of admitting a territory "peopled by inhabitants, whose habits, language, religion, and laws, are repugnant to the genius of our government." *Ibid.*, June 8-16, 1813. For documents bearing on the first and second proposed amendments drawn up by Dane for the convention's use, see Morison, *Otis*, II, 193-95. Most of this list of amendments was urged and anticipated by Pickering in a letter to John Lowell, Jr., Nov. 28, 1814, Pickering MSS, MHS. See also *Palladium*, Nov. 8, 1814.

[5]For an earlier proposal in this vein, see *Mass. Resolves*, June 20, 1809, and Herman V. Ames, *The Proposed Amendments to the Constitution of the United States During the First Century of its History* (Washington, 1897), pp. 264-329.

mense population . . . remote from immediate danger will not be averse from the occasional disturbances of the Atlantic states"—would have prohibited waging offensive war without a two-thirds vote of both houses of Congress. The sixth, "subordinate in importance," would have retained the nation's traditional hospitality toward foreigners but declared the naturalized citizen ineligible for Congress and any civil office under national authority.[6] And the seventh, upon which, noted the report, "it is superfluous to dilate," prohibited a president from succeeding himself and outlawed the election of a president from the same state in successive terms.[7]

The report closed with a set of resolutions which embodied the amendments and the proposals regarding defense. The convention "recommended" their adoption by the state legislatures or by conventions of the people, and urged the states to "persevere in their efforts to obtain such amendments, until the same shall be effected." Then, as much to reassure New England Federalists as to warn the administration of its resolve, the convention went on record in favor of a second convention to be held in Boston in mid-June—during the first session of what at that time promised to be a tumultuous General Court—if these petitions to the government were rebuffed, if war should continue, and if New England's defenses were still neglected. Finally, it authorized Cabot, Chauncey Goodrich of Connecticut, and Daniel Lyman of Rhode Island to call another meeting of the convention. By giving themselves the authority to reconvene the convention without the

---

[6]This amendment was proposed and adopted for consideration on the convention floor long after the other six had been sent to committee for drafting. On earlier versions of this amendment, see Ames, *Proposed Amendments*, pp. 30, 74.

[7]New England Federalists had sought since 1800 for some way to prevent a long succession of presidents from the same state and to immunize the choice of president from the populace. See, e.g., Noah Webster's draft proposals for amendment, marked for introduction into the October 1807 session of the Connecticut legislature, in Webster MSS, NYPL.

express consent of the legislatures, the moderates intended to preserve their initiative, insure their control, and divert any movement for a second and more radical gathering.[8]

Many reasons can be cited to account for the convention's failure to endorse secession or to recommend a separate New England peace with Britain. John Lowell, closely acquainted with the party captains, ascribed the party leaders' prudence to their fears of hazarding career, fortune, and standing in uncertain ventures.[9] Separation would have severed their last chance for preferment at the national level and would have ruptured the intimate and indispensable economic links between New England and the rest of the nation. Manufacturing interests, most of them born of embargo and war and requiring large tariff-free markets outside the Northeast for their existence; shipping interests dependent upon the carrying trade in Southern produce to foreign and domestic ports; strategically-placed Federalists, such as party leader Thomas Handasyd Perkins, holding a stake in the national debt; and, as the Republican press pointed out, the colleges, insurance companies, widows, and investors dependent upon the income from government securities—all these would have been threatened by

---

[8]A second convention would probably have yielded formally to interposition and either have declared New England neutral for the duration of the war and opened her ports, or have made a separate peace with England and ceded, as many hoped, the northern half of Maine. See Otis to Robert Goodloe Harper, Oct. 27, 1814, Harper MSS, LC; *Centinel*, Sept. 10, 1814; and the sentiments of the Newburyport town meeting in John J. Currier, *History of Newburyport, Mass. 1764-1905* (2 vols., Newburyport, Mass., 1906), I, 64-65. A disturbing portent of what might have occurred was the one-man embassy sent by Strong to Canadian officials in Nov. 1814 to inquire about a New England armistice. The embassy is chronicled in J. S. Martell, "A Side Light on Federalist Strategy During the War of 1812," *AHR*, XLIII (Apr. 1938), 553-66. Morison believes the emissary was Thomas Adams, a Castine, Maine, Federalist and a member of the General Court. Morison, "The Henry-Crillon Affair of 1812," *Massachusetts Historical Society Proceedings*, LXIX (1947-50), 218*n*, which documents the doings of two notable scoundrels.

[9][John Lowell, Jr.], *Gov. Strong's Calumniator Reproved . . .* (Boston, 1814), p. 17.

disunion.[1] Add to these considerations the written threats of violence received by leading party figures, the probability of civil war within New England if secession occurred, and rumors that the administration planned to mount an offensive against the Northeast upon the first move toward independence, and the impediments and inhibitions to disunion must have appeared insurmountable.[2]

But no convention member, nor for that matter many reflecting Federalists, ever seriously contemplated disunion as an alternative in 1814. They retreated from separation because, at bottom, they were profoundly attached to union. This is not, however, to say that their opposition to secession was, in their minds, inconsistent with state interposition. Nor did it

---

[1] These points are convincingly made and amplified by Robert A. East, "Economic Development and New England Federalism, 1803-1814," *New England Quarterly*, X (Sept. 1937), 430-46. Israel Thorndike was tempted to lend money to the government, reasoning that without public support of national credit property values and private credit would be crippled, but he held off until July 1815. J. D. Forbes, *Israel Thorndike, Federalist Financier* (New York, 1953), pp. 111-16. Perkins's contribution of $25,000 is established in *American State Papers, Public Lands* (Washington, 1832), I, 846-47. The founding by Charles Tracy Jackson and Francis Cabot Lowell of the Boston Manufacturing Company in Waltham before the war's end was of course a striking vote of confidence in the union by two high-standing Federalists and suggests that the more heavily ⁊n individual had invested in ventures whose success depended on factors outside New England, the less likely he was to be an extremist. The conflicting sentiments regarding contributing to government loans can be traced in Morison, *Otis*, II, 66-67; and James Lloyd, Jr., to Otis, May 17, 1814, Thorndike to Otis, Apr. 23, 1814, Otis to Cabot, July 2, 1819, Cabot to Otis, July 3, 1819, and Charles Willing Hare to Otis, Apr. 26, 1814, Otis MSS, MHS.

[2] For a threat of bodily harm, see, e.g., "Union" to Theodore Dwight, Dec. 15, 1814, Dwight Family MSS, NYPL. Fears of civil war are revealed in Otis to Rutledge, Mar. 15, 1813, Rutledge MSS, UNC. One curious sidelight of the convention was its constant surveillance by U.S. Army Colonel Thomas S. Jessup, a war veteran under special orders from War Secretary Monroe. Jessup's reports to Madison contain frequently conflicting testimony, which attests not so much to confusion in the convention's plans as to confusion in the public mind as to what it intended. Jessup's letters to Monroe from October 1814 through May 1815, will be found in Ingersoll, *History of the Second War*, II, 234-37, in the War Department microfilms, and in the Jessup MSS, LC.

seem so to the large and approving Federalist public. The influential Newburyport town meeting, for instance, when resolving to accept the Convention Report, proposed that if by spring conditions had not improved, Federalists should "consider our State Legislature as the sole, rightful & bounded judge of the course which our safety may require, without regard to the persons still assuming to be the National Government" and that the officials at Boston should "declare that our resources shall be appropriated to our defence, that the laws of the United States shall be temporarily suspended in their operation in our territory, and that hostilities shall cease towards Great Britain on the part of the free, sovereign & independent States of New England."[3]

Nothing better illustrates the moderate nature of the report than the disillusionment of the "warm bloods," as Theodore Dwight called them, who had hoped for something stronger. "They have done what they ought to do," wrote one observer of the convention members, "but they certainly have not done as much as was expected of them by the great Body of the people of this State."[4] Yet, if the rank and file remained ahead of the party leaders, informed and respectable Federalist opinion throughout the Northeast, hardly inclined to welcome a statement of radical principles, was almost unanimous in

---

[3]Labaree, *Patriots and Partisans*, pp. 198-99. Historians have liked to emphasize, as if to offer proof of secessionist intent, a declaration in the Nov. 9, 1814 *Centinel*, just after the appointment of delegates from Connecticut and Rhode Island, which read, "Second and Third Pillars of a new Federal Edifice reared." The headline had nothing whatsoever to do with disunion. "Federal" meant "Federalist," and the paper was applauding the ostensible reinvigoration of party fortunes.

[4]Theodore Dwight to Timothy Pitkin, Jan. 9, 1815, Pitkin MSS, Huntington Lib.; and Ephraim Lock to Cyrus King, Jan. 10, 1815, Cyrus King MSS, Columbia. See also William Cullen Bryant to Austin Bryant, Feb. 5, 1815, in Parke Godwin, *A Biography of William Cullen Bryant* (2 vols., New York, 1883), I, 134-35. The convention members, it was reported by Connecticut's Simeon Baldwin who spent Christmas with some of them, "did not calculate to satisfy the most zealous partizans," only "that the sober and discreet part of Society would acquiesce in the course they should pursue." Simeon Baldwin to Ebenezer Baldwin, Jan. 5, 1815, Baldwin MSS, Yale.

praising the report as a statesmanlike declaration of New England's special grievances. High-placed partisans in Massachusetts and Connecticut lauded the report as "moderate but firm" and reported wide approval in their circles. Word came from old-schoolman John Jay and young Daniel Webster praising the results. Newspapers in New York as well as New England offered their approval. And even Timothy Pickering was moved to acclaim the report as bearing "the high character of wisdom, firmness, and dignity."[5]

By the time the General Court convened for its winter session late in January, optimism was the growing mood. Serious negotiations were known to be taking place in Ghent. Congress had already taken up the matter of state defense and, in apparent conformity to the convention's wishes, it was about to authorize the raising of state forces and their compensation by the national government.[6] All of this had quickly restored confidence in the party leadership and created the impression that the voice of New England Federalism had once again been heard in the land. Indeed, so great and rapid was the decline in public fever that Otis, ascribing the calm to the

---

[5]Theodore Dwight to Timothy Pitkin, Jan. 9, 1815, Pitkin MSS, Huntington Lib.; Roger S. Baldwin to Ebenezer Baldwin, Jan. 8, 1815, Baldwin MSS, Yale; James Hillhouse to Pickering, Feb. 7, 1815, Pickering to Robert Beverly, Jan. 12, 1815, to Lowell, Jan. 23, 1815, Pickering MSS, MHS; Pickering to Hillhouse, Jan. 14, 1815, Hillhouse MSS, Yale; and Gore to Strong, Jan. 14, 1815, Lodge, *Cabot*, p. 560. See also John Jay to Roger Minott Sherman, Jan. 31, 1815, Jay MSS, Columbia; Jay to Richard Peters, Mar. 14, 1815, Peters MSS, PHS; Daniel Webster to ?, Jan. 11, 1815, Misc. MSS Colls., Harvard; and Roger Minott Sherman to David Daggett, Feb. 4, 1815, Chauncey Goodrich to Daggett, Jan. 17, 1815, Daggett MSS, Yale. Even Gouverneur Morris approved. Morris to Moss Kent, Jan. 10, 1815, Sparks, *Morris*, III, 326. Throughout January 1815 and later, the *Centinel* and *Palladium* indicated their approval. The New York *Evening Post*, whose editor William Coleman socialized with convention members in Hartford, noted that "the tone of this report, though in our opinion sufficiently high for the occasion, is, I know, from the most authentic information quite inferior to the public feeling in the Eastern States. The people there are in advance of their leaders." Quoted in *Centinel*, Jan. 11, 1815. Coleman's presence in Hartford is indicated in Goodrich, *Recollections*, II, 35-36.

[6]Adams, *History*, VIII, 280-85.

tranquilizing effect of the report, now feared a return to public torpor. On the eve of the January 1815 legislative session, he found it hard to believe that critical matters were up for decision: "I should fear from appearances," he wrote from Boston, "that a state of apathy had been the result."

In his opening speech before the General Court, Governor Strong praised the Hartford Convention as preventing a "fatal excess" of zeal when "the passions of the multitude are inflamed." The legislature passed without delay a resolution expressing full confidence in the work of the convention and authorized Strong to appoint three commissioners to carry Massachusetts' case to Washington. Finally, as if to symbolize the organization's role in the entire affair, the governor immediately appointed Otis, William Sullivan, and Thomas Handasyd Perkins, all Central committeemen, to represent the state's case in Washington.[7] The party organization was to finish what it had begun.

None of the three ambassadors wished to undertake the trip. Now that the public zeal had cooled, they saw no reason to risk humiliation in Washington and wished the administration to make the first move toward conciliation.[8] But, under pressure from Boston, they left with a commission from Strong to "endeavor to effect an arrangement whereby this State separately or in concert with neighboring States may be enabled

---

[7] Otis to Gore, Jan. 21, 1815, reproduced in Morison, "Two Letters of Otis," p. 28. The General Court proceedings, the appointment of the delegates to Washington, and the outcome of their travels is outlined in Morison, "The Massachusetts Embassy to Washington, 1815," *Massachusetts Historical Society Proceedings*, XLVIII (1914-1915), 343-51, and Morison, *Otis*, II, Chap. XVII and pp. 195-99. Strong's speech is in the *Centinel*, Jan. 21, 1815. Regarding Congress's passage of an act permitting the president to accept for national service and pay men raised for state armies, Massachusetts Federalists believed that this yielded the central demand of the convention. Otis later argued that had Congress approved the act earlier, the convention would not have met. *Letters in Defence of the Hartford Convention and the People of Massachusetts* (Boston, 1824), p. 53.

[8] On their reluctance to assume the trip, see Otis to Gore, Jan. 21, 1815, Morison, "Two Letters of Otis," p. 28; and Sullivan to Otis, Jan. 29, 1815, Misc. MSS Colls., Boston Public Library. See also Gore to Rufus King, Apr. 11, 1815, King MSS, NYHS.

to assume the defence of their territories against the enemy." They were also to seek permission to collect the national taxes within the states and pay them into the state treasuries to defray defense costs. Nothing was said in their instructions about the amendments.[9] Since Congress had authorized the federalization of state forces, the only demand they had to press in Washington was the reimbursement of defense expenditures.

And they had little hope of securing even that. Their trip commenced on February 3rd, just two days after Boston had received the first word of Jackson's victory at New Orleans. With confused emotions they moved south, fearing on the one hand that Jackson's victory would harden an already obdurate administration, heartened on the other by the prospects for peace. Arriving in Washington on the 13th, they found themselves the next day in a town celebrating the official peace report from Ghent. On the 15th, Boston heard the news. Irrelevant and ridiculed by the opposition press, the three commissioners remained in Washington long enough to argue their claims before a skeptical administration and then returned home.[1] Peace had rescued the party leaders and rendered gratuitous any thought of what another convention might do. But, like the commissioners themselves, had the Hartford Convention been irrelevant too?

From a national perspective, the convention reinforced the image of Federalist obstructionism and deepened the wide-

---

[9]On Feb. 10, 1815, the General Court approved all seven amendments recommended by the Hartford Convention and sent them on to the Massachusetts senators and congressmen for presentation before Congress. *Mass. Resolves*, Feb. 10, 1815.

[1]*Centinel*, Feb. 1 & 15, 1815; and Thomas Handasyd Perkins to John P. Cushing, Feb. 16, 1815, in Thomas P. Cary, *Memoir of Thomas Handasyd Perkins* (Boston, 1856), p. 219. Some tavernkeepers of Old Hampshire, in anticipation, it seems, of either interposition or disunion, had pledged not to remit excise duties and on this account were sued by the national government. The commissioners did manage at least to obtain a nol pros in the matter. On these expectations, see Joseph H. Lyman to William Sullivan, Feb. 14, 1815, Misc. MSS Coll., Columbia; J. E. A. Smith, *History of Pittsfield* (2 vols., Springfield, Mass., 1876), II, 249-50; and Morison, *Otis*, II, 196-97.

spread conviction that the Federalist way was inappropriate to an expanding and democratizing nation. It did nothing to hasten peace negotiations nor the conclusion of peace itself. Despite Federalist belief, it played little part in convincing the administration of the need to accept into the national service at national expense detachments of state defense forces; the collapse of national recruiting efforts and the obvious and immediate need for armed protection had already done that among reasonable men of both parties. Nor did the convention succeed in persuading Congress and the other states even to consider its proposed amendments to the Constitution. The only enduring bequest of the convention gave no solace to the friends of union: it nationalized the doctrine of interposition and in so doing gave it a legitimacy which it had lacked before.

When viewed from the perspective of Massachusetts, however, the convention proved highly useful to party purposes and perhaps indispensable for the nation as a whole. To begin with, it enhanced the electoral prospects of the Federalist Party. Rather than engendering any lasting and injurious schism within the party ranks, it preserved the party's cohesion, made possible a continuity of leadership, and provided a moderate platform upon which Federalists of all stripes could run. Never before, not even after 1797, had the party been able to look forward to eleven uninterrupted years in the statehouse; and even though Federalism had no national base after 1815, state Republicans could not successfully challenge the party until 1823. Like the Southern Confederacy a half-century later, the Hartford Convention became a "Lost Cause" which possessed an arresting appeal to a people with so keen a sense of exclusiveness. Whatever its real consequences, the convention seemed to give New England a rejuvenated role in national affairs, and the Federalist Party of Massachusetts reaped the political harvest.

The convention also preserved the future of moderate politics in New England and thus contributed to preserving the union. Political apathy had always made it easy for entrenched elitist cliques to dominate the Commonwealth's political life, but with the end of public complaisance and the resulting rise of a kind of rough internal democracy in party affairs, the politics of deference was endangered and with it the moderate, if unresponsive, leadership provided by the old elites. The end of apathy created the need for a new kind of political manager, fearful no less than the clique figure of the force of democracy, but practiced in its exploitation. Yet exploiting it meant risking the very discipline the manager sought, and it was this surfeit of democracy which in the end imperiled his control over the rank and file. Thus the same political mechanism which had been created to stimulate the participation of the electorate had to be called in to subdue the people; without organized politics, neither political democracy nor moderate politics was possible. In serving both purposes of the party captains, the Hartford Convention was the chief monument to the democratization of Federalist politics.

Yet its ultimate significance lay elsewhere. The Hartford Convention originated above all in a consistent vision of republicanism. Like the Battle of New Orleans, with which it was exactly contemporaneous, it was a product of the American Revolution, whose ideology inspired it. And like that battle, it represented an attempt to come to terms with the conditions of a larger revolutionary world from which the United States was able, only in 1815, to begin to withdraw. That the convention never possessed, like Jackson's victory, an inspirational appeal for the nation and that its members generally won the opprobrium of their countrymen should not blind us to their place within the main currents of our history. For they drew upon the principal attitudes and concerns which Americans of the day—Federalists and Republicans alike—so earnestly debated and which have never lost their timeliness. If the Massachusetts Federalists and the Hartford Convention are to be arraigned by history, they must be arraigned for their fidelity to the republican faith.

Appendices

Appendix I

Reproduced below is a hitherto unattributed and unpublished letter from the William Griswold Lane Collection at Yale University. From internal evidence and handwriting, I conclude that its author is Harrison Gray Otis and its recipient Roger Griswold of Connecticut. Otis left the letter unsigned, possibly through inadvertence but most likely to conceal his authorship from the prying eyes of Republican postmasters. Along with Otis's letter to Josiah Quincy of December 15, 1808 (a full text of which is most conveniently available in Edmund Quincy, *Life of Josiah Quincy* [Boston, 1868], pp. 164-5), this letter is the most important single piece of evidence which has come to light regarding plans for an 1809 New England convention.

The letter is printed here with the permission of the Yale University Library.

[Harrison Gray Otis] to [Roger Griswold]

Boston 4 Jany 1809—

My dear Sir,

Since writing to you a few lines last week, I have been in daily expectation that I or some of our friends should receive from Hartford some communications upon the interesting subject of your last favor, but nothing of this kind has yet come to hand.[1] Impressed with apprehensions similar to

---

[1]Neither Otis's letter to Griswold, nor a letter from Griswold or another leading Connecticut Federalist to Otis in January 1809, has been found. But George Cabot was in correspondence with Connecticut Governor Jonathan Trumbull, Jr., in the same period (Cabot to Trumbull, Feb. 5, 8, and 10, 1809, and Trumbull to Cabot, Feb. 15, 1809, Trumbull MSS, Connecticut Historical Society), and Griswold and Cabot also exchanged letters (Cabot to Griswold, Feb. 6, 1809, William Griswold Lane Coll., Yale; Griswold to Trumbull, Feb. 12, 1809, Trumbull MSS, Connecticut Historical Society).

yours, I had written to our friends in Congress, some weeks since, apprising them of our wishes that they would devise some plan of proceeding for the legislatures of the Eastern States in which they might probably be agreed.[2] This they have not yet done, and it is probable they will at last refer to the discretion of the legislatures the decision which we wish them to make in our behalf. I presume the legislature of this State will convene with a disposition to adopt any course which is deliberately recommended by the leading members, and in a temper not so much requiring excitement as prudent restraint, and it is a very embarrassing question to determine the precise extent, to which their measures of disapprobation shall be carried. Unless measures of an explicit and energetic character shall be adopted, our people are enslaved and our country ruined. And on the other hand the assumption of ground, on which the people upon due reflection will not sustain their legislatures, would be equally fatal to our cause and to the public interest. It is a crisis demanding the wisdom and concurrence of all good men, and I lament that their means of comparing opinions and digesting a practicable and efficient system are not better prepared.

You intimate that your State would follow our example. I believe I may with confidence return the compliment, and I am satisfied that your taking the lead would be more effectual and much less obnoxious. You need not to be informed of the artifice and stratagem, by which it is attempted to stigmatize Massachusetts as the hotbed of opposition, and *Boston* as the source of the corruption of the State. The eternal nonsense, that an Essex or a Boston Junto give the cue to the Eastern States, and that the Federalists in those States are our Dupes and tools, has been propagated with studious care, & with too much success. Would you believe, that we have received formal remonstrances and reprimands from the *Federal Comm'ee* of New Hampshire for countenancing doctrines unfavorable to the *Union of the States,* and declaring themselves shocked by the essays in *our* Federal

---

[2]The letter to which Otis refers here is his own to Josiah Quincy—Edmund Quincy, *Life of Josiah Quincy* (Boston, 1868), pp. 164-5—recently made available in manuscript form in the Quincy Papers, Massachusetts Historical Society.

papers?[3] It is amazing to observe how few of our own party have penetrated to the depths of the Cabinet policy, and understand its true origin and destructive tendency. Their fears are for the most part limited to the immediate consequences of what they deem temporary measures, and their efforts have as yet no other object than temporary opposition & relief. Unless however this whole section is smitten providentially with blindness or stupified by infatuation, the madness of our rulers and the sufferings of the Country must rouse them to action, and it is of immense consequence to give a sure and temperate impulse to this action when they are prepared for it. To prevent insurrection, civil commotion, fruitless opposition, or a convulsive severance of the union, must be objects of immense importance, and I wish the system could be devised, matured and promulgated by your State. It is most obvious that the administration calculate upon the existence of such minorities in the Eastern States as will paralyze all our measures and leave them at full liberty to try out their experiments untill a State of war growing out of their measures shall enable them to enforce them by military power, and penal sentences, and hitherto they have but too much ground for such confidence. Nothing would more effectually undeceive them than a well concerted plan for convening and ascertaining the sentiments of the Eastern States upon their own peculiar interests. We have therefore thought, that it will be indispensable for our legislature, in some mode, to address the people, and to publish under the sanction of authority, a clear analysis of the causes of our difficulties, a review of leading measures, with temperate reflections upon the motives and unequivocal warnings of the tendencies & effects.[4] Still the difficulty of the remedy, of the ultimate measures, recurs. Shall means be devised for calling a convention of the Eastern States & inviting N York to join (for the purpose of *more efficient remonstrance and*

---

[3]No copy of this remonstrance has been preserved.

[4]Such an address to the general public, along with other documents, was eventually published under authority of the Federalist-controlled General Court as *The Patriotick Proceedings of the Legislature of Massachusetts, During their Session from Jan. 26, to March 4, 1809* (Boston, 1809).

more certain amendment to the Constitution) by the present legislatures? Or shall they merely express their opinions of the expediency of this course and recommend to the people to make their next elections with that view? Or shall they forthwith declare certain laws unconstitutional and not binding on their citizens? This last would in my opinion be imprudent and in all views improper. I have rather thought something like the second would be advisable, and our friends here generally concur. We think that an authentic statement of our situation from authority, published in all our towns and read in all our churches would open the eyes of a great majority & secure a great ascendancy in our legislature, or prove that we are devoted to ruin by the judgments of God, &, that of consequence opposition would be vain.

I repeat that if in this, or some similar course of proceedings you would lead, you would be supported with alacrity & firmness, and we should have the best reason for acceding to your proposals. We should avoid the cry of mad dog, and New Hampshire, Vermont & Rhode Island would follow with less jealousy and repugnance. This might be concerted. The plan of a convention to meet at *Hartford* or elsewhere for the purpose of procuring amendments to the Constitution essential to our best interests, and if these could not be effected at our joint instance, *other consequences,* might be met with prudence, circumspection, and such preparation as would avert violent commotions & civil war.

This my friend, are as you see, but *crude* hints for you to improve upon. Let your central Comm'ee write to ours without reserve. Or which would be better, let two or three of them come to Boston for a couple of days.[5] No time should be lost. When does your Genl Court meet?

I am my dear Sir

with great esteem & respect
yr friend & obedt Sevt

---

[5]Roger Griswold and Calvin Goddard, a member of the Connecticut Federalist organization and later a delegate to the Hartford Convention, actually laid plans to go to Boston in pursuance of this suggestion but were prevented by illness and other complications from doing so (Griswold to Jonathan Trumbull, Jr., Feb. 12, 1809; Trumbull to George Cabot, Feb. 15, 1809; and Cabot to Trumbull, Feb. 18, 1809, Trumbull MSS, Connecticut Historical Society).

Appendix II

TABLE I: Political Affiliations of Massachusetts Towns with No Dissenting Strength, 1806

County	Per cent Distribution of Votes in Each County		Political Affiliation of Towns without Dissenting Strength*					Total
	F	R	OF	SF	D	SR	OR	
Suffolk	61.0	38.9						
Essex	57.9	41.9	4	1	2	1		8
Middlesex	40.9	58.5	1	3	4	12	10	30
Norfolk	40.6	59.0		3	1	6	1	11
Plymouth	45.0	54.4			2	2	1	5
Bristol	53.7	42.9		3	1			4
Barnstable	40.9	58.6	3	1		2		6
Dukes	47.2	51.5						
Nantucket	44.9	55.1						
Worcester	60.7	39.0	10	9	4	2		25
Hampden	49.1	50.6	2	1		2	1	6
Hampshire	74.7	25.1	10	5	1			16
Franklin	66.6	33.1	3	1		1		5
Berkshire	43.9	55.6	1	1	1	2		5
York	31.2	68.6				1	2	3
Cumberland	49.0	50.8		2		3	1	6
Lincoln	48.6	50.8		1	1	1		3
Kennebec	32.7	66.9		1	2	1	4	8
Oxford	36.3	63.5	2	2	1	2	2	9
Somerset	38.4	61.3		1	2	2	3	8
Hancock	29.6	69.9		1	1		4	6
Washington	73.0	27.1	1	1		1		3
Massachusetts	50.2	49.3	37	37	23	41	29	167
			(74)		(23)	(70)		

*OF = Overwhelmingly Federalist: 75 per cent or more of town vote was Federalist.

SF = Strongly Federalist: 55 per cent to 75 per cent of town vote was Federalist.

D = Divided: neither party received more than 55 per cent, nor less than 45 per cent, of the vote.

SR = Strongly Republican: 55 per cent to 75 per cent of town vote was Republican.

OR = Overwhelmingly Republican: 75 per cent or more of town vote was Republican.

The figures in parentheses indicate the grand totals of Federalist, Republican, and politically divided towns without dissenting strength.

The tabulations in Tables I and II are based upon the rosters of Massachusetts and Maine churches and religious societies contained in *The Massachusetts Register and United States Calendar* (Boston, 1800-1815) for the years 1800, 1805, 1810, and 1814, and the census of Baptists in David Benedict, *A General History of the Baptist Denomination in America and Other Parts of the World* (2 vols., Boston, 1813), II, 497-508, 549-50. For the purposes of the tabulations, I have included only those towns which in Benedict's compilation were recorded as containing no Baptists and which in the four issues of the *Register* were shown to have no Baptist, Methodist, Episcopalian, Presbyterian, Quaker, Shaker, Lutheran, Universalist, or Catholic churches or ministers. I have thought it best to adopt the most rigid definition of dissent, that is, membership in any non-Congregational denomination.

TABLE II: Political Affiliations of Massachusetts Towns with No Dissenting Strength, 1813

County	Per Cent Distribution of Votes in Each County		Political Affiliation of Towns without Dissenting Strength*					
	F	R	OF	SF	D	SR	OR	Total
Suffolk	70.1	29.1						
Essex	63.8	36.1	5	1	2			8
Middlesex	47.5	52.3	2	3	3	16	5	29
Norfolk	46.9	52.3	2	2	4	1	1	10
Plymouth	56.0	43.8	1	1		1	1	4
Bristol	63.0	36.9	2	1	1			4
Barnstable	66.1	33.9	5			1		6
Dukes	48.8	51.0						
Nantucket	49.5	49.8						
Worcester	64.2	35.6	12	9	3			24
Hampden	53.7	46.2	3		1	1	1	6
Hampshire	82.7	17.2	12	4				16

TABLE II (Cont.)

County	Per Cent Distribution of Votes in Each County		Political Affiliation of Towns without Dissenting Strength*					Total
	F	R	OF	SF	D	SR	OR	
Franklin	70.5	29.4	3	1				4
Berkshire	51.2	48.8		4				4
York	43.1	49.2		1		1	1	3
Cumberland	55.3	44.4	1	1	1		1	4
Lincoln	50.7	48.8		1	1	1		3
Kennebec	42.6	57.3		3		4		7
Oxford	37.5	62.1	2	2	1	2	2	9
Somerset	50.6	49.1	2	1	3		2	8
Hancock	46.6	53.1	2		2	2		6
Washington	52.5	47.5		1	1			2
Massachusetts	46.6	42.7	54	36	23	30	14	157
			(90)		(23)	(44)		

*OF = Overwhelmingly Federalist: 75 per cent or more of town vote was Federalist.

SF = Strongly Federalist: 55 per cent to 75 per cent of town vote was Federalist.

D = Divided: neither party received more than 55 per cent, nor less than 45 per cent, of the vote.

SR = Strongly Republican: 55 per cent to 75 per cent of town vote was Republican.

OR = Overwhelmingly Republican: 75 per cent or more of town vote was Republican.

The figures in parentheses indicate the grand totals of Federalist, Republican, and politically divided towns without dissenting strength.

TABLE III: VOTING PARTICIPATION IN MASSACHUSETTS GUBERNATORIAL AND PRESIDENTIAL ELECTIONS, 1800-1815

	Per Cent Adult White Males Voting	Total Votes	Change in Total Votes
1800 (G)	32.5	39,059	
1801 (G)	37.2	45,816	+6,757
1802 (G)	39.3	49,583	+3,767
1803 (G)	33.7	43,409	−6,174
1804 (G)	41.4	54,409	+11,090
(P)	42.0	55,346	
1805 (G)	51.3	68,986	+14,487

TABLE III (Cont.)

	Per Cent Adult White Males Voting	Total Votes	Change in Total Votes
1806 (G)	54.7	75,216	+6,230
1807 (G)	58.1	81,516	+6,300
1808 (G)	56.6	81,147	−369
1809 (G)	63.9	93,322	+12,175
1810 (G)	61.0	90,813	−2,509
1811 (G)	55.4	83,917	−6,896
1812 (G)	67.7	104,156	+20,239
(P)	50.8	78,250	
1813 (G)	64.1	100,223	−3,933
1814 (G)	64.9	103,163	+2,940
1815 (G)	59.4	95,963	−7,200

The figures in Tables III and IV have been derived from the manuscript "Returns of Votes for Governor and Lieutenant Governor," Massachusetts State Archives, Boston, and from the 1830 compendium of the Official Returns of the Census. In order to arrive at percentage figures, I have interpolated the size of the adult white male population for years between each decennial census by subtracting the total of each census from the succeeding census, dividing the difference by 10, and adding the result to the figure for each preceding year. Because the early census does not provide a category for males over 21, I have taken the figures for males aged 16 to 26, divided them in half, and added half the result to the estimates for males aged 26 to 45 and 45 and over.

The tabulations, especially those for the total votes and for the level of participation, differ at some points from those developed by J. R. Pole, "Letters to the Editor," *William and Mary Quarterly*, 3rd Ser., XV (July 1958), 412-16, and Pole, *Political Representation in England and the Origins of the American Republic* (New York, 1966), pp. 544-52. Many of the internal totals and grand totals of the official voting returns as they exist in the Massachusetts State Archives are incorrect. I have refigured these totals and used the new results in my computations. In most cases, the corrected errors have not appreciably altered the figures for the level of voter interest indicated by Pole. But for 1805, my figures differ sharply from his. Based on a total vote of 64,100, the number legally attested by a Federalist-controlled joint committee of the General Court appointed especially to certify the election returns of a hotly contested election full of shenanigans, Pole's figure for participation is 47 per cent. But I have used a vote total of 68,986, the total which the manuscript returns show were actually cast, even if not counted by the joint committee. In no other case was the discrepancy between votes cast and votes counted remotely so large. In any case, based on a total vote of nearly 69,000, participation in 1805 was 51 per cent, a level which emphasizes more vividly than Pole's figure the effect of party organization upon electoral activity.

TABLE IV: DISTRIBUTION OF VOTES IN MASSACHUSETTS
GUBERNATORIAL AND PRESIDENTIAL ELECTIONS, 1800-1815

	Fed. Per Cent of Total Votes	Rep. Per Cent of Total Votes	Total Fed. Votes	Total Rep. Votes	Change in Fed. Votes	Change in Rep. Votes
1800 (G)	55.4	43.6	21,649	17,019		
1801 (G)	55.6	44.1	25,452	20,184	+3,803	+3,165
1802 (G)	60.5	39.3	29,983	19,443	+4,531	−741
1803 (G)	67.3	32.0	29,119	13,910	−864	−5,533
1804 (G)	55.0	44.1	29,993	24,006	+874	+10,096
(P)	46.7	53.3	25,832	29,514		
1805 (G)	51.0	48.6	35,204	33,518	+5,211	+9,512
1806 (G)	50.2	49.3	37,740	37,109	+2,536	+3,591
1807 (G)	48.1	51.5	39,234	41,954	+1,494	+4,845
1808 (G)	48.9	50.8	39,643	41,193	+409	−761
1809 (G)	51.3	48.4	47,916	45,118	+8,273	+3,925
1810 (G)	48.5	51.3	44,079	46,541	−3,837	+1,423
1811 (G)	47.8	51.6	40,142	43,328	−3,937	−3,213
1812 (G)	50.6	49.3	52,696	51,326	+12,554	+7,998
(P)	65.2	34.9	50,978	27,272		
1813 (G)	56.5	42.7	56,754	42,789	+4,058	−8,537
1814 (G)	54.8	45.1	56,510	46,502	−244	+3,713
1815 (G)	53.4	46.5	51,099	44,505	−5,411	−1,997

TABLE V: Representation in the Massachusetts House, 1800-1815

Session and Controlling Party	Eligible Towns	Towns No.	Represented Per Cent	Representatives
1800-1801 (Fed.)				
1	419	222	53.0	248
2	419	230	54.9	254
3	419	232	55.4	266
1801-1802 (Fed.)				
1	443	256	57.8	283
2	443	258	58.2	286
1802-1803 (Fed.)				
1	447	200	44.7	221
2	447	205	45.9	225
1803-1804 (Fed.)				
1	448	224	50.0	251
2	448	226	50.0	253
1804-1805 (Fed.)				
1	455	237	52.1	273
2	455	238	52.3	278
3	455	237	52.1	277
1805-1806 (Fed.)				
1	470	266	56.6	348
2	470	264	56.2	346
1806-1807 (Rep.)				
1	471	327	69.4	480
2	471	326	69.2	477
1807-1808 (Rep.)				
1	476	271	56.9	382
2	476	273	57.4	385
1808-1809 (Fed.)				
1	477	321	67.3	488
2	477	317	66.5	486
3	477	315	66.0	484
1809-1810 (Fed.)				
1	477	363	76.1	574
2	477	360	75.5	585
1810-1811 (Rep.)				
1	477	389	81.6	644
2	476	381	80.0	635
1811-1812 (Rep.)				
1	476	392	82.4	652
2	566	379	67.0	687
1812-1813 (Fed.)				
1	570	417	73.2	722
2	570	410	71.9	739
3	570	410	71.9	737

TABLE V (Cont.)

Session and Controlling Party	Eligible Towns	Towns No.	Represented Per Cent	Repre-sentatives
1813-1814 (Fed.)				
1	574	378	65.9	636
2	574	381	66.4	634
1814-1815 (Fed.)				
1	577	327	56.7	515
2	577	323	56.0	512
3	577	327	56.7	519

These figures, like those in Table VI, are derived from *Massachusetts Senate Documents*, 1854, Doc. 56, pp. 55-89. I have been unable to discover any compilation of statistics indicating the total number of representatives who were eligible to sit in the General Court at any one time. Fragmentary evidence regarding single localities does not provide an adequate basis for generalizing what percentage of those eligible actually took their seats. Furthermore, the source of these figures fails to indicate whether the towns represented were represented for one day or for an entire session or how long individual deputies remained at their posts.

TABLE VI: REPRESENTATION IN THE MASSACHUSETTS HOUSE, 1800-1815, BY SECTION

Session and Controlling Party	Representatives per Section					
	East		West		Maine	
	No.	Per Cent	No.	Per Cent	No.	Per Cent
1800-1801 (Fed.)						
1	128	51.6	83	33.5	37	14.9
2	139	52.7	86	32.6	39	14.7
3	138	52.6	88	32.8	40	14.6
1801-1802 (Fed.)						
1	133	47.5	98	34.7	52	18.3
2	133	46.5	98	34.3	55	19.2
1802-1803 (Fed.)						
1	135	53.8	78	31.1	38	15.1
2	135	52.9	80	31.4	40	15.9

TABLE VI (Cont.)

Session and Controlling Party	Representatives per Section					
	East		West		Maine	
	No.	Per Cent	No.	Per Cent	No.	Per Cent
1803-1804 (Fed.)						
1	119	47.4	77	30.7	55	21.9
2	119	47.0	79	31.2	55	21.8
1804-1805 (Fed.)						
1	128	46.9	93	34.1	52	19.0
2	131	47.1	95	34.2	52	18.7
3	130	46.9	94	33.9	53	19.8
1805-1806 (Fed.)						
1	175	50.3	111	31.9	62	17.9
2	175	50.6	110	31.8	61	17.8
1806-1807 (Rep.)						
1	221	46.0	145	30.2	114	23.8
2	220	46.1	145	30.4	112	23.5
1807-1808 (Rep.)						
1	190	49.7	104	27.2	88	23.1
2	191	50.4	106	28.0	88	21.6
1808-1809 (Fed.)						
1	221	45.3	153	31.4	114	23.3
2	221	45.5	153	31.5	112	23.0
3	221	45.7	152	31.4	111	22.9
1809-1810 (Fed.)						
1	256	44.6	170	29.6	148	25.8
2	262	44.9	177	30.1	146	25.0
1810-1811 (Rep.)						
1	298	46.3	186	28.9	160	24.8
2	297	46.8	178	28.0	160	25.2
1811-1812 (Rep.)						
1	312	47.9	170	26.1	170	26.0
2	312	45.4	205	29.8	170	24.8
1812-1813 (Fed.)						
1	311	43.1	198	27.4	213	29.5
2	330	44.7	197	26.7	212	28.6
3	330	44.8	196	26.6	211	28.6
1813-1814 (Fed.)						
1	280	44.0	176	27.7	180	28.3
2	275	43.4	177	27.9	182	28.7
1814-1815 (Fed.)						
1	225	43.7	171	33.2	119	23.2
2	221	43.2	171	33.4	120	23.4
3	228	43.9	170	32.8	121	23.3

TABLE VII: Composition of the Massachusetts House, 1800-1815

	Fed.		*Rep.*		*Unknown*		*Entire House*	
	NO.	PER CENT	NO.	PER CENT	NO.	PER CENT	NO.	PER CENT
Distribution by Occupation:								
Lawyers	144	14.7	34	5.1	12	3.7	190	9.7
Doctors	53	5.4	44	6.6	19	5.9	116	5.9
Clerics	18	1.8	24	3.6	17	5.3	59	3.0
Merchants	203	20.7	98	14.7	45	14.0	346	17.6
Captains and Masters	67	6.8	60	9.0	29	9.0	156	7.9
Artisans	101	10.3	86	12.9	26	8.1	213	10.8
Farmers	415	42.4	346	52.0	180	56.0	941	47.9
Other	232	23.7	156	23.5	74	23.1	462	23.5
Occupation Listed	979	88.2	665	84.8	321	82.5	1965	86.1
Distribution of College Degrees	104	9.4	29	3.7	8	2.1	141	6.2
Other Public Service:								
Revolutionary Service	40	4.0	29	4.0	21	6.0	90	4.0
State & National Constitutional Conventions	36	3.0	23	3.0	10	3.0	69	3.0
Other Service	95	8.0	69	8.0	7	2.0	171	8.0

TABLE VII (Cont.)

	Fed.	Rep.	Unknown	Entire House
Party Affiliation				
Numerical Distribution	1110	784	389	2283
Average Birth Dates				
All Massachusetts	1762.7	1762.6	1760.3	1762.3
Massachusetts Proper	1761.7	1762.1	1756.5	1761.2
Maine	1766.6	1764.1	1763.0	1764.8
Per Cent With Age Listed	87.9	85.0	81.2	85.8

These figures with the exception of those concerning party affiliation—which are drawn from sources too numerous to name—are derived from the biographical register of General Court members, Massachusetts State Library, State House, Boston. In the biographical registry of the General Court, some members are listed with two occupations. Unable to determine which was the principal calling, I have listed both. Hence, the total occupational distribution of each party and of the House as a whole comes to more than 100 per cent. Under occupations, "Other" refers to a miscellaneous group of callings—from banker to fisherman—the listings for each of which are insignificantly small.

TABLE VIII: PATTERNS OF INCUMBENCY IN THE MASSACHUSETTS HOUSE, 1800-1815

General Court	General Court Representation				Per Cent of Incumbents			
	FED.	REP.	UNKNOWN	TOTAL	FED.	REP.	UNKNOWN	TOTAL
1800-1801 (Fed.)	128	66	57	250	55.8	52.4	40.9	53.4
1801-1802 (Fed.)	156	103	22	281	68.9	79.5	13.8	65.2
1802-1803 (Fed.)	122	73	29	224	55.5	51.1	31.4	50.8
1803-1804 (Fed.)	137	82	35	254	56.4	50.4	31.3	52.3
1804-1805 (Fed.)	140	123	16	279	50.0	61.4	9.7	51.2
1805-1806 (Fed.)	170	145	31	346	54.0	53.1	22.7	49.5
1806-1807 (Rep.)	211	222	44	477	81.5	74.1	40.5	73.0
1807-1808 (Rep.)	135	201	42	378	38.4	66.5	28.6	49.4
1808-1809 (Fed.)	255	197	28	480	60.5	53.1	18.5	61.8
1809-1810 (Fed.)	309	226	54	589	66.2	66.7	27.6	61.8
1810-1811 (Rep.)*	302	264	76	642	66.8	50.6	47.0	66.2
1811-1812 (Rep.)**	219	275	66	660	56.6	60.2	32.9	55.3
1812-1813 (Fed.)	408	259	82	749	67.2	66.3	75.0	67.0
1813-1814 (Fed.)	417	199	12	628	66.8	55.6	66.7	63.5
1814-1815 (Fed.)	355	151	9	515				

Derived by interpolation from rosters of General Court membership contained in annual publications of the *Resolves of the General Court of Massachusetts, 1800-1815*, and from tabulations of party affiliations drawn from many other sources.

The incumbency ratios represent the proportion of members of the immediately preceding General Court returning to office.

*Inasmuch as the Republicans were able to elect the House Speaker in the General Courts of 1810 and 1811 and thereby are assumed to have been in control, the figures for identified party affiliation above are of interest as suggesting that Republican votes for Speaker came from among those members whose affiliation I have not been able to ascertain and which is therefore listed as "Unknown."

A Note on Sources

THIS brief bibliographic note is intended to draw the reader's attention to the sources which I have found to be of particular importance to my own thinking. It is not meant to be an exhaustive survey of items, both primary and secondary, which I have used, all of which have been cited in the footnotes.

Primary material relating to Massachusetts Federalism is abundant. The Harrison Gray Otis, Timothy Pickering, and Theodore Sedgwick Papers at the Massachusetts Historical Society, the Adams Family Papers in the possession of the same society, the Rufus King Papers at the New York Historical Society, the John Rutledge, Jr., Papers in the Southern Historical Collection at the University of North Carolina at Chapel Hill, and the Oliver Wolcott, Jr., Papers at the Connecticut Historical Society are indispensable. All of these collections contain many letters—especially from Fisher Ames, George Cabot, Christopher Gore, and Josiah Quincy—which have never before been published or used. Moreover, many that have been published have not been printed fully or accurately. This is especially true of the King, Rutledge, and Wolcott manuscripts. In all these collections, one will find letters omitted from the notoriously unreliable Octavius Pickering and Charles W. Upham, *The Life of Timothy Pickering* (4 vols., Boston, 1873), and from the more reliable but scarcely complete *Works of Fisher Ames*, ed. Seth Ames (2 vols., Boston, 1854); Henry Cabot Lodge, *Life and Letters of George Cabot* (Boston, 1878); "Letters of Stephen Higginson, 1785-1804," ed. J. Franklin Jameson, *Annual Report of the American Historical Association for the Year 1896* (2 vols., Washington, 1897), I, 704-841; Charles R. King, *The Life and Correspondence of Rufus King* (6 vols., New York, 1894-1900); Edmund

Quincy, *Life of Josiah Quincy* (Boston, 1868); and George Gibbs, *Memoirs of the Administrations of Washington and John Adams, Edited from the Papers of Oliver Wolcott, Secretary of the Treasury* (2 vols., New York, 1846). The letters of George Cabot, long considered lost or destroyed, and of Fisher Ames are to be found throughout these collections. Further unpublished Ames letters are contained in the Fisher Ames Manuscripts in the Dedham, Massachusetts, Historical Society. I have also found the John Holmes Papers and the Noah Webster Papers at the New York Public Library, the Cyrus King Manuscripts and the Van Schaack Papers in the Special Collections Division, Columbia University, and the Caleb Strong Papers in the Forbes Library, Northampton, Massachusetts, to be of great use. The Adams Family, Pickering, and Rutledge Papers are now available for wider use on microfilm; and the Ames Manuscripts at the Dedham Historical Society may be secured on microfilm through the Society.

Besides manuscript collections, no sources yield more information on the genesis, structure, and operations of the Massachusetts Federalist Party and on the thought of its leading members than the printed broadsides and circulars contained in the broadside collections of various libraries. The catalogued and uncatalogued broadside collections at the American Antiquarian Society remain unsurpassed. Almost as useful, however, are the similar collections of the Library of Congress, the Massachusetts Historical Society, the New York Historical Society, and the New York Public Library. The recently-available William Smith Shaw Papers at the Boston Athenaeum contain many significant manuscript and printed party broadsides, circular letters, and other items relating to party activities. Many broadsides and circular letters are also contained in the John Holmes Papers at the New York Public Library and in the Waldo and Ward Manuscripts at the American Antiquarian Society.

For insights into Federalist thought and party operations, newspapers are as useful as private correspondence; and, because they offer continuing commentary by a wider variety of people and are directed at the general public, they contain somewhat more characteristic and less elitist utterances than private letters. I have relied chiefly upon the principal Federalist papers of Boston, the *Columbian Centinel* and the *New England Palladium,* as well as the capital's chief Republican counterpart, the *Independent Chronicle.* Regional papers of both political persuasions—both continuing journals and transitory electioneering sheets—are available in the Readex Microprint Publications series of Early American Newspapers, 1704-1820. A useful list of Federalist papers is printed in David Hackett Fischer, *The Revolution of American Conservatism: The Federalist Party in the Era of Jeffersonian Democracy* (New York, 1965), Appendix III, pp. 413-29. A full catalogue of contemporary newspapers is contained in Clarence S. Brigham, *History and Bibliography of American Newspapers, 1690-1820* (2 vols., Worcester, Mass., 1947). For the attitudes of the Federalist men of letters, I have used the *Monthly Anthology and Boston Review*—the predecessor of a more successful journal of higher quality, *The North American Review.*

Official documents relating to the government of Massachusetts during the Federalist ascendancy are found in both manuscript and printed form. These include the manuscript "Returns of Votes for Governor and Lieutenant Governor" in the Massachusetts State Archives, State House, Boston, and, especially important for understanding the mood of 1814, the manuscript petitions from towns to the General Court in manuscript Senate Document series 4820, also in the State Archives. Essential printed records include the *Acts and Laws Passed by the General Court of Massachusetts,* 1790—; *Resolves of the General Court of the Commonwealth of Massachusetts,* 1790—; *Reports of Cases Argued and Determined in the Supreme Judicial Court, of the Commonwealth of Massachusetts,* 1804-15; *Massachusetts Senate Documents,* 1854; *Boston Town Records, 1796-1813* (Boston, 1905); and *Boston Town Records, 1814-1822* (Boston, 1906). What could form the basis of a unique study of the history of a legislative body from the Revolution to the present is the remarkably informative biographical file of members of the General Court in the State Library, State House, Boston.

Equally revealing as both newspapers and official publications are the scores of contemporary printed documents, most of them partisan in nature. I have cited many addresses, orations, discourses, and electioneering speeches throughout the book. The most useful and revealing are [Stephen Higginson], *The Writings of Laco* (Boston, 1789); [Jonathan Jackson], *Thoughts Upon the Political Situation of the United States of America in Which That of Massachusetts is More Particularly Considered* (Worcester, Mass., 1788); [Theophilus Parsons], *Result of the Convention of Delegates Holden at Ipswich in the County of Essex . . .* (Newburyport, Mass., 1778); *The Patriotick Proceedings of the Legislature of Massachusetts, During Their Session from Jan. 26, to March 4, 1809* (Boston, 1809); and Caleb Strong, *Patriotism and Piety, The Speeches of his Excellency Caleb Strong, Esq. . . . from 1800 to 1807* (Newburyport, Mass., 1808). Most of these materials, along with most other items dated before 1820 cited in the footnotes, are available in the Readex Microprint Publications series of Early American Imprints, 1639-1819.

Aside from the efforts at self-vindication of individual contemporary Federalists, the historiography of Massachusetts Federalism—which often becomes the historiography of all Federalism written simply with a New England accent—begins with the printing in 1809 of the one-volume commemorative *Works of Fisher Ames* (Boston, 1809), superceded forty-five years later by the two-volume edition already cited. Throughout the nineteenth century and into the early years of the twentieth, filio-pietistic memoirs, biographies, and collections of letters were the style. Since the second decade of this century, however, a large body of secondary literature, which takes a more critical view of its Federalist subjects, has come into being. Indeed, so substantial has been the production of historians and especially of the students of Jeffersonianism and the Democratic-Republican Party that the older Northeastern elitist bias in favor of the Federalists has given way to a now general historiographical bias which celebrates the Jeffersonians. Belatedly but effectively, the Republicans have triumphed over the spirit of their old Federalist enemies.

Among the most useful of the early collections of letters and documents, none of which, however, were compiled and edited with the completeness, care, and accuracy of modern standards, are those of the Ames, Cabot, Higginson, King, Quincy, and Wolcott correspondences, already cited in this note, and *Documents Relating to New England Federalism, 1800-1815*, ed. Henry Adams (Boston, 1905). Adams's volume marked the close of the first period of Federalist historiography. Adams and his good friend Henry Cabot Lodge, George Cabot's editor and biographer, fought out in the pages of their works a decorous but always sharp historiographical war of ancestral vindication, to which Ames, King, Pickering, Quincy, and others were accessories. Lodge opened innocently enough in 1878 with a defense of his great-grandfather against persistent charges of wrongdoing and even treason in the role of Hartford Convention president. Lodge's volume should also be seen as an attempt to distinguish Cabot from the radical and less gracious likes of Timothy Pickering, whose life and letters had been published five years earlier in a manner which inaccurately played down Pickering's secessionist schemes. Lodge tried both to exculpate Cabot and more fully to implicate Pickering. But the straightforward Lodge—himself a sort of later-day embodiment of Federalism: bluff, exclusivist, nativist, prejudiced, and all—was no match for Henry Adams, the master of the ironic style.

Adams began his great *History of the United States of America During the Administrations of Jefferson and Madison* (9 vols., New York, 1889-1898) about a decade after Lodge offered Cabot to posterity; and if Pickering, Otis, Quincy, Gore, and the others came off rather badly in Adams's account, so did Cabot. The argument, though wonderfully subtle, had a familiar ring: the charge that all Massachusetts Federalists, including Otis, Cabot, and the rest, had verged on treason at

Hartford with a view to establishing a separate New England Confederacy was not unlike that made publicly and privately in the late 1820's by Henry Adams's own grandfather, John Quincy Adams, the apostate from Federalism. As if to leave no doubt about John Quincy Adams's accuracy—and the others' complicity in disunionist activities—Henry Adams in 1905 published John Quincy Adams's private 1829 account of Federalist doings, along with supporting documents, in his *Documents Relating to New England Federalism, 1800-1815*. Henry Adams, however, omitted without notice a few of John Quincy Adams's deepest thrusts at his distant cousin, Harrison Gray Otis; they can be found in the original manuscript of the "Answer to the Appeal of Certain Federalists. 1829," pp. 122-23, 226-27, now available on reel 246 of the Adams Family Papers microfilm.

A major event in Federalist historiography occurred soon after with the publication in 1913 of Samuel Eliot Morison's *Life and Letters of Harrison Gray Otis, Federalist, 1765-1848* (2 vols., Boston, 1913). While indulging in his own sort of filio-pietism—the author was a descendant of Otis—Morison nevertheless was critical of his subject and of the party he led and epitomized. This in itself was a large step away from the older mode of Federalist history. But equally as important as shunning most of the old Federalist antagonisms and controversies was Morison's pioneering achievement in writing party history and his full and candid account of the Hartford Convention. Although preceded in his examination of party organization by George D. Luetscher, *Early Political Machinery in the United States* (Philadelphia, 1903), Morison was the first to explore in any detail the structure and operations of a state party organization. Moreover, the first lengthy account of the Hartford Convention had been written in the old self-congratulatory manner by the convention's secretary, Theodore Dwight, in his *History of the Hartford Convention* (New York, 1833), an effort which merely reiterated the standard Federalist position and which is useful today principally for its inclusion of the convention report and journal. But Morison was the first to write dispassionately of the convention, albeit somewhat too much from Otis's perspective, and, as a Massachusetts man himself not altogether unsympathetic to his ancestors, to chastise its backers and participants. That Morison exonerated Otis of disloyalty to the union may be accepted as a predictable outcome of yet another ancestral account, but I have found no reason to challenge the general outlines of his portrait of Otis. Since 1913, Morison has added some useful glosses to his earlier study of Massachusetts Federalism, and I have cited them in the text. Regretfully, however, he has reduced or omitted much of his description of the Massachusetts Federalist Party and of the Hartford Convention in his new edition of Otis's life, *Harrison Gray Otis, 1765-1848: The Urbane Federalist* (Boston, 1969).

Since Morison originally wrote, the historical study of political parties has grown immensely, although the student of Federalism must acknowledge that the admirers of Jeffersonian Republicanism have captured the field by force of numbers. For general histories of American parties, one should begin with Wilfred E. Binkley, *American Political Parties: Their Natural History* (4th ed. enlarged, New York, 1962), and Roy F. Nichols, *The Invention of the American Political Parties: A Study of Political Improvisation* (New York, 1967). The two works of Noble E. Cunningham, Jr., on the Republican Party are authoritative: *The Jeffersonian Republicans: The Formation of Party Organization, 1789-1801* (Chapel Hill, N.C., 1957), and *The Jeffersonian Republicans in Power: Party Operations, 1801-1809* (Chapel Hill, N.C., 1963). There also exist studies of Jeffersonian Republicanism and of the Democratic-Republican Party, but not of the Federalist Party, for virtually every state in the nation before 1815. The standard account of Massachusetts Republicanism is now Paul Goodman, *The Democratic-Republicans of Massachusetts: Politics in a Young Republic* (Cambridge, 1964). For Federalism, one should start with Joseph Charles, *The Origins of the American Party System* (Williamsburg, Va., 1956), Manning J. Dauer, *The Adams Federalists* (Baltimore, 1953), Stephen

375

G. Kurtz, *The Presidency of John Adams: The Collapse of Federalism, 1795-1800* (New York, 1957), and William Nisbet Chambers, *Political Parties in a New Nation: The American Experience, 1776-1809* (New York, 1963), and end with Shaw Livermore, Jr., *The Twilight of Federalism: The Disintegration of the Federalist Party, 1815-1830* (Princeton, N.J., 1962), and Richard P. McCormick, *The Second American Party System: Party Formation in the Jacksonian Era* (Chapel Hill, N.C., 1966). David Hackett Fischer's *Revolution of American Conservatism*, already cited in this note, is a major work, compelling attention to the shape and activities of the party and to the effects of its operations upon voting behavior in its middle period between 1800 and 1816.

Some of the most provocative work in American historiography in the last decade and a half has concerned the history of the suffrage. Perhaps the most controversial of the works is a study of Massachusetts: Robert E. Brown, *Middle-Class Democracy and the Revolution in Massachusetts, 1691-1780* (Ithaca, N.Y., 1955). Richard P. McCormick's studies, especially "New Perspectives on Jacksonian Politics," *American Historical Review*, LXV (Jan. 1960), pp. 288-301, and Chilton Williamson, *American Suffrage from Property to Democracy, 1760-1860* (Princeton, N.J., 1960), have made important contributions, upon which I have depended heavily. Besides the relevant sections of Fischer and Goodman, cited earlier, J. R. Pole's "Suffrage and Representation in Massachusetts: A Statistical Note," *William and Mary Quarterly*, 3rd Ser., XIV (Oct. 1957), 560-92, as corrected in "Letters to the Editor," *ibid.*, XV (July 1958), 412-16, are important, as is Pole's longer study of voting and representation, *Political Representation in England and the Origins of the American Republic* (New York, 1966), especially pp. 169-249. In a category of its own is James Sterling Young, *The Washington Community, 1800-1828* (New York, 1966), which implies as much about matters the author has chosen to ignore as about those he has illuminated so strikingly.

The study of Federalist thought—though not of the

thought of the party's principal figures, John Adams and Alexander Hamilton—has not received the attention it deserves. Much of the reason lies in the failure to see the unity of the entire era of Revolution from 1765 to 1815 and to place the Federalists squarely within this Revolutionary tradition. Much remains to be studied after the ratification of the Constitution in 1788, but Bernard Bailyn, Gordon S. Wood, Cecilia M. Kenyon, John R. Howe, Robert R. Palmer, and Marshall Smelser have brilliantly pointed the way. See Bailyn's *Ideological Origins of the American Revolution* (Cambridge, 1967), *The Origins of American Politics* (New York, 1968), and "Political Experience and Enlightenment Ideas in Eighteenth-Century America," *American Historical Review*, LXVII (Jan. 1962), 339-51; Wood's *Creation of the American Republic, 1776-1787* (Chapel Hill, N.C., 1969) and "Rhetoric and Reality in the American Revolution," *William and Mary Quarterly*, 3rd Ser., XXIII (Jan. 1966), 3-32; Kenyon's "Republicanism and Radicalism in the American Revolution: An Old-Fashioned Interpretation," *ibid.*, XIX (Apr. 1962), 153-82; Howe's "Republican Thought and the Political Violence of the 1790's," *American Quarterly*, XIX (Summer 1967), 147-65; Palmer's *Age of the Democratic Revolution: A Political History of Europe and America, 1760-1800*, Vol. I: *The Challenge* (Princeton, N.J., 1959); Vol. II: *The Struggle* (Princeton, N.J., 1964); and Smelser's "The Federalist Period as an Age of Passion," *American Quarterly*, X (Winter 1958), 391-419. Richard Hofstadter has recently explored the origins and development of the notion of party in his *The Idea of a Party System: The Rise of Legitimate Opposition in the United States, 1780-1840* (Berkeley, Calif., 1969). Much further study should be given to the conceptions of politics, politician, democracy, and the like.

The state of Federalist biography and, somewhat less curiously, of local history is lamentable. Besides Morison's studies of Otis and the more recent but less satisfactory and less ambitious lives of Ames and Sedgwick—Winfred E. A. Bernhard, *Fisher Ames: Federalist and Statesman, 1758-1808*

(Chapel Hill, N.C., 1965), and Richard E. Welch, Jr., *Theodore Sedgwick, Federalist: A Political Portrait* (Middletown, Conn., 1965)—there are no dependable accounts of the lives of Caleb Strong, Christopher Gore, Josiah Quincy, George Cabot, Stephen Higginson, Jedidiah Morse, and Theophilus Parsons, to name the most important. One need not try to make a case that these are "major" figures on the national scene in order to insist that studies sensitive to the historical significance of their careers, their business and party affairs, and their family and social milieus, as well as their thought, could reveal much about the life of the Massachusetts upper class and of the institutions and practices of party, law, commerce, religion, and education in the early republic.

After having tried, usually without success, to exploit some two hundred local histories, one can only applaud the industry of the antiquarian and colorist and bewail the abdication of the historian in this field. Rather, however, than emphasing the failure to ask the right questions of abundant local sources, it is preferable to underscore the value and readability of two recent studies of Newburyport—Benjamin W. Labaree, *Patriots and Partisans: The Merchants of Newburyport, 1764-1815* (Cambridge, 1962) and Stephan Thernstrom, *Poverty and Progress: Social Mobility in a Nineteenth Century City* (Cambridge, 1964)—the first of which was of most use in this study, and of Richard D. Birdsall's *Berkshire County: A Cultural History* (New Haven, Conn., 1959). All three suggest the many possible varieties and rewards of this genre of historical research and writing.

Index

Adams, Henry, 159n., 178n.,
304n., 309n., 326n., 373–4
Adams, John, 5, 25n., 116–17,
218, 224, 243, 288; and election
of 1800, 145, 217, 226
Adams, John Quincy, 6, 14,
65–6, 74–5, 103n., 178, 224n.,
231, 246n., 279, 295n., 301n.,
304n., 305n., 331, 374; Federalist view of, 79–80, 150–1
Adams, Samuel, 6, 12, 217, 218
Adams Federalists, 217, 220–1,
223, 225
Alien and Sedition Acts, 89,
97–8, 218
aliens: Federalist view of, 89–
99, 284n., 340–2; see also
immigrants, nativism
American Revolution, 6, 7,
123–5, 289, 291, 350; ideology
of, xi, 35–46; effects of, 9,
153–4, 182, 191–2; as "Augustan Age," 36
Ames, Fisher, 6, 35, 144, 147,
151, 180, 183, 207–8, 221,
296n., 373; views of, 18n., 25,
37–41, 50, 58, 60, 67–9, 85–6,
94, 120 and n., 124–5, 128–32,
145–6, 174, 223, 272; and
Federalist Party, 88, 132–4,

136, 251–2; and newspapers,
134–5, 258–9
Ames, Nathaniel, 187, 190, 207–8
Anthology Society, 148–52
anti-intellectualism: of Federalists, 128–30
anti-slavery: Federalist view of,
104–9; see also Negroes,
three-fifths clause
apostasy: Federalist view of,
78–80
aristocracy: Federalist view of,
127–8
artisans, 8–9; party affiliation of,
172n., 291

Baldwin, Loammi, 96–7
bankers: party affiliation of,
192–3
Baptists (Mass.), 7, 14; rise of,
153–4, 198–9, 208–14; and
Republicans, 169, 213–15; see
also dissenting religion
Barnstable County, 169, 285
Bavarian Illuminati, 200; Federalist fears of, 43, 155–6
Bentley, William, 171, 182–3,

Bentley, William (*Continued*) 202–3, 232; on religious dissent, 208, 210, 214*n*.

Berkshire County, 180, 217–18, 223*n*., 224–5, 265 and *n*.; Republicans of, 170*n*., 173, 176

Beverly (town of), 116, 177*n*., 256–7

Bigelow, Timothy, 229*n*., 243, 295, 305, 306*n*., 313, 326*n*., 336

Blake, Francis, 324, 329

Bliss, George, 336–7

Boston (town of), 13, 19, 171, 174, 176, 187, 201–3, 218–19, 235, 247, 253–4, 290, 301, 316, 322, 354; parties and politics in, 169, 224*n*., 233, 248, 257, 263*n*., 264, 283, 309; representation of, 283, 287–8; *see also* Suffolk County

Bowdoin, James, 6, 9, 12

Bristol County, 226, 290

Bryant, William Cullen, 108*n*., 139, 140*n*., 174

Buckminster, Joseph Stevens, 149, 202

Cabot, George, 6, 9, 46, 49, 92*n*., 120*n*., 121, 124, 136–7, 139, 141, 147, 167, 168, 179, 190, 204, 219–20, 236–7, 298, 301, 337, 342, 373; views of, 37, 67, 68*n*., 71, 120, 129–30, 132, 272, 312*n*.; party service of, 66, 133–4, 135*n*., 137*n*., 146*n*., 258, 260*n*., 295–6, 311*n*., 353*n*.; and Hartford Convention, 327–43 *passim*

Cambridge (town of), 116, 206–7

caucus, congressional, 296*n*.

caucus, legislative, 221–39 *passim*, 292, 295, 308, 311; composition of, 223; functions of, 228 *ff*.; moderator of, 229; committees of, 229–30; and Central Committee, 238 *ff*., 246*n*.; and Hartford Convention plans, 319, 322–3

caucus system, 232 *ff*., 249–55 *passim*, 283; old-school contribution to, 135; and ward caucuses, 233–4; "grand" caucus, 233–4; and conventions, 261

Central Committee, Conn., 303, 356

Central Committee, Mass., 230–1, 238–51 *passim*, 264, 281–2, 310*n*.; and caucus, 238 *ff*.; size of, 239; members' tenure, 240; staff of, 242–3; dangers to, 255; and 1808 convention, 296; and Hartford Convention, 322–3; *see also* committee system

charity, Federalist view of, 62; *see also* sacrifice

Charlestown (town of), 174*n*., 176

clergy: role of, 56; party affiliation of, 291

clergy, Federalist, 152–67, 298, 307, 330

Clinton, DeWitt, 146*n*., 232, 310–12

Clinton, George, 299, 304*n*.; and 1808 election, 295–7, 303

Codman, Stephen, 136, 251–2

commerce: Federalist view of, 49–51

committee, caucus, 229–30

committee system: old-school participation in, 135–8, 255; rise and operation of, 237–57; and county committees, 251–4; and town committees, 253–7; and conventions, 261; effects of, 266–7; *see also* Central Committee

Congregational clergy, 17–19, 34, 56, 156 *ff*.; and Federalist Party, 152–7

Congregationalists (Mass.), 7, 14, 161, 184, 197–214, 276–8; political affiliation of, 169, 204 *ff*.

Connecticut River Valley, 169, 196, 201–2, 210, 221, 262

conspiracy theories: of Mass. Federalists, 43–5

Constitution, Mass., 7–8, 10–11, 269, 280–1

Constitution, U.S., 6–8, 11, 27, 36, 289; Federalist view of, 41, 102, 118–21, 139, 216; proposed amendments to, 316, 335 *ff*., 355–6

conventions, Federalist Party, 260–6, 292

conventions, national nominating, 232; of 1808, 295 *ff*.; of 1812, 310 *ff*.

conventions, New England: plan for 1809, 294–306, 353–6; plan for 1812, 308 *ff*.; *see also* Hartford Convention

corruption: Federalist view of, 25, 37–45

Crowninshield family, 182, 192

Cumberland County, 309*n*.

Cutler, Manasseh, 88, 116, 196

cyclical theory: Federalist espousal of, 33–4

Dana, Francis, 124, 221

Dane, Nathan, 104, 124, 136, 314, 329, 336*n*.; and Hartford Convention, 327–38

Dawes, Thomas, 113–14, 308, 319*n*.

Dedham (town of), 207–8

Deerfield (town of), 173

deism (Mass.), 14, 18–19

democracy: Federalist view of, 38, 42–3, 71–2, 130–2, 150; significance of in Mass., 349–50

democracy, electoral; rise of in Mass., 268–79

Democratic-Republican Clubs, 19, 266

Democratic-Republican Party: *see* Republican Party

Derby family, 124, 180, 182, 192

despotism: Federalist view of, 25, 40–2, 316–17

Dexter, Samuel, 104, 240*n*., 263, 301*n*., 309–10, 320, 322

dissenting religion, Mass.: rise of, 7, 14–15, 154, 156, 170; and politics, 182*n*., 197–9, 208–14; causes of, 209 *ff*.; *see also* Baptists, Methodists, Quakers, Religious Freedom Bill of 1811, Unitarians

disunion: Federalist view of, 109–21, 299, 301, 304, 304–5*n*., 321, 333, 343–5

doctors: party affiliation of,
187–91
Dutton, Warren, 258–9, 311*n.*
Dwight, Theodore, 311*n.*, 334–
5*n.*, 345, 374–5
Dwight, Timothy, 174*n.*, 195,
200, 259*n.*

education: Federalist view of, 55
election of 1800, Mass., 217–18,
224–6
election of 1800, U.S., 14, 109,
226 *ff.*; as "revolution," 37;
effects of, 66–7, 112*n.*, 245,
273–4
election of 1808, U.S., 295–300
election of 1812, U.S., 310–12
election of 1828, U.S., 279*n.*
elections, Mass.: methods of,
226 *ff.*, 237; scheduling of,
274*n.*; *see also* voting
elitism: Federalist view of,
127–8, 130–1, 268–9
Embargo of 1807, 14, 41, 44, 116,
231, 246*n.*, 275, 285, 290, 292,
294, 298, 301*n.*, 306; effect of,
8, 25*n.*, 166–7, 171, 192, 195,
199, 211, 264
Embargo of 1813, 313, 320
embargoes: Federalist view of,
325, 341
Emmons, Nathaniel, 26–7, 56,
62*n.*, 157–8, 201
Enforcement Act of 1809, 275,
299–300
enterprise: Federalist view of,
67–72; and party affiliation,
191–3
Episcopalians, Mass., 184, 200,
207–8

equality: Federalist view of,
54 *ff.*, 106
Essex County, 12, 171, 205,
223*n.*, 285, 290, 324*n.*; parties
and politics in, 169, 170 and
n., 173, 176, 183, 219, 252, 263,
307–8, 309*n.*
"Essex Junto," 219, 303, 354
Eustis, William, 101*n.*, 190, 218,
224*n.*
exclusiveness, myth of, 84–9
expansion: *see* territorial
expansion
experience: Federalist view of,
128–9

factions before 1795, 12
family: Federalist view of, 54–5
farmers, 196*n.*; party affiliation
of, 110, 183, 195–7, 290
Federalist Party, Conn., 259,
303, 306*n.*, 310–11, 328, 353–6;
and Hartford Convention,
328, 334*n.*
Federalist Party, Mass., ix, 4, 6,
72 *ff.*, 88–9, 120–1, 169–75, 225,
299*n.*; schism in, ix–x, 120–2,
145–67, 211–14, 221 *ff.*, 279*n.*,
313–14; ideology of, x, 3–167,
216; origins of, 23–52; and
union, 84–121 *passim;* and
nativism, 89–99; and three-
fifths clause, 99 *ff.*; and slavery, 104–9; and territorial
expansion, 109–13; and secession, 116–21; leadership of,
122–67; old-school members,
123–38; young members, 139–
47; family bonds of, 141–2,
179–81; and marginal politi-

cians, 147–67; literati in, 148–52; composition of, 168–215; support of, 171–3; and lawyers, 184–7; and doctors, 178–91; and businessmen, 191–3; and maritime trades, 193–4; and "peace" label, 212; growth of, 216–67; structure of, 216–67; succession crisis in, 218 *ff.*; nominating methods, 220 *ff.*; caucuses of, 221–35; and conventions, 260–6; effects on voting, 271–9; effects on representation, 279–89; demise of, 279*n.*; representatives of, 289–93; and plan for 1809 New England convention, 294–306, 353–6; leaders' predicament, 297 *ff.*; and Hartford Convention, 327–50
Federalist Party, Pa., 297, 310, 311*n.*
Federalist Party, R. I., 306*n.*, 328, 356
Federalist Party, South, 106–7, 120*n.*, 331
Federalist Party, Vt., 329, 356
France: purported U.S. conspiracy with, 44–5
Franklin County, 170, 271*n.*
French Revolution, 266; response to in Mass., 17–21, 81, 154–5

General Court of Mass., 8, 11, 218, 226; composition of, 184, 190, 193, 288–93, 362–6; representation in, 278–93; 362–4;

requirements for, 280–1; reapportionment of, 286–8; incumbency in, 292–3, 367; divisions in, 320; and Hartford Convention, 323–4, 346–7
general ticket, 226–37 *passim*
Gerry, Elbridge, 6, 12, 101*n.*, 221, 224*n.*, 225–6, 270*n.*, 275–6, 278, 286, 306
"Gerrymander," 211, 265*n.*, 270*n.*, 275–6, 286*n.*, 309*n.*; Federalist attack on, 231*n.*; effect of, 310
Gill, Moses, 218–19, 220–21, 223–5
Goddard, Calvin, 311*n.*, 334*n.*, 356*n.*
Gore, Christopher, 141, 146, 165, 231, 275, 302, 305*n.*, 373; on parties and politics, 66 and *n.*, 136, 137*n.*, 240, 295–6, 304, 311*n.*, 312*n.*, 333–4*n.*
government: Federalist view of, 46–51, 57–60, 313, 333
Gray, William, 80, 182–3, 192
Great Britain, 20–1, 51–2, 91–2
Griswold, Roger, 140–1, 311; and 1809 New England convention plan, 303, 353–6

Hadley (town of), 316–17
Hamiltonian Federalists, 217, 220–1, 226
Hampden County, 271*n.*
Hampshire County ("new"), 170, 252, 271, 309*n.*, 311, 314–16
Hampshire County ("Old"), 173, 174, 180, 183, 223*n.*, 314–16, 348*n.*

Hancock, John, 5, 6, 9, 11–12, 75–6
harmony of interests: Federalist view of, 10–12, 27–9, 53–4
Hartford Convention, viii, x–xi, 279*n.*, 286, 306–50, 356*n.*, 373–5; significance of, vii–xii, 25*n.*, 52, 121, 350; report, 95, 98, 103, 109 and *n.*, 112, 120–1, 139, 337–43; origins, 263, 267, 309, 314 *ff.*; prefigured, 294–306; plan for, 324; called, 325–6; members, 325, 326–9; purpose, 333; journal, 334–5*n.*; debates, 335 *ff.*
Hatfield (town of), 317
hierarchy: Federalist view of, 61
Higginson, Stephen, 46, 124, 147, 179, 192, 219–20, 236, 257*n.*; views of, 18*n.*, 55, 67, 71, 75–6, 100, 145, 146*n.*
Hillhouse, James, 336–8

ideology: *see* American Revolution, ideology of; Federalist Party, Mass., ideology of
immigrants, Mass., 13, 14, 98; Federalist view of, 29, 39, 93 *ff.*; *see also* aliens, nativism
interposition: Federalist doctrine of, 118–21, 300–1, 339–40, 349
Irish, 14, 94*n.*, 97

Jackson, Jonathan, 180, 219; views of, 54–5, 58

Jay Treaty, 20–1, 154
Jefferson, Thomas, 25*n.*, 48*n.*, 204, 306*n.*; Federalist view of, 34–5, 38, 44, 45–6, 129–30, 203, 211, 216
jeremiad, 32–6
Jessup, Thomas S., 344*n.*

Kennebec County, 247
Kirkland, John T., 135*n.*, 149, 180; views of, 26, 203–4

lawyers: party affiliation of, 291
legal profession, Mass., 184–7
Lloyd, James, Jr., 86*n.*, 240*n.*, 295–6, 320*n.*
Louisiana Purchase, 14, 109, 236; effect of, 25*n.*, 93–5; Federalist view of, 111–14; *see also* territorial expansion
Lowell, John, 124, 135*n.*, 136, 179, 219–21, 223
Lowell, John, Jr., 179, 330, 343; views of, 28, 68, 113, 117, 325, 327–8
Lyman, Joseph, 88, 201, 309*n.*, 314–15, 325*n.*, 327
Lyman, Theodore, 29–30, 279*n.*, 325, 334–5

Madison, James, 28, 29*n.*, 262, 306, 312, 321, 344*n.*; Federalist view of, 18, 41, 129*n.*, 323

Maine, District of, 15–16, 183, 192, 196, 198, 223*n.*, 278, 284*n.*, 285, 321, 325*n.*; population, 13, 169–75; representation of, 287–90, 320*n.*

manufacturers: party affiliation of, 192–3

Marblehead (town of), 176, 194

maritime trades: party affiliation of, 291

Massachusetts, Commonwealth of, 5, 9–10, 115–21, 208–14; population, 4–5, 13–14, 91, 171*n.*; influence, 4–6, 13–14, 99–109; unity of, 6–12, 75; divisions in, 7–8, 11, 287–8; Federalist view of, 84–9

Massachusetts proper, 13, 15–16, 169–70, 172–3, 198, 289–90

medical profession, Mass., 187–91

merchants: party affiliation of, 191–2, 290

Methodists (Mass.), 7, 14, 153–4, 198–9, 208–14; *see also* dissenting religion

Middlesex County, 183, 204–5, 226, 264, 309*n.*, 313

militia: Federalist view of, 55–6

Morse, Jedidiah, 135*n.*, 155–6, 200, 201, 204; views of, 57, 68, 90, 97*n.*, 104, 106, 116, 164–5

Nantucket (island of), 173*n.*, 194, 313

nativism: of Federalists, 4, 89–99; *see also* aliens, immigrants

Negroes: Federalist view of, 104 *ff.*, 276; see also anti-slavery, three-fifths clause

New England: Federalist view of, 84–9; influence of, 93, 99–109, 114, 315, 349; secessionist tendencies in, 101, 115–21; sectionalism, 109–21; defense of, 322 *ff.*, 333, 335 *ff.*, 339

Newburyport (town of), 9, 44–5, 119, 180–1, 191, 196*n.*, 247, 253; parties and politics in, 176, 233, 254, 271, 300, 345

newspapers: Federalist use of, 159–60*n.*, 162, 174–6, 257–60

nominations: methods of, 220 *ff.*, 233

Norfolk County, 204, 226, 252, 325*n.*

Northampton (town of), 28, 102, 261; Federalist Party in, 262, 298, 307–8

occupation: and party affiliation, 183–97

old-school Federalists, 142–3, 219–21, 236, 273*n.*; and party organization, 133; views of parties, 142; on Central Committee, 135–8

Old Hampshire County: *see* Hampshire County ("Old")

Osgood, David, 32, 201

Otis, Harrison Gray, 6, 46, 108*n.*, 121, 141, 145–6, 147, 165*n.*, 168, 180, 185, 204, 220, 231, 243, 246 and *n.*, 292, 301*n.*, 305, 306*n.*, 318–21, 337, 373–5; views of, 37, 44, 47–9, 67, 68*n.*, 93–5, 97–8, 107*n.*,

Index

Otis, Harrison Gray (*Cont.*)
108, 112, 139–40, 144, 146, 272;
as party leader, 146, 218, 229,
240–1, 263, 311*n.*, 312*n.*; and
1809 New England conven-
tion, 294–6, 302–4, 353–6;
as Hartford Convention
leader, 316–47 *passim*
Oxford County, 285

Parish, Elijah, 57, 201, 204, 307
Parsons, Theophilus, 6, 124, 136,
147, 180, 185, 186, 240, 288;
views of, 28, 33–4, 63, 127–8,
312*n.*
parties: Federalist view of, 29,
38, 65–6; origins of, 16; spread
of, 174; support of, 177–8;
growth of, 177–8, 216–67; and
religion, 203–15; effects of,
268–93; *see also* Federalist
Party, Republican Party
Perkins, Thomas H., 180, 240,
343, 344*n.*, 347
petitions: use of, 298–9*n.*, 300,
313, 315–17
Phillips, John, 240*n.*, 326*n.*
Pickering, Timothy, 6, 43, 92*n.*,
108*n.*, 124, 125, 137, 140–1,
145, 196, 204, 231, 304, 309*n.*,
310*n.*, 329, 341*n.*, 373; views
of, 27, 38, 44, 66, 79, 103*n.*,
114–15, 164*n.*, 298, 318–19,
327–8, 346; disunionist views
of, 115*n.*, 116–17, 120, 304–5*n.*,
308*n.*, 330
Plymouth County, 174, 290;
parties and politics in, 169,
263, 309*n.*

politicians: *see* old-school Federalists, young Federalists
politics: Federalist view of, 127,
150–2
popularity: Federalist view of,
72–5
power: Federalist view of,
29–30, 126–7, 141
Presbyterians (Mass.), 7, 184,
197
professions: and party affiliation, 183–97
property: Federalist view of,
58–60, 63–5
public service: Federalist view
of, 65 *ff.*, 125–6, 144

Quakers (Mass.), 7, 194, 198–9,
212–14; *see also* dissenting
religion
Quincy, Josiah, 6, 49, 108*n.*, 144–
7, 180, 224*n.*, 245, 298, 310*n.*,
331, 334, 373; views of, 41, 67,
74–5, 93, 102, 103*n.*, 111, 139,
326*n.*; political activities of,
146*n.*, 218, 240*n.*, 303–4

religion: Federalist view of,
26–7, 157–9; and party in
Mass., 197–215; membership
in Mass., 198–9
religious dissent: *see* dissenting
religion
Religious Freedom Bill of 1811,
211–15, 265*n.*, 275–6, 286; *see
also* dissenting religion

representation: effect of parties on, 79–88; taxation for, 284; levels of, 362–4

republican experiment: Federalist view of, 25–6, 31

republican ideology, vii, 111; influence of, 20–2; nature of, 24 *ff.*

Republican Party, Mass., 72, 75–82, 156, 171, 176, 217–18, 224*n.*, 226, 235–7, 244–5, 273–7, 281–3, 284 *ff.*, 320, 325–6*n.;* ideology of, 3, 22, 43, 58–9, 104, 131; religious ties of, 152*n.*, 182*n.*, 197–215 *passim;* composition of, 174, 180–3, 184, 187–91, 191–7; and General Court apportionment, 287; representatives of, 289–93

Russell, Benjamin, 156*n.*, 196*n.*, 258*n.*

sacrifice: Federalist view of, 26, 60–3, 71–2

sailors: as youths and Republicans, 172*n.*

Salem (town of), 174, 180, 182, 192, 202, 247, 253, 276; parties and politics in, 176, 232–4, 248, 254–5, 257, 283, 324*n.*

Scotch-Irish: in Mass., 7, 197*n.*

secession: *see* disunion

Sedgwick, Theodore, 6, 39, 47, 49, 126, 136, 137*n.*, 141, 144, 217–18, 245–6, 288, 304, 311*n.;* views of, 63, 67, 104*n.*, 129*n.*, 300; political activities of, 133, 221–2, 296–7

Shaw, William Smith, 68, 95, 242–3, 282

Shay's Rebellion, 19, 266, 289; effect of, 5–6, 7–8, 11, 12

ship captains: party affiliation of, 193

slavery: *see* anti-slavery

social structure: Federalist ideal of, 53–4

South: Federalist view of, 85, 99–109, 112, 339

Strong, Caleb, 11, 49, 124, 137, 180, 221, 223–4, 225, 231, 265, 288, 306, 308, 320–23, 343*n.;* views of, 26–7, 29, 55, 59, 112, 126, 312*n.*, 347

Strong, Lewis, 262, 309*n.*, 315*n.*

Suffolk County, 290; parties and politics of, 170*n.*, 183, 252, 254, 263; *see also* Boston

suffrage: *see* elections, voting

Sullivan, James, 6, 274–5, 298

Sullivan, William, 156*n.*, 241*n.*, 324*n.*, 328*n.*, 331; political activities of, 240, 310*n.*, 311, 325*n.*, 347

Sumner, Increase, 218–19, 220–1

Taggart, Samuel, 137; views of, 25, 42, 73, 111

Tappan, David, 26, 27, 34, 135*n.*

territorial expansion: Federalist view of, 27–8, 39, 110–13; *see also* Louisiana Purchase

Thacher, George, 104, 136, 319*n.*

Thorndike, Israel, 328*n.;* 344*n.;* political activities of, 136, 240, 311*n.*

three-fifths clause, 5, 13, 100, 109, 315, 341; Federalist view of, 101 *ff.*; Hartford Convention on, 325; *see also* antislavery, Negroes

towns, Mass.: representation of, 279–88; incorporation of, 284 *ff.*; political affiliation of, 357–9

tyranny: *see* despotism

Unitarians (Mass.), 7, 14, 149, 157*n.*, 164, 200, 202, 203; *see also* dissenting religion

Van Schaack, Henry, 141, 224–5, 247

violence: political, 22–5; ideological, 51–2

Virginia and Kentucky Resolutions, 25*n.*, 100, 118, 340

virtue: Federalist view of, 26–7, 39–40

voting, 198, 232; participation, 10–11, 270–9, 360–1; views of, 132; practices, 217, 247–8, 253–4, 256 *ff.*, 268–79; requirements, 269–70; in England, 272*n.*; and election schedules, 274*n.*; town requirements, 276; *see also* elections

war: Federalist view of, 30

War of 1812, viii–ix, xi, 28, 35, 45, 166–7, 204, 275, 277, 278, 286, 290, 292, 321–2; effect of, 8, 25*n.*, 189, 192, 211, 214, 264, 306 *ff.*; Federalist loans for, 69*n.*

Washington Benevolent Society, 241, 264–5

Washington County, 170*n.*

Webster, Noah, 149*n.*, 333*n.*; and Hartford Convention, 308–9, 314–16, 325

West: Federalist view of, 109–21, 340–1

"Whiskey" Rebellion: effect of, 19, 154

Worcester County, 183, 223, 287; parties and politics in, 170, 244, 252, 262, 263, 309

York County: parties and politics in, 176, 252

young Federalists: 235–8; on Central Committee, 239–41

"Young Federalists": origins of, 248

"Young Republicans": origins of, 248

youth: appeal of Republican Party for, 172–3

A NOTE ABOUT THE AUTHOR

James M. Banner, Jr., was born in New York City in 1935 and graduated from Yale University in 1957. He received his Ph.D. from Columbia University in 1968 and is now an assistant professor of history at Princeton University. He is married and the father of a daughter.

A Note on the Type

The text of this book was set on the Linotype in Janson, a recutting made direct from type cast from matrices long thought to have been made by the Dutchman Anton Janson, who was a practicing type founder in Leipzig during the years 1868–87. However, it has ben conclusively demonstrated that these types are actually the work of Nicholas Kis (1650–1702), a Hungarian, who most probably learned his trade from the master Dutch type founder Kirk Voskens. The type is an excellent example of the influential and sturdy Dutch types that prevailed in England up to the time William Caslon developed his own incomparable designs from these Dutch faces.

The book was composed, printed and bound by The Haddon Craftsmen Incorporated, Scranton, Pennsylvania. Typography and binding design by

WARREN CHAPPELL